# STRUAN

First published in 2000 by

Right Words, 14 Bedford Road, St. Albans, Herts AL1 3BQ
Telephone: 01727 766822



ISBN 0-9538721-0-6

Printed and bound in Great Britain by
Unwin Brothers Limited
The Gresham Press, Old Woking
Surrey GU22 9LH

# STRUAN

## THE EXTRAORDINARY STORY OF

## KARL AND EILEEN FUCHS

RICHARD BROWN

## *Acknowledgements*

The biggest debt is to Eileen, who welcomed me into her home, talked tirelessly into a recorder and set up meetings. She also made photographs, press cuttings and books freely available, corrected drafts and nudged politely when it seemed that the process was coming to a halt. Of the immediate family, Lisi, supported by Davie, and Lisa gave generously of their time. All spoke with commendable frankness of their Struan times.

Particular thanks are due also to people who subjected themselves to the cassette recorder or put up with my note-taking; Eric Langmuir, Clive Freshwater, Frith Finlayson, Eilif Moen, George McLeod, Norbert Uist, Charlie Walpole and Miree Hewlett. People too numerous to list wrote to me with Struan anecdotes and impressions. All of their contributions have fed, one way or another, into the book and I am most grateful for these inputs.

Apart from the immediate Fuchs family, three people kindly read portions of the text and suggested corrections; John Knowles, Norbert Uist and Konrad Bartelski. All three also provided great encouragement. I thank them for their time and for providing that much needed extra impetus.

In the process of writing and production, Anna Reynolds has provided invaluable editorial support. Her assistance is very much appreciated. Thanks are due, also, to Philip Prestianni who did some of the research.

I further gratefully acknowledge the many individuals and organisations who very kindly gave permission to quote material. In many cases the usual reproduction fees were waived in recognition of the special purpose of this book. Those deserving of heartfelt thanks are:

*1. Books and Journals*

Konrad Bartelski for permission to quote from 'Konrad Bartelski, the autobiography of a skier'.

Frith Finlayson for permission to quote from 'The Ski Teacher'. (This autobiography is available from William Culross and Son Limited, Coupar Angus, Perthshire PH13 9DF, tel: 01828 627266).

David Hayes of Landmark Press, Carrbridge, Inverness-shire PH23 3AJ and Myrtle Simpson, author, for permission to use material from 'Skisters'.

Victor Gollancz, the Orion Publishing Group Ltd, Orion House, 5 Upper Saint Martin's Lane, London WC2H 9EA, for permission to quote from Tom Patey's autobiography, 'One Man's Mountains'.

The Scottish Mountaineering Club for allowing me to quote from one of the guides to the Cairngorms.

The Scottish Ski Club for permission to use material first published in their journal.

*2. Newspapers and Journals*

In alphabetical order:
The Daily Express, The Daily Mail, The Daily Telegraph, The Evening Express, The Glasgow Herald, The Guardian, The Inverness Courier, Mirror Syndication International – a Trinity Mirror Business, The Observer, The Press and Journal, The Scotsman, The Strathspey and Badenoch Herald.

Finally, there must be a posthumous 'thank you' to Karl. If this book succeeds in capturing some of his vision, energy, sense of humour and generosity of spirit then it will have been well worth the writing.

**Richard Brown**

## 1. Prologue

'I was lucky once.

It was midnight at the Struan Hotel and the music, and the crowd, were wearing thin. Time was running out for the special licence, which lasts only as long as the music. It seemed the ceilidh was drawing, unfulfilled, to a quiet close.

Then up jumped a player, not heard before. He set the place alight. Faster and faster he played, louder and louder the watchers cheered, harder and harder their feet banged on the bare boards. Beer mugs slammed on the flooded tables, talking couples turned, silent at last, to listen, the accordion and guitar trailed away, as still the fiddler built up speed. Faster still, until, as we held our breath, within an ace of an explosion, he stopped.

Tumultuous, joyous, careless applause - and then we were all on our feet. The ceilidh magic had come, and for an hour we were magic, too.'
*(Simon Tisdall, The Guardian)*

★★★★★★

Located in a small, unremarkable, Scottish highland village, Struan House Hotel had few pretensions yet among its many hundreds of patrons were; knights and their ladies, generals and admirals, world-famous climbers, Olympic skiers, best-selling novelists, film-makers and distinguished journalists. It generated a sturdy loyalty. People have travelled half way round the world to attend reunions. It changed lives radically. It spawned many weddings. 'Struan' is a significant segment of experience for hundreds of people. There are some who can scarcely say the word without smiling and plenty whose eyes prick with nostalgic tears at the mere mention of the name. The 'magic' was part of the place, there to be tapped into whenever circumstances were right.

The power was palpable. Clive Freshwater, founder and Director of a substantial water-sports complex on Loch Insh, a man who knows the time and area better than most, says of Struan; 'It was a potent force, the place where the proper development of Scottish skiing started.'

Frith Finlayson, former Director of the Ski School d'Ecosse, author of the recently published autobiography Ski Teacher, comments; 'It was so exciting at Struan House.'

Eric Langmuir, who for many years was Principal of the prestigious Glenmore Lodge outdoor pursuits centre and a major influence in the area, refers to the hotel as 'the Mecca.'

Eilif Moen, long time Director of the Scottish Norwegian ski school and a frequent visitor to Struan, fondly speaks of going to 'a powerful place'.

George McLeod who, when not undertaking tours of duty in the Antarctic, worked at Glenmore Lodge, testifies that Struan 'made the whole area sit up' and that little Carrbridge was 'the place to be'.

Tom Patey, Ullapool doctor, amongst the elite of climbers, pioneer of many winter ascents in the Cairngorms, 'inventor' of the televised climbing spectacular and author of 'One Man's Mountains', would travel in his beloved, trusty Skoda the many miles of single track, wintry roads just for a taste of the Struan magic.

★★★★★★

There are numberless forces operating in the world, pushing objects and people in ever-changing directions. Struan became a powerful place because some particularly strong currents came together there, to form a mighty stream. One of these factors stemmed from the hotel's location in the beautiful Spey Valley, close to the ancient, wild, brooding Cairngorm mountains. The area hums with natural power.

Another element was the spirit of the times. In the 1960's and early 1970's there was an atmosphere of freedom which allowed almost unbridled individual expression. Most of the hundreds upon hundreds who came to the place felt able to be themselves, to unleash some of the personal power which is normally locked safely away. Writing about the development of skiing in the area, Frith Finlayson says, 'We all played a full part of what was a self-generated, never to be forgotten and never to be repeated...experience in our lives. These were magical times!'

But the strongest forces of all were those brought by the hotel's founders, Karl Fuchs and Eileen Knowles.

It would be difficult to imagine a more unlikely couple.

Because of the circumstances of his life, Karl had very limited schooling. Eileen was an honours graduate of Cambridge University. He was a superb skier, a member of the 1948 Austrian Olympic team; she never progressed in the sport beyond the level of a competent intermediate. She was an administrative Civil Servant; he was a policeman. She played the violin and the piano to an accomplished standard and sang in classical choirs; Karl's musical expression was limited, when they met, to picking out a few Austrian folk tunes on the mandolin and brief but passable episodes of yodelling. Eileen learned to speak German fluently with a determinedly English accent; Karl developed a largely impenetrable language of his own, which became known as 'Scotstrian'.

A journalist wrote of them, 'They're devoted, efficient, and professional, and there's a quality about their hospitality - they've created their "paradise" between them but they include the outsider - which is true of very few private paradises.'

The story of their meeting is romantic in the extreme.

## 2. Eileen

Eileen Knowles was born on May 30th, 1920 at her paternal grandmother's house in Ashford, Middlesex, where her grandfather was headmaster of the county school. As a baby she was not robust and her parents, Maurice and Lilla, moved three times in the first three years of her life because of their daughter's recurrent pneumonia. From a bungalow on the Thames they went to a cottage at Laleham in Surrey, thence to a house in Ashford until they settled finally in Purley where Eileen's brother, John, was born.

Maurice and Lilla had not had the easiest of starts to their life together. They met in East Yorkshire, where she was a student at the High School and he was a boarder at Bridlington Grammar. Maurice came close to being expelled because he so frequently disobeyed instructions not to go walking on the cliffs with his local sweetheart. The teachers failed to keep the young lovers apart but the First World War took young Maurice off to Malta, Egypt and the Sudan. Lilla filled the lonely hours by teaching the piano whilst her fiancé enjoyed his adventure but the quality of life changed dramatically for Maurice when he was ordered to join the Gallipoli invaders. He was involved in the Suvla Bay assault and had to swim for survival through water-filled trenches before being sent home on sick leave.

Whilst recuperating, Maurice made inquiries about the newly formed Royal Flying Corps. To Lilla's intense dismay, he was accepted for training. She could see that the primitive aircraft were hazardous even without presence of enemy planes with machine guns strapped to their fuselages.

The learning experience confirmed Lilla's fears. Whilst attempting a landing in an unprepared field, her beau contrived to put the propel on the ground before the wheels, a manouvre not recommended in the manuals. To the dismay of the instructor, who buzzed angrily off in his own aeroplane, the flimsy machine flipped and collapsed into not a few of its component parts. Luckily the trainee pilot was undamaged in body and confidence. Putting a piece of the snapped propeller over his shoulder as a souvenir he made the cross-country journey back to base. The beautifully shaped piece of wood would, he thought, make an excellent holder for a barometer and so it subsequently did.

Lilla suggested that the trenches of France were sure to be safer than the uncertain skies but Maurice had caught a new and apparently incurable disease. Flying had become much more than just another way to defeat the enemy; it was a provider of unlimited excitement. He carried on training without further mishap and was soon awarded the coveted wings which, with a heavy heart, Lilla sewed onto his army uniform. The new pilot was immediately posted to the muddy morass of death which was known, to the sacrificial victims who were sent there, as the Western Front.

The business of aerial combat served only to heighten the flow of Maurice's adrenaline. In the exciting business of downing the enemy he had his share of success until, early in April 1917, he came up against a man whose aircraft seemed faster, whose manouvres were unprecedented, who seemed to anticipate and counter every trick that was tried. Finally helpless, Maurice knew that he was fixed in the centre of the enemy's sights.

Bullets ripped through the thin fabric. Anticipating searing pain, Maurice concentrated on the techniques of piloting. No agony came; it was almost as though the opponent was going for the machine rather than the man. The single engine emitted a large cloud of smoke before sputtering to silence. It seemed to Maurice, as the wind became the loudest noise in the immediate environment, that his conqueror waved before zooming off to try his consummate skills against another inferior warrior.

It was possible, Maurice knew, to make a good powerless landing. He was unhurt and the flight controls all seemed to be working. He had survived the crash in training; with skill and luck he would survive this. It was only of secondary importance that, when he stepped out of the aircraft, he would be deep into enemy territory.

*The Apprentice Flyer*

Trimming constantly, searching for the optimum landing strip, he brought the craft down. There were bumps and jolts but when the machine came to a halt Maurice had suffered nothing worse than a thorough shaking. He stepped out of the aeroplane and, as instructed, immediately set it on fire.

Watching German soldiers arrived too late to do anything about the blaze but they removed any thoughts Maurice had about making an escape. They pointed guns and shouted at him in a language he did not understand. The meaning was obvious. He raised his arms in the universal gesture of surrender.

The captive was taken to a makeshift prison. His immediate thoughts were of Lilla. She would not know that he had survived the battle. He would be reported as missing, presumed killed The thought of her misery was considerably more painful than his own temporary discomfort.

Deep in contemplation about strategies for escape, Maurice was surprised when the door of his cell was opened to admit an immaculately uniformed German. The man spoke excellent English. It was impossible not to respond to the outstretched hand of greeting. The cultured voice announced that Maurice was in the presence of his conqueror. Smiling, the pilot said, 'My name is Lieutenant Frankl and you are my one hundredth victim.'

There was, Maurice thought, some small consolation in that.

The men talked; about flying, naturally. Their shared passion for the new form of transport easily overcame nationalistic enmity. To Maurice's astonishment, the German was soon inviting him to dinner which they ate in an expensive restaurant. At the end of the surreal meal, Lieutenant Frankl reached into a pocket and produced a postcard. He summoned one of the waiters, demanded a pen and was not too pleased when he was given a pencil. Nevertheless, he wrote on the back of the card and handed it to his guest.

Maurice took the proffered gift. The picture showed his conqueror, looking handsome and intense, with a shining silver cross pinned to his jacket. Modestly, Lieutenant Frankl translated the inscription above the image which held him to be, 'Our most successful flier'. The words on the back referred, he revealed, to the gallantry of his opponent and to Maurice's admirable aeronautical skills. There was an improbable bonding and a strange sadness as the two said their farewells.

*Maurice's conqueror*

The most unwilling captive was moved to a prisoner-of-war camp where he began the life of privation. There were no arrangements for making contact with family and friends; his worry about Lilla intensified. Perhaps sensing that their new prisoner was a potential escapee, the Germans soon transferred him to the notorious Holzminden. Whilst there he heard, through the prisoner-of-war camp grapevine, that Lieutenant Frankl had been killed in action. Those who conveyed the news were elated and they found it hard to understand why Maurice was not joining in the general rejoicing.

Everything about prison life was anathema to Maurice. He came to loathe the language of his captors, associating it with all his misery. Unlike many of his fellows, who seemed dulled into inactivity by their plight, he watched and planned. When the opportunity to escape presented itself, he seized it.

Packing as much as possible into his pockets, he went out for an apparently innocent walk across the compound at a time when a truck was being loaded with the camp's accumulated rubbish. Timing the move to perfection, he leapt aboard and burrowed into the stinking ordure. Breathing was a penance but he made sure that he was deep enough into the pile to avoid being seen when the gate guards ran their routine glance over the departing vehicle. As soon as the truck had roared and jolted some way from the prison, Maurice cautiously pushed his head out into the sweet, fresh air. Fighting nausea, he breathed deeply. The driver in his cab was totally oblivious to the fact that he had a passenger. He drove very slowly, perhaps worried that his rattling vehicle might fall to pieces if he went at speed over the bumps. It was safe and easy for Maurice to leap out at a point where a dense wood afforded immediate cover.

Luckily, his clothing was not too badly soiled; he was able to brush most of the debris away. He then made a careful survey of his surroundings and noted the position of the sun. The plan was to head for the Dutch border. He knew that there would be people in Holland who would be only too willing to assist an escaped prisoner. For an experienced airman, navigation should not be too much of a problem.

Travelling by night, sleeping in drainage ducts or forests by day, Maurice made his cautious way northwards. There was food to be foraged from the fields, berries to be gathered from the hedgerows, water to be supped from streams. On more than one occasion he was forced to swim in the darkness across rivers to avoid the heavily guarded bridges.

For Lilla, this was a desperately anxious time of unknowing. All she could glean from official sources was that her fiancé had failed to return from a mission. It was very natural to assume that someone who had been forced down into enemy territory could not have survived but she kept hoping that Maurice's indomitable spirit would have carried him through.

She learned that her trust was justified in a most extraordinary fashion. It was not the military authorities, nor the Red Cross, which brought evidence that Maurice was alive. The glad tidings came from the downed airman's bank.

Like everyone else who heard the story, Lilla could scarcely believe that one of her fiancé's cheques, written and presented in Germany, had been conveyed for clearance. How could it be that, even though half the world was locked in the most appalling of all conflicts, the processes of international commerce were still working? She saw the slip and confirmed that it bore an apparently genuine signature. It was difficult, in spite of the anxiety, not to laugh. Maurice was alive and, typically, he was swanning into a bank as though he were on a peace time tour.

Perhaps unsurprisingly, the German authorities caught up with the cheeky fugitive and conveyed him at pistol point to a more secure prison. He had no option, then, but to suffer frustration until the conflict was over.

The post war joy of reunion was still fresh when the couple ran into their first obstacle. In spite of his harrowing experience of aerial warfare, Maurice was so enamored of the business of flying that he wanted to remain in military service. He planned to be one of the band of pioneering pilots when the Royal Air Force was formed

Lilla began her campaign. The long months of uncertainty and the almost unrelieved tension had fixed her mind. It was out of the question that she could be married to an airman. She tried rational argument, she added emotion, she used all her wiles. Maurice could not be shifted; there was an adventurous future beckoning and he longed to follow the trail.

In the end, Lilla had to issue her ultimatum. She loved Maurice utterly and could scarcely tolerate the thought of being without him. Yet she knew that this very intensity of love would make existence unbearable if he were to be hazarding his life day by day. In the deepest dread, she announced that if he did not change course she would not go through with the wedding.

They were married in April, 1919.

Reluctantly, Maurice joined the Government Actuary's Department. The work demanded a high level of computational skills and involved great responsibility but the new civil servant felt trapped. His mind was too lively and his sense of adventure too keen for him to be happy with routine. He climbed steadily up the ladder of promotion, doing well for his beloved wife and children whilst all the time yearning for a greater freedom.

There were many compensations, of course. The family was able to afford a good standard of living. There were weekend outings and active holidays. The children, bright, inquisitive, inventive, were a source of huge delight. Their intelligence shone through their schooling. After the primary years Eileen moved on to become a diligent pupil at Croydon High School and all too quickly she developed into a very pretty, engaging adolescent who, given the chance, talked incessantly. John went to Epsom, rather too orthodox a public school for his liking. However, academically it enabled him to make progress matching that of his sister. Both of them were spoken of as potential Oxbridge candidates.

*Schoolgirl Eileen*

In the summer of 1939, during Chamberlain's hard-purchased peace, the elder of the Knowles children fulfilled her promise and went to Cambridge to read history.

Her father was also facing a life change. As for many men of his generation, the potential onset of the second great war provided Maurice with his escape route from the routine. He was deemed too old for active service but keen minds were needed in the Ministry of Food which was facing the urgent task of organising an efficient system of rationing. Released from his interminable calculations, Maurice began to enjoy his working hours.

For Eileen, wide-eyed in Cambridge, the coming conflict was then a most unreal prospect. The university could still offer wonderment to the newcomer. Newnham College had 'maids' to perform domestic chores; there were clubs, societies and parties. It did not seem possible, then, that Hitler's pernicious power would ever extend to the inner sanctums of establishment England.

It was the Dunkirk retreat which established the realities of war. Students were unprecedentedly sent home a week early at the end of term. Eileen recalls sitting in a library Reading Room just before leaving for the break and seeing, with great shock, a map in *The Times* which showed how far the Germans had advanced.

On that same day she was given a telephone message from a young woman in her college who had gone hastily on pre-embarkation leave with her very new, volunteer solider husband. In the confusion of the times the woman had left her engagement ring behind and she wanted Eileen to make sure that it was safe. Just a very short time later the young man who had given her the band was one of the many slain on the frantic retreat through northern France. War was no longer a distant drama.

For the first year of the fighting the Knowles family continued to live in Surrey but as the military crisis deepened it was decided that the Ministry of Food should move away from London. At home on vacation, Eileen innocently asked her father where the family would be going. Security rules allowed him to reveal only that they were destined for a location code named 'UJ'. It was a thinly cryptic device. It did not take long to realise that 'UJ' was the car registration combination used in Denbighshire.

Lilla travelled to Wales by train to look for suitable accommodation. She found a house in Glan Conway which was soon to be vacant and then located an immediately available temporary home, a bungalow in Penrhyn Bay. The mission completed, she returned to Surrey where, it had been agreed, she would have to stay until new schooling arrangements could be made for John. His immediate goal was matriculation and it would be necessary to find a suitable academy as near as possible to the Knowles' new home. This could not be achieved overnight.

Eileen and her father set off together in the summer of 1940 to take up residence in North Wales. Maurice, concentrating on driving down narrow, winding roads, expected his daughter to navigate, which she did to the best of her ability under the trying circumstances of all the road signs having been removed to frustrate an invading enemy. They made many three, five and even seven point turns before they arrived, exhausted and tetchy, at their temporary home.

Needing money to tide her over the long summer break, Eileen found temporary employment. Her improbable employer was the Bacon Importers' National Defence Association Limited. Without having the least idea as to why importers of pig meat needed to defend themselves, Eileen put some of her energies into BINDAL. The most impressive aspect of her short stint with the organisation was that she learned to use a finger stall for turning pages. In characteristic Knowles fashion, she soon demanded, and was awarded, a pay rise from two to three pounds per week.

Shrewsbury School agreed to take the displaced John for the period up to the crucial examination and he stayed in lodgings there, delighted to be freed from what he saw as the petty restraints of Epsom. Lilla was thereby able to make the move to Wales. She brought with her most of the family possessions, including the slightly puzzled black cat.

*Maurice and Lilla, 1940, North Wales*

Eileen returned to Cambridge and continued with her degree studies. John moved on to be a boarder at Rydal School, temporarily in a hotel high above Conwy and the Irish Sea. It was ideal for an evacuee with opportunities to walk and climb in the Welsh mountains. In time he passed the Oxford entrance examination and joined his sister in the higher halls of learning.

The war then entered its most desperate phase. Unknown to all, at that time, Lilla contracted the leukemia that within a few years would kill her.

John went to Oxford for two terms to reserve a place for after the war. He could then choose which service to join. It was natural to follow his father's footsteps and to try for the Royal Air Force.

Lilla, through her brother who had been a student at Cambridge, had high connections. She used these to procure an interview with a senior air force officer. John was asked the inevitable question as to why he preferred the newest of the services. After strategically mentioning his brave, literally ground-breaking, father he said that he had another reason for favouring the RAF. The commander smiled in anticipation. 'What's that, then?' he asked brightly. John confidently replied that he had heard that pilots had less imposed discipline than the members of the other organisations.

The smile faded, the brows beetled. John was not selected for the Royal Air Force.

The young man turned to the navy which subjected him to rigorous physical tests and discovered that one of his eyes was less than perfect. John would not, they declared, be acceptable as a seaman but he could be useful to them as a writer. This was no problem as he still had the experience of two and a half years on seagoing ships during the war, a spell which included the famous attack on the Tirpitz.

Knowing that communication between them would thereafter be limited, father and son devised a code. 'Anglesey' meant 'aircraft carrier', 'Denbigh' stood for 'destroyer'. Once training was complete, John conveyed that he was heading north and destined for an aircraft carrier. Maurice understood that Scapa Flow was the intended destination.

Aboard the huge vessel, John did his patriotic bit, managing to avoid death and serious injury, seeing much of the world and cultivating a reputation for being a ready questioner of futile orders.

Eileen completed her studies in 1942. Because women were still not officially acknowledged at Cambridge, she was not allowed the dubious privilege of wearing a graduate's gown but this, and the other absurd sexist restrictions, did not affect her career prospects. However, the other broader social circumstances did.

There were but three options open to her at that stage of the hostilities. She could teach, she could join the armed forces or she could become a civil servant. Neither the classroom nor a life in uniform appealed; for her there was only one realistic route.

The usual entrance examinations for government service had been suspended and someone with Eileen's qualifications could enter directly at a reasonably high level. There was, however, a preliminary in the shape of a gruelling interview with a body known as the Waterfield Commission. This hurdle was negotiated and Eileen knew that, like her father, she was destined to work in one of the Ministries.

For two delightful summer weeks she was a temporary Assistant Principal at Board of Trade premises in Bournemouth, staying in lodgings and walking to the office along the sea front. It was like a holiday which ended abruptly when the entire department was moved to London. It was an odd manouvre, given that the Germans were making the capital a very dangerous place to be, but the authorities must have had their reasons.

Eileen soon discovered that the overseas enemy was not the only hazard which she faced. She was billeted in a hostel run by white-cowled Catholic nuns, members of an order called the Sisters of Charity. 'Insisters on Chastity' might have been more appropriate.

The new civil servant was not hostile to religion but her family tradition in matters relating to the Almighty was very much of the Protestant persuasion. The holy women, who imposed an eleven o'clock curfew and expected their residents to behave with the utmost decorum, were alien creatures. The huge white reflectors around their pious faces concentrated the force of their religious zeal. One by one, Eileen's fellow hostellers confessed, 'I've been converted!'.

Seeking relief from the pressure, Eileen gladly accepted a social invitation from one of her former Cambridge supervisors. The evening passed pleasantly until, even earlier than Cinderella, the female had to return to her open prison. It was just approaching the curfew hour as Eileen knocked on the door. The Mother Superior herself responded. Anticipating a censorious look and a dismissive nod towards her escort, Eileen was astonished when the two greeted each other warmly. Against all normal procedures the man was not only admitted into the residence but taken at once to the chapel. He, it turned out, had also been converted to Catholicism a few years earlier. It was evident that forces were ranged against the freethinker from all directions; she would have to flee. A friend who was living in Purley came to the rescue. She knew someone who was looking for a lodger.

Eileen went to investigate and thereby met a woman of Swiss nationality who had married a very much younger Englishman called Palmer. Mrs. Palmer was a skilled dressmaker who, according to Eileen's vivid report, smoked 'tremendously'. Her house was Alpine-neat but very welcoming. There was no hesitation on either side as the deal was agreed.

Alas, all was not well in the Palmer household. The husband had grown weary of the older woman's ways and had taken up with a local temptress who used to telephone quite frequently. Eileen and the abandoned Mrs. Palmer became allies against this invasion. In the kitchen, where the lady of the house produced astonishingly good meals on the meagre rations then available, the two talked and became quite close. Mrs. Palmer revealed that the one consolation in her trying circumstances was that she much enjoyed her voluntary work in a nearby club for officers. The military men greatly appreciated her culinary genius.

The first blow came when those in charge of the club decided that, even though Switzerland was a non-combatant country, Mrs. Palmer was a danger to security. She was summarily banned from her place of deepest fulfilment.

The second devastation came from an entirely different direction.

Purley was on the flight path of the dreaded flying bombs. These monsters droned in with their lethal loads and people took cover as they could. If the engine of the nearest invader continued running, those beneath it were relatively relaxed. That one was going overhead, to maim and maybe kill some other poor victims. It was when the rumbling roar stopped that hearts began to beat at twice the normal rate. That one was about to crash down and anyone immediately underneath was at very serious risk.

In her ninth floor office in Dolphin Square Eileen could see the bombs going by. Sometimes during meetings everyone would, without a word, dive under the table. The noise had stopped! They would stay there, jumbled up, until a nearby explosion told them that someone else had borne the brunt. Then they would emerge and carry on with the discussion about clothing coupons.

Quite frequently telephone calls would be interrupted. 'Hold on, I'm going under the desk,' one or the other of the conversing parties would say. If the two telephones were in adjacent buildings the other might say, 'Yes, I'm going too!' Generally, after the crash and roar, the talk would be resumed but sometimes there was silence. At best the lines were down, at worst the fellow civil servant had been hit.

On the train, coming up from Purley, Eileen would every day see fresh gaps in the buildings. In the street she would join others in falling to the ground whenever the overhead racket ominously stopped. In buses passengers would dive to the dirty floor. There was, she remembers, a marvellous atmosphere of comradeship. In the Underground, where the huge steel doors under the Thames would usually be closed against the risk of flooding, there could have been claustrophobic panic but instead there was humour and mutual support.

The cruel device which ran out of flying power over Purley came at night, two years or so after Eileen first lodged with Mrs. Palmer. Eileen had done some washing and hung it near the fire to dry before, unusually, going to bed in the steel Morrison shelter which took up much of Mrs. Palmer's dining room. Her hostess and another lodger had gone to their familiar beds. The nightmare drone of the lethal machines began but the Purley residents were accustomed to it. It was possible to sleep through the racket but on that night everyone was suddenly awake, not because of a noise but because of the absence of it.

There was nothing they could do but tremble. An engine had cut out early. The ghastly swooshing noise told that one of the canisters was at that moment tumbling from the sky and would, within a second or two, hit somewhere, explode, devastate and kill.

The awful blast, when it came, shook the house. The front door was propelled violently from its hinges. It is likely that there were screams and curses but nothing could be heard at first save the explosion and the crash of falling masonry. It seemed that they had sustained the worst but when a pale-faced Air Raid Warden suddenly appeared where the door had been, he told them that it was a near neighbour who had suffered a direct hit. He asked if they were injured and when Eileen said 'no' she was surprised to be told that blood was streaming from her nose.

It was June and already there were strong hints of daylight as the three women staggered out. They could see then that the Warden was right. The house whose garden abutted onto the rear of theirs was a pile of smoking rubble. At first it looked as though the inhabitants had survived because there were figures around the Anderson shelter on the lawn but then the terrible news was relayed. The children had been under the stairs, perhaps to keep them warm. They had been killed.

Unable to do anything to help, the women went back to the house. All of the windows were missing. Inside was devastation; every ornament was smashed. Mrs. Palmer was stoical. At least they were alive. Oddly, Eileen noticed almost immediately that her spare pyjamas were missing. They must, she supposed, have been sucked up the chimney and she struggled to repress a giggle at the idea of her night garments swooshing upwards into the midsummer sky.

Mrs. Palmer suggested that tea and toast would be welcome. The women cooperated and then sat amongst the chaos with their steaming, brimming mugs and a plate of buttered toast before them. Eileen took a welcome bite and immediately felt sharp pain. Inside her mouth was the taste of blood. She cried a warning to the others and Mrs. Palmer peered anxiously into the remnants of the butter. It was, she declared with horror, impregnated with tiny shards of glass. The enemy had robbed them of even this simple treat.

A male voice was heard as they finished their unsatisfactory breakfast and the women called in welcome. A Czechoslovakian pilot, Eileen's current boy friend, made his way through the debris. He was a member of the Caterpillar Club which was open only to those who had parachuted to safety from a stricken aircraft. He had endured many tribulations but it was clear that the evidence of domestic damage was upsetting. He had come, he said, to make sure that they were safe.

There was nothing the caller could do but he asked Eileen if she cared to take a walk. They made their way to the village green and joined the small crowd of people who were watching the anti-aircraft battery trying to shoot down the doodlebugs which continued to stream high overhead. There was some satisfaction, at least, in seeing the effort to counter the mindless menace.

The house was uninhabitable. Eileen was forced to move once more, this time to Highgate which, being to the north of the city, was relatively free from the perils of flying bombs. The accommodating friend could offer space only for a short time so Eileen then found a room in Belsize Park in a house largely populated by elderly German-speaking Jewish refugees. One of these, for no evident reason, used to spend much of her time craning her head out of a window and staring into Eileen's third floor room, an unnerving habit.

Whenever there was a threat of bombs all the residents would gather in the lounge where, it seemed to Eileen, she was the only anglophone. She recognised that the women were speaking their first language but it was difficult not to dislike the sound. At the time the young civil servant would have scoffed mightily at the idea that the time was not too far off when she would be a fluent German speaker herself.

As soon as Mrs. Palmer was rehoused, her lodger returned. Many of the original comforts were missing but the Swiss woman's residence was still the nearest thing Eileen had to a home in the London area.

Throughout all these disruptions, the serious work continued. Being sharp-witted and diligent, Eileen was eventually promoted to take charge of a section. Her department dealt with the implementation of the Consumer Rationing Order and her particular group had responsibility for the extra coupons given to people who had lost clothing as a result of bombing.

There were problems. An adult was granted twenty six clothing coupons per year, just sufficient to acquire a man's suit. Careful choices had to be made and people could not afford to use their personal allowance on work items. Generally, those in 'dirty' work were allowed ten extra coupons but the gas workers were not content with this and went on strike in protest. Worse off were the paramedical staff who had been omitted from the scheme altogether. To solve this latter problem, Eileen devised a voucher system which successfully stretched the regulations.

Eileen's main concern was with providing ration coupons for those who had been bombed out of their homes but she dealt also with immigrants and those who, through misfortune, had become separated from their rightful allocation. If the loss were accidental then no replacement could be made but there were many borderline cases which demanded great interpretative finesse. For example, a man wrote on behalf of a female relative who, finding herself in a lavatory with only her ration book for paper, felt justified in using it in pursuit of hygiene. Could this be described as an accidental loss? The case went all the way to the President, the famous Sir Stafford Cripps, who found in favour of the benighted damsel. The woman's sudden biological need might have been an accident, the absence of proper paper might also have been a matter of chance but clearly the decision to divert the precious coupons was deliberate and, under the circumstances, entirely forgivable.

Eileen was not surprised by Sir Stafford's humane judgement. She had met him several times because he made a point of visiting everyone employed within his domain. He was perhaps the kindliest of the Presidents during Eileen's eleven years at the Board, a distinguished company which included Hugh Dalton, Hartley Shawcross, Hugh Gaitskell and Harold Wilson. Just why all the first names of the Cripps successors had to begin with the same letter was one of life's minor unsolved mysteries.

Work was taxing in many ways but Eileen made sure that it did not deprive her entirely of a social life. She remembers a very lively party in Cheyne Walk, organised to celebrate the first anniversary of the

Consumer Rationing Order, after which she enjoyed a flirtatious but essentially innocent stroll along the Embankment with a very high ranking official. There were also events such as the dances at the RAF officers' club and Eileen found cultural self-expression through playing in amateur orchestras and quartets. Life was by no means dull and it was significantly enhanced by a government ruling that restaurants could charge no more than five pounds for a meal. People who would normally think very carefully about patronising London's elite establishments were suddenly able to dine, and in some cases dance, at the Cafe Royal, the Ritz, the Savoy and the best that Park Lane could offer. Eileen took full advantage.

As the war drew towards its end, Maurice was restored to uniform, granted an official car and given the task of following the advancing armies. His brief was to report on the needs of the starving Belgian and Dutch citizens. As always, he performed this task with great enthusiasm and efficiency. He located an apartment in Brussels and exhorted Lilla to join him but, much as she would have wanted to share the adventure, her illness was draining all energy. Disappointed, but determined to be with her, Maurice applied for a transfer and was given a senior post with the Wines and Spirits Department, a role that was not altogether displeasing to one who had a cultivated taste for Scotch whisky.

When peace came, it brought the reinstatement of the Civil Service examinations. Those who had been working throughout the hostilities were not granted exemption. Along with other experienced administrators, Eileen was summoned to the college at Stoke D'Abernon for a three day ordeal.

Before setting off, candidates had to take tests in English and arithmetic. Eileen had no qualms whatsoever about the former of these but throughout her life the manipulation of numbers had posed problems. In mild terror she fled to her father whose training as an actuary would surely prove invaluable.

The family had by this time moved back to Surrey. The house had suffered some damage during the war but it was habitable. Under great stress because of Lilla's illness, Maurice made time for his daughter, explaining, setting exercises, marking, but the sessions became fraught.

Not for the first time the reluctant student wondered why anyone was interested in calculating the total area of a complex of gravel paths, or why the owner of the leaking bath did not simply mend the wretched thing rather than waste precious time trying to work out how long it would take to empty. There were tears of frustration as Eileen struggled to overcome the inexplicable mental blocks but the struggle was worthwhile; she acquired sufficient expertise to scrape through the test

Relieved that the worst part of the ordeal was over, Eileen went to Stoke D'Abernon. The first shock was the discovery that participants were expected to wear numbers on their chest and back. The second was that they were to be under observation at all times, even during meals and breaks. The third was that everyone was enjoined to deliver a ten minute speech on a topic drawn out of a hat. By the end of the first day Eileen was so frazzled that she had been in the nearby public house for over half an hour before she realised that she was still wearing her identifying numbers.

On the second day, the candidates were told to imagine that they were on an uncivilised island. Their task was to create a structure of governance from scratch.

There was, Eileen recalls, a wonderful comradeship amongst the victims of this selection system. They were aware that methods evolved during the war years for officer recruitment were being tried out on them. Some thought that this was not entirely appropriate but their careers depended on cooperation. With considerable inputs of humour, they set about creating their kingdom.

Ironically, given her uncertainty with arithmetic, Eileen found herself with the task of devising a banking system. Maybe the actuarial spirit of her father provided inspiration because the Eileen Knowles Island Bank was deemed to pass muster.

On the third day the candidates made their speeches and then the psychologists were given free rein. Their war-honed technique included a searching interview which seemed to have no conventional limits. Eileen was asked; 'What do you associate with the word "mother"?'. What the candidate actually associated, at that time, was anxiety and grief. It was a taxing moment. Presumably the questioner did not want to hear a personal lament along the lines of, 'Well, actually, my mother's dying'. Fighting for self control, she gave what she hoped were psychologically acceptable responses. Eileen was so mentally bruised by the ordeal that she cried copiously when she got home and visibly shook for three entire days.

The outcome was not satisfactory. Eileen had not failed but she was placed on a waiting list. After all the highly successful efforts with the Consumer Rationing Order it was a frustrating decision.

There was the problem of what to do in the waiting period. As ever, Eileen's father was stalwart. One of his previous superiors had become Secretary General of the British Tourist and Holiday Board. There was little difficulty in finding a niche for Eileen within the department.

She was very soon entrusted with the setting up of a new travel organisation for Wales. Having lived in the Principality, and loving the place, Eileen addressed her task gladly. The problem, she swiftly discovered, was in establishing any level of agreement whatsoever amongst the Welsh. It was impossible even to achieve a consensus as to where in Wales the preliminary meeting should take place. In the event it was held across the border, in thoroughly English Shrewsbury.

Once the new body was established, Eileen was delegated to supervise the flow of catering supplies to hotels and guest houses. One of the primary problems in this area was the allocation of sheets. Although she had no way of knowing it, this was not to be the last time that this basic commodity would be of important concern to her.

A period of light relief from these duties came when the secretary of the Board's senior executive became ill and Eileen was asked to deputise. Day to day working in the office soon revealed that her superior's name, when it was uttered by his subordinates, was invariably preceded not by his knightly title but by the word 'bloody'. This was not because he was a difficult manager but because of his ineradicable propensity for swearing. No sentence, however simple, was complete for him without a mild expletive. It was just his way.

Eileen quickly discovered that the man was colourful in more aspects than his language. A central part of her new post was time management in relation to her boss's wife and mistress. Diplomacy and discretion were requisite. Under other circumstances this might have been invidious but the good baronet was one of those male charmers, a maverick, for whom the normal rules of social conduct seemed irrelevant. Everyone acknowledged that he was 'a bit of a lad' and for him almost anything was possible.

A few months after Eileen had started to work at the Tourist Board it was announced that those who had been placed on the waiting list after the Stoke d'Abernon ordeal could seek an interview to be considered for entry to the Special Departmental Grades of Labour Exchange Managers and Income Tax Inspectors. The latter was utterly abhorrent but there would, Eileen thought, be something honourable in helping people to find work. She went through the process, doing her best to make her feelings clear and was thus utterly astonished when she was offered a post with the Inland Revenue. She refused, as she recalls, 'not only on the grounds of innumeracy but because I couldn't bear to do a job which would cause the public to hate me.' Like her brother she revealed her feelings to the interviewers and, predictably, they were shocked.

*Eileen on a visit to Cambridge soon after women were officially acknowledged by the university in 1948.*

Another period of waiting ensued but at length the Civil Service Commissioners came routinely to the name of Eileen Knowles on their reserve list. She was offered the post of Assistant Principal in the Board of Trade and, having enjoyed her wartime stint in that department, she accepted the opportunity readily.

She worked initially in the areas of tyres, silk and other fabrics. This unpromising ground provided her with what she describes as 'marvellous trips' to the likes of Macclesfield and Wolverhampton. In spite of the equalising effects of the war, she was invariably the only female at meetings. She was treated as a member of an exotic species. Out of four thousand members of the First Division Association, the 'trade union' of high-ranking civil servants, there were but four hundred women. Within the civil service women were generally treated equally but it was different in the commercial world. Eileen was, for example, excluded from the Tyre Manufacturers' Conference purely because of her gender.

After the mandatory six months probationary period she was promoted to the rank of Principal and given the task of servicing the operations of the Central Price Regulating Committee. Her office was in Queen Anne's Mansions, very close to where her father was working. Regularly they met for lunch at the English Speaking Union. There, Eileen recounted her triumphs and complained bitterly about her superior, a man called March, whose attitude towards women was antediluvian.

The work was interesting, even challenging at times, and Eileen would have been perfectly content with her lot were it not for the peculiarities of her new superior. Ostensibly in the furtherance of good staff relationships this misogynist would organise tea parties at which he would indulge himself with one or both of his obsessions. At the best, he would show dull holiday photographs at which everybody present was supposed to exclaim delightedly. On the bad days he would indulge his morbid fascination with human blood.

There were no satanic rituals, no actual woundings, just recitations of what came to be known as Mr. March's 'gory stories'. It happened that his brother was a Home Office pathologist. What a rich source of stomach-churning anecdotes this unhappy circumstance proved! But Mr.

March was not content with second-hand material. He either caused accidents to happen, or was gravitationally attracted to them. He seemed to have an inexhaustible stream of episodes in which blood featured mightily. His very briefcase, consigned to the overhead rack on the commuter train, became an instrument. As the train braked suddenly, the case fell. It was probably full of family photographs and purloined forensic documents. Whatever, it was heavy and the clasp gouged a deep groove in an unfortunate fellow passenger's head. Mr. March was publicly contrite but it was clear to those who knew him that he was, in truth, utterly delighted.

Eileen's distress at Mr. March's antics was doubtless exacerbated by the fact that her mother's illness was becoming ever more acute. The misery of her father added to her woes. Maurice had returned to the Government Actuary's Department. He was working all hours on the implementation of the radical Beveridge social security scheme but it was clear that the distractions of the task were nowhere near sufficient to dull the pain of seeing his wife in so much anguish. Their dream of a retirement home in North Wales, for which they had already acquired a plot of land, was evidently never to be realised.

When Lilla died in 1949 it seemed to Eileen and John as though she took a large part of their father with her. His normally limitless energy dwindled, his optimism and sense of fun departed. The children were glad on his behalf when he announced that he was being sent temporarily to New Zealand to establish reciprocal arrangements with their pioneering social security system and further delighted when, as a result of his efforts, was made a Commander of the British Empire. As his children had hoped, these diversions helped to restore some of their father's spirit but there was still much ground to be regained.

Looking for further revival, Eileen and John investigated a new organisation called the Austrian Alpine Club which offered cheap but excellent facilities for hikers. Foreign currency restrictions were severe and the AAC promised the rare prospect of a continental holiday within the limits. The three of them took the plunge and enjoyed the experience so much that they repeated the exercise the following year. It was the start of a family love affair with Austria.

A very busy social diary and the foreign holidays made life very enjoyable but Eileen was coming to the end of her tether at work. She was on the point of asking for a permanent transfer to another branch of the Civil Service when Mr. March himself was moved. In his place came a man called Douglas Markwick who was utterly different from his predecessor. Life at the Board of Trade became suddenly enjoyable.

Douglas Markwick gave Eileen responsibility for the section which dealt with 'Miscellaneous Goods'. Immediately she found herself embroiled in complex negotiations about funerals. The austerity caused by the war had removed choice; there was but one standard funeral which cost twenty pounds. There was a standard coffin too. Swiftly Eileen got to know the officials of the combined trades associations, Mr. Hands, Miss Hurry and Mr. Hotter. The curse of the 'H' was not confined to presidents of the Board of Trade, it seemed. Shrouds and coffin linings became her daily concern and when Douglas Markwick was invited to the annual conference of funeral directors in Scarborough Eileen was not entirely surprised to learn that the ceremonial cake was shaped like a coffin.

'Miscellaneous Goods' also included sanitary products. Eileen could not resist implanting a few tasteful jokes in her formal papers, innocent jests which would have driven Mr. March to apoplexy but which generally met with amusement and approval under the new regime. Perhaps as a subtle, humorous, punishment for her temerity it fell to Eileen's lot to accompany the Chairman of the Central Price Regulation Committee to a meeting about sanitary towels. This goodly citizen had, for a time, been Director of Public Prosecutions. He was a bachelor, in semi-retirement, a gentleman of the old school still devoting himself to public service.

Eileen strolled alongside this august figure towards the building where the meeting was to be held. They exchanged commonplaces. He was, she discovered, entirely pleasant, almost shy. Apparently reminding himself of the topic for the morning's meeting he said, 'Er, Tampax is it not this morning, Miss Knowles?'

Eileen confirmed. The good knight cleared his throat. They were approaching the doorway.

'Er, Miss Knowles?' the Chairman said, halting his stroll for a moment but looking fixedly ahead, 'er, could you tell me, er, could you say, what are Tampax?'

The product was, in fact, relatively new and the ignorance was understandable. This did not help Eileen, however, who was faced with a delicate task. Turning a nervous giggle into a convincing cough, she delivered what she describes as a 'careful definition' which, so far as she could tell, did little to enlighten the mystified old bachelor.

Such challenges, under the benign control of Douglas Markwick, became ever more enjoyable and the Board generated a social and cultural life which made the non-working hours also pleasantly busy. Eileen's primary recreational focus was the choir. She joined as a singer and swiftly progressed to being secretary. There were weekly rehearsals but much time was taken up with peripheral organisation, especially when the fame of the ensemble began to spread. Each year they sang carols round the Christmas tree in Trafalgar Square and, unusually for those early days of the medium, they were invited to participate in a television programme.

This period of peace could not last. The civil service is notorious for transferring staff regardless of their preferences and, quite often, careless of their qualifications. Eileen would not have minded being asked to learn some new discipline but she did resent being reunited, as she perversely was, with the odious Mr. March.

Her new specialism was hosiery. As a way of learning about the process of sock production she was sent to the Aristoc factory in Nottingham, Eileen was met at the station by a gleaming, chauffeured Bentley. The manufacturer treated her like royalty. Once sufficient knowledge had been gained, Eileen was given the brief, if such an ambiguous word is appropriate, of making a sock plan for the next war. This seemed a touch pessimistic, almost futile, but there was a dubious perk in the guise of a visit to Leicester, the heart of the hosiery industry.

Eileen duly produced the report but when, six months later, another dull treatise on socks was required she felt that it was time for a change. She had heard of a course in trade and industry at Vienna University. A sabbatical year in her beloved Austria would provide just the break she needed. Without much difficulty the arrangements were made.

One minor snag was that Eileen spoke no German. Indeed, during the war years when she had lain on the floor surrounded by chattering biddies, she had come to loathe the sound of the language. The lack, she told her employers, was not a problem. She would learn sufficient German on the train. In fact, in the time before her departure, Eileen arranged for some conversation classes but these gave only the rudiments.

The leave was not to be a paid one but Eileen had savings and Lilla had bequeathed modest amounts to her children. The main financial hazard was that only a very limited amount of foreign currency could be purchased in those days of tight fiscal restrictions. Eileen, determined to make a change in her life regardless of difficulty, guessed that there would be ways of managing.

Whilst Eileen engineered this major upheaval there was a similarly large scale, and oddly parallel, shift in her father's circumstances.

Ever since their mother's death, Eileen and John had worried about their father. The New Zealand trip and the Austrian holidays had been very beneficial and he had subsequently picked up some of his old zest yet it was evident that the prospect of a life of retirement without Lilla was subduing his spirits. His children talked often about encouraging him to find a second career. Then, all at once, a moment of inspiration came.

Through the mountain excursions the family had come to know Major Ingham, the founder of the Austrian Alpine Club. The children suggested to their father that he might ask this new acquaintance for a job.

Maurice could see drawbacks. For one thing, he also spoke no German which, up to that point, he had habitually referred to as 'that damn language'. For another he had a serious problem with one of his knees which stuck out at an angle not intended by nature. The trouble stemmed from an accident sustained whilst playing football in a prisoner of war camp and had been much exacerbated by a fall from a wireless mast in 1935. The ligaments had been badly torn. The 'treatment' then prescribed, of six weeks inactivity, had probably been the worst possible course.

His children were not to be gainsaid. Eileen was planning to learn German from scratch and so could he. As for the leg, he never allowed it to get in the way of walking miles and dancing for hours on end. The Austrian mountains would be no match.

Major Ingham, when approached, saw no difficulties at all. He was delighted to have someone so personable as Maurice as one of his representatives. And so it came about that as Eileen made her final preparations for temporary migration Maurice was negotiating with the university in Innsbruck to take a language course. Father and daughter would, if he was accepted, be some distance apart but at least they would be in the same country and facing the same learning task.

It was the autumn of 1953 when Eileen set out on her journey into the unknown. She was thirty three years old. She heard, just before she left, that Mr. March had been relieved of responsibility for the hosiery department but she had no second thoughts about going. It was time for a change and there was no knowing where this new adventure might eventually lead.

## 3. Karl

Karl's life started on May 22nd 1924 in Steiermark, Austria. He was born in his grandmother Rinnerhofer's house which was a long way up a very steep mountain track, a few kilometres from the industrial town of Bruck an der Mur. His father worked as a smith at the Boller steelworks. When Karl was two the family moved to Bruck.

*Karl's parents*

In the aftermath of World War One, Austria was a tempestuous place. Like its neighbour, Germany, it endured economic recession, high unemployment and bouts of extreme price inflation. Politically, the country became polarised. Violent confrontations between left and right wingers were commonplace.

Karl's first ten years were dominated by this underlying uncertainty. His father was a leading member of a trade union which was fighting hard to improve the lot of labourers. Herr Fuchs was often away at meetings which, to the young Karl, had secret purposes. There was an atmosphere of conspiracy, fear and fierce determination. The name 'Karl Marx' was often uttered and the boy must sometimes have wondered if he had been named after this mysterious hero.

An only child, Karl worshipped his father. The loyal son adopted the hatred of the oppressor with uncritical zeal. Priests were loathed just as much as the rich and the fascist politicians. In winter, the local man of God was fair game for snowballs, his black cassock making him a highly visible target against the glaring white. In the warmer months the pious form attracted high velocity gobbets of golden dung. Generally Karl was too agile and fleet to be caught but on one occasion, when he was spotted and chased by the enraged cleric, an old woman hid him under her voluminous skirts. She evidently shared the boy's antipathy towards things Roman.

There was a feud, also, with two young girls who lived in the apartment below the one inhabited by the Fuchs family. Driven to the limits by their teasing Karl responded by raining urine down upon them from his balcony to theirs. He agreed with his father; when the balance of force is mightily against you there is every justification for using dirty tricks. The rift cannot have been serious because the child enemies became lifelong friends although the teasing and bantering never stopped.

Around the time of Karl's tenth birthday, the turmoil was reaching new heights. All the adults were talking about a man called Hitler who was promising a re-birth of the devastated German nation. Some of the local people seemed to admire this saviour, others mistrusted him. At school the boys argued, taking their cues from their parents. Karl was of the Schutzbund faction, the enemy was the Heimwehr, left versus right, peasants versus lords.

There was a third force in the country, the Christian Socialists led by Englebert Dollfuss. In contradiction to their name, these people, who formed the democratically elected government, were right wing. They were not as extreme as the 'home defence' Heimwehr but were resolutely determined to forestall any attempt to mount a Marxist revolution.

In spite of their shared antipathy towards the left, neither Dollfuss, nor Fey, the Heimwehr leader, embraced Nazism. They felt threatened by the propaganda which Hitler had begun to filter into the country. The key question of the time was; would the Schutzbund use their considerable stocks of arms in defence of their country in the likely event of a German invasion? More probably, the right-wingers believed, the Marxists would use the opportunity to attempt to seize power for themselves.

In the face of what they saw as potential treason, Herr Fey and his Heimwehr decided on direct action. The left-wing Schutzbund had to be neutralised. Fey made a rousing speech in a town near Vienna on the 11th of February, declaring: 'Tomorrow we will go to work and we will do the job properly for our Fatherland'. The following morning this belligerent promise was kept. There were dawn raids in Linz, primarily on the Hotel Schiff, the main stronghold of the Schutzbund in the city. It seems that Fey had anticipated an easy victory but what resulted was nothing short of civil war. Wherever they had armaments, the workers took up the fight. Dollfuss was forced to join in on the Heimwehr's side. History books tell of the Schutzbund taking on the police, the gendarmerie and, eventually, the regular federal army.

The conflict lasted only four days and the outcome was entirely predictable. The pro-government forces lost one hundred and five men, with over three hundred wounded. The Schutzbund suffered one hundred and thirty seven fatalities with over four hundred wounded.

Karl was to remember for the rest of his life the aftermath of the Bruck battles. As soon as it was safe to do so, he went in search of his father. Broken, bloody bodies were strewn in the streets. Running, desperate, the ten year old boy ascertained that none of the dead was his father but he recognised one or two of the lifeless faces. Maybe his father was lying somewhere else, maybe he was injured, maybe he had been captured by the enemy. At the very best he would be in hiding.

It was some time before news emerged that Herr Fuchs had managed to get out of the country. Given that nine alleged ring-leaders of the Schutzbund were executed, it was a huge relief to Karl and his mother that their hero was safe. Once the worst of the retribution was over, the exile risked a secret return and was almost immediately arrested. His fate was imprisonment, not death. Frau Fuchs and her boy were at least spared the horror of execution but they found themselves in dire economic circumstances.

British sympathisers with the Austrian workers' cause were filtering financial aid through the Protestant churches. Karl's mother was Catholic according to her birth certificate but she swiftly made a strategic transfer of religious allegiance. It was no time to let ideology dominate. With occasional inputs from the fund, and with money she was able to earn, the two of them survived.

Dollfuss, who had banished the Nazis because they threatened Austria's independence, was murdered by right wing fanatics. Hitler annexed Austria a few years later in 1938. Many welcomed the Anschluss. The Fuhrer was promising economic revival, a gift he seemed capable of delivering given the evidence of Germany's resurgence. The price to be paid for this economic coat-tail ride was the disappearance of all political freedoms. The young Karl Fuchs, son of a Marxist agitator, imbued with the spirit of free-thinking, was trapped in a fascist, Catholic state.

One of the punishments inflicted on the worker rebels was the removal of the rights of their children to a secondary education. At thirteen Karl was compelled to leave school but he was fortunate enough to be signed up for an apprenticeship with a local locksmith. His resourceful mother had found regular employment which provided sufficient income for her to be able to put money aside for the anticipated time when the man of the house would be released. Above all Frau Fuchs was determined that one day they would build their own house.

Apart from the loss of his father, which Karl felt grievously, these prewar years were pleasant enough. Generally, young teenagers are not overly affected by politics. Life continued; indeed, people began to prosper as Hitler's economic miracle spread to the conquered country. An older cousin, Herman, who lived nearby, became Karl's main playmate.

Karl was a small youth, bereft of body hair. It was as though the normal path of physical development had been cut off, perhaps by the shock of losing his father. His chief delight was to go high into the mountains.

He had been given skis at the age of four and in the winter he would venture far and fast. With Herman and other friends from the neighbourhood he would race down the steep Alpine slopes, careless of danger. When not skiing, Karl would swim, sprint, play football and climb the challenging rocks and limestone faces The physical world was his domain; he had no time for scholarship. He rarely walked anywhere, he would always be running, treating the parked cars as slalom poles.

This youthful, carefree interlude came to an abrupt end as the new war developed. The German army needed men. They had already forced Herman into uniform. He was, as far as the family knew, in Norway. With the minimum age of recruitment becoming ever lower, Karl's moment of destiny arrived all too quickly.

To his mother it seemed absurd that anyone could imagine turning her son into a soldier. A neutral observer would probably have guessed his age as twelve. He was puny, there was still no trace of body hair and his face was scarcely beyond the baby stage of development. Yet it was undeniable that his birth certificate told the truth. He must either be a soldier or be summarily shot.

Karl had heard of men who, rather than succumb, had taken to hiding in the mountains and of others who had managed to escape across the border but the prospects of years of cold, hungry loneliness, or of being hunted and shot like a wild animal were not appealing. Many Austrian men of left wing views were adopting the policy of seeming to go along with the German demands but of resolving never deliberately to kill one of the 'enemy' unless such action was inevitable in pursuit of self-defence. This was Karl's strategy.

The boy-soldier was assigned to the artillery section of the Gebirgesjager whose badge was an Edelweiss. He was sent to the Kaisergebirge close to Kufstein in Tirol for basic training. This daunting group of rocky peaks had been the haunt of many of Austria's finest mountaineers. The troops selected for mountain warfare were expected to negotiate some of the toughest ascents as part of their learning process. This was no imposition as far as Karl was concerned; climbing was one of his greatest joys.

Perhaps in recognition of his immaturity, the Germans put Karl to work at the nearby Kneissl ski-making factory where he was set to painting the laths white, ready for winter warfare. Like the climbing, the job suited Karl to perfection. In the free periods he tested the equipment on the slopes and impressed his employers mightily with his skill. His physical slightness also caused him to be chosen to exercise a racehorse which had been presented by the Arab King Farouk to the colonel.

Karl's accelerated journey of maturation started there in Kufstein. The physical work developed his body and the contact with older males forced him to face the realities of life. Close to the manufacturing plant was an establishment which, Karl soon discovered, housed young women. They were there partly for the gratification of officers of the notorious SS but their main role was to produce 'pure' children, the future citizens of the purged fatherland. The talk amongst the workers about this baby factory answered many of his adolescent questions. The 'facts of life' were laid before him crudely and unavoidably.

*The boy soldier*

The physical drills of the military training built muscles, the focus on killing and avoiding death forced Karl quickly into adulthood. By the end of this three month induction into warfare, the reluctant soldier was deemed ready to join the ill-fated Axis incursion into Russia. His expertise with horses determined the nature of the posting. He was assigned to the task of looking after the stoical beasts which pulled the heavy guns.

Up to that point, being a German soldier had been something of a game. Karl was just a youth of very limited experience. Like most other Austrians, he loathed the fact that his country's sovereignty had been stolen. Like his father, he resented the power of the wealthy and the excessive influence of the Catholic church but he had not fully registered the implications of these things.

The long, cold journey towards Stalingrad concentrated his young mind. A further, dreadful, lesson in reality came when he learned, via a letter from his mother which astonishingly reached him, that his cousin Herman had been killed in Norway. Karl knew that he was neither German nor fascist but he knew also that power was concentrated against the likes of him and his father. There was no hope of providing a realistic resistance. He would have to play a careful game, seeming to go along with the tide but all the time looking for his own survival. If called upon to fight, he would fight, not to further German imperialism but simply to avoid disaster.

Numerous books tell of the daily proximity of death from cold, starvation, disease and enemy action during that wretched, futile campaign. Karl was spared the worst of the Russian nightmare because when his company reached Odessa, the ignominious German retreat was already under way. Instead of marching towards Stalingrad, as they had expected, the fresh soldiers were ordered south but there was still the shortage of food, the lack of adequate clothing and the constant threat of attack.

They marched, usually uncertain about their destination, acutely anxious about survival, drifting according to the changing patterns of the war. They went to the Caucasus, Crimea, northern Greece, Albania and, finally, Yugoslavia. According to Karl's reckoning, their meandering journey covered over four thousand miles. At the Yugoslav border they were at last loaded onto trains. The carriages were cattle trucks but the men packed into these, grateful for the chance to rest blistered, frost-bitten feet.

*Winter warfare*

In Yugoslavia, the communist partisans, led by Tito, were causing much trouble for the remnants of the occupying Axis forces. Through the slats of the carriages the soldiers could see, as the conveyance clanked and jolted along, the dangling, twisted bodies of resisters who had been hanged from every telegraph pole and signal gantry.

At first this theatre of war was much the same for Karl as the Russian one had been. Arrogant, brutal officers issued mindless orders and anyone who dared to demur faced immediate execution. The partisans were infuriating the occupying generals with their hit and run tactics. Unable to catch and kill the enemy, the Germans ordered a programme of gross attrition. Villages were completely destroyed. Reluctant soldiers such as Karl, hardened by war but still capable of being appalled, did what they could to minimise the damage but there were always the bloodthirsty psychopaths who really did shoot with lethal purpose. It is reported that for every German soldier killed, one hundred civilians were executed regardless of age and gender.

A kind of relief from the war misery came in the form of illness; a bout of cerebral malaria and jaundice contracted, so Karl believed, in the Greek phase of his wanderings. He was sent to a hospital and stayed there several months before the doctors pronounced him fit to return to active service.

Ever more empathetic to the partisan cause, Karl soon found himself involved in action in Bosnia. The partisans had launched an insulting offensive at Mostar and the Axis troops organised a huge reprisal which they called 'Operation Schwarz'. There was a bridge over the River Neretva close to Mostar which, for German strategic reasons, had to be demolished. Here was a task which Karl could accomplish without killing the innocent and which would defer any doubts the commanders might have about the loyalty of this particular Austrian soldier.

At great risk to his own safety, Karl played a prominent part in the operation. The military authorities were so impressed that they mentioned the hero in despatches and suggested that he should be awarded the Iron Cross. Although Karl was totally opposed to all that the Axis forces represented, he was proud when this honour was bestowed. He saw it as a tribute to his personal skill and courage. The decoration would give the young soldier status; it would be difficult from then on for any officer to question his commitment.

This new position of strength was further confirmed when, in an abortive raid on the island of Korcula, Karl was blown out of the boat by a partisan shell. He swam to safety, enhancing his reputation as a brave and resourceful soldier.

In the winter, Karl's expertise on skis ensured that he was always based in the mountains. Here, the battle against the partisans was very different from the massed confrontations on the Russian plain. Wit and agility were more important than pure might. There is nothing, Karl would occasionally say later in life, better able to refine slalom skills than the circumstance of an enemy firing an automatic rifle with lethal intent. Under the new circumstances, the boy who had been so uncertain of himself on the way to Stalingrad turned rapidly into a young man to whom others looked for leadership. Often the decisions required of him were crucial to survival. Less frequently they involved winning internal battles against their German masters.

It was on one of these latter occasions that Karl was partly instrumental in daringly diverting a goat which was destined for the officers' mess. The beast was killed, cooked and eaten by the men in record time. Karl was proud of the ingenuity with which he and his comrades eliminated all traces of the animal. 'Goat, what goat?' they were able to say to the investigating officers without a twitch of hesitancy.

More seriously, he was also involved in a patrol which for once had the fleeing Marshal Tito in their trap. Nobody wanted to present the Germans with this much coveted prize. Taking their time, the soldiers alerted the colonel who, against strict instructions, had taken his boots off for the night. His slowness in putting them back on gave the Yugoslavian patriot all the time he needed. Between them the pursuers failed to make the best of their advantage and Tito escaped.

As the battle developed, the occupying troops were forced ever more completely into adopting the strategy of the enemy. Apart from the constant fear that death might come suddenly, Karl began to enjoy the contest of wits. He admired the partisans greatly; they were mountain men. They too could ski and shoot and live off the land just as he could. As the German defeat became inevitable the conscripts who were sympathetic to the partisan cause had ever more opportunity for cooperation with the erstwhile enemy. A curious comradeship developed.

It was no great trouble to Karl when his band of nomads was captured. As prisoners of war, but more like companions in hardship, they wandered about the mountains. Because most of them were expert hunters, they ate well but often they had to sleep without shelter. They packed their disintegrating boots with newspaper and never took them off but still many of them, including Karl, succumbed to frostbite. The worst cases were taken to a makeshift hospital where a surgeon conducted wholesale amputations of fingers and toes. Karl took one look at the well-meant butchery and fled; he had no intentions of parting willingly with any of his digits.

When the end came, Karl was in Hungary, near Lake Balaton. The only clothing which he possessed was his uniform. There would, obviously, be great danger in continuing to wear this. Bartering with what little he had, his rifle, the iron medal, the few provisions which they had managed to annexe, he and a few other of his countrymen acquired ill-fitting, fraying garments from Hungarian farmers. Once they had disguised their immediate past, the Austrians turned to Karl. His maturation had been so rapid that from being a timid youth he had turned into a natural leader. In response to the question as to what they should do next, Karl told them simply; they would have to walk home.

The ragged band, trusting Karl's sense of direction and mountaineering skills, followed as he led the way, through the Russian lines, unerringly over four hundred miles to Graz and their newly liberated land.

At home Karl found that his bedroom was occupied by a billeted Russian general. Not too long ago they could have been trying to kill each other. The former enemy was gracious. He seemed to understand the difficulties which the young Austrian men had faced. With great dignity and sorrow he told how his own son, more or less of Karl's age, had been killed at Stalingrad. Instead of acting vindictively, as might have been expected, he congratulated the returning soldier on his survival and promptly vacated the room.

Karl's mother, who had not seen him for four years, scarcely recognised her only child. Apart from the strange clothing, the weather-worn face, the unfamiliar stubble on his chin and cheeks he had, it seemed, almost doubled in bulk. His formerly puny shoulders were broad and thick, his arms bulged with muscles. In the face of this instant manifestation of manhood, Karl's mother became childlike in her behaviour. The experience of reunification was too potent, her self-control simply fell away.

His father, from whom the separation had been much longer, was a stranger. They embraced, of course, and slapped each other's backs but they had to start almost from scratch in building a relationship. As soon as the first breathless phase of story-telling was over, Franz Fuchs suggested that his admirable son might like to join the police force. A respected, popular pre-war leader, Franz Fuchs had much influence in the local community. When Karl heard how keen the law-keepers were on encouraging sporting activity amongst its members, he accepted the chance with alacrity.

Karl took to being a policeman. He was used to uniform and enjoyed playing a part in a hierarchical system but more than this, the job pleased him because the sporting opportunities exceeded his most optimistic expectations. In the summer he ran and swam competitively. Life became intensely enjoyable. He and his companions competed amicably, ever pushing each other to fresh feats of daring. Their chief delight when the weather was hot was to treat weekend strollers to heart-stopping thrills by diving expertly from a dizzyingly high bridge into the river. It must have seemed to Karl that there was no limit to his physical prowess.

In the winter Karl played football for the Bruck team and skied whenever he could. At his number one winter sport he quickly became national police champion and this honour, much appreciated locally, produced ever more generous periods of leave for training. He was, in some measure, a professional sportsman. He acquired and re-furbished an abandoned mountain hut and turned it into a retreat. Whenever there was free time, he would take food and drink with him and linger for as long as possible amongst his beloved hills.

There were few ski lifts. For the most part enthusiasts had to walk up the slopes, carrying everything they needed. The race hills were always steep ones because skis were slow. A sharp incline was needed to set them going at the kind of speeds that keen practitioners craved. As a result, Karl's athletic body developed even further. His shoulders and arms grew from the effort of carrying, his legs from the uphill trudging. The conditions of war had, however, set the basis of some weakness. Frostbite had damaged one foot considerably and blood circulation was not what it should be. When Karl consulted a doctor about the spread of varicose veins he was told to abandon his running. The advice was that ideally he should cut down on the skiing but this was impossible. The snow was his first love, his escape, his place for physical poetry. He would rather die than desist.

His success in police skiing competitions led to invitations to participate in other races. Officials in the sport took notice. With winter Olympics due in 1948 the Alpine countries were all looking for new stars of the slalom and downhill. Karl was drafted into the Austrian squad. All at once he was in the company of national heroes such as Ernst Spiess, Erika Mahringer and Ernst Hinterseer. The trainer, Heli

Lantschner, seemed to have no doubt that Karl was worthy of his new status.

Determined to secure his place in the elite squad, Karl extended himself ever further in the training until, one dark day on the Zugspitze, he made a minuscule mistake and crashed at very high speed. Equipment and safety measures were rudimentary by modern standards. Karl broke a leg so comprehensively that he was forced to spend nine months in hospital. It was there, miserably trapped between the starched white sheets, that he heard the radio announcement of the chosen few. He was glad for all those who had succeeded but felt his loss bitterly.

Had there been no war, no waste of sporting years, Karl would doubtless have had several chances to find Olympic glory. At twenty four years old, twenty eight by the time of the next competition, he was unlikely to have the skills and fitness to beat the new generation of dedicated racers.

Although he took part in local competitions once he had recovered, Karl decided to make ski teaching and touring the main focus of his career. He needed, for economic reasons, to continue being a policeman but he enrolled on the new nationally approved course for teachers. He was amongst the first batch to receive the treasured qualification. He also won the right to be an official ski guide. One day, he believed, when skiing had recovered from the devastation of the war, he would be able to resign from the directing of traffic and spend all of his working days on his beloved snowy slopes. His dream was that, with luck and good management, he would find a place in Austria where he could open a ski school.

It is difficult to focus on long term ambitions when life is pleasantly filled with exciting events. In the February of 1954, with his thirtieth birthday looming, Karl was still very much enjoying the regular round of racing. An event on the Hochswab was his focus, offering challenging runs against some serious competitors. At the back of his mind, no doubt, was the looming change of personal decade and the uneasy notion that if his dream were to be realised then he should soon take purposeful action. But Karl Fuchs was still living too fully in the present to worry consciously about the long term future.

He went blithely to that event on the Hochschwab, having not the slightest inkling that his life was on the point of being irrevocably changed.

## 4. A Meeting, a Marriage

Eileen was enjoying herself in Vienna. The course was almost an irrelevance. Mainly she was learning German and meeting other students who came from many parts of the world. The expected source of extra income had materialised in the shape of fees for English lessons. Life was pleasantly busy.

With an American, she founded a foreign students' club which arranged social events and outings. Money was made available for study trips to factories which seemed to compete with each other to lay on the most lavish hospitality. There were banquets and visits to beer cellars. It was all very satisfactory after the years of austerity. She also found people with whom she could make music, not a difficult feat in a cultured city such as Vienna.

She was living in a room with a family which had more or less adopted her as one of their own. The man of the house, a retired lawyer called Dodi Pichler, had been one of the first Austrians to take up ski-jumping and had been permanently crippled as a result. His wife, Soso, nursed him devotedly.

There were other students in the house and Eileen's personal space was very small. This she did not mind; the tiny coal stove kept it comfortably warm as the winter began to bite and there was a constant atmosphere of conviviality amongst the guests. The Viennese world seemed exciting, full of possibilities.

Some of these possibilities were unforeseen. Eileen was heavily preoccupied with her various social activities and it seemed that the daily domestic trivia, as though competing for attention, developed a dramatic potential of their own. For example, she would set some bread by the fire to toast and before she could hum two bars from Don Giovanni it was bursting into flames. She would boil handkerchiefs to bring them to a brilliant whiteness and perversely the pan would be dry and scorching the delicate cloths black in the time it took her to look up a couple of difficult German words in the dictionary. Whereas others seemed to persuade the coal-heated bath to deliver an inviting pool of tepid liquid, with her the fire was instantly so fierce that the water boiled as though ready to make tea. The gas-powered iron was no better. For the most part people managed to light it without incident but for Eileen it popped, spat, jumped and came close to outright explosion. Dodi and Soso, who might have been irritated, laughed. They called her 'The Incendiary', a title which she did not in any way resent. It was true, she thought; fiery accidents were attracted to her.

Maurice called to see her in November, en route for Innsbruck, and naturally a party was organised to celebrate. In February, Eileen visited him and they discovered, to their delight, that they were working from the same textbooks. They practised their new language, sorting out the intricacies of the convoluted German grammar as they conversed. When they tired of studying, they went to join the tobogganers and skiers on the Patscherkofel where, it quickly became evident, Maurice already had a very lively social base with the young students. His damaged knee precluded skiing but Eileen, who had previously been on a ski course in Norway and a winter sports holiday in Obergurgl with Board of Trade colleagues, ventured onto the slopes. In the evenings they enjoyed student cafe life and the Fasching dances.

Although he was by no means an ordinary holidaymaker, Maurice was limited to the annual allowance for tourists, then set at twenty five pounds. As far as she could, Eileen helped but Maurice was, as always, spiritedly determined on the maximum of independence. He decided that since the ration of money did not stretch to the purchase of coal he would manage without. With his still slim figure bulked out like a scarecrow's with a miscellany of garments he would sit in his room, hunched over German grammar books, his breath frosting as it emerged.

Both of them continued to develop their contacts with the Austrian Alpine Club, Maurice partly because his beckoning career lay in that direction and Eileen because there were so many interesting people involved in the organisation. One such was a plain clothes detective whose police task was to escort the distinguished visitors who came to Vienna. His connection with the AAC was that he acted as an external supervisor of a mountain establishment called the Sonnschein Hutte. When he learned of Eileen's interest in winter sports, he invited her to join him and his wife for the weekend following a routine inspection. There would, he assured Eileen, be plenty of good skiers around who would be willing to provide instruction.

Accepting gladly, Eileen made her own way to the hut carrying recently purchased skis. The ascent did anything but generate enthusiasm. It was a long slog through deep snow; a strength-sapping climb even for someone as fit as Eileen. To make matters much worse, the usually reliable sun was absent. Low cloud clung to the mountain. The picture was very far from the one shown on all the postcards.

Eileen reached the hut which, in common with most of the AAC establishments, was more like a hotel than a simple refuge. There were dozens of people milling about. Against the sturdy wooden walls of the building, skis were propped. She sought out her policeman friend and registered her arrival with the staff.

Once she had settled the immediate business, she went with her companions to the main downstairs room which acted as bar and dining area. A stove poured out heat, generating a delicious atmosphere of cosiness. There was a smell of gluhwein thick enough to be intoxicating. This was an aspect of skiing which Eileen loved, the conviviality, the comradeship of shared danger, the anticipation of adventures yet to come. She surveyed the scene appreciatively.

And then, all at once, her eye was caught by a tall, good-looking young man who seemed to be the focus of much attention. Her gaze lingered for a moment. The policeman by her side noticed the fact and nodded affirmatively.

'If you want lessons,' he said, 'there's the man to give them to you.'

She learned that the potential tutor was one Karl Fuchs, also a policeman but in nearby Bruck not Vienna. He was a nationally famous skier, a member of the 1948 Olympic squad, a frequent winner of races. He had come up the mountain for a competition which bad been cancelled because of the bad weather. Eileen's informant quickly pointed out, though, that he was not recommending Karl on the basis of his downhill speed but because he was a stylist beyond peer, a natural demonstrator, a most patient and properly qualified instructor. Being willingly led, Eileen was introduced.

There was an immediate difficulty. By this time Eileen's German was moderately fluent. Karl, to her delight, seemed to focus flatteringly on her but as he spoke she could understand but one word in ten. Her friend, well accustomed to the local dialect, acted as interpreter. Karl was puzzled. The very attractive English woman was able to transmit competently but seemed incapable of receiving messages. She excused herself on the grounds that her skills in the language were limited and begged him to speak slowly.

Never one to falter before a challenge, Eileen asked Karl directly if he would be her instructor. He said that, as the race had been cancelled, he certainly had some time to spare. He would be delighted to show her a few tricks of the snow.

Eileen changed into her outdoor wear and followed Karl. Her earlier attempts at skiing had convinced her that she would never be a champion but she had enjoyed the sport immensely. As they fitted the skis and readied for the first manoeuvres, she prayed that she would remember enough to impress. It seemed very important, all of a sudden, that her instructor should approve.

The lesson began and within moments Eileen was laughing. Karl, she discovered, was an inspiration. He made what had sometimes been painful exercises thoroughly enjoyable. He had teaching techniques which were new to Eileen, he could demonstrate like a dream.

When the session was over she asked him if he would be able to continue the lessons on the next day. Karl was apologetic. His duties as a policeman called him back to Bruck. He had been given time off for the race but he could not stay indefinitely. He could though, he said, come back the day after next.

Already there was a tantalising understanding between them that something much more than ski instruction was afoot. Smiling, her eyes conveying more than her words, Eileen said that she would be very pleased if he did come back. Karl said that in that case he would.

Trying him out, testing to see if her intuition about their rapidly developing relationship was correct, Eileen hinted at doubt about his fidelity. He would not, she suggested, want to repeat the long trek up the mountain for the sake of a solitary pupil.

With a smile which broadened all the time, Karl took off his hat and swiftly removed a badge. He proffered it to Eileen. It was, she realised, his teacher's badge, a most treasured possession. Karl told her that he would personally collect it from her and she knew then that the waves of fate were rolling.

In the hut Karl had a quick final drink and then made preparations for the fast ski down the mountain. Naturally he wanted to reach the road before darkness fell. With a last few words, and a wave to everyone, he was gone.

Eileen, whose starry state of love was evident to all, was the subject of some good-natured teasing. The chuckled remarks made it evident that she was not the only young woman to find the racer very attractive. One or two suggested that Herr Fuchs might not, after all, be making the promised ascent to the Sonnschein Hutte but then someone noticed the glint of metal in Eileen's hand. 'Karl's left his badge!' the man declared.

There was a huge, guttural roar of laughter. All of Karl's associates knew; he would be back! And everybody there knew why he would be back. Eileen was not alone in being in love!

The next day she went out with another young man, determined to improve her skiing skills so that Karl would be impressed. The cloud had parted and Eileen was reminded why it was that for many people, skiing was tantamount to being a religion. The mountains in their winter mode were mesmerising. The air was brilliantly clear almost to the point of pain. The tall trees seemed greener, the snow whiter, the sky bluer than anything she had seen before. And, although the ungainly planks strapped to her feet felt often like enemies, she had seen the purest poetry of Karl's movements, full of inspiring grace.

On the third day of her short holiday she was struggling to master the contortions of the snow-plough when Karl appeared. He was walking fast with a rucksack on his back and pair of long, powder-blue Kneissl skis over his shoulder. For a moment Eileen thought that there might be an awkward confrontation between her temporary instructor and the object of her deep desire but the interloper deferred immediately. It was very clear that Karl was king. As befitted a man with such power he exercised it with natural dignity. He took over the running of the private lesson and Eileen was bubbling with excitement.

The magical day vanished but Eileen knew that it was inevitable that she and Karl would meet again. Another trip to the Sonnschein Hutte was arranged and, as Eileen recalls, '...before long I was counting chamois, a kiss for each one.' Almost without negotiation it became clear that they would marry. A longer holiday amongst the snowy mountains was arranged which they both saw as a pre-wedding honeymoon. It was understood that once they were married they would scour Austria for a suitable spot for a ski school and hotel which they would run together. Eileen's days as a civil servant and Karl's as a policeman were very surely over.

Geographically separated for a time, they wrote. Karl's first letter was a work of art, composed impeccably in the classical Kurrentschrift with its ornately embellished lettering. To Eileen, accustomed to the more mundane Lateinisch, it was, like much of Karl's speech, disappointingly unintelligible.

Desperate to know what the pages contained, she took them to a close friend who began to read aloud. The first few sentences caused the interpreter's face to turn a vivid red. By half way down the first page she was collapsing into helpless laughter. The flowing love talk was too much for her composure and Eileen realised at once that just as she would have to learn Steierisch so she would have to become competent in Kurrentschrift. Highly motivated, she accomplished the educational feat in record time.

The 'honeymoon' began and the relationship developed apace. Both of them were fired with enthusiasm for their shared ambition. It mattered not that neither of them had the slightest experience of running a ski school or a hotel; they would learn by doing. The important factor was that Karl had his teaching qualification. Customers would come for the excellence of the tuition and the two of them would quickly acquire the ancillary skills of catering.

*The young couple*

It seemed important that Eileen should become at least competent as a skier. When their pupils began to arrive she could keep the beginners fruitfully occupied whilst Karl taught the more advanced. The one-to-one lessons acquired a deeper purpose than mere recreation.

She discovered that, even beyond her first impressions, Karl was a very gifted teacher, patient, inventive, endlessly encouraging. The sadness for Eileen was that she was by no means the perfect pupil. What seemed so completely effortless for him was a huge task for her. Nevertheless, it was gratifying that by the end of the holiday she had reached a stage where Karl was confident that he could nurse his pupil down the mountain.

He swooped down the steep track and stopped. She ploughed, coming frequently to bone-jarring halts. Very slowly they descended. Karl invented further kissing games, claiming that there was a tariff, one for the sighting of a common bird, two for a rarer one, a dozen for a crested eagle. Eileen did not mind this in the least. She tumbled often and they laughed.

Close to the bottom he went, with her blessing, on a liberating, whooping, swooping run. The track was still steep and to Eileen's right there was a very sharp, densely forested drop. The tops of the trees were at the level of her skis. Unfortunately for her, the left turn was the one with which she had most difficulty. Tired but happy beyond her imaginings she let the skis run a little. She could hear Karl's yodelling cries ahead of her. The tips of her instruments of torture headed for the drop. Weight, weight, weight! on the right ski! on the right, right, right ski!!!!

She was exhausted and the wretched lath would not come round. She let out an involuntary shriek of despair and fell. She thought that death might be the outcome but when she dared to open her eyes she found that she was lying bridged between the track and the spiky summits of the tall pines.

Karl, sensing her difficulty, came up at a run, skis over his shoulder. Once he saw that she was safe and unharmed he laughed, though with no malice whatsoever. Tenderly he gathered and held her, replacing her fatigue and anxiety with an overwhelming burst of love. He put his arm around his future wife and skied for both of them until the track became less steep.

On the last section, when Eileen felt that her energy was close to being drained completely, the way became a nightmare of rutted ice. The runnels were like tram tracks, determining where the skis would go. Karl seemed oblivious, he floated over them.

One of the pernicious hollows trapped Eileen's right ski and led it inexorably, like the wheels of a vintage car caught in tramlines, towards an exposed tree root which was sticking out at shin height. The collision was utterly inevitable. At first she was convinced that the bone had broken but Karl, running once more to the rescue, tenderly explored the wounded area and assured her that the worst outcome would be no more than a lurid bruise. The flood of solicitous love was more potent against the pain than any analgesic and Eileen was able to continue the journey with laughter in her heart.

They stayed for a while at Karl's family home. His mother's

Catholicism seemed to present no problems to their sharing a room but with Eileen's hosts in Vienna, old-fashioned, conventional people, they had to be more circumspect. Karl very soon met Maurice whom he declared delightedly, and only allegorically, to be Colonel Graham, the British commanding officer in Karl's part of Steiermark. They established an immediate rapport. One of the many aspects of Karl's personality which delighted Eileen was his ability to identify one or two key qualities of people and thereby to characterise them. This he did with no malice at all but usually with a deep, wry humour. His names for people were funny but, in relation to his friends at least, they were always profoundly respectful.

As far as practicable, the new couple spent time together. Eileen travelled to Bruck where they would take a bus to the mountain track and trudge for four hours or more to the place of their first meeting. Karl continued to teach her, even though her progress was disappointingly slow. He knew, almost from the outset of her skiing career, that she would never be a competent practitioner of parallel turns but this did not matter. For Karl, then as in the future, what mattered was that people fulfilled their natural potential and that in so doing they enjoyed his chosen sport to the very maximum.

Maurice came to their mountain too, where he wore snow shoes and tramped determinedly. When the lovers introduced him to the plan to open a ski school somewhere in Austria, he was immediately enthusiastic. Having endured years of economic slavery himself he was delighted that his daughter was escaping to something far more romantic.

In the quieter times, Eileen repaid Karl's ski tuition by introducing him to the rudiments of English. He was a hopeless student. On most occasions he would simply fall asleep. His progress in the language was far slower than hers in skiing. She chided him that if their proposed venture were to be successful then it would be just as vital for him to be able to communicate with all the British people who would flock to them as it would be for her to be able to take the occasional ski class. Karl acknowledged the logic but failed to put in the effort. He was of the opinion that he would eventually pick English up naturally, just by doing it.

Their other lives had, of course, to continue. Karl performed his policeman duties in Bruck whilst Eileen resumed the enjoyable Viennese round. Her musical skills were developing, she was becoming ever more fluent in German and the educational excursions were delightful. All the theory about international trade was just the inconvenient price to be paid for such a fulfilling lifestyle.

By Eileen's design, one educational trip took the group of students to Bruck. In a foundry, randomly selected as far as most of the visitors knew, a sweating, burly figure came from the fires of hell and flung his arms around the party leader. There were those present who were ready to defend the betrothed woman's honour until she delightedly explained that the man who hugged her was her future father-in-law.

Later, in the streets, she watched Karl directing traffic. Someone in the group was buying ice creams and on an impulse Eileen took one to her lover standing proud and handsome in his conductor's box. It was the first time she experienced his anger. Karl, she discovered, was an absolute stickler for propriety. He was on duty! He could not be seen to be eating ice cream.

He forgave her, of course, and sweeter than any confection was the making of peace between them.

The distractions of the new relationship increased Eileen's proneness to fire-related accidents. She also, uncharacteristically, managed to book two visits to factories for the same day. This might have been manageable but for the fact of hospitality. No tour was complete without a feast and politeness dictated that everything put before the students must be consumed with every evidence of pleasure.

The first meal of a substantial soup with bread followed by schnitzel, mountains of mashed potato and fried onions followed by strudel and cream was most acceptable. The second, identical, repast an hour or so later was like torture. As one of the leaders of the group, Eileen had to set an example. She ate mightily and, on the journey back, realised that she was heading for a serious illness.

The doctors said that her stomach had been stretched far beyond its natural capacity. That was why she was internally bleeding and suffering excruciating pain. The prescription was that she should eat only very modest amounts of biscuits and milk for at least three weeks. This, or just the normal healing processes, brought her gradually back to health but the ridiculous ailment introduced a measure of unhappiness to a time which otherwise was illuminated by the bliss of new love.

When Easter came, Maurice, Eileen, John and Marion Dalton, one of Eileen's friends from the Board of Trade, set off on holiday. In those days of underdeveloped tourism they planned an adventurous trip. Sadly Karl's duties kept him in Bruck but he was excited that his fiancée was going to visit some of the scenes of his wartime exploits. They took the train to Split in Yugoslavia and travelled by boat down the Dalmation coast to Dubrovnik, sailing very near to the spot adjacent to the island of Korcula where Karl's boat had been sunk. They then flew to Sarajevo with its primitive 'tin hut' airport and were fascinated by the Turkish quarter where fez-wearing men beat copper into utensils. In Zagreb, on the way back, they visited a cinema which was showing a British comedy with Serbo-Croat subtitles. There were few travellers in Yugoslavia in the mid 1950's and the locals were puzzled as to how four members of the audience managed to appreciate all the jokes before they had time to read the punch lines.

Their Vienna-bound train stopped for a time in Bruck and Karl was there to meet them, agog to hear of how things were in the place where he had spent so many difficult months. The sharing of the territory was a strongly bonding experience.

As soon as she was settled back in the capital, Eileen set about arranging the marriage. This turned out to be a tricky business. There was immediate suspicion that she was marrying an Austrian purely to gain citizenship. She pointed out that this would bring few, if any, advantages for her. There was no suitable employment for her in Austria whereas back home she had a well paid post. Then the authorities found it hard to believe that one so educated was marrying a policeman, not even a senior one at that. Eileen begged them to accept that she really was, in true romantic tradition, in love with her ski instructor. She spent hour after hour in dull offices, clutching her birth certificate, her passport and all the other documents demanded by the suspicious state.

Then, when it seemed that all parties were satisfied, the problem arose about the tithes unpaid by the Fuchs family. According to Karl's mother's birth certificate she was a Catholic and should, therefore, have been paying regular sums to Holy Mother Church. The fact that, all the time her husband had been in prison, Frau Fuchs had been officially a Protestant made matters even worse. She had become liable to pay taxes to the other church as well. Whilst this wrangle was going on, Eileen managed to persuade one key official that since Karl, the man of the moment, was in fact a resolute atheist the niceties of Christian division were irrelevant. Through Eileen's power of persuasion the problem of tithes was forgotten but it was instantly replaced by another one.

Austrian law had it that a foreigner marrying a citizen had to pay a substantial tax on any assets which they owned. The sums being talked about were so vast that, if delivered as demanded, the couple's hopes of setting up a business would have been seriously damaged. It would have been simple to claim that they had no assets but there was a snag with this defence. For the marriage licence to be granted, they had to persuade the authorities that Eileen had sufficient private means to ensure that she would never be a burden on the public purse. It was a difficult conundrum. It was of no use claiming that she would be supported by Karl's wages as a policeman, she had to have the wherewithal to survive, presumably to cover a possible breakdown in the marriage.

Once more Eileen went into action. She visited the Ministry of Justice and sought the highest ranked official who would give her time. She blessed her experience in the Board of Trade; she knew how to deal with bureaucrats! She explained; she had savings, not huge amounts but sufficient to form a safety net. However, they were in England and, under currency export regulations, they could not be transferred. Neither could a tax be paid, for the same reason. All the same, if, heaven forbid, the marriage turned out to be a mistake she would simply go home. Thus she both had and did not have the requisite sums of money, if the official got her meaning.

A compromise was reached. A nominal sum was agreed for tax purposes. The licence was issued.

Conveniently, Eileen lived very near the square, the Rochusplatz, which contained the chosen Registry Office. She made all the arrangements. Her father was, of course, coming over from Innsbruck but her brother John had used up his meagre annual allowance of foreign currency on the Yugoslavian holiday. Sadly, he had to miss the great event.

Karl's parents, who had never before been to Vienna, were determined to be there. Eileen arranged accommodation for them and they arrived a day or two before the ceremony. She showed them around their capital city which they treated like a delicate flower. They moved very slowly, gazing at almost every building and caressing the rough stones in reverence.

The bridegroom arrived on the motor bike which the couple had recently acquired. In the early evening before the wedding they paid a romantic visit to the Vienna woods and then Karl turned the twisting descent to the city into a tar macadam slalom run. With absolute confidence in his skill, Eileen experienced a wonderful excitement. There were challenges ahead, of course, but life seemed so utterly carefree in those thrilling moments.

After the ride, Karl went dutifully to keep his parents company whilst, in traditional fashion, Eileen had her final 'hen night', an event she describes as being 'interesting', perhaps because all of the assembled poultry were male. Her companions were fellow musicians who had agreed to provide entertainment on the day of the wedding.

The next morning, the simple service was over quickly and the nuptial group went first to Eileen's lodgings where Dodi and Soso provided a delicious nuptial lunch. Once the meal was over, everyone decamped for a heurigen party in the woods of Grinzing. The musicians, as promised, delivered a suitably Viennese serenade to accompany the festivities.

The honeymoon was to be spent camping in the Dolomites. Friends gathered to wave the new couple off and one insisted on tying a small tin dish to the rack on the back of the motor bike to provide a traditional racket. Entering into the spirit, Karl let in the clutch and roared off, the tin bashing noisily against the cobbles.

They called at the flat, to change out of wedding clothes into touring ones, and then set off for Bruck. Maurice, and Karl's parents, travelled by train with the luggage. The couple's first wedded night was spent in Bruck with Maurice 'camping' on the sofa. After seeing the bride's father onto the return train to Innsbruck, they spent one more night in Bruck before remounting the machine and readying themselves for the journey to Semmering.

*The happy day*

They stopped after a while for a drink. Eileen took off her goggles and wondered why people were glancing at her and giggling. It was of no comfort that Karl, too, was grinning mischievously, neither did it help when he told her that she looked like the devil. She rushed to the mirror on the handlebars of the bike and peered in horror at her black-circled eyes. There were drawbacks to this motor cycling!

The next day they motored through the extreme south east corner of Austria towards Italy. Disappointingly, it rained. They reached their first campsite and erected the simple two-person tent kindly loaned by John. The downpour intensified. Soon there was a stream running through the middle of their temporary residence. Both struggled to make light of this disaster. It might have been tolerable if the water coming from the skies had been warm but it seemed possible that it might soon turn to snow. The nearby lake, which would have been idyllic had the weather been true to the season, was considerably warmer than their personal river. It was a relief to go for a swim and only marginally wetter than being inside their shelter.

*Setting off*

This was a test for a new marriage! There was also the matter of priorities. Eileen wanted to linger wherever the fancy took her, she longed to spend a day or two wandering through Venice. Karl's only ambition on the trip was to reach the mountains above Lake Garda.

He did allow a diversion to the city of her dreams where they found themselves in a vile, crowded campsite with dirty elephant's feet toilets and blaring radios. They were at least near the sea and the sun came but, as it turned out, too powerfully for comfort. In search of relief, Eileen took her inflatable air bed to the gentle waves and lay on it. Three hours later she was wincing in the agonies of acute sunburn. The newly-weds had gone, it seemed, from one extreme to another but they had yet to face the worst.

Karl allowed his wife a mere twenty minutes sight-seeing in Venice claiming that there was a parking restriction. They then, in Eileen's graphic description, 'shot through lovely places' to Lake Garda, thence to a smaller lake at altitude. There they spent several happy days and attended a picturesque village dance before going via Bolzano to yet higher pastures beside the beautiful lake of Carezza which mirrored the pink Dolomites in the evening sunshine.

They pitched the tent in considerable cold. As night approached they added to their layers of clothing. The hours of darkness were silent but when they woke it was to a white wilderness.

The snow was so deep that they could not travel. It was crazy, being so trapped at the height of summer. This was supposed to be their honeymoon! Yet they supported each other, finding humour, pointing out the positives. They survived one day, then another. The blanket showed no signs of melting.

On the third day, they packed up and hauled the bike onto the road. They slithered downwards, Karl's feet almost constantly on the slippery sheet beneath them. Having not anticipated such iciness, Eileen used socks as gloves but still froze. When, at last, they reached a village shop which promised much needed sustenance, they stopped. Eileen rolled off the pillion, almost too stiff to walk, and staggered towards the lifesaving store. Karl pointed out, with a touch of impatience, that she was still wearing socks on her hands. Eileen, never one to be cowed, declared that she did not care. Her husband was not pleased, his strong sense of propriety was offended but she was not about to sacrifice her tiny morsel of comfort for the sake of some supposed rule of mountain etiquette.

They were down to their last reserves of money but happily they had arranged another tryst with Maurice, who was by this time working as a representative for Inghams. He was being paid in schillings and so his cash-flow problems had been solved. Naturally he invited his frosted daughter and Karl to have some refreshments. For the motorbike driver the beer was a life-saver but all Eileen wanted was to eat chocolate which her father duly provided.

On the face of it, the honeymoon had been something of a disaster yet they had coped with the crises, had resolved their various disagreements and had contrived a high level of enjoyment. They recounted the saga to Maurice who laughed mightily. It was just the kind of tempestuous experience he would have expected his headstrong daughter to have.

Over a meal, Karl outlined his strategy. Once they were settled in his Bruck apartment, they would spend every free day roaming over Austria, searching for the perfect venue for their business venture. It was obvious that, in spite of the rigours of their recent trip, he could scarcely wait to be reunited with his motor bike.

## 5. A Move

For two months the newly-weds devoted every spare hour to swerving and swaying across all the hillier parts of Austria, sometimes abandoning the motorcycle to range on foot. Once or twice they thought that a suitable site had been found but always the property was too expensive or the established competition too fierce or the skiing potential not quite to Karl's liking. For a while they considered a different idea, opening a cafe in Vienna, but they soon realised that Karl could never be happy away from his beloved mountains.

When they were not on their travels, Eileen spent considerable time with Karl's parents who were unostentatiously kind. Frau Fuchs imparted all the skills of Austrian cuisine. The new wife became adept at stretching strudel pastry and at preparation of tender, tasty schnitzels, acquiring skills which would surely make the cuisine at the hotel as attractive as the ski teaching.

In spite of this enduring kindness, and of the excitement of being married, Eileen began to experience homesickness. Bruck was very limited in comparison to Vienna and without the social distractions she began to fret. She had been away from England for a long time and yearned for its familiar sights and sounds. Whenever her father was in Austria she saw him as much as possible; when he was home, she wrote.

Maurice began to be concerned that the search for suitable premises might never succeed. It seemed that Karl and Eileen had tried everywhere. He pointed out, also, that there were dangers in setting up a business in a country where the communist Russians still wielded considerable power. There was no guarantee that one day Karl's native land would not be annexed and turned into another Bulgaria or Poland.

Helpfully, Maurice made investigations of his own. He had read something, which he vaguely remembered, about an outdoor activity centre in Scotland which had occasional ski lessons. His researches brought up the name; Glenmore Lodge.

Eileen wrote, enquiring about vacancies for instructors. She had never even been to Scotland but she thought that she and Karl could perhaps make a start at the Lodge, investigate the possibilities and maybe, if there were sufficient commercial potential, eventually open a hotel.

The reply was disappointing. The Glenmore priorities were climbing and hiking. Apparently one of their instructors sometimes taught basic ski technique but there was no obvious demand for full time winter sports instruction and certainly no available funding to employ a new trainer.

Maurice was not to be diverted. On a short break from his summer duties escorting hikers he met the couple once more and suggested that they should go to Britain anyway, even if only for a touring holiday. It was time for Karl to have a taste of his wife's native culture. They could do the round of relatives and friends whilst, at the same time, exploring ski possibilities. Maurice generously said that he would make his car available and even act as guide and chauffeur if the couple so wished.

Karl was keen. He took leave from his duties and, in September 1954, the introduction to British ways began. They stayed for a few acclimatising days at Purley. Karl was not allowed to drive until he had taken a test, so Eileen took him to see the local sights. The weather was generous. They lay in the sun on Box Hill, and repetitively discussed the idea of risking a teaching venture in Britain. Karl said that if they could find suitable terrain he would be willing to do the pioneering work. Eileen rejoiced. She loved Austria but she had no hesitation as to where she wanted her permanent place of residence to be.

As prearranged, they drove to Dover to pick up Maurice whose summer season was over. Eileen could tell, as they passed through the quaint Kentish towns and villages, that Karl was puzzling over something. Every now and then he twisted in his seat and stared, muttering soft sounds of wonder. Intrigued, Eileen asked him to explain his bewilderment. He was silent for a while but then pointed excitedly. 'Look!' he insisted, 'another one. Poison! Why do so many English shops sell poison?'

It took just a moment for the linguistic connection to be made. She laughed outright, knowing that Karl would not be offended. In German the word for 'gift' is 'poison'. Poor Karl had been imagining that he was in a country of licensed mass murderers when all he was seeing were peddlars of harmless trinkets. She explained and then Karl laughed too.

The language lesson was not Karl's only learning experience on that trip to the coast. At one place where they stopped he ventured out in his customary Austrian clothes and was quite rudely accosted by a man demanding to know whether his 'uniform' was that of the Irish Republican Army. The episode was all the odder because at that time Ireland was a tranquil place and the IRA had, by many people, been forgotten.

Maurice derived intense amusement from the stories of Karl's progress through southern England and was evidently delighted at the prospect of the grand tour which the three of them were just about to make. To make the costs manageable they were to camp, using two small tents and an impressive array of aluminium equipment. They would, the veteran said, always pitch beside stream, lake or river and they would spend most of their evenings snugly in a local cinema regardless of what was on the programme.

They went first to Wales which was Eileen's ideal venue. Karl was highly impressed with the beauty of the scenery and declared that many of the hills would be suitable for ski instruction. They made enquiries about snow and received very discouraging responses. Some years, they learned, there was no long-lasting cover at all, even on the summit of the principality's highest peak. Despite all its manifest advantages, it was clear that Wales was not a suitable place for Britain's first ski school.

Disappointed, they drove north to the Lake District where the message about conditions was the same. There were suitable slopes by the hundreds but snow in sufficient depth and longevity came rarely. It was clear that they would have to venture even further north, into Scotland, maybe to the very limit of the mainland.

*The explorers*

In Edinburgh they called into the offices of the Scottish Council for Physical Recreation. An official there was at first a little startled at the idea of a permanent ski school but suggested that there were three potentially suitable areas; Glencoe, where enthusiastic weekenders already skied, Ben Lawyers and the north facing aspect of the Cairngorms close to a small village called Aviemore.

More in a spirit of lukewarm enquiry than determination they visited an estate agent which specialised in hotel properties. The only place which seemed to be available within the areas suggested by the SCPR, of a size commensurate with their budget, was in a tiny village called Carrbridge. They learned that the owner of the Struan House Hotel, who was running the establishment as a holiday centre for diabetics, was wanting to sell the business. The £5000 price, given their savings and a promised loan from Maurice, was manageable. They asked the agent to arrange for a viewing a few days hence and resumed their northward journey.

In the late summer sunshine, all of them were enchanted by the beauty of the lochs and bens. Karl was like an animal returning to its territory. He sniffed the air and clambered eagerly up such hills as they had time to conquer. They looked at Glencoe, they surveyed Ben Lawyers.

Killin seemed a possibility; the searching trio learned that the Scottish Ski Club used it as a base. They heard, also, that a small hotel within reasonable distance of these tried and tested slopes would soon be coming onto the market. This was obviously a tempting prospect but they decided that before seriously considering it they would take just a look at the Cairngorms and Carrbridge.

They drove up the narrow, twisting, hilly ribbon of tar macadam which connected Braemar, the Lecht, Tomintoul and Grantown on Spey. Over an obvious hump-backed bridge Maurice drove deliberately fast, causing the wheels to leave the ground and Eileen to all but vanish through the roof. Sobered somewhat by her screech, he maintained a more sedate pace as they went through the sleepy place called Aviemore and then turned off onto a minor road which, according to the map, would bring them to the mountains.

The way was metalled as far as a hamlet called Coylumbridge. A sign pointed down a well-used track to Glenmore. They turned the nose of the hard working car in that direction and lurched along through the forest. Soon, on their right, Loch Morlich glistened. Its sea-like beaches beckoned. They stopped and sat on the sand, gazing at the block of mountains laid out across the water before them. The air was fortuitously calm and the black water reflected the hills vividly. Near the summits of the immediate peaks they could see brilliant strips of residual snow.

Karl produced powerful binoculars and scanned the upper reaches. There was nobody, as far as he could see, taking advantage of the wonderful wilderness. All three of them began to experience a generalised excitement. There was a silent agreement that the search might be over. Karl had already seen, to the left of Cairngorm, a steep, narrow corrie running down the flank and had decided that a filling of snow would turn that feature into a brilliant intermediate ski run. From their sandy vantage point he could see other slopes, some of which would test the skills of an expert. This place was thrilling like none other they had seen.

They returned to the car and bumped along to the hayfield which marked the end of the trail. 'Perfect for beginners,' Karl noted before once more turning his attention to the hills above them. After a long inspection he pronounced himself well satisfied. Provided that the snow was plentiful enough to cover the grass and heather there would be magnificent skiing.

Thinking of future customers, Eileen pointed out that access to those upper slopes would involve a two-hour climb at the very least. Karl shrugged off this minor inconvenience. He countered that for the most part they could use much lower areas but he said that in any case, an early morning uphill hike was good for skiers; it would loosen them up.

Karl was for setting off walking up the mountain track but there was no time for further exploration. The imperative was to keep their viewing appointment at Struan House. They dragged themselves reluctantly back to the car and lurched down the track towards Aviemore. The unspoken prayer, as they emerged onto the metalled road, was simply; 'Please let Struan House be suitable!'

Having half-made the crucial decision, they looked more carefully at Aviemore as they returned through it. There seemed to be little to the place, apart from the charming wooden station building, a few uninspiring shops and an imposing hotel. If this was, as their map suggested, the local metropolis there could be little of note in Carrbridge.

Slightly tense, because they were coming head-on to a life-determining moment, they drove the half dozen or so miles to their destination. The road undulated pleasantly through patches of forest and past richly green fields. To their left were tree-topped hills, to the right, the lush valley of the Spey with the quiescent Cairngorms marking its far boundary. Every now and then an intriguing small loch enhanced the wonderful scenery. They manoeuvred round a difficult set of bends under a bridge. Karl muttered, 'Railway'. Eileen had already ascertained that it was possible to take a train directly from Euston in London to Inverness, stopping at Carrbridge and this was a single tracked part of that long route. The village was linked to some very large concentrations of potential customers.

Their destination was invisible until they turned a sharp, left handed bend. Maurice slowed down. They had been advised that Struan was one of the first properties on the right. They spotted it almost immediately, even though the board announcing its presence was unostentatious. Just as her heart had lifted at the first sight of Karl, so there was a surge of excitement for Eileen when Struan came into view.

They were slightly early for their appointment and they filled time by driving into the village.

They immediately discovered that Carrbridge was indeed considerably smaller than Aviemore. There was a church and a shop flanked by a few houses. Most of the property seemed to be strung beside the road although there were one or two side turnings which suggested greater depth of development. About half way down the main street was a small hotel, the 'Rowanlea'. A sign declared that this establishment owned a bar which was open to non-residents. The estate agent had said nothing about Struan having such a facility and a thought came to Eileen; skiers would surely want to relax in a bar after their exertions. What, she wondered, would it take to acquire a licence?

The narrow trunk road to Inverness, which at this part of its twisting, hilly, hazardous path formed the main street, widened slightly towards the end of the village and turned very sharply left. A minor road, signposted to Grantown-on-Spey, branched right. A small, grassy, triangular traffic island marked the junction and the unwary motorist might easily mistake the priorities. The top of the T could very easily be seen as the main thoroughfare.

Stopping just short of a modern bridge over a small river, the three of them stepped out of the car. To their right, in one of the ninety degree angles of the junction, was an impressively large, grey building which declared itself to be the Carrbridge Hotel. Directly ahead, beyond the tarmacadam, was a golf course and, further away, the rounded contours of the Monodliath Mountains. Opposite the hotel was a building which looked like a small village hall.

Having taken all this in, they stood above the rushing torrent and looked upstream. To their left was a narrow road which, according to the signpost, headed towards a place called Dalnahatnaich. Within a few yards there was a remnant of a previous crossing point, a complete stone arch. It seemed that all but the last layer of this structure had been plundered and it was a wonder that there had not been a collapse. They were glad that there had not because, against the tree-lined ravine carved by the water, the bridge looked very picturesque.

*The old bridge*

Whilst Maurice and Eileen scanned the map. Karl walked towards the remnant. The obvious assumption was that the river must be the 'the Carr but it was not so. It was the Dulnain and the map-readers noted that further downstream there was a village labelled Dulnain Bridge.

Engrossed in the local geography, Eileen was momentarily unaware of Karl. When she looked up it was to see him standing erect on the residual arch, very close to the edge. Her heart pumped. She called his familiar name, 'Karli', sharply. The stones would surely give way! He laughed and then said something which was impossible to hear above the noise of the torrent. She had seen the bridge from which he had often dived in Bruck and for a ridiculous moment she thought that he was contemplating going head-first into the rock-strewn, swirling stream. He waved and then walked calmly down the steep incline. Within a moment he was reassuringly linking his arm through Eileen's.

They turned the car around and cruised very slowly back to Struan. It looked as though the establishment had originally been a very substantial, double-fronted house with a small, tower-like feature. Although they said nothing, both Karl and Eileen were aware of a shared excitement as they approached. The attraction which the building had for them was akin to that which had drawn them so precipitately together.

The vendors provided tea and cakes in the lounge, situated in one of the front, downstairs rooms. Another of the front rooms was a bedroom whilst the third was where the guests ate their meals. After tea the potential purchasers were shown the kitchen with its solid-fuel cooking range, the dining room, the small laundry and the downstairs bathroom. Upstairs they saw the seven bedrooms, all but three of which had wash basins. Some of them, Eileen noted with satisfaction, were large enough to accommodate small families. The touring party inspected the two communal bathrooms and the various storage cupboards. Having no experience whatsoever of running a residential establishment, Karl and Eileen had to rely on native wit to make their assessment of the facilities. The determining factor was that the place was already running as a hotel so everything must, at root, be satisfactory.

*Struan House*

As they stood on the landing Eileen asked about the possibility of setting up a bar, perhaps in the lounge. The vendor was honest. He explained that it was impossible to obtain a licence. The right to sell alcohol was granted solely on a 'local need' basis. The Carrbridge and Rowanlea hotels already provided public bars so what, the authorities argued, was the point in opening another one in such a tiny village? It is possible, Struan's owner said, that their attitude towards drinking was influenced by the presence of a substantial number of 'Wee Frees'; members of the Free Church of Scotland, a Presbyterian faction which strongly opposes licentiousness.

They went outside. The inspection team imagined the space between the boundary wall and the front of the hotel filled with tables and chairs, with motorists stopping for afternoon tea. In Karl's mind were fluttering flags, beckoning people in; Eileen's thoughts were of colourful umbrellas. Both of them were already dreaming of bringing something of the European style to this northern outpost of the continent.

Down one side of the building was a driveway, easily wide enough for motorised traffic. This gave access to parking space behind the hotel and, on the left, some outhouses which the newcomers thought could be converted into living space should the need ever arise. The last of these detached buildings, a gardener's shed, was, in Karl's imagination, already being converted into an office and shop. He pointed and said simply, to Eileen, 'Ski shed.' In his mind it was filled with neatly arranged equipment and a workbench. The decision about Struan had already been taken. There was also a garage, a reminder that if they were to commit themselves they would have to acquire a car.

Behind the house was a well-tended lawn, with surrounding flower beds, and then a very large kitchen garden. At the bottom of this was a grey, weathered, wooden building which immediately put the young couple in mind of cowboy accommodation in the Wild West. The vendors explained that this was 'The Annexe' which, so they understood, had been built by Polish refugees during the war. The style of the structure was more Eastern European than American it seemed. There was a veranda, with a 'hitching-rail', giving access to a row of small rooms. Further inside were much larger rooms. Most of these were filled with beds but one, with an adjacent kitchenette, was set out like a cafe. Electricity and mains water were evidently connected. If, if, skiers started to come in large numbers here was the perfect place for those on tight budgets!

Once more in the lounge, over further cups of tea, Eileen poured out the questions which tumbled at random into their heads. Karl's English, still minimal, was nowhere near good enough for him to join in directly but his new wife translated expertly. Naturally a key question concerned the snow. The vendor shrugged. He said that, yes, of course, there was often heavy snow, and there were drifts which lingered in the corries well into the summer but nobody could predict.

Afire with excitement, the three set off to find a campsite for the night. There were many anxieties, of course, but the mountains seemed so promising and Struan had the most extraordinary potential. It was a shame that the hotel was so far from the higher ground, it was a nuisance that they would not be permitted to run a commercial bar but these deficiencies were not fatal to the project.

Back in Purley, they talked the proposition over. It was pure madness, really. Apart from the information imparted by the hotelier and the SCPR they knew little about the climate. There would surely be times when there was snow only at the higher levels. On these occasions, guests would have to make a long drive, part of it over a rough track, then undertake an arduous uphill hike carrying equipment and essential supplies with them. It was a far cry from the Alpine village, with snow on the doorstep and mountain-top hostelries. Would anyone, even the keenest skier, tolerate the Cairngorm conditions?

There were further drawbacks and questions. Karl still knew almost no English and neither of them had any experience of running a hotel. How would they go about attracting customers? It was also true that there were no shops in the vicinity selling the kind of articles which skiers needed. Until they could afford to set up their own retail outlet, what would they do to replace torn gloves, lost goggles and collapsing boots?

There was about Karl and Eileen a positive impetuosity. Maurice, too, was a man for the unknown. He always relished an adventure. The worst that could happen was that they would lose some money. With a strong sense of unreality they decided to take their outrageous gamble.

Karl, still on leave, had to return to Austria in order to be formally discharged from the police service. He declared that when he returned he would bring skis and boots in assorted sizes. Eileen stayed in Purley so that she could accomplish the formalities of purchasing the property and make plans for the removal.

They parted with deep regret but also with hope. They had found their venue. However the venture turned out they would be together, supporting each other, complementing each other's skills. They had faith, abundant energy, indefinite resourcefulness and a broad array of talents to their credit. Objectively, what they were proposing was impracticable almost to the point of insanity. There were no dedicated ski hotels in Scotland, there was no professional ski school. Many would conclude that they were embarking on a gross folly. But they had felt something, a magic in the mountains, a strong sense of destiny, that gave them confidence. Against all the disincentives, they would make Struan House succeed.

## 6. Mountains

Had Karl and Eileen had the time and inclination to undertake a thorough research of their chosen area they might have gone back to motorcycling around Austria.

In the summer, with the River Spey bubbling and sweeping grandly along and the many lovely lochs glinting in the sunshine, the countryside around Aviemore is seductively beautiful. Perhaps because of the sharper angle of the incident light in such a northern location, the colours seem to be more varied than anywhere else in the British Isles. There are unusual shades of green, brown, yellow, red, purple, silver - too many hues to list completely - which contrive to be both subtle and intense at the same time. A warm day and a light breeze can suggest that the climate is benign. The waters of the shallower lochs are easily warm enough for swimming. Speyside can seem like a province of paradise. The Scottish Mountaineering Club guidebook to the region refers rightfully to; 'magnificent remote hills and a wealth of river, loch and forest scenery that cannot be matched elsewhere in Britain'.

Many visitors testify to the glory and the grandeur of the place. There are days when the sky is blue like no other sky, when the silvers and browns of the birch trees, the reds and purples of the flowering heather, the hues of the evergreens and of the dense ferns produce an effect which is almost overwhelming. There are deer and lovely, furry highland cattle, capercailzie and ptarmigan, eagles, oyster-catchers and ospreys. There is an abundance which can seem paradoxical in such a northern place.

All along the course of the Spey are farms and fields, crops and cattle, granite-built towns and villages. There are huge hotels, erected by the

Victorians to cater for the new, Walter Scott-reading breed of rich Highland-lovers. Carrbridge has one such establishment, Nethybridge another, Grantown-on-Spey boasts several. Their confident solidity suggests calmness, permanence and prosperity.

Even in the winter, with the hoar frost thick on the branches of the silver birch trees, the tall pines blindingly green against a cloudless sky and the ice thick upon the lochs, it is very easy to see the forests as vast temples. The blue above is like a divinely determined ceiling, the thick trunks are akin to stately, intricately carved columns and the limitlessly varied vegetation suggests icons and statues acceptable to any creed. Some of the waters freeze to total clarity such that the pebbly depths can be seen by those who venture onto the ice. These are the treasure vaults, the containers of mystery.

What the bold couple had not seen, in their brief summer visit, was that the northern winters can be relentlessly dark. What they had not had time to tap into was the folk-memory of struggle against viciously harsh conditions and cruel invaders.

Close by the road which Karl and Eileen took from Aviemore to Carrbridge is a small, very beautiful loch hidden from the passers-by. A visitor, sleeping one hot summer's day on the sandy beach of this exquisite, tree-encircled stretch of water, dreamed of dreadful drownings. He awoke, crying out, shivering with fear and appalled by the contrast between the beauty around him and the nightmare. He told a local person of the experience and learned that the waters are called 'Loch Vaa' which translates as the 'loch of the wails'. Centuries ago people built houses there on stilts as a defence against enemies. One black night a mighty wind pushed the structures over and many drowned.

Tension between the sublime and the terrible is characteristic of the region. It is also not unusual for people to 'sense' events in a way which, generally, modern humans cannot do. Many visitors to nearby Culloden, scene of a military slaughter, claim that it is the most chillingly atmospheric historic site of all. Not a few have come away choking with a transmitted misery at that scene of barbarism. It is as though the turbulent history of the locality is somehow recorded in the rocks in such a powerful form that it bursts through the normal mental barriers.

*The Cairngorms from Loch Morlich*

There are also plenty of more tangible reminders of the rape of Scotland by the wealthy, of the 'clearances' of peasants from the land, of the wars with their brutal bonfires of furniture and effects, of the massacres of women and children whose menfolk chose to resist. Vast estates now stand where once there were smallholdings. People with grand titles put fences round their properties, sealing off beauty which was once accessible to all. The wholesale theft is not dignified merely by the bestowing of grand titles and the passage of time.

Vivid evidence of the military power which brought a portion of the misery is provided by the remnants of the road, built by General Wade's men, which snakes improbably across the wildness. There are bridges in remote places, part decayed but still strong enough to take the weight of walkers. Once soldiers marched over these, on their way to keep the local people in their English-appointed places.

There is sturdy sign, too, of rebellion and banditry. On an island in Loch an Eilean, one of the most beautiful lakes imaginable, is a small castle which once the Wolf of Badenoch used as a retreat. He had other fortified places in other lochs. The Wolf roamed and took whatever he wanted just as the rich and powerful stole the people's land.

It is scarcely possible to be in the region for any moderate length of time without sensing that the exquisite scenery hides a history of sadness. In the darkest times of winter, when the brief passage of the sun's travel across the sky can be obscured day after day by grey cloud, the human spirit can very easily be repressed.

These contrasts of the valley are even starker in the mountains.

They are generally known as the 'Cairngorms' although, according to the Scottish Mountaineering Club guidebook, this is only a nickname which should, in any case, be pronounced 'Cairngoroms' rather than in the usual two syllable version. The true, gaelic title is 'Am Monadh Ruadh', which translates to 'The Red Hills', a name emanating from the observation that, on a clear evening, the granite screes which can be seen from Aviemore glow warmly red. At the time Karl and Eileen arrived there, the proper name was apparently still being used by the older inhabitants of the region but most, locals and visitors, carelessly used the 'Cairngorms' designation. On a good day, with the red glint enriching even further the dazzling array of local colour, they give no hint of the other side of their complex character.

The hills are geologically ancient. Once they towered to heights in excess of Everest. Through millions upon millions of years they have been worn down to rounded, residual stumps. Mainly they are composed of schist and granite which has weathered uniformly save for the deep corries, some of which were formed by the moving and eventual melting of the ice-age cap. It is, perhaps, this unimaginable history which provides the massif with its undeniable power. Maybe the turbulent evolutionary history of the Earth has been recorded, just as the social annals of the valley have been imprinted.

The peaks, though small by Alpine standards, are literally awe-inspiring. They can engender an almost mystical excitement but they can also cause dread. On a darkening evening, in one of the decaying forests, with rotting silver tree stumps, damp, despairing vegetation and dark, cold stones it can feel as though all the helplessness of chaos is contained within the scenery. Tom Patey, world renowned climber, pioneer of many of the major winter routes in the area, a man who loved the region and who was the very antithesis of a coward, captured some of this feeling when he wrote:

'Most gullies are unpleasant. A Cairngorm gully is doubly so. It is the sort of place you would incarcerate your worst enemy; a dank gloomy prison where moisture seeps from every fissure and "all the air a solemn stillness holds" - save for the constant drip, drip from many a greasy, moss-enshrouded chockstone and the occasional dull thud as another ledge sloughs away in a welter of slime and rubble.'

Unlike the Alps, which have habitations at high altitudes and a complex network of roads, the Cairngorms are almost untouched by the hands of humans. They are not at the centre of the continent but at its periphery. They are, and feel to be, isolated. It is easy to understand why the infamous 'Loss of Gaick' came to be seen by the locals as the work of Satan.

It was one windy day in January 1800 that Captain John MacPherson of Ballachroan, known as the 'Black Officer', was leading a party of four through the mountains. They sheltered overnight in a remote, primitive hut erected by sheep farmers. Nobody knows for certain what happened during those dark hours but when the soldiers were next seen, their bodies, grotesquely broken and twisted, were distributed yards away from where the hut had been. Parts of the structure itself were found almost one third of a mile away. Speysiders readily came to the conclusion that such devastation could be wrought only by the devil.

A more rational explanation is that a rare phenomenon known as an 'airborne avalanche' was responsible. A weighty mass of snow, lifted and formed by the tempest, probably smashed into the hut, tearing it and its human contents apart. Given that wind speeds well in excess of one hundred miles per hour have been recorded in the mountains, this seems to be the most likely account.

There is a ready explanation, too, as to why a further five soldiers, walking from Edinburgh to their homes in Abernethy, died in the Lairig an Laoigh just before Christmas 1804. They were overwhelmed by a snowstorm which simply buried them.

But there are further mysteries to feed the speculations of the irrational. Mostly the bodies of those who have died in the Cairngorms from exposure, climbing accidents or drowning have been found without any unexpected deformations or markings but in not a few cases people have vanished without the slightest trace. The mountains have their own versions of the 'Picnic at Hanging Rock' but there is a story even more perplexing than the total disappearance of humans.

On a September day in 1938, a stalker was in very remote territory on the south face of Ben Avon looking for a wounded stag. In a stream he came across a badly decomposed human head. Higher up, the stalker found the associated body dressed in what was once a smart, dark suit with a light check. Nearby was a walking stick and a briefcase of brown leather which contained a pair of pyjama trousers, two collars, a toilet roll, a pair of scissors, a box of safety matches and a handbill advertising Simpson's two-day tours. On a ledge of rock, for all the world like a bathroom shelf, was set out all the paraphernalia of shaving; brush, soap and razor. Next to this was everything else a gentleman might need for a morning toilette; comb, toothbrush and toothpaste. The assemblage of personal effects was completed by a bowler hat.

The pathologist who eventually examined the remains was sure that the man had been dead for at least six months. Manufacturer's tags on the collars suggested a possible link with Aberdeen but a thorough and long-lasting police exercise failed to unearth a single piece of further information about this man.

As Karl bustled about in Austria, formally ending his employment as a policeman and acquiring essential equipment for the Scottish venture, his mind was doubtless filled with memories of the alluring beauty of the Cairngorms as he had seen them on that hasty visit. Little, if any, of the darker side of the picture would have been there to trouble him. It is fairly certain, also, that his anticipation was of sunny slopes like the ones that he was used to. He knew and loved the mountains. In his wartime wanderings he had seen many, many hills and valleys but, in fact, he had seen nothing like the Cairngorms.

The Scottish Mountaineering Club guidebook explains that; 'The general appearance of the landscape, the landforms, the soils, weather, vegetation, invertebrates and birds are all much more akin to stony hill ground in high arctic Canada, Iceland or the arctic tip of Norway than they are to the Alps, the Caucasus or Rockies.'

Neither had Karl experienced the Cairngorm weather. The guide-book warns;'One of the main dangers of the plateau is the wind. These tops are often swept by gales and winds of hurricane force, especially in the winter. The writer has often seen small gravel blowing in the wind and plants torn out by the roots, and the strongest man can be blown right over and thrown to the ground, or reduced to crawling on all fours.'

The wild wind was not the only hazard unsuspected by Karl. The guide continues;'When a gale is accompanied by thick storms of ground drift, or worse, by heavy falling blizzards plus ground drift, or worse still, by mist as well, conditions can be extremely serious on the plateau, making it suffocating and difficult to breathe, hard to open your eyes, impossible to see anything beyond your own feet, and unable to communicate with your party except one at a time by cupping an ear and shouting into it. In these respects the blizzards on the Cairngorms can be as bad as anywhere in the world. They can be severe not only on the high plateaux but also on the lower plateaux and moors. From November to early February the days are so short and the weather so often stormy that ski tourers or hill walkers who head for the highest summits should leave early in the morning and be prepared for very severe weather.'

Hamish McInnes, a very experienced mountaineer who climbed in many parts of the world, says of the Cairngorms, 'I have known conditions there to be even more severe than in the Alps, the Caucasus, and even the Himalayas. Conditions can change like a flash. Winds of up to almost 150 mph have been recorded. At times it can be quite frightening for even experienced mountaineers like me.'

An author and explorer, Tom Weir, who has also climbed all over the world, asserts that there is, 'nothing anywhere to compare with the savagery of a Scottish mountain when it lets itself go.'

In a piece written for the Observer, Chris Brasher confirms these views. He writes;'We talk of the mild British climate yet the only accurate description of the climate on that plateau is sub-Arctic. Some men who have been to the Antarctic and the Himalayas say that the worst conditions they have ever experienced have been in the Cairngorms.'

These references to blizzards and Arctic conditions might have alarmed Karl had he known about them but at least he could have felt reassured, as he collected skis and boots from the manufacturers, about the reliability of snow cover. Surely there would be no problem with bare slopes in the depths of winter?

The Scottish Mountaineering Club guidebook removes even this comfort, claiming that; 'In most years good heavy snowfalls in November and December are often followed by great thaws and even January snowfalls may be unreliable. Indeed, in the mildest years there may be far less snow on the hills in January and February than in June of other years.'

Had Karl been able to peruse this particular publication he would eventually have found some consolation; 'Beautiful weather can, however, come at any time in winter with frost, blue skies and much calmer air than in summer. At these times, ski touring from powdery white glens up through snow-laden pines to the highest ground shows the Cairngorms at their finest; waves of frozen hills stretching for many miles and great cliffs plastered white or creamy in thick ice, snow and hoar frost. In April or May the storms can be as bad as in December, but with long hours of daylight and usually more reliable weather, you often have days when it is like a scene in the high Arctic, with strong sun, deep blue skies, bright colours on thawed patches of vegetation, a beautifully uniform snow surface, and the odd ptarmigan croaking lustily on its chosen snowfree patch.'

The Alps have, of course, their share of tragedy. Climbing accidents and avalanches take their toll but what seems to mark the difference between the continental ranges and the Scottish one is the savagery of the weather. There are many instances where people have died not because they fell, or because a mass of snow engulfed them, but purely because the meteorological conditions became too terrible for survival. There are dozens of examples but one, which happened many years after Karl and Eileen settled in the area, serves to illustrate that for all their stark beauty the Cairngorms are very serious mountains where safety, even on the best of days, or on the most organised of expeditions, can never be taken for granted.

Along with most of the national newspapers, the Daily Mail of November 23rd 1971 devoted its entire front page and considerable space on the inner pages to the story. One of the interior articles spelled out the details of the tragedy.

**'Six die in a raging blizzard on a survival course that went wrong. Nearby was the shelter that could have saved them.**

'The dangerous slopes of the rugged Cairngorms claimed six victims yesterday - five children and a young teacher.

'They died in a raging blizzard 4,000ft up on the mountain in a 'survival exercise' which went wrong. Only two, the 20-year-old leader, Cathy Davidson of Edinburgh, and a 14-year-old schoolboy survived. The others perished from exposure huddled in a small bivouac tent with all their supplies lost. Their bodies were left on the mountain overnight. Attempts to bring them down will be made today.

'The party, from Ainslie Park Secondary School, Edinburgh, left Aviemore on Saturday morning with a covering of snow on the mountain and clear skies. But the forecast spelled out what they were going to face over the weekend with a warning of strong winds, and heavy snow. They didn't see the men of the Glenmore rescue station who later came looking for them and so they didn't get their warning not to attempt the climb.

'Twelve hours later they were in deadly trouble. Unable to reach their destination - a tiny hut deep in the mountains - they were forced to shelter behind a makeshift snow wall from the unbelievable force of the storm. Their supplies, enough for them all for several days, were lost when their rucksacks were buried in the snow. It was all that the two girls and the children could do to stop themselves from being buried as well. Eventually exhaustion overcame them. They did not return on time and the much-practised rescue teams went into operation.

'Cathy was found alive but frostbitten and taken to hospital in Inverness. Several hours later, the RAF mountain rescue team from

Kinloss, Morayshire, found her seven companions huddled in the snow. Six were dead.'

It is tempting to believe that with the modern wonder of the helicopter available a simple rescue could have been effected but the account given by the crew which lifted Cathy shows the limitations. They speak of being constantly on the verge of disaster and of having only seconds to bundle the young woman aboard before being trapped in a swirling bank of dense cloud. The report tells of the acute difficulty of handling the machine, of the near impossibility of seeing what they were doing and of the men having to wade and crawl through drifts which came up to their waists. The crew, clearly shocked, said that they had been operating at the absolute limit.

A few days after the disaster, the Scottish Daily Express gave Cathy Davidson the chance to make public her version of the story.

'Her blackened, frost-bitten hands suspended in protective muslin 'stockings', the 20-year-old student teacher relived the 46-hour diary to disaster step by step. And the slim, blonde-haired Edinburgh lass vowed: "Given the same conditions and the same type of children I would go out again".

'She spoke slowly - every word a torment - but comforted by an occasional reassuring smile from her mother and sister Margaret who sat by the bedside in a screened-off section of a special care unit in Raigmore hospital. In the ward next door lay the only other survivor, 15-year-old Raymond Leslie, alive because a freak breath hole kept him from suffocating beneath a 3ft blanket of snow.

'Cathy told of the fury of the blinding snow which prevented them reaching a shelter hut, her endless hours of tearing away the suffocating, powdery snow from the children's faces and her hands-and-knees crawl over the swirling wastes in a last desperate bid for help.

"With darkness falling I had a decision to make, whether to go on and try to find the hut or make such shelter as we could in what remained of daylight. I decided to make shelter. I knew the hut could get snowed-in completely and we could miss it. The snow was too soft to make a snow hole - a sort of snow cave that you can get inside for protection from the biting wind. Instead we had to build a semi-circular wall about

3ft. high and get behind this in our sleeping bags and protective polythene bags. We were still in good spirits but I was annoyed at not being able to reach the hut. The children were tired but otherwise we were perfectly OK at this time."

'She told the children to kick their legs to shift the snow off their bags. But the snow became so heavy on top of the children they couldn't move. Time and again she cleared the ceaseless fury from their hands and faces resting every few moments back in her own sleeping bag to get warmth and strength back for her desperate fight.

'But by Sunday morning the weather was worse and their spirits began to flag. With 15-year-old William Kerr - the only other one who had managed to stay near the surface - she set out for help some time on Sunday. But they got just 25 yards through the waist-deep snow before they were forced back exhausted. She gave William her own sleeping bag because his had got wet. Two of the girls managed to wriggle out of their snow trap and she climbed into a communal bag beside them to keep them warm.

'Cathy's eyes watered as she recalled: "I knew I had to try for help again in the morning. We saw the flares of a search party and shouted and yelled but nobody came. By Monday morning everyone was buried except for one girl and William. I tried to get him to go with me for help. But he was too weak even to stand up. I was faint and dizzy. When I left them I could still hear them shouting from under the snow. I lost all sense of time and direction, but I remember I was crawling on my hands and knees when I heard a helicopter overhead".'

Events were to prove, quite quickly, that Karl and Eileen had little idea that they were facing such daunting conditions on the Cairngorm slopes. In addition to the hazards of entering the entirely new trade of hotel keeping, of running a business for the first time, of working in a part of the world which was largely alien to both of them, they were going to have to deal with one of the most savage micro-climates on Earth.

It was perhaps just as well that they had this area of ignorance. With full knowledge, Karl might have decided against loading his mountain of equipment onto that Austrian train and beginning the trek to join his eager British bride.

## 7. Forerunners

There had, of course, been British interest in skiing long before Karl and Eileen made their exploratory journey.

One of the earliest references to the sport occurs in the Saturday Magazine of January 1836. This article, entitled 'The Skating Soldiers of Norway', refers to the use of the technique by the Norwegian army but it took Nansen's account of skiing in Greenland in 1888 to stimulate British interest to a significant extent. A Colonel Napier, with a Norwegian 'servant', allegedly brought the first pair of skis to the Alps.

Five years later, Conan Doyle was reported as being the first British person to make a full day tour, climbing and gliding from Davos to Arosa over the Furka Pass. He wrote an article about the adventure for the Strand Magazine and predicted that; 'The time will come when hundreds of Englishmen will come to Switzerland for the "skiing season".'

At about the same time, Scottish pioneers were active. In her book 'Skisters', Myrtle Simpson tells of Glaswegians taking the train to Kirkintilloch in March 1892 with skis as unprecedented luggage. The ash planks, seven feet long and four and a half inches wide, had leather straps attached which the experimenting skiers fixed around their everyday boots. Three years later, in Aberdeenshire, a doctor called to a woman in childbirth used skis to make his way through otherwise impassable snow drifts.

Towards the end of the century Henry Lunn was facilitating the travel of the first of Conan Doyle's 'hundreds' but whilst the Lunn customers were blazing the Alpine trails, Scottish skiers were exploring their own intriguing territory. Myrtle Simpson quotes an account in the Scottish Mountaineering Club Journal of an expedition made by a man called Wigner on Ben Chonzie; three hours up to two thousand five hundred feet, one and a half hours down. Wigner's description of his exploit is close to ecstatic.

Among the Alpine experimenters was one E. C. Richardson, born and educated in Scotland, who in 1903 found that he had sufficient support for the creation of a Ski Club of Great Britain. He instigated the first recorded ski lesson in the Highlands by persuading the Scottish Mountaineering Club to use their 1904 Easter meeting for the purposes of learning the new sport. A German was prevailed upon to act as instructor. Full of enthusiasm, Herr Rickmers travelled with his Scottish-born wife from London to Fort William. In 'Skisters' he is quoted as describing skiing as 'the finest form of mountaineering' and of rhapsodising;

'Having ascended a hill, who can describe the feelings of the downward slide, the exuberant joy of the swaying motion - in short the whole rippingness of a good run? Having partook of our wholesome food at the summit, how do we delight in the view, so deep, so clear, that crystal purity wherein seems to float the promise of eternity. Survey with pride the many windings of the clear cut line of ski tracks - what man-made beauty.'

It will come as no surprise to those familiar with Scottish skiing that for the first four days of Rickmer's course there was steady rain. The students persevered on wet snow. Rickmer reports that they took their picnics, 'where the water seemed most driest'. It will further be anticipated by the experienced that on the fifth and last day the sun emerged. Rickmer took his pioneering party to the top of Ben Nevis and rejoiced at the vista of snowfields better, or so he claimed, than any he had come across in the Alps. In the distance the sea was blue. The party exulted and swooped two thousand feet.

Sadly for one Miss Macpherson, the final turn, the one which was necessary to avoid an unscheduled visit to a loch, proved a manoeuvre too many. In she shot, long skirt and all. She would have stayed there, standing but stuck, weighted down by freezing water creeping sinisterly up the fibres of her voluminous costume, had it not been for a gallant doctor called Inglis who waded in and fumbled in the freezing fluid to remove her impediments.

Rickmers, after recording the gallantry of the medical man, provided a summary of the experiment; 'The ground and snow is excellent but the climate extremely discouraging. The only real drawback in Scotland is the question of good approaches and comfortable lodgings close to snow - not insoluble. However, in fine weather, two hours walk to the snowline is a mere nothing to a ski runner. The question for skisters in Scotland is not one of the ground and snow, but rather 'the sky above.'

Undeterred by the 'sky above', the pioneer instructor advertised the following year;

**Mr. W. Rickmers offers to teach SMC members and their ladies to ski. Terms: None. Conditions: Enthusiasm and Discipline.**

As an earnest of his good intentions, Rickmers generously donated twelve pairs of skis to the Scottish Mountaineering Club. These were the newly-developed Alpine variety, shorter and thinner than the Scandinavian ones, with a hinged metal plate for a binding. One club member was sufficiently enthused by the technical development to write that; 'The sport of skiing is here to stay'.

Scottish pioneers began to visit the Alps in greater numbers where they discovered that a hermetic Austrian called Zdarsky had, allegedly alone and untutored, invented a new way of turning on skis which he called the 'stem christie'. Being, it seems, a natural lunatic, he issued a friendly challenge to the Norwegians to a race from the summit of Mont Blanc. He wanted to prove the superiority of the new technique over the old.

Wisely the Scandinavians declined on the grounds that they would be too ill from vertigo to make the telemark turns which their countrymen had used from time immemorial. Undaunted, Zdarsky offered them a lower slope but this was still too steep. Zdarsky wheedled and cajoled and placed forty tempting sticks at intervals, thus casually inventing the slalom two decades before Arnold Lunn's intervention. Nordic honour was thus challenged and the race was on. Zdarsky, with his idiosyncratic technique, won by a matter of minutes. Not wanting anyone to feel slighted, the genial innovator presented all who completed his course with a prize regardless of which hour or day they glided gratefully through the finishing gate. Soon almost everybody was using the Zdarsky method for downhill skiing.

Myrtle Simpson records that a Scot called Allan Arthur was one of the first to be influenced by Zdarsky. He also brought home the idea of using two hand-held sticks rather than one long one. With other aficionados, Arthur would catch a weekend evening train from Glasgow to Pitlochry and then wait until four in the morning for a connection to Kingussie. Using a combination of telemark and christie turns, the sleep-deprived maniacs then ranged over the adjacent hills until it was time to make for the station to catch the return evening train.

In 1906 two skiers exploring the Cairngorm slopes came, by chance they claimed, on an 'easy gully' known as Coire Cas. This is the first recorded reference to skiing in what was to become a familiar fold to thousands of beginners. These two originals were so delighted by their experience that when they returned to Kingussie they approached a local distillery and acquired barrel staves which they fashioned 'after the continental manner' into rudimentary skis. With these, they conducted classes at which, it was claimed, many adults and boys showed considerable skill. Espying a commercial opportunity, a local joiner called Stewart started making skis out of pitch pine. He declared, probably with good justification, that he was the first ski maker in Great Britain.

Encouraged by all this activity, a member at the annual general meeting of the Ski Club of Great Britain proposed that there should be a competition to be called 'The Championships of the British Isles' to be held on native ground. The club began to circulate notes to its members about the best way to enjoy Scottish skiing. Reinforcing the almost universal presence of medical practitioners in the development of the sport, the Dr. Wigner who had disported on Ben Chonzie a few years previously produced a guide. He recommended Aviemore as the best place from which to approach the Cairngorms though he warned, with resonance for the future, that he had been refused service at a Coylum Bridge establishment 'for breaking the Sabbath'. He had been seeking food, not the ungodly alcohol, but apparently the Almighty did not approve of skiing on His appointed day.

The Zdarsky-influenced Arthur skied often with another pioneer, W. W. Naismith, the founder of the Scottish Mountaineering Club. Both were badly afflicted with what Arthur called 'ski fever'. In Arthur's opinion even Father Time had no cure for this particular disease. The two men, seeking group support rather than an antidote, set up a meeting in Edinburgh in November 1907 with a view to the formation of a National Ski Club for Scotland. A polar explorer by the name of Bruce, another medical man, was invited to take the chair, which, appropriately enough, was situated in a facility known as Surgeons Hall. Dr. Bruce had the distinction of owning a pair of Nansen's skis which had mysteriously turned up one day at Dundee docks. This connection brought about the election of the great Norwegian explorer as the first honorary member of the new association. Since he had become his national ambassador in London and Rector of St. Andrews University, the honour was apt.

The newly formed Scottish Ski Club set about persuading hoteliers that winter sports offered unparalleled opportunities for business in what was otherwise a dead part of the year. The Great British counterpart, based in London, stepped up its efforts to encourage its members to think about skiing at home rather than going to the Alps.

Then, adding to the momentum, the army became involved through the agency of a Colonel Malcolm who lived in Inverness. He had met the pioneering E. C. Richardson in the Alps and had been much impressed by the fluidity of his stem christies and the readiness with which he launched himself into the air over bumps in the snow.

The good Colonel decided that ski training would be excellent for the moral fibre of his men. He invited Richardson to Scotland and the man came 'home' gladly, bringing with him a fanaticism about the beneficial effects of jumping which boded ill for nervous beginners. He declared; 'In the course of quick runs, leaps, turns attempted, one learns how to keep cool and collected when travelling at speeds hitherto unapproached and finds that a fall taken when travelling is not a serious matter after all.'

Every beginner will, of course, agree. Richardson went on, 'To overcome nervousness, practice on a steep slope.'

Of course! The steeper the better! He went on; 'Build the take off high and scoop out lots of snow immediately below it, so as to make it look as alarming as possible, then you go over anyhow and will be surprised how easy and harmless such a dreadful looking thing can be.'

This is perhaps the historical origin of the sadism which those who have been to ski school will recognise as an important characteristic of a significant proportion of instructors.

The poor young soldiers entrusted to the care of Colonel Malcolm were subjected to this mad method. Seventy years later the army was still clinging to this approach to a first day of skiing characterised by the routine order: 'We are *here*, men, at Point A. Your objective is to get to Point B, *there*, as fast as possible? Ok? *Go!*'

Point B was, of course, the bottom of the mountain. Doubtless Colonel Malcolm's sacrificial victims were no different from their successors. Obeying orders they would have nervously pushed off, thirty per cent of them falling over immediately, another third careering into one another and embracing in ways generally anathema to military men, at least in public, the remainder wobbling, curving, cursing and crashing far enough to take out a dozen innocent, more cautious civilians unsuspectingly trying out their newly acquired stem christies below. One soldier, maybe two, perhaps reached Point B, entirely by luck and with eyes firmly closed. The Colonel, with his Alpine experience and the insensitivity of 'good' breeding, doubtless sashayed past his fallen flock, uttering praise and condemnation as the mood took him and ordering his slaves to get up and do the whole suicidal exercise again.

If confirmation of this account is needed, 'Skisters' has illustrations of soldiers training in the 1940's. A slight satisfaction is that in one of them a person, clearly the officer because he is dressed in snazzy white whilst the other ranks are in their khaki uniforms, is flat on his face on the snow with his skis in the very painful 'snowplough-into-splits' position which is never adopted by choice. Further delight can be obtained by observing that the officer, naturally more intelligent than his men, has quickly hit upon the pretence that he intended to fall in order to 'fire' the surrogate rifle, really his ski stick, at an alarmed enemy.

It is possible, of course, that the officer is pretending to *indicate*, rather than shoot, that is, making it precisely clear what he means by Point B, but if either of these exculpatory explanations is true, why are the two men at the extremes of the observing group grinning so obviously? Point B is not funny, neither is shooting at some loon who is probably going to shoot you. No. But an officer falling flat on his face is very, very funny indeed. The one in authority has clearly made the foolish mistake of saying, 'Follow me, lads', and has paid the price for the sin of pride.

The original ski-crazy Colonel was so taken with the 'jump to destruction' style that, no doubt to the terminal despair of his men, he caused a moveable wooden structure to be created. This he placed on the moors at Dalwhinnie. It is claimed that all his friends wanted to try it out but, if they did so desire, it is a fair bet that they were not first day beginners. Probably most of them hated the instrument of torture but did not want to be branded cowards by a serving soldier. Malcolm tried to persuade the Ski Club to erect transportable jumps all over the Highlands but happily for newcomers to the sport it seems that funds did not run to such an extravagance.

The Ski Club, whether because of the Colonel or as an antidote is not clear, began to get into its stride. Posters appeared at many English railway stations exhorting the sassenachs to stop being fops and to face the bracing challenge of the Scottish winter. The famous, forthright Richardson had compiled a series of eight instructional cards so there could be no excuses about not knowing how to ski. (Why he needed eight is a mystery. One would have sufficed, saying; 'Find the steepest possible slope, build a terrifying jump and go!' with perhaps a simple illustration on how to construct a cliff). The leading newspapers, caught in the wave of enthusiasm, began to print special weather forecasts on Fridays and Saturdays. Herr Rickmer's 'sky above' was not allowed to be a deterrent either.

There was, by this time, the problem of fashion. For men, the normal huntin', shootin' gear was appropriate but what was an eager young gal to do if she did not want to end up a waterlogged statue in a loch like Rickmer's unturned pupil? An advertisement in 1911 solved the problem. They could wear, 'a two piece woollen Norfolk suit with knickers similar to boys' and a short unlined skirt to be carried in the rucksack for donning before reaching the station or the hotel'.

'Short' was, of course, used in the context of the time as, indeed, was 'knicker'; knicker as in bocker and short as in, ankles are erogenous zones. It was all extremely decorous.

One of the women, who had witnessed poor Miss Macphersons's involuntary dip on Ben Nevis, had further good counsel for members of her sex. From the lofty position of President of the Scottish Ladies

Climbing Club she pronounced; 'My advice to ladies is to commence at once and pass from stumbling beginner to expert to whom the wonderful snow scenes unfold a new page of the world's mystery'.

She was not herself a doctor but she was married to one. It sounds, though, as if she might have been happier with an army Colonel as far as skiing is concerned. From 'stumbling beginner to expert'; yes, the goal of every tyro. If only it were that easy!

Mrs. Inglis had thought of other things too. Women should, she suggested, carry a length of rope which could be criss-crossed over the skis for uphill travel; indubitably a worthy idea. 'With this,' the good woman claimed, 'one can go straight up a slope as steep as the roof of a house - an invaluable device for cross country skiing, as long as one remembers to slip it off for ski running downhill.'

Well, yes. Although one person, and a man at that, found that when it came to untying the knot, the rope was frozen to his skis beyond manipulation. After breaking several nails and teeth he was reduced to chopping at his expensive gear with a knife, bringing to mind the frenzy of the frustrated Eyore with his alphabet sticks.

This sufferer would, as compensation for his shredded equipment, by then have had the wherewithal to take other steps to increase velocity of descent. There are few things more frustrating in the entire world than to trudge up a snowy mountain, anticipating with every gained metre the thrill of the downward dash, only to find from the first push-off that the wretched white stuff is clinging to the soles of the skis like glutinous mud. To eliminate this hazard, the Allan Arthur who had communed with christie-inventor Zdarsky had imported the idea of waxing. This normally required the use of a flat iron but for emergency application on the slopes a champagne cork was recommended, this being, of course, the accessory which every working class Scot would carry with them as a matter of routine. But at least champagne corks were locally obtainable by those with the wherewithal; prior to a piece of Scottish enterprise, the wax was not.

It was a member of the Ski Club committee who began the process of resolving this difficulty. During the course of his trials he contrived to render unusable the greater part of his family's supply of saucepans but this inconvenience was amply justified by the eventual production of a viable composite. The cerebral work of invention completed, the innovator handed larger scale production to a chemist who, by chance or more likely by the Happy Families Eponymous Effect which accounts for chauffeurs called Driver, poets called Wordsworth and hairdressers called Trim, was a Mr. Speedy. It is said that this humble practitioner 'perfected' the recipe, although very likely he changed it completely. Regardless, he began to turn out tablets and tubes of handy 'Speedolin'.

Disputes began to arise between the 'true' skiers, those who came to the sport from a mountaineering background, and the newcomers who were not interested in touring but who simply wanted to go as fast as possible. The ubiquitous Dr. Wigner wrote, 'There is more to skiing than sliding on a patch of snow close to the railway line.'

Henry Lunn's son, Arnold, doubtless agreed but not for Dr. Wigner's reasons; he was not of the touring faction. In spite of an accident in Wales which had left him with one leg shorter than the other, he had made good use of the skis given to him by his father. He wanted to nudge skiing into the realm of competitive sport and on Jan 7th 1911 (some say 1909) he organised a race, which was held on the Plaine Morte glacier at a place called Montana. This is often claimed to be the first properly regulated slalom.

Lord Roberts of Kandahar donated a cup. Kandahar is in Afghanistan and has nothing directly to do with skiing. Lord Roberts just happened to have had his most glorious moment there in the Afghan war and had chosen the name when ennobled. However, slightly peculiarly perhaps, the Kandahar name instantly entered the world of skiing.

The Scottish Ski Club, firmly in the grip of the Wignerian purists, was unimpressed by such artificiality. The club refused to allow membership to those who had not toured extensively according to complex rules which must have defeated those without extensive mathematical expertise. Height ascended, distance travelled, weight carried, proportion of mileage on snow; everything was specified and all journeys had to be witnessed.

The dispute between the purists and the commercially-minded worsened. Because the Ski Club of Great Britain seemed to be siding with the travel agent, the various local ski clubs which had sprung up formed a new association, the National Ski Union.

The 1914 war put an end to ski development in Britain. Apart from some very minor episodes, the technique did not play a part in British military effort. The Scottish Ski Club ceased to function and in spite of efforts to revive it in 1920 it was not until almost a decade later that business was resumed.

In the Alps it was a different story. Arnold Lunn, doubtless with an eye to commercial advantage, was very active. By 1923 the British Ski Championships, held always in the Alps and mainly of interest to European-based skiers, were including a slalom. In 1924, Lunn used the Kandahar name for a new club which he established to promote ski racing.

The Scandinavians were not pleased that a Briton should be muscling in on something they had been doing for millenia and neither were most of the Alpine skiers entirely glad that someone from a comparatively flat, largely snow-less, country should be taking such a leading role. But Lunn had an Austrian friend, Hannes Schneider of the Arlberg ski club in St. Anton, and together they organised, in 1928, an international race known as the Arlberg-Kandahar. The event comprised slalom and downhill and was deemed to be an immediate success. By 1930, Lunn's approach to ski racing had been internationally accepted even though the Nordic countries persisted with their objections.

Scottish-born skiers were prominent in the early races. One man, C.E.W. Mackintosh, won the 'Roberts of Kandhar' four times. Many judged him to be the best in the world for a time. Another, Harold Mitchell, won what was then the longest downhill race, the 'Inferno'.

The widening base of motor car ownership helped to re-generate Scottish skiing. Enthusiasts could at last free themselves of the constraints imposed by railway lines and bus timetables. Those who had experienced Alpine conditions brought back news of developments in equipment and technique. It was not always the case, however, that they out-skied the natives. Many discovered to their cost that conditions in the Highlands were very different to those in Austria or Switzerland. Myrtle Simpson notes that home-based practitioners needed two types of turn, a stem and a 'lifted' stem which helped to avoid rocks and protruding clumps of heather. She quotes one contemporary as recording that;

'Snow slopes in Scotland take on a most puzzling kind of surface glare which defies the most hawk-eyed of skiers and reduces the short-sighted runner, with moisture on his glasses, to a state of dithering funk. The run and crash type of skier will have a thin time in Scotland because even if the slopes are well covered caution would be necessary. With uncertain snow, heather, rocks, windswept ice and all kinds of bunkers placed in the most awkward and trying positions, fast running is mere folly.'

The global financial crisis of the early 1930's provided a boost for the home-grown product. Those who could no longer afford to go abroad travelled north for their sport. 'Skisters' provides the sad account of a hotelier in Braemar who, for Hogmanay 1934, invested heavily to create the convenience and comforts which had become commonplace in Alpine resorts. He even went to the expense of hiring a band of musicians and a Swiss instructor.

The crowds gathered, the band played, the Alpine hero paraded and what did the fates deliver?

Nae snae.

That year it snowed heavily in Barcelona. Kent was rendered invisible by blizzards. But there was no snow in Braemar until the middle of March.

This was bad news for more than the unlucky hotelier. The Scottish Ski Club, encouraged by Arnold Lunn, had arranged to hold the first ever British slalom race. In February there were but a few streaks of whiteness at the highest altitudes and the event was cancelled. With the March redemption, the race was suddenly reinstated.

Myrtle Simpson's account of the event tells a typical Scottish skiing story of triumph over adversity, of chaos not quite prevailing, of snobbery and earthiness, of humanity and of all-pervading humour. In summary the event went as follows:

**Weather:** High wind, driving snow, very cold. (i.e. typical)

**The start:** Confused by the appearance out of the mist of unlisted, seriously hung-over, sleep-deprived revellers (a normal condition) who were determined to take part come-what-may and who did.

**The starter:** Lady Raeburn (essential, gung-ho, aristocratic component).

**Gatekeeping:** Reported to be 'Disgraceful' (but forgivable since nobody had ever kept a gate before and in any case it was impossible to see more than a yard or two).

**Press coverage:** The *Scotsman* lost interest when it learned that insufficient people with titles would be present. The *Glasgow Herald* telephoned the organiser on the day *after* the race to ask where its photographer should stand.

**Animal involvement:** Several dogs (not racing but lolloping about, snuffling, throwing snow in the air with their noses, chasing randomly selected skiers, barking at nothing and waving their tails in ecstatic circles).

**Race winner:** Patricia Raeburn. (No relation, surely!)

**Post race dinner:** 55 guests, great merriment, hang-over reinforcement.

**Cup presentation:** "Er, sorry, we forgot to get a cup".

The committee, perhaps not uninfluenced by the celebrations, decided on a subtle approach to the swift acquisition of a trophy. They sent a telegram; 'Fifty five members of the Scottish Ski Club present their compliments to their oldest member and intimate that Miss Patricia Raeburn has won the first open slalom race held in Scotland. At present no cup.'

The 'oldest member', the recipient of this piece of diplomatic nicety, was a Mr. Pitman. With admirable promptitude and generosity he responded that he would, of course, donate a cup and the Pitman Quaich was duly brought into the British winter sports world.

Indigenous skiing was once more on an upward curve. Myrtle Simpson records that so many people were trying out their turns in the Lawers district in the mid-thirties that a notice appeared in the press asking them to go away. They had become, in some people's estimation at least, a nuisance.

There were other racing innovations, one involving dubious handicapping and a massed start which surely led to premature deaths though none seem to be recorded. Another, instigated by Arnold Lunn's Kandhar club, was for a downhill. It had been thought, until the recent improvement in levels of skill, that a mad dash down a Scottish mountain would prove fatal for many but confidence had reached a new high. The race started at the summit of Beinn Ghlas near Killin and then, after a painful slog across a plateau, it dived down a vertiginous gully. A report on the event was sent to the editor of the Scottish Ski Club Journal, accompanied by a letter from which the following startlingly honest quotation is drawn.

'I enclose herewith the official report of the Scottish Kandahar race, for which you asked, but it is impersonal and does not give you any idea of the absolute horror with which I, and no doubt many of the other competitors, viewed the little string of flags which marked the course down what is, to all intents and purposes, a precipice! I have often been to Beinn Ghlas and have even occasionally looked down this south gully but have always recoiled from the edge of it with sick horror, and certainly, the idea of racing down in a mist had never occurred to me, even in my wildest nightmares.'

The fatalism with which this masochist, and dozens of others, threw themselves off a precipice in the dark prompted a bemused foreign visitor to comment; 'Skiers in Scotland are afraid of nothing. I have seen them ski down slopes which elsewhere would have been recognised as meadow, but no, here it is considered an excellent skiing slope, just as long as there is a little snow buried between the grass. Adaptability and agility are truly great virtues.'

It is obvious, from the informal race report, there was no lack of *fear* but against this there was the determination not to retreat and to extract the maximum of enjoyment from the most unpromising conditions.

The competitors in the crazy race had, of course, to find their own way to the starting point but as Alpine countries began to experiment with mechanical uplift there was pressure for Scotland to follow suit. In a very limited way, motor vehicles were pressed into service but, off the road, these were not very successful and even on the macadam they were often stuck when, higher up, skiing conditions were at their best. Clubs, such as the one formed in Dundee in 1936, devoted much effort to finding locations for skiing which were accessible by road in most circumstances.

When the second major conflict with Germany began in 1939 the effect was not, as it had been in 1914, to eliminate almost all skiing. It was anticipated that many of the coming battles would be fought in Arctic Norway. There was an urgent need to train troops who could match the enemy experts.

Refugee Norwegians were billeted in Drumintoul Lodge, in the forest of Rothiemurchus which decorates the foothills of the Cairngorms. British troops were stationed at Forest Lodge near Nethybridge, amongst them the famous climbers John Hunt and Frank Smythe. In Skisters Hunt is quoted as writing;

'It proved a novel experience of not unmixed pleasure. A great expanse of heather, not much snow, stupendous loads and fierce Cairngorm blizzards. On one occasion, fighting the way up to Loch Etchachan in the teeth of a gale, I watched Smythe lifted by some gust and deposited forty feet below the track in a snow drift.'

The haphazard nature of army ski-teaching is recorded by Frank Sutton who simply responded to a circular asking for those with experience. His was very limited indeed but, since he had been on skis once or twice, it was greater than that of most of the others. He became an instructor instantly. Confirming the prevailing services philosophy he writes;

'There was little snow and what there was lay on north and east facing slopes towards Macdhui. The men made good progress. They were miners from Lanarkshire who had never been in the mountains before. When I had my first squad lined up on the top of a small, gentle slope I thought I would make myself popular and said "There is nothing in it boys, just push off, close your eyes and wait for the crash". Which I did, but opened my eyes when I stopped with a snow plough, but they did not. The result was a bit of a shambles, so I never said that again.'

Two things are certain in connection with this recollection. One; the slope on Ben Macdhui was by no means gentle. To the beginners it was close to being a cliff. Two; those miners from Lanarkshire were swiftly promoted to instructors and they used the death or dishonour method no matter what Frank Sutton might have subsequently done.

If confirmation is needed of the rudimentary nature of wartime troop training it is provided by a man called Chris Lyon who was a member of the Glasgow-based Craig Dhu climbing club. Several members of this famous institution, formed during the 1920's Depression by unemployed artisans and labourers, had experimented, since 1938, with skiing in Glencoe but the hostilities took away their MacBrayne's bus service; the vehicles were not permitted to carry futile recreational equipment. He and a friend, Bob Clyde, managed to get themselves to the Cairngorms in 1942 where, to their delight, they found German prisoners of war who were willing to provide ski lessons for the fee of a few cigarettes. This input was quite sufficient for the British army commanders to approach the two Scots and invite them to become instructors. In Chris Lyon's words they 'laughed like drains' at the suggestion.

The Norwegians doubtless used a more sophisticated approach and the wartime saw an expansion of skiing in terms of numbers of participants and levels of skill. There was also a marked improvement in the infrastructure in the Cairngorm area. Bridges were built and new tracks established. The army also addressed the problem of adequate clothing for the conditions, introducing string vests and longjohns as part of the standard kit.

None of the troops trained in winter warfare ever used their skills in combat but it is severally claimed that the benefits of the exercise were far-reaching. In this, as in many other areas of life, the war was a leveller. Men who would never have dreamed of venturing onto the snow gained crucial experience. Many enjoyed recreational skiing on periods of leave and carried on once the hostilities had ended.

A leader in this area was none other than Field Marshal Montgomery who had enjoyed Scottish skiing a great deal before the war. He conceived the admirably egalitarian mission of introducing army conscripts to skiing regardless of its potential military value. Pulling rank and reputation in all directions he persuaded Colonel Grant, main landowner in the Cairngorm area, to provide a site for a hut, the Nuffield Trust to provide finance and the War Office to donate the labour. A wooden shelter was built in the Larig Ghru, the great pass which cuts across the Cairngorm range, and opened with due ceremony. An Army Ski Association was formed.

There was a further boost to British skiing brought through the war. Many soldiers had experienced Alpine conditions during their periods of rest from grappling with the enemy. No doubt they would have chosen to return to these happy hunting grounds but they could not because foreign currency was in very short supply. Even though the distance from the south of England to the Alps is much the same as it is to Scotland, the new enthusiasts had no choice but to head north.

The Scottish Ski Club, which had been in abeyance, revived itself through the device of a cocktail party at the pre-war secretary's house. This was, arbitrarily according to 'Skisters', turned into an official meeting. During this multi-purpose gathering it was agreed that returning soldiers were unlikely to fulfil the stringent, mathematically taxing, touring qualifications and so these were summarily dropped. Membership became open to all who were interested.

One of the most experienced of the pre-war skiers, Dick West, felt impelled to warn the newcomers. He wrote; 'The weather is always indifferent to bad and the great mistake lies in waiting for the good day, as it seldom happens. Great enjoyment is always available once the art of indifference to the weather has been mastered. The wind is a greater trial than the rain and cannot be surmounted without strength. Never sit down. Sandwiches must be eaten while walking up and sweeties may be sucked on the way down. A header sometimes spirits the sweety away but it tastes even better if the owner should chance to retrieve it from its snowy grave.'

That was the spirit! and is the spirit to this day. Never sit down!

Ex-army equipment was generally available at reasonable cost. A handicap was the severe petrol rationing which limited the use of the private car but buses were pressed into service and these fostered a spirit of comradeship.

The travel restrictions which caused this post-war surge of interest in Scotland also led to the brief functioning of the first professional ski academy. An army man, Bill Bracken, who had learned his skills in Austria where his parents had a chalet, could no longer rely on customers getting to the school in Zermatt which he had operated since 1936. He relocated to Drumochter. Bracken had been a successful racer in his time and was, according to Arnold Lunn, who might not have been entirely disinterested, the first person to perfect the parallel turn.

The school operated for one season only. There was a race at Easter at which, through a combination of canniness and courage, locally based Scottish Ski Club members took the first five places.

One of those involved in the Drumochter venture, Earl MacEwan, commented on Bracken's swift return to Switzerland in terms which might have driven Karl and Eileen Fuchs straight back to the Alps. It was 'just as well' Bracken abandoned his Calendonian venture, claimed the noble Earl; '....as no similar organisation could ever operate successfully in Scotland in a year when skiing in Switzerland was possible. Are people going to travel from, say, London to Newtonmore for some very spartan skiing when it is permitted to spend £35 at Davos or Scheidegg?'

This pessimistic member of the aristocracy was doubtless thinking about the ever-expanding systems of mechanical uplift on the Continent, about the new practice of piste preparation and about the mountain-top bars and restaurants. It must have seemed impossible then that Scotland could ever compete.

Those British people who did manage to reach the Alps in the late 1940's would probably have been forced to agree. The prepared slopes were creating a new breed of skier with modified styles and adapted equipment. The leisurely swings which were possible with wooden skis on un-pisted snow simply led to disaster on the polished tracks. 'Checking' to make a base for a turn was impossible without steel edges.

But what the Earl was not thinking about, perhaps characteristically for a member of the aristocracy, was the likes of Frith Finlayson.

In his autobiography, 'Ski Teacher', Frith Finlayson gives a very moving account of how he and his friends, impoverished boys from the tenements of Glasgow, 'discovered' the countryside around the grimy industrial city, very locally at first, then venturing to Loch Lomond. From walking in the hills they graduated to climbing and thereby became involved in the Craig Dhu club.

Frith tells how, in 1950, he had his first sight of skiers when he was roaming above Rannoch Moor. The attraction was immediate. A friendly soul offered a chance to try the sport. Nailed boots were tied to the laths and the initiate took his first carefree slide. It was the beginning of something close to an addiction.

Subsequently, Frith went with a large Craig Dhu contingent to Glenmore where they hired a lorry as a conveyance and stayed in the huts formerly used by the Norwegians. Close to where they were staying was Glenmore Lodge which the Central Council for Physical Recreation had purchased just after the war and turned into an outdoor pursuits centre for children. On the staff there was a man called Jack Thomson who was appointed in 1950 specifically to teach the rudiments of skiing. Frith records that Thomson, '..... has the honour to be teaching skiing longer than any other person in our not so short history in skiing'.

By this time, some of the hoteliers in the Cairngorm area were becoming alert to the commercial potential of skiing. Frith writes; 'It's true to say however that skiing came to the attention of hoteliers in Speyside through the early efforts of Jock Kerr Hunter running his first courses in skiing and climbing from the Aviemore Hotel.'

According to this account, up to one hundred and twenty people took part in what Frith describes as the 'first two weeks of organised ski teaching on Cairngorm.' The manager of the Aviemore Hotel was an enthusiastic supporter. He could evidently see that there was potential for a significant expansion of trade.

There were other initiatives at this time. Eric Langmuir, who for many years was in charge of Glenmore Lodge, recalls that a man called Arthur Kumar, who was Secretary of the Scottish Youth Hostels Association, introduced ski instruction at the Glen Isla hostel and possibly at others too.

It was not, therefore, that Karl and Eileen were heading into completely virgin territory. There were keen skiers about in Scotland and there were people who could see that there might be commercial potential in winter sports. What was lacking was a point of focus, a person with sufficient credibility and charisma to turn the vague aspirations into something tangible. Unbeknownst to the incomers, the stage was most definitely set.

## 8. A Cairngorm Lesson

Karl arrived at Victoria Station in November 1954 accompanied by three piles of luggage. He had his own personal belongings, a considerable quantity because he was in effect migrating; he had Eileen's residual effects from her long stay in Austria and he had no less than eighteen pairs of skis with associated sticks and boots. In Vienna the load had broken the roof of a taxi.

In those days, customs formalities were performed at the London terminal. Understandably daunted by the volume of the Austrian's baggage, an officer asked politely to see the import licence for the winter sports equipment, thus getting the great adventure off to a worrying start.

Karl was at a significant disadvantage because he spoke almost no English but at least he was allowed through with the trunks and cases. The skis stayed behind.

After greetings suitable to newly weds who had been separated for a time, Eileen went to plead with the official. She explained what the skis were for and that they would not be sold, all to no avail. The customs man was adamant; without a properly stamped import licence the winter sports equipment was staying put.

Feeling entirely like the supplicant she was, Eileen took a taxi to the Board of Trade, leaving Karl forlornly guarding their belongings. It might have been politic to play the innocent but in her determination to free the skis, Eileen let it be known that she had once been a person of some rank in the Board. Immediately she realised that she had made a mistake. The official she was dealing with was of the solid British 'fair play to all' tradition; there could be no special favours, not even if Eileen had been the Prime Minister. The petitioner had to use all her negotiating skills to rescue the process and she was, as she recalls, 'very unpopular' as she left the building clutching the precious licence.

At last they were at the taxi rank with all their belongings. Eileen insisted that, regardless of expense, they would use two London cabs; she did not want tiresome claims for damages to mar the start of their adventure. By spreading the load they safely reached the Knowles' house at Purley.

Karl was happy to be there. He was excited by the coming challenge. Eileen guessed that he would suffer sometimes, as she had done, from homesickness but the circumstances were different. They were about to build a home of their own. They were both going to largely unknown territory far from where they had been brought up. It would be a shared adventure.

At an expense they could ill afford they hired Carter Patterson, a company of removals experts, to convey their more substantial belongings, including Eileen's piano, but on the overnight train from Euston they transported as much as they could, including the skis. They had booked couchettes and as they re-entered Scotland they were both deeply asleep.

They awoke, as if alerted by a warning, at the moment the train clanked to a halt at Dalwhinnie, the highest station on the route. They were in the heart of the Drumochter Pass, on the high level route which links Perth with Inverness. Karl flicked up the blind and immediately exclaimed in huge delight. There was snow! masses of it, deep, drifted snow all around them and thick upon the surrounding slopes. So much snow and only early November; it was a happy portent!

Drumochter is a wild spot. For many travellers, the way through the mountains is daunting. On a dark day there can be a false sense of leaving civilisation behind. Atavistic fears about survival come to the surface. The long, gloomy winters threaten depression, the bitter cold causes anxiety about fuel supply failures. For the faint-hearted sassenach it is often tempting to turn and run towards the comparative safety of the south.

Of course, the two adventurers were far from being faint hearted but in any case, once the transition is made, once the traveller reaches a comfortable hotel or a warm, welcoming house, the anxiety quickly dissipates. Life in this northern quarter of the British Isles is much as it is in the other parts. People go about their business in more or less the same fashion as do those living in Surrey or Sussex. But some of these troubling thoughts must have been with Karl and Eileen as the train moved on. Their first brief view of the area had been in late summer; now they were surrounded by all the evidence that winter would be fierce. They knew nobody in Speyside; they were not going for a short, comfortable holiday where others would look after them; they were facing the totally unknown; they were going to have to cope with the setting up from scratch of an entirely new way of life.

There were several stops to go before they reached their destination. As the clanking train approached Aviemore they had their first full sight of the slopes which, only a few weeks earlier, Karl had judged to be suitable for a ski school. He twisted in his seat, his face close to the window. 'Mah!' he exclaimed more than once. Cairngorm was a rounded mound completely covered in snow. The potential ski runs which he had spotted a few weeks earlier were looking exceedingly inviting. Eileen had discovered, from the map, that the long declivity to the left of the Cairngorm summit was called Coire na Ciste. The gruesome translation underneath the Gaelic name was 'Corrie of the Coffin'.

The train jerked back into motion. The next stop, half a dozen or so miles up the line, was their destination.

Carrbridge station is set slightly apart from most of the village buildings, up a narrow, dead end road which heads past the cemetery towards a tiny place, a few miles away, called Dalnahatnaich. On that cold November morning there were few people alighting at Carrbridge. Karl and Eileen stepped onto the platform and looked about them. The halt seemed to be in the middle of a forest. Karl dumped their overnight cases on the long, snow-covered platform and then hurried to the guard's van to off-load all the equipment. The ticket collector, having reaped the bulk of his meagre morning cardboard harvest, obligingly came along with a trolley.

'Ye'll be Mister and Mrs Fuchs,' he said in the slow, elegant, long-vowelled vocal manner of the region. Word had already spread! It was wonderful to be locally famous before a single ski had been strapped to a boot.

The previous owner of Struan House was waiting for them. Anticipating bulky luggage he had kindly taken the trouble to fix a trailer to his car. They stowed their belongings and clambered into the warm, leather-smelling interior. Slightly disorientated by the protracted journey, Karl and Eileen gazed about them as they bumped towards the village and cautiously turned right onto the A9. It struck them that the main street had an unexpectedly large number of people along its length and that most of these were stationary in the cold. All of them stared, one or two with open mouths. 'The rumours were true!', their expressions declared, 'there really is going to be a ski hotel!'

In fact, this was not the very first time that skiing had impacted on Carrbridge. It is reported that a Norwegian au pair had brought skis to the village just after the war. To the astonishment of all, she had skied on the golf course but the villagers, by their evident amazement, seemed to be saying that to have one lone, temporary skier is one thing, to have a permanent ski school is absolutely another.

The popular attention brought reality home to Karl and Eileen. This was it! What had been akin to a vague dream was now unavoidable. Fear and excitement competed for dominance. What if nobody wanted to come to little Carrbridge for the skiing? But what, oh what! if people *did?*

The new owners were given breakfast and were then treated to a thorough induction into the ways of the establishment; the skills of lighting the stove, the tricks of coping with uncertain electricity supplies, the arguments to be used with guests when they complained about the peaty colour of the silky-soft water, the method for rectifying the occasional blockage of drains.

When the hand-over was completed, and the departing vendors gone on their journey, Karl and Eileen plunged into work. In the short term, she needed to become familiar with the kitchen, cleaning and laundry arrangements. Karl set about mastering the mysteries of power and water supplies and assessing what needed to be done to create his continental style ski shed. As he roamed about their newly acquired property, Karl made mental notes as to how he would transform the building into a proper ski hotel. This could be done only stage by stage but he was very eager to start deploying timber

Within a few days, their first guest arrived, an elderly woman. She migrated the few hundred yards from the Carrbridge Hotel which was closing for the winter. Karl and Eileen learned, in confidence of course, that she was there, in that lowest of low seasons, mainly because she was totally in love with the Carrbridge Hotel's dog. It was divulged that she would often telephone from London simply to 'talk' to this creature.

Eileen cooked her first diabetic meal. Karl, dressed in full Austrian costume and with a napkin neatly over one arm, served the food silently to their one guest, relishing every moment, making waiting-on an art form. For Eileen the first experience as hostess was not a particularly pleasant one. The woman was amicable enough but she was unduly fussy; not at all what they anticipated from skiing clientele. One of her several fads was that she had to have several hot water bottles in her bed, all precisely positioned. They were glad when the doting dog-lover departed, leaving them six weeks or so to convert the hotel into a ski base. Through word of mouth they had secured at least two paying customers for the Christmas period and more for New Year. Everything had to be in place by then.

It was a hard but happy time. They worked, sometimes together, often separately, making their preparations. With difficulty, Eileen persuaded her husband to stop for tea breaks. They smiled at each other often. It was just the two of them, the civil servant and the policeman, beginning to create.

Maurice had very generously offered to buy them a car as a wedding present. They took the train to Inverness and acquired a Lea Francis shooting brake. Mr. Henderson, who sold them the vehicle, was married to a woman from Eastbourne and Eileen found this fact very comforting. Somehow the presence of another southerner made her realise that she was not as far from home as she had thought.

Karl had still not taken the British test but he was able to drive as a learner as long as a qualified person was with him. Since they went almost everywhere together this was not unduly restricting. Using the new conveyance, they called on other establishments and introduced themselves. Few if any of the hotels in the area stayed open in the winter, apart from Hogmanay, and the prospect of a ski school was interesting. Perhaps the commercial season could be considerably extended. In Grantown on Spey, Colin Sutton at the Craiglynne and David Ross at the Ben Mhor expressed great excitement at the injection of Alpine expertise.

*The Lea Francis outside a snowy Struan*

Another part of the work, similarly pleasurable, was exploring the area in search of suitable slopes. At first they looked locally. Karl had already spotted the potential of the Carrbridge golf course; beginners would feel very safe on its unthreatening inclines. They tried it out. Eileen was still at a fairly elementary stage so Karl used her as a prototype customer. In return, she shouted English translations of his instructions which he then attempted to repeat. The results were not impressive but at least the essential words 'knees' and 'bend' entered the teacher's English vocabulary. Colin Sutton and David Ross came over with their wives and quickly learned enough about skiing to be able to cope with the enquiries of potential guests should they eventually decide to try a winter season.

Karl and Eileen ventured in the car along the main road towards Inverness and found, close to the Slochd Pass which cuts through the Monodliath Mountains, an ideal teaching area. Their customers would be spared the long drive to Glenmore and the even more tedious uphill hike provided that the snow came to a reasonably low level. They ventured, too, along the road towards Grantown-on-Spey and, turning left towards Forres, Nairn and Elgin, discovered a hill known as the Giant's Face which also had useful areas.

Partly guided by the map, partly just using Karl's infallible sense of direction, they made a circular tour on skis via Aviemore. It was a long trek by most people's standards but they were both supremely fit and they made light of it. Eileen enjoyed the langlauf style where speed control was not so much of an anxiety. On the way back to Carrbridge they came across a stretch which was the flattest they had found. They skimmed merrily across it, marvelling that nature had created a perfect plane in such a hilly area.

Intrigued, Eileen brought out the map and studied it as they sipped their welcome-home cup of tea. After a moment she said 'Karli?' He grunted to show that he was listening.

'You know that flat field we skied across?' Eileen continued.

Karl grunted once more.

'It was a loch.'

This elicited much more than a neutral noise. Karl bounded over to look at the evidence. It was obviously true! They had skied across the frozen Loch Alvie. Just as well, they agreed, that there was no sign of a thaw.

Then came the day when they felt ready to make their first skiing excursion to Cairngorm. For a while Karl had been trying to persuade his wife to abandon her familiar, comfortable boots. They were very loose and thus partly responsible, so he said, for her difficulties with certain skiing manoeuvres. There was a brand new pair, brought especially from Austria. He insisted that the Cairngorm baptism demanded proper footwear.

Eileen protested that she had tried the boots within the hotel and was sure that they were too small and stiff. Karl would have none of this. They were her exact size and his mother had considerately hiked around Bruck for days on end, wearing them in. The leather was at a perfect consistency, he claimed.

Conceding, Eileen put the boots on. Karl was probably right as he generally was in such matters. On the hill they would doubtless form about her foot and give that extra support which would make her unpredictable stem christies into demonstrator's models of the technique. It was, in any case, a perfect day. The snow had lingered and the sky was blue. It was impossible to be unhappy.

They drove to the limit of the road and began the walk. In spite of Karl's confidence, Eileen felt discomfort from the first step but the day was glorious and she did not want to spoil it by complaining. Karl set a taxing pace; he was eager to reach the steeper slopes. After a few hundred feet of hectic climbing she dared to mention that something unpleasant was happening to her heels. The leader of the expedition simply refused to believe his sole follower. There was no time for diversion; the corries above them were too inviting.

Risking a further muttered grumble about her heels, Eileen dutifully followed. The target field looked a mite taxing for her unreliable technique but she trusted Karl absolutely. With skis balanced on shoulders they trudged very steeply up towards what would one day be a famous ski run called White Lady and came, breathless but triumphant, to an intermediate ridge. On the far horizon were a few puffy clouds but above them the blueness was dazzling and the air clean and crisp. The sun was still shining. Far below, the rough rectangle of Loch Morlich glinted.

For the moment Eileen forgot the demons which were slicing at her heels with razor blades. The innovators began to imagine. A ski lift to the summit, Eileen suggested. 'No', Karl said, 'a *railway*, a funicular from Aviemore. A restaurant at the top station.' In their imaginings were hundreds of brightly clad skiers happily swooping all over the high level bowl. This *could* work. This *would* work.

The next thing Eileen knew was that something like a giant, invisible sea wave had hit her and she had fallen. Her skis were whipped away but luckily they went like fat javelins into the snow. Probably she screamed but nothing could be heard. She saw Karl staggering, fighting to stay upright. The wind whistled and screeched about them. Eileen made some way on hands and knees as Karl struggled over. He helped his stricken wife to her feet and shouted that they should go further up where another ridge would provide shelter.

With several stumbles and falls they reached this landmark and, as Karl had suggested, there was a degree of protection. Eileen was just thinking that they might, after all, have the promised lesson when another unforseen hazard hit them. Driving, blinding snow whipped into their faces and with it came a terrible darkness. Mist swirled. Karl vanished.

Instantly, Eileen's sense of direction abandoned her. Even though they were not far apart it seemed impossible that they could find each other in the deep, grey gloom.

It would have been easy to panic but instead she began to calculate. There was no point in shouting, no way whatsoever of communicating with Karl. It was tempting to believe that as long as she headed downwards she should eventually reach some part of Glenmore. The difficulty with this was that it was impossible to see which was down and in any case there were probably smaller bowls and valleys on the descent. A wrong line out of one of these and she could be heading in entirely the wrong direction, into the wilderness.

Karl, his clothes flapping as though for take off, his body being pushed once, then again, into an involuntary kneel, came within her range of vision. She gasped her gratitude for the sight of him but he knew nothing of this. He shouted directly into her ear. 'We go down a little'.

Incredibly, he was still intent on completing their mission.

For a short while they went through the motions, Karl contriving to demonstrate steadily in spite of the hurricane and the almost zero visibility, Eileen falling often. She was glad when he yelled that they would make for a hut which he had seen over to their right as they had ascended.

They began the precarious journey. Eileen had not the least notion as to the direction in which the hut lay. She could see nothing. Karl seemed to be reassuringly confident. She followed.

In spite of the ferocious coldness and the fear that they might be buried before reaching the shelter, Eileen was once again aware of the torturers in her boots. There was a sadistic satisfaction, even there, in knowing that she had been right; the pain had not been imaginary. It was not, though, the time for triumphalism.

She had no idea how Karl knew where to go. There were no visible features. The entire world was dark grey. Somewhere the mist ended and the settled snow began but Eileen could not distinguish between the two. She stayed close, blind to everything except Karl's battling figure. They must have returned to the ridge because the wind suddenly increased in ferocity. When the colossus toppled, as twice he did, she fell too. She also fell when he did not but he seemed to sense this and always turned to help. Often her skis came off. When fixing skis whilst on a slope the rule is; always put the lower ski on first. But which *was* the lower ski? Where *was* the slope?

Karl knew. She copied him, shivering with cold and deep emotion. At the best of times it was difficult to deal with the crude Kandahar bindings.

In such conditions, not uncommon in the Cairngorms, it is very easy to lose all emotional control. Dizziness, physical and psychological, takes over. The toughest of people can be reduced to helpless tears. The point of persisting seems to vanish. There is no hope whatsoever because there are no cues. The skis seem to be moving. You make a manoeuvre to stop and discover, or believe you discover, that they had not been moving at all. You fall over. It is very difficult to get up again because you have no idea where 'up' is. If your ski has come off, as very likely it has, you struggle with frozen fingers to clear the snow from the binding. Because you have no idea which way the slope is going, if indeed, there is a slope, you have no idea where to put the ski to prevent it running off without you.

Without Karl it is very likely that Eileen, close as she was to hut, would have become one of the Cairngorm cautionary tales. He seemed to have penetrative eyes, his spirit was indomitable. The wind had apparently lost its power over him. Exaggerating every movement of his body as though demonstrating to an imbecile, he executed a perfect stem turn. Eileen copied him as best she could. The manoeuvre was not elegant, she ended in an undignified crouch, but still Karl yelled extreme encouragement. It was probably her bravery rather than her technique which brought forth the praise.

'Soon at the hut,' Karl screamed. She did not entirely believe him.

He seemed never to hesitate, never to doubt. Yet, Eileen thought, these are not his mountains. How can he know?

The 'soon' was a relative term. They stemmed, they ski-walked, they glided, they side-stepped until, as Karl had predicted, the hut was there. When it became visible they were almost close enough to touch its comforting wooden walls.

Later they were to learn that it was known as 'Jean's Hut', a refuge erected by the father of Jean Smith who had died whilst skiing there in 1948. It was probably as well that the macabre provenance of the shelter was not known to Eileen at that time; the Cairngorm conditions were quite sufficient to generate fear.

They had a long walk ahead because the snow cover towards the bottom of the mountain was not suitable for Eileen's standard of skiing. After a drink from the flask in Karl's rucksack and a rest they set off. Eileen knew that they had, as she suspected, been through something extraordinary because for once Karl broke his rule that she should carry her own skis.

All the way down she wanted nothing other than to go to sleep. They were sheltered from the worst of the wind but the cold seemed ever more intense. Karl began to sing, expecting a duet. She could not give voice. The pains in her feet were no longer apparent. Maybe Karl had been right; maybe her judgement of the boots *was* 'rubbish'.

In the car she could not keep awake. Once they reached Struan she had barely the energy to take off the contentious footwear. Wearily she dealt with the laces. She began the pulling and the first shafts of renewed agony caused her to cry out. Karl glanced at her, perhaps ready to suggest that she was making a fuss about nothing just to support a worthless point. Eileen looked into the boot and, smiling for the first time in many hours, she handed it to him.

He looked impatiently inside and then at her, his expression very altered. The evidence was blatant. On the inner sole there was a minor lake of blood.

The damage to her feet was substantial. It took three weeks to heal properly. Penitentially, Karl gently bathed the wounds that evening and covered them with plasters. As he did so he talked about their experience. He acknowledged that he had learned a crucial lesson; that the Cairngorms are different mountains. No such rapid weather change would have happened in his native hills, no wind of such ferocity would have made standing up impossible. Henceforth the Carrbridge Austrian Ski School would be maximally cautious on the hills. Nothing there, it seemed, could ever be taken for granted.

## 9. First Season

Skiing was out of the question for Eileen, even walking in normal footwear was acutely uncomfortable. Whilst she nursed her gory heels and hobbled gingerly about doing her domestic chores, Karl began redecorating the hotel and making the changes which would turn it into a winter sports centre.

His main priority was to create a ski shed, where equipment could be stored and where maintenance work could be carried out. The ideal would have been to erect a building at the back of the yard but there was neither time nor money for this. He decided that he would press the Annexe tea room into short term service whilst he converted one of the outhouses at the side of the property. The first task was the building of racks. Using the garage at the front of the drive as a workshop, Karl began the sawing, gluing and hammering

Eileen was in the kitchen one late morning, preparing lunch for the two of them, when the carpenter came staggering in. His face was the colour of the cabbage which was being chopped and there was a white foam bubbling from his mouth. His skin was wet with sweat but when Eileen rushed to him, she found that he was icy cold. He collapsed onto the floor and became unconscious.

The first thought for the highly alarmed wife was that she had married an epileptic. Had she been in London or Purley she would have immediately dialled for an ambulance but she imagined that the nearest emergency vehicle would be twenty five miles away in Inverness. Needing urgent advice, she rushed to the next-door cottage which was owned by a delightful old couple called Panton. They had had some brief contact with them already so Mrs. Panton at least knew who Eileen was. When she heard the alarming tale of Karl's collapse she went immediately to the telephone and called the Grantown-on-Spey doctor. 'So,' Eileen noted to herself, part of her mind still cool in spite of the crisis, 'that's what to do in a medical emergency.' It was not an entirely reassuring thought.

Mr. Panton and Eileen hurried back to the Struan kitchen where they were mightily relieved to see that Karl was just beginning to come round. The two did what they could to make him comfortable until the doctor arrived.

By the time Jimmy Gow came briskly and reassuringly into the kitchen, the patient was able to talk. The doctor asked for a full description of the circumstances of Karl's collapse. Eileen translated. There was puzzlement on Dr. Gow's face for a moment and then there was enlightenment.

'Carbon monoxide!' he said.

It transpired that because it was so cold in the garage, Karl had started the car so that, every now and then, he could slip into the driver's seat and enjoy the benefits of the heater. What he had forgotten to do was to provide sufficient outlet for the car's exhaust fumes. He had been taking in deep breaths of poisonous gas.

There was relief all round that the crisis had an obvious cause but Dr. Gow stressed that Karl had survived only because of a strong constitution, a high level of fitness and the good luck that he had fled just in time.

Over a cup of recuperative coffee, Karl told the doctor, via Eileen's translation, of the plans for the ski school. Jimmy Gow declared himself to be very keen on learning to ski. He became, in that moment, Struan's inaugural fee-paying ski school customer. This was the first benefit of Karl's poisoning.

The second was that Jenny and Sandy Panton turned from neighbours into friends. Both professed themselves to be too old to indulge in winter sports but Sandy was one of those men who understood *things*. He had an Aladdin's Cave workshop where there was always a tool or a spare part which could remedy any malfunction. He had already, in those early days of the medium, built his own television. He never despaired of fixing a broken implement no matter how hopeless the case seemed to be. He was constitutionally incapable of throwing anything away. He was the technician supreme and yet he was also a humanitarian and a lover of nature. When blackbirds chose to nest in his boxes of screws he refused to disturb them.

*Sandy Panton*

Just as the doctor became the first customer, so Sandy Panton became Struan's first employee. He seemed to understand, without the need for language, what Karl wanted. A simple sketch and a few waves of the hands would set Sandy off installing the timber that gradually turned Struan from a relatively genteel private hotel into an Austrian-style winter sports centre.

It usually seemed, to new visitors, that the transition was inspired by an architect or, at the least, by someone with a clear theme, an overall vision. Eileen asserts that this was not so. Karl did not consciously set out to replicate something from his homeland; he simply did what he knew best. As the process continued, people donated pictures and objects which fitted in. The 'Austrianisation' was an organic, subconscious process and this, perhaps, is why Struan seemed so unpretentious and welcoming. It was a place which grew incrementally and which changed according to the whim of its creators. It had a built-in personality.

And if, as some people claim, materials absorb something of the attributes of those who work on them, then the wood which was added to the hotel's fabric was imbued with a goodness. The two men who worked so hard were positive men who loved what they were doing. Their benignity was recorded in the materials.

By Christmas time, when the first residential guests arrived, Struan was well into its unlikely transformation. The two young people, Ruth and Bert, doubtless unaware that they were in at the birth of something monumental, expressed delighted approval. The snow had, as was and is its wont, dwindled so there was no option but to take the duo up to the higher reaches of Cairngorm. To those with the energy of youth the climb was as nothing. Completely alone on the hill at that stage of the season, Karl showed them the basics. Both made good progress except that Bert had a pedagogical blockage in the elementary discipline of the kick turn.

The manoeuvre has, mercifully, largely gone out of fashion but the idea is that a stationary skier, standing on a slope of almost any steepness, can turn neatly on the spot. The trick is useful for those who had come to an involuntary halt facing a pile of rocks or a patch of heather. Generally this is the result of having chickened out of an attempted turn but it is important to convey nothing of this involuntariness to anybody who might be watching, that is, everybody else on the slope. The kick turner needs to suggest, by body language alone, that the halt has been made deliberately, to allow a period of view-admiration or to permit the adjustment of equipment.

The drill is simple.

**One:** Whilst facing down the hill with skis together across the slope, put ski sticks into the uphill snow and lean gently on them. (This is the moment to look contemplative and superior whatever the thumping in one's chest suggests).

**Two:** Shift all weight to the upper ski, lift the lower ski to a vertical position then put it back on the snow facing in the opposite direction to its fellow. (One should try, at this crucial juncture, to appear as though it is natural to people other than ballet dancers to have one foot pointing in entirely the opposite direction to the other).

**Three:** Transfer all weight to the lower ski and simply swing the other one round, shifting weight for the last time as it comes into contact with the snow. What was the upper ski thus becomes the lower ski.

Easy! and ready to glide confidently off....

.....except that there are hazards. It is important, as will be self-evident, to have the skis firmly based on a platform of snow. The idea, for the beginner at least, is that no forward or backward motion should be made during this manoeuvre but equipment and snow slopes have their own conspiracies. All too often a ski which seems to be level, and firmly stuck, contrives a sudden loss of friction and finds an improbable downward line. It was not uncommon, in the days of frequent kick turns, to see a dismayed intermediate skier careering despairingly across the piste with one ski pointing one way, the other the other.

And it is not only skis and slopes which contrive the downfall of the unwary. Sticks can be just as vicious. In theory they should, in the kick-turn operation, have nothing much to do other than prop but, unobserved, they move such that tip of the ski which is being dragged round becomes trapped behind one of them. This, theoretically, is impossible but theory and practice have relatively little to do with each other as far as skiing is concerned. The *Law of the Perversity of Things* applies almost universally on the slopes. The would-be kick turner whose tip is stuck begins a frantic, usually overbalancing, rugby-like rucking movement and generally falls backwards in a pic-a-stic tangle which takes an age and a patient ski instructor to rectify.

Naturally there were, not long after beginner Bert's time, nauseating types, always lithe and sun-tanned, who could insouciantly do linked kick turns *on the move* but many people came to grief. On at least one White Lady occasion, an Achilles tendon snapped under the strain of a failed effort at the skill.

Bert's problem was that he could manage Step One, the languid leaning bit, to perfection and could complete Step Two, albeit with difficulty. Then, through a process which defied analysis, he would set off, not in a neat if perverse traverse but in a dizzying spiral, turning and turning with his skis facing in directions opposite to each other until he subsided gracefully onto the snow. Had freestyle skiing been in vogue in those days he would have won rich prizes.

As Old Year's Night 1954 approached there were nine guests, all young people, in Struan's warm embrace. Maurice, bubbling as ever with excitement, came to inspect the new venture at first hand. His ebullient personality complemented those of the new owners. His eyes were always twinkling, he was ever ready to have fun, his constant good humour added to people's enjoyment. He was vibrant, life-loving and possessed of limitless energy. At the new year celebrations he led the singing and joined in the dancing in spite of the difficulties posed by his right-angled knee.

He was there, with snow shoes in his rucksack, looking at every moment as if his leg would collapse, as the enlarged party made the ascent for their first experience of skiing. Eileen too, even though her heels were still very painful, joined the group to act as translator.

For the less fit guests, the walk was rendered difficult by the burden of skis and lunch packs. Karl worked assiduously; encouraging, somehow managing to make people laugh even though most of the group had no knowledge of German. Maurice added his brand of fun, offering translations with witty embellishments of some of Karl's hilarious remarks.

When they reached Jean's Hut, their leader took from the heavy rucksack, which he had carried with apparent ease, supplies for making a variety of hot drinks. The party took refreshment, recouped their energies and then continued to the flatter upper reaches of Coire Cas.

Other skiers appeared. Jack Thomson from Glenmore Lodge had his first class of the season on the slopes. There were some servicemen hurtling down on edgeless skis and crashing spectacularly in true heroic British army tradition. There was a man called Tom Mackenzie from Aviemore, a few members of the newly formed Highland Ski Club and a couple of British-based Norwegian students.

Karl and Eileen introduced themselves to everybody, explaining what they were about to do, yet all of them stared in astonishment as Karl put his pupils through a rigorous warm-up exercise to commands shouted in German and then demonstrated ski techniques rarely if ever seen on that particular hillside. Thereafter he devoted great attention to each student, clearly demonstrating their bad skiing habits and then showing the approved method for contrast. He had a range of educational tricks which brought people to an understanding of what they were doing.

Above all, he made the process enjoyable. It was a revelation.

When the morning class was over, and the participants safely grouped at Jean's Hut for lunch, Karl's students begged him to make a demonstration descent, to show what it was they were hoping one day to achieve. Not averse to letting his skis run, Karl climbed back up the slope and waved as he pushed off, yodelling gleefully.

It is important to remember that there were few, if any, truly competent skiers in Scotland at that time. George McLeod, who was then working at Glenmore Lodge before going off for the first of several stints in the Antarctic, confirms that Jack Thomson was the only Cairngorm-based instructor and that his standard of skiing was, at that juncture, rudimentary. For the most part the occasional Lodge pupils learned how to snow plough. George recalls Karl as a 'magical man' who made the Scottish ski world 'sit up'. Nobody, he says with confidence, could ski properly before Karl came.

Eric Langmuir confirms George McLeod's estimation. Eric, who was later to take charge of Glenmore Lodge, had been one of Jack Thomson's pupils and had also done some cross-country skiing in Norway. In the mid-fifties he was a regular visitor to the Norwegian huts and he remembers the day he first saw Karl demonstrate the stem christie. The word Eric uses to describe the Fuchs style is 'regal'. 'I've tried many times to copy him but I never could,' Eric says, 'in fact, I've seen nobody who was able to demonstrate as well as Karl.'

Frith Finlayson also testifies that the levels of competence were low. His first ski lesson, conducted not long before Karl arrived and entirely in the military tradition, consisted of the instructor saying; 'Point your skis straight down the hill, holding yourself back with the points of your sticks dug into the snow in front of you. To christie to the right, you move off, gain speed and bend down over the left ski, straighten up quickly then down again over your right ski, and that's all there is to it.'

Frith recalls that the first time he saw what he came to describe as a 'good skier' was in 1953 at the British Ski Championships. The man who so impressed was Allan Crompton, the winner of the competition, who had learned his skills in the Alps. Frith was astonished by Crompton. He writes, 'I don't know what seeing him did for me but half an hour later I was lying with a broken leg'.

Undeterred by this, Frith eventually took himself off to Switzerland in order to learn how to excel but he says of himself and his companions in the mid-1950's: 'None of us could be compared with good skiers of the day. We had a very long way to go.'

It is not surprising that the gap existed. Frith and his highly motivated, mainly Glaswegian friends, had come to skiing relatively late in life. They had understandably picked up bad posture habits through incompetent teaching. By comparison, Karl Fuchs had been skiing from the age of four and training for many years with the best practitioners. He held the Austrian state ski teaching qualification. He was a professional. That was why the people on Cairngorm stopped to watch as the maestro began his run.

Some years later there was an advertisement for Shell petrol which depicted a face looking one way, then the other. There were blurred linking lines to suggest that the person was following a very fast moving object. Eileen likens those watching Karl for the first time to that image. Their mouths opened, their jaws dropped and they realised that, for the first time in their lives, they were seeing proper skiing. Karl plummeted down that slope, leapt athletically over the burn at the bottom and executed a slick series of wedeln turns on the other side in what looked to all the observers like a patch of snowless heather. His students broke into spontaneous applause.

To Karl's great delight, Jack Thomson paid a courtesy visit to Struan soon afterwards. Far from feeling threatened by the significantly greater expertise of the incomer he was keen to learn.

Word spread. When, a little while later, Karl created a slalom course through the trees above the village golf course there were, so the Struan couple later discovered, some members of the local community furtively watching the proceedings through binoculars. The speed of the Austrian's descent became the stuff of local legend.

The highly impressed and enthused New Year visitors left just in time to avoid a huge blizzard which cut Carrbridge off for several days. Two young women who were stranded in the village stayed at Struan and they became Karl's first commercial golf course pupils. As soon as the roads were passable, the travellers continued their journey, vowing to come back soon for a proper holiday. The Fuchs set off for Grantown to replenish supplies.

The outward trip was completed successfully but whilst they were shopping, a new blizzard began. On the way back, the road was blocked by a stuck vehicle. Karl and Eileen helped the motorist on his way but then discovered that it was their turn to be stranded. All the repressed, unspoken fears of struggle for survival became active.

There was sufficient light for them to see some telephone wires which, with difficulty, they followed to a cottage. In response to their call, a man called John Ross from the garage at Dulnain Bridge came in a four wheel drive vehicle to attempt the rescue but by the time he reached them the snow was so deep that all he could do was pass a bottle of whisky through the window of the immobile Lea Francis. Karl, not averse to alcohol but not at all keen on whisky, politely refused the offer and expressed himself shocked when Eileen took a healthy, grateful swig.

It would perhaps have been sensible for them to have abandoned the car and to have retreated to Dulnain Bridge but against all reason Karl insisted that they would eventually resume their journey. He tried all the tricks; reducing the tyre pressure, putting twigs under the wheels, 'rocking' the car by changing from reverse to forward drive repeatedly but the Lea Francis refused to rise from its self-created ruts.

It was dark, with snow drifting up to the roof, before Karl would admit to defeat. Sense suggested a return to the nearby cottage which would surely provide shelter for the night but Karl was determined to get home. There was a six mile hike to be accomplished, in the blackness, in feet-thick snow and with the road largely obscured but he knew that his astonishing sense of direction would not let them down. Insisting on the singing of duets as they forced their way through, he kept their spirits buoyant.

Eileen was exhausted to the limits as they trudged down the middle of the deserted A9 road through Carrbridge. For the last couple of miles her thoughts had been exclusively focused on the pleasures of a steaming bath and a crackling fire. How delighted she was that they had no guests!

There were no street lights. Even in the familiar environs of the village Eileen was glad of Karl's guidance. She exclaimed with relief as she could at last make out the shape of their new home. The water should still be hot, it would take moments to set the logs a-crackling. Karl put the key into the front door lock.

It was the signal for the ambush! People appeared from the outer darkness. There were distant cries of relief and the sounds of car doors slamming. More strangers converged on Struan. They were, they announced, stranded and in urgent need of shelter. All Eileen's hopes of personal comfort were instantly banished. The hosts had to be bright, self-sacrificing, hard working, inventive in the kitchen. They were learning, all too quickly, about some of the hazards of their trade.

As with the two who had earlier been stranded, some of the involuntary guests reacted very positively to the Struan atmosphere. Word circulated even further. In spite of very minimal advertising, enquiries began to come in. From then on, there were times when the hotel was full and none when it was entirely empty. The Annexe was pressed into service. There were those who, for a reduced rate, were very willing to put up with a lower standard of comfort. It was preferable to camping; there was running water, there was lighting and there were bunks. What there was not, however, was any form of heating.

In truth, the building had never been intended for cold weather use. The previous Struan owners had, like most of the local hoteliers, closed the entire establishment for winter. Nobody had ever considered the needs of skiers. Heating had not been anyone's priority.

For a time, the hardy, stoical souls who opted for the Annexe coped with the conditions but inevitably, expectations began to rise. It was unpleasant, returning wet and cold after a day on the mountain to a building which seemed chillier than the outside. The point about discomfort was made dramatically to Karl one morning as he huffed condensing moisture in his make-do ski shed. A woman, who had rinsed out an item of underwear the night before and who, a mite optimistically, had laid it out to dry, appeared clutching a pair of totally stiff knickers. She snapped them dramatically as though they were made of balsa. From then on the laying of a new, higher duty, cable became one of the priorities for the summer schedule of improvements

*The Annexe*

As the first weeks went by, Eileen experimented in the kitchen and gradually devised a pattern of menus that prevailed for many years. There were no frills in the Struan dining room. Soup, main course, dessert, cheese and biscuits, coffee; apart from those who had special dietary requirements there were no variations. Everyone ate the same food and guests sometimes helped with the distribution and the clearing up. It was in some ways more like a club, or a superior hostel, than the standard idea of a hotel but the conditions were perfect for the creation of a convivial atmosphere. After a hard day on the slopes people would sit, their limbs aching, their faces glowing, eagerly discussing the day's triumphs and disasters. Differences in class, politics, religion and education were largely subsumed under the common endeavour. For a week contention could be forgotten. What mattered was the next stage. The first successful snow plough, a tentative stem; these were the preoccupations.

Later in the evenings, guests would gravitate to the lounge to read or play board games. If the mood were for something more expansive they would stroll down to the bar of the Carrbridge Hotel at the end of the village where the Grantown road forked or to the nearer Rowanlea.

Given that she had had absolutely no experience of catering for large numbers of people, and no relevant training, Eileen coped remarkably well. In fact, many of her problems were not so much in the kitchen but in the pantry. With suppliers being so far away, and deliveries infrequent, it was difficult to order with precision. Even with the local sources there were problems. The village baker was, according to Eileen, 'tyrannical'. At public holidays customers had to order five days' worth of bread. The Struan chef was reduced to collecting huge quantities in a pram and in those days before deep freezers there was an inevitable hazard of staleness.

In spite of all the countervailing factors, Struan quickly began to develop a reputation for its hospitality and, just as swiftly, the ski school made its mark. Karl was thrilled when a senior army officer arranged for some of his men to receive instruction. This went well and there was promise of much more military trade to come. This eventually took the form of an annual instructor-training course in the first week of December. Drawing on his extensive military experience, Karl treated this as a complete exercise. The soldiers were expected to undertake general fitness training, including cross-country running, as well as learning ski technique.

*Chefs!*

There was other institutional interest. The Royal Navy became a much-valued regular customer. Karl was further delighted by this and was equally pleased when the prestigious Gordonstoun public school asked if he would teach some of their pupils. The golf course was pressed into service for these young beginners and a useful long term business contact was established.

The weather was good to them. According to the Scottish Mountaineering Club Guide, 1955 was one of the most severe winters on record. For much of the season the golf course had sufficient snow to conduct excellent classes. Eileen, moderately expert by this time, recalls a particularly alarming schuss on the slope behind the fairways which culminated, if disaster were to be avoided, in the need to hit precisely a narrow, unguarded plank across a stream. For variety, or if weather conditions suggested a change, the entire school would decamp to the Slochd where longer runs were possible.

These extreme conditions helped considerably the process of settling into the area. With snow lying at a low level for most of the season, Karl began to teach some of the local children on the village slope. This soon turned into a regular Wednesday afternoon group with instruction and equipment being provided free of charge. The families of the hoteliers from Grantown who had been so welcoming often joined in. Very quickly, skiing became a community focus and Karl something of a local hero. In spite of the communication difficulties people were charmed by the newcomer's enthusiasm and kindliness. 'Daisy the post', delivering mail on her bicycle in daunting conditions, was a most efficient advertiser.

It would have been very easy, in these highly conducive conditions, to slip into complacency but Karl was a very rapid learner as far as the ways of Mother Nature were concerned. He knew that, unlike Austria, full Cairngorm snow cover one day could turn to patchy conditions almost overnight. Blue sky in the morning could mean a near hurricane by lunchtime. He learned, also, that the constant melting and re-freezing of the snow resulted in very slippery patches to negotiate on the walk up to the slopes and, once the clients gained their goal, there were thin icy caps on deep bogs which trapped the unwary. A ski leader needed to be constantly alert in order to warn pupils of hazards and to anticipate difficulties which might otherwise threaten safety. Karl came, with remarkable swiftness, to understand and anticipate better than many who had long experience of the Cairngorms. Some innate quality, a natural empathy with wilderness, provided him with insights which were denied to most others.

He tried, one bright winter's morning, to warn a group of soldiers who were on a training exercise that the weather was about to deteriorate. Through Eileen's interpretation he suggested that they should stay where they were, in the relative comfort of Jean's Hut, rather than move upwards into the bleak interior as they were planning. The response was predictable; they were soldiers, they were learning to survive. Bad weather was a bonus against which they could test themselves and their equipment.

The conversation with the Fuchs was the last one these people had outside their own party. In the blizzard which Karl had sensed, they mistook their direction. Finding a river tumbling down a steep hillside they reasoned that it must lead to civilisation. What it led to was Loch Avon, deep in the heart of the range, very far from shelter or assistance. Well equipped though they were, they died there, in that deep, steep valley.

This shocking loss of life temporarily diminished enthusiasm but the skiing momentum was too powerful to be slowed for long. Karl's classes filled with keen beginners, some of them destined to become excellent skiers, others who seemed to have little hope of achieving competence. Karl treated them all equally, extending great patience where necessary, offering encouragement for every advance, however minor. He took his work very seriously, trying always to ensure that every individual maximised their potential but never forgetting that skiing is a recreation not an endurance test, a thing to be enjoyed. Using humour as a sugar to the bitter pills of learning, he considerately showed people how they looked to an objective observer and then demonstrated what they had to do to achieve the norm. As his ski-English improved, he invented a series of vivid descriptions. He had only to shout, 'heavy wheelbarrow!' to a passing pupil to create, in the student's mind, an image of erroneous body posture. With a 'make a pretty picture' to someone about to set off he created a template of the ideal which helped to shape the effort.

People had their tumbles, of course, but Karl was ever careful to keep his students within their current limits. They could expand these without taking undue risks. Serious injuries were very rare. Indeed, the worst wound in those early days was self- inflicted. One of Karl's less promising pupils fell frequently in a particular way. In this man's back pocket was a tobacco tin which, against Karl's gentle suggestion, he refused to move. Before long the buttock next to this hard object became discoloured and indented. At dinner the man was in considerable discomfort but the next day he persisted with his folly. To a degree, Karl admired him. There was, at least, a determination to cure the trauma by learning not to fall rather than by changing other habits.

The resilience and enthusiasm of the tobacco tin man and all the others, the delight of the Carrbridge children and the excitement of the Grantown hoteliers combined to form a new force in the area. The very fact that an Austrian of such exalted skiing status was pledging his future to the area provided an immense psychological boost. In 'Skisters', Myrtle Simpson records that at the time the Fuchs couple were establishing themselves in Struan, Jock Kerr Hunter was strongly voicing his belief that the time had come to build a lift in the Cairngorm area. What had been an entirely casual, amateur affair was turning into something different. Kerr-Hunter argued forcefully that if the likes of Karl Fuchs were to be retained, then facilities would have to be improved. In the long run, he maintained, the boost to the tourist trade would make the investment extremely cost-effective.

Naturally, the Sutton and Ross families supported Kerr Hunter but there were those who vigorously rejected the proposal. The fact that a lift was being planned for Glencoe was seen as no threat at all. Some refused to believe that the facility would actually be built but the sceptics maintained, in any case, that the existing Cairngorm arrangements were what people wanted. Myrtle Simpson quotes a letter, published at the time by a newspaper, in which these diehards are roundly castigated. The extract concludes; 'King Canute could not keep the tide from rolling in, but a lesson or two in the working of a Swiss resort might show the Cairngorm hoteliers how to stop the tide rolling out.'

One problem for the progressives was that new currency restrictions were on the side of complacency. British nationals were limited to £25 per year which meant that those wealthy enough to take two or more holidays abroad were being forced to have one trip only. Those who gave priority to a summer break were then left with no option but to travel to Scotland if they wanted to ski. Even if the Glencoe development took place it could not, the complacent ones maintained, cater for everybody in the British Isles who yearned for winter sport.

Jock Kerr-Hunter and the other activists were not to be deterred. It was decided to make a fresh approach to the Badenoch District Council. Kerr Hunter once more pointed out the general economic benefits to the area of a skiing development. He suggested that even if a lift was, for the time being, out of the question then at least the road could be extended part of the way up the hill so that most of the long hike would be eliminated. With a car park at, say, two thousand feet and a couple of temporary tows operating, the Cairngorms would offer at least some competition to the proposed Glencoe facility.

With predictable response the Council set up a small working party to examine the feasibility of this proposal. The ensuing report was also not entirely unexpected. It was to the effect that the road could be built if only the money could be found. It was suggested, however, that 'other interested parties' might consider the idea. This note of slight encouragement led nowhere. What Kerr Hunter referred to as the 'four mile trachle up the glen' was likely to be the lot of Cairngorm-based skiers for a long time to come.

The Fuchs' answer to this was to recognise that, for the time being, it would be sensible to focus on slopes more accessible than those of the high Cairngorms. In their view Kerr-Hunter was right, the 'trachle' could easily become a deterrent, especially for older clients. Slochd, though by no means as high as Glenshee or Glencoe, seemed to be the natural answer and, in that winter of copious snow, it was their most frequently used arena.

Karl realised, though, that Slochd had its drawbacks. Even in good years, the length of the season there would be curtailed purely because of altitude. It was also true that the runs were limited in severity. As people improved they would demand something more testing. An exploratory expedition up the Findhorn valley revealed some alternative snow pastures and these were added to the ski school's repertoire.

Learning day by day, the new hoteliers kept their venture going. Karl varied the skiing venues according to the weather and the snow conditions, always doing the best he could for the pupils. If the elements made skiing impossible he would take the customers walking. They were never allowed to be idle for long.

By Easter time, the ski school had twenty and more pupils. Over the winter months Karl had trained Tom Mackenzie from Aviemore, and Simon Fraser, a night nurse at the Craig Dunain mental hospital in Inverness and a member of the Highland Ski Club, to a level where they could coach beginners. He was able to split large groups up into clusters according to ability and thereby focus his efforts.

There came a morning during the holidays when the Carrbridge Austrian Ski School was scheduled to have its largest attendance. Unfortunately the assistant instructors could not be present because there was to be a race on Cairngorm, the prestigious Scottish Kandahar. Tom and Simon needed to be there. Karl was at a loss. This was the busiest day in the history of their enterprise and he had nobody to whom he could delegate.

*Teacher training! Karl watches Eileen*

It was through this crisis that Eileen found herself suddenly promoted. She was cook, cleaner, laundress, receptionist, publicist, customer relations manager and many other things; now she had to become a ski instructor.

She was, as she recalls, not much beyond the beginner stage herself but in her role as translator she had very often seen Karl at work. She could not hope to demonstrate as he did but she could readily tell people what to do. It was only fair, and within the spirit of their joint enterprise, that she should help out.

Not a little nervous, she agreed to do her bit. She knew that Karl's feet were twitching anyway. He longed to join the race but he was excluded on the grounds that he was a professional. 'Amateurs only' was the prevailing British rule. The least she could do was to alleviate some of the teaching pressure and to distract Karl's mind from thoughts of nearby slalom poles.

Rather than hike all the way up the mountain, where the racing would be all too temptingly visible, Karl took the huge group and his new instructor colleague to a natural arena known, with workaday but accurate imagery, as 'The Sugar Bowl'. It was lower down the mountain than Coire Cas, a fact for which those who had to toil up the hill were grateful.

The director of the Carrbridge ski school picked out Eileen's rabbits and was on the point of moving a little distance away with his more experienced students when a stranger approached, hurrying and calling out Karl's name. The maestro skied over to greet the intruder. From a distance, Eileen saw an urgent conversation taking place. Karl nodded vigorously and her spirits dived. He turned and shouted. The race organisers wanted a vorlaufer, someone to ski the course before the racers, imprinting the way. It was a request which Karl was constitutionally incapable of refusing.

Karl quickly gathered all the pupils around him and explained, through Eileen, that he had been offered this honour. So eloquent was he, or his translator, that everyone insisted; he must go! They would manage. Thus, from being assistant instructor (beginners only) Eileen became Chief. She remembers that all of her pupils were, mercifully, at a lower standard than she. The lesson was a fruitful one in spite of the absence of the one true expert.

The first season drifted towards its end. There had been many moments of dismay but overall Karl and Eileen had coped magnificently. Everyone had been fed and watered, those who wanted to learn to ski had all had lessons. The enterprising pair had been kept busy to an extreme degree. When Karl had not been teaching he had worked on the ski equipment, made improvements to one of the rooms or undertaken essential repairs. Eileen had dealt with all the domestic matters as well as seeing to correspondence, promotional material, the keeping of accounts and all the other myriad tasks involved in running their establishment. They had often been extremely tired but their gamble was showing signs that it would pay.

*The skiing snow hare*

Encouraged, Karl and Eileen began to plan for 1956. Karl created a badge using the old bridge with a skiing snow hare. This became the hotel's emblem. A simple brochure was produced and circulated to anyone they knew who might be able to generate interest. In the spring. Karl took his driving test in Grantown. To the lasting and totally illogical irritation of a local gamekeeper who failed, he passed first time. As he revelled in the new freedom, Karl reviewed the first season with considerable satisfaction. The Austrian Ski School had not exactly made a fortune but it had more than survived and there was every prospect that little Struan would quickly grow into something quite unique.

## 10. Uplift

Had Karl been more aware of developments elsewhere in Scotland, he might not have been quite so optimistic. As the Fuchs' second season approached, the brief history of Scottish skiing uplift, which had centred round a rivalry between Glenshee and Glencoe, was taking a very significant westward lean. An objective adviser would probably have suggested that Cairngorm was not the place for the new ski school at all.

The first Scottish attempts to convey skiers up the slopes were made just after the war. Imported 'weasels', the tracked vehicles which the army introduced to the Cairngorms, were pressed into service. They were not an unqualified success. On one occasion at Glenshee such a machine burst into flames, singeing the trousers of the Dundee Ski Club's President, on another it fell over into a snow drift, unceremoniously dumping all its passengers. They were unable to right the vehicle so they opted to use it as a windbreak whilst they ate lunch.

The President was not the only one to suffer incineration. One Club member was so traumatised by his weasel experience that he felt compelled to share the nightmare with the wider world. He wrote to a newspaper;

'On my first and probably last voyage in this perilous contraption - the weasel - I seated myself initially in a position where I was rapidly gassed. Rising for air I was thrown onto a portion of the vehicle which proceeded to scorch the seat of my trousers. Moving then to perch on one of its sides, I endured a process of being corrugated where previously I had been singed, till, reaching the limit of my endurance, I collapsed heavily onto a cleat in the floor. Before I could release my hand from under a nailed boot in order to rise, a roof stanchion collapsed, depositing three passengers who had been holding onto it in the pit of my stomach. Without wishing to decry the efforts of those striving to solve the difficult problems of mechanisation, I venture to suggest that as far as the Scottish Ski Club is concerned, painless elevation has yet to be achieved.'

There were many who argued against the contraptions which, so it was claimed, defiled the purity of the sport but the old brigade of ski idealists had lost most of its power. The younger generation was looking for the thrills of speed rather than a mystic communion with nature. Mechanisation was a trend which could not be stopped.

Recognising this, the Dundee Ski Club purchased a second tracked vehicle. This proved more reliable and it was pressed into service one Easter for the Scottish Kandahar race. The perverse beast developed clutch trouble at the moment of its greatest glory but, as one newspaper reported, it provided a significant step forward from the previous arrangements where competitors had to undertake a major uphill hike before starting the race.

There were still those, however, who were wary. The race starter, a member of the nobility who doubtless had public school memories of scorched buttocks, refused to travel in the notoriously incendiary weasel. With everyone else lurching up the hill at half a dozen miles per hour and the key official toiling up at two, there was an inevitable disparity of arrival times. The race organisers, fearful that the last runners might be trying to find their way down in the dark, decided to cut the time between departures from thirty to fifteen seconds. Had everyone been wonderfully expert, had the rankings and thus the start order been fantastically accurate then this simple ploy might have worked. As it was, there were collisions galore. Fallen skiers became additional gates. Those who were moving at more or less the same speed wove in and out, more intent on avoiding impact than on posting a brilliant time. The weasel worked its wickedness in its own devious fashion.

Skiers with European experience soon realised that the unreliable vehicles were unlikely to provide the final solution to the problem of uplift. Driven by Alpine dreams, the Dundee enthusiasts determined to create a tow. By 1948 they had erected two huts at Glenshee which provided a base for their efforts and in the following year they persuaded the landowner that a ski tow would not significantly add to the despoilment. Cautiously, the laird agreed to the proposal but only on the condition that the device was de-mountable. It was not until the start of the 1950 season, however, that the plan was put into effect. A simple rope tow, powered by a petrol engine mounted on a sledge, was installed. It worked well although there were, naturally, some problems. The following season, an improved version was used and the Scottish Ski Club felt justified in erecting a similar device at Killin.

Enter an Edinburgh man called Bill Blackwood who, dissatisfied with the design of existing tows, determined to create a superior device of his own. In his garden he constructed a prototype which worked wonderfully. With enthusiastic supporters he transported the engineering masterpiece to a snowy hill. The Secretary of the Scottish Ski Club, Donnaie MacKenzie, tells the sorry tale, albeit with some confusion, common enough, between Frankenstein and his creation.

'It had a massive engine and looked like a raft with two lorry wheels and long shafts to guide it. There was no clutch and a pole forced the engine towards the drive shaft. At that point, the monster got under way and out of control. It was all right in Blackwood's garden but on its first trial on the hill, this Frankenstein got its own back on its creator. It took off with three of us hanging to the shafts and Willie trying to get level with the engine to switch off. Bodies flew in all directions as "Mark One" roared down the hill on its own and disappeared into a peat bog. All except Willie were for burying it where it lay.'

Undeterred, Bill repaired home to dream of other versions. The next exemplar of his engineering prowess was tried out on the Fiacaill Ridge on Cairngorm. It failed ignominiously, as did efforts involving decrepit tractors and an ex-army tracked vehicle. Persuaded by others to try a change of venue, Blackwood used Glencoe for his piece de resistance. Installation involved manoeuvring an old Studebaker limousine to a position of altitude on Meall a' Bhuiridh. The American car, piloted by a part time racing driver, was assisted in its uphill efforts by two tracked vehicles. Donnaie MacKenzie was, of course, there to witness the struggle against nature.

'The operation took two days and the final traverse entailed building a hundred yards of track across a steep slope. It was only Blackwood who knew how "Mark Three" was going to work on site. We eventually discovered it was to drive a wire rope on a drum fixed in place of a rear wheel with an opposing lay wheel as a tensioning device. The rope actually went to the top of the mountain being supported by three legged pylons which sat on top of the snow. The skier attached himself to the rope with a pole with a hook on the end, rather like the tool for lopping high branches of trees. It was a great day when the rope actually started to move uphill and disappeared out of sight over the crest. The first of the happy band attached themselves to the rope with the long poles and moved up. Had gravity finally been conquered? It had been for one or two until disaster struck. Somehow the return rope had got fankled in a pulley at the top, unknown to the engine operator. The top pylon proceeded downhill, collecting its brothers en route and the operator only knew all was not well when a load of pylons came charging over the crest and downhill at him. It was a sad moment for Blackwood because he knew he had to go back to the drawing board....'

Being endlessly resourceful, Bill did just that and by the time Karl was taking his first classes in 1955 he had developed a model which worked tolerably well.

There were some, however, in the Scottish skiing world who by this time had determined to move even further from the honourable British tradition of amateurism and to seek professional help.

Since the end of the war there had been three main areas of ski activity. Cairngorm, with its acute problem of access, was not popular. Nobody wanted to hike upwards for a couple of hours in order to ski when they could drive to altitude and begin their sport within a few yards of the road.

Highest up the social ladder of the favoured venues was Ben Lawers, where the mainly middle class and traditionalist members of the Scottish Ski Club spent their weekends. Glenshee, to the east, was the playground of the Dundee faction and, to a lesser extent, the Perth branch of the Scottish Ski Club. Then there was Glencoe.

The 'Coe' was, as Frith Finlayson relates in his autobiography, largely the preserve of the Glaswegians. He was not the only one to be bitten by the ski bug and in 'Skisters', Myrtle Simpson records that there were tensions at first between those who were loyal to the climbing tradition and those who were straying. For the 'true' mountaineers, skis were merely a form of transport. For the converts, they were the equipment of a totally new sport. Eventually a breakaway organisation was formed with the name of the Glencoe Ski Club.

There was another Glasgow climbing club, the Lomonds, which also used Glencoe as its playground. Whereas the members of the Craig Dhu were predominantly working class, the Lomonders were mainly teachers and technicians. There was intense, though generally friendly, rivalry between the two groups. The Lomonds also had their split between climbers and skiers and this produced the White Corries Rescue Patrol.

Had the picture remained like this, with three main areas being used and all the disparate groups pursuing their own aims then it is likely that Glenshee, the first to have a rope tow, would have been in the forefront of development. But, as Myrtle Simpson explains, there was a significant shift. She writes; 'The majority of the Scottish Ski Club had meanwhile abandoned Ben Lawers and the Killin area in favour of Meall a' Bhuiridh in Glencoe.'

They did so mainly because the newly favoured site offered more reliable snow and runs which were more challenging to ever-improving techniques. The unintended outcome was, however, a crunching clash of cultures. Frith Finlayson recalls:

'Even within their nativeness their cultures were very different. Ours grew out of a background which could be considered austerity, where luxuries had to be carefully sought after. It was only now, with the changing times, that we would be more expansive in our outlook to better opportunities to come. Because of this background we had very strong views on how the world "worked". The other part of this new skiing equation was the established Scottish Ski Club members. All the things we thought were extras, they accepted as everyday necessities. They had cars, they stayed in hotels, spoke differently, their demeanour and obvious confidence bespoke of a comfortable background. And, like ourselves, most were nice folks. By pure chance we were all together at the beginning of a new epoch in skiing in our own country.'

In spite, or perhaps because, of the class divide, the combination proved potent. With increased numbers, with the energy and determination of the ex-climbers added to the business expertise of the newcomers, there was an excellent basis for progress.

One of the main instigators of change was a Scottish Ski Club official called Phillip Rankin. As editor of the club journal he wrote a piece describing the early 1950's state of Scottish skiing. In part he explained that:

'Scottish skiing is at that awkward stage between pigtails and perms when lemonade is no longer good enough and our legs cannot stand cocktails......The Cairngorms above all need extensive development of hut accommodation, alas none exists yet, nor does it seem likely that it will until the general popularity of the sport brings large numbers of people to Scotland. The extensive erection and maintenance is at present beyond the combined resources of the ski clubs and there is no other organisation likely to interest itself in the foreseeable future.'

This strikes a pessimistic note but, with others, Rankin began to use the combined forces at Glencoe to press for investment. Enthusiasm took a cruel knock when, in January 1953, three people on a ski tour in the Glencoe area died of exposure but there was too much momentum for the setback to be permanent. Painstakingly, funds were gathered until a point was reached where Rankin offered to undertake the organisation of a proper, Continental-style lift installation if the Scottish Ski Club agreed to make £2000 available. Lewis Drysdale and Robert Finlay, a ski fanatic who lived in a Loch Lomond-side castle, were enthusiastic supporters as was George Donald who, at the age of 84, made a contribution to the fund whilst publicly doubting that he would ever get the full value out of a season ticket.

Helped by yet another special appeal to club members and a substantial loan, the ski lift fund reached its target of £5000 just as Karl and Eileen were facing their first summer as hoteliers. A company called Breco, which was prepared to quote a keen price because the project was experimental, was offered the contract. In keeping with the best traditions of Scottish skiing, the club members provided much of the hard labour.

A six wheeled truck and the infamous weasels were used to convey materials. The laying of concrete foundations and erection of pylons was a huge task for an inexperienced workforce. Philip Rankin described the attempt to haul parts of the pylons up a ropeway.

'Just as the load was nearing the top, the order was given to "heave" and we did so with such good effect that with a loud "twank" the rope parted. Four eighteen foot organ pipes went shooting back whence they came, giving clear and audible warning of their progress. It is claimed that no stag ever covered the ground on Meall a' Bhuiridh as fast as the foreman down below as he saw his consignment returning "expresso"......The only damage done was to one pole which was riveted up in the shape of a snake charmer's tooter.'

Frith Finlayson tells of meeting three of the Breco professional fitters in the Kingshouse Hotel. They were complaining bitterly about the daily hike up what they called Thrombosis Slope. Gravity was not their only enemy. They were contending with persistent rain, clouds of vicious midges and ground so glutinous that it sucked their boots off.

In spite of all the difficulties, the installation continued and Philip Rankin eventually wrote, exultantly, 'Scottish skiing is on the march, even if we hope that means exactly the opposite of what it says'. Frith, empathising with the workers, writes more sombrely; 'How they ever got that first lift up and onto the hill amazes me,' but by the start of the 1956 season it was operating.

A definition of a ski lift might be: '...a satanic contraption designed by sadists, located in an impossible place, operating under hellish conditions and patronised by masochists.'

The new Glencoe lift was of the Poma variety. Someone of this company had hit upon the brilliant idea of starting with a Bill Blackwood-style rope and lifting it twenty feet or more into the air on pylons. Dangling down from the rope were aluminium poles with round buttons on the end. All skiers had to do was grab hold of one of these rods, slip it smoothly between the legs, allow the button to come softly to cushion against defensively clenched buttocks and away they went.

Modern versions of these inclined altitudinous merry-go-rounds have 'reservoirs' of poles which click into action as they are grabbed. The earliest versions were continuous in operation. The poles on the prototypes never stopped. Skiers queued to grab one of these as they began their upward journey. Kindly ski tow managers would often employ someone to do the grabbing. These shivering operatives then handed the rod to the skier. Whether the apparatus was self-grabbed or politely handed, the machine could, and most frequently did, then perpetrate any number of tortures, amongst them:

1. Pole slipping out of the skier's grasp and going up the hill without an attached body; an event which could evoke guffaws and jeers from those who had been queuing half an hour and who strongly resented every lost opportunity for uplift.

2. Pole slipping out of the skier's grasp and spinning round in a dervish-like circle, whacking either the skier or the operative on the shin, creating instant invalids.

3. Skier getting a grip, setting off and being jerked in the air because the sadistically built-in slack in the system, which had induced a false sense of security, came to a sudden end and delivered a force on the posterior equivalent to several mules-worth. The unwary operative got to be swatted on the head with flailing sticks. Equipment distributed itself humiliatingly all over the track.

4. Centrally located abrasion. There are gender differences here. Some humans seem to have nothing but positive regard for a stiff pole deep between the thighs. They smile sweetly as they ascend. Sometimes they even sing. Others, with different anatomical arrangements, are reminded of tailors asking them which side they dress.

5. Roughness of track, including deep gouges and tram lines, which whip the skis in directions not intended by their wearers, and frozen waves which cause manic rising and falling, crashing and slapping.

6. Meteorological problems. Wind tipped people off, high velocity sleet insinuated itself into allegedly storm-proof clothing. Whenever the sun came out, which it did rarely, it shone blindingly into unaccustomed eyes causing tears and confusion in equal quantities.

7. Ascentus interruptus; on the steepest part of the track, the damn thing stopped and everyone slid backwards. Not a few fell off.

8. Premature ejaculation; an ignominious exit before the proper place

which involved the risk of being ground to powder by the following herd.

9. The not-so-graceful exit which meant for some, letting go of the pole too soon, for others, not letting go soon enough and, for the truly unfortunate, finding that letting go was impossible because the pole was caught in clothing.

According to Frith Finlayson, the first Glencoe version of this monster was of a poor design. The poles kept coming off. This constituted Hazard Number Ten for many punters. For Frith and his friends, Bob Clyde and Tommy Paul, however, it was a bonus. As the most accomplished skiers amongst a very inexperienced clientele, they were recruited to retrieve the fallen poles and bring them back to base. For this service they were granted free rides and, with the vastly increased mileage, their skiing started to improve.

But for all its failings, the Glencoe installation posed a real threat to Karl and Eileen's fragile venture. They had been very lucky in their first season. Snow had covered the lower ground for much of the winter. What would happen, though, at the times when Slochd and the Giant's Face were bare? A few dedicated followers might return to Struan for the quality of the life and the instruction but surely many would want to avail themselves of easy access to the slopes and effortless uplift. It was strongly rumoured that Glenshee was not far behind in the erection of its own lift. What price then the Cairngorms and the fledgling ski school?

## 11. The Snowball Rolls

The need for Karl and Eileen to make their position more secure was very significantly increased in the October of 1955 when, to their intense delight, a baby boy arrived. They called him Peter. Hitherto, the adventure had been just theirs; failure would have meant a sale of the hotel and a retreat to think again. Economic hardship would not have been an unbearable burden. Now they had the welfare of a child to consider.

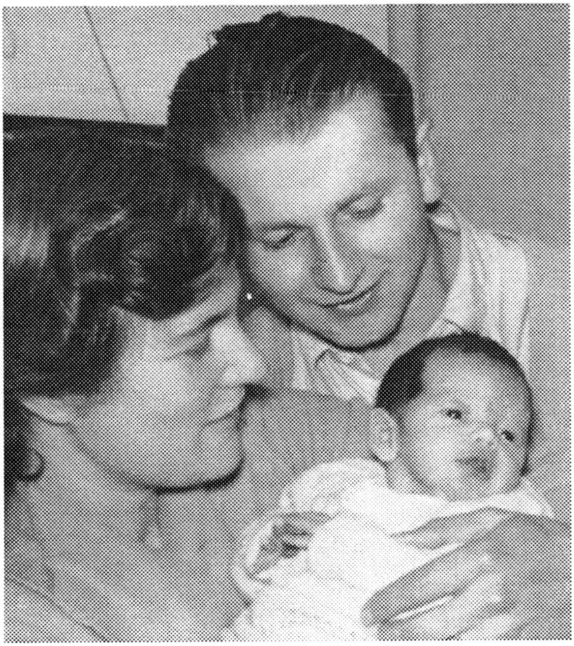

*Proud parents*

Happily, the meteorological climate was once more kind to them. For very many days during the 1956 season it was possible to avoid the long Cairngorm ascent. Slochd and Findhorn provided excellent teaching slopes and the lure of Karl's expertise outweighed, for many people, the attractions of the unreliable Poma at Glencoe.

There was another, unexpected, bonus. Early in the season Donnaie Mackenzie, who had become friendly with Karl and Eileen, introduced Bill Blackwood to the Austrian Ski School. Thereafter there were many occasions when mechanical uplift was available, even though it was on a less ambitious scale than the westerly version.

For all that he often missed his homeland, Karl was carried along with the excitement of treading new territory. Donnaie Mackenzie was by no means the only person of importance in Scottish winter sports to make contact. The Austrian was already something of a celebrity and there was the beginning of a feeling that, with his weight behind the process, Cairngorm would eventually see significant development. There was nothing definite but some believed that one day there could be a road up the mountain and a Poma to rival the one at Glencoe.

Eileen, too, derived a great deal of pleasure from the prospect of Karl's ski vision being realised but for her the economic worries were more immediate. The tasks of looking after a new baby meant that she had no option but to acquire some paid help in the hotel. Local women were employed on a part time basis and proved themselves to be excellent workers. Nonetheless, all at once there were wages to be paid. To keep the costs to the minimum, Eileen continued to do as much as she could in the hotel.

She also carried on with her unexpected career as a ski instructor. Teaching had become an essential part of her load because the ski school was catering not only for the residents but for an ever growing crowd of locals which, to Karl's delight, included a farmer who saw skiing as a useful technique for conveying fodder to snowbound sheep. Tom Mackenzie was often available to take some of the pupils but Simon Fraser's work frequently kept him away. Eileen filled the vacancy.

To cope with the increased clientele, the business acquired a Bedford minibus and this, supplemented by private cars, carried up to twenty people to wherever Karl had decided to conduct the day's lessons. It transported the faithful to Slochd one day towards the end of the second season and Eileen had finished teaching when she sustained a fall which caused more pain than the usual tumbles.

She hauled herself upright and found that although the assaulted leg seemed not to be broken, it was at least badly sprained. On a previous occasion when she had incurred an injury Karl's advice had been to 'jump on it'. She had done so without benefit but the thought of taking the crude remedy to this latest injury was inadmissible. The pain was already acute.

Luckily she was at a point where it was possible to drift carefully down, keeping all the weight on one ski. Back at Struan she struggled to take the boot off, wincing at every touch. Karl watched empathetically. Expressing a mountain of emotion in one word he said, simply, 'Broken.'

Eileen called the surgery and spoke not to their pupil, Doctor Gow, but to a new incumbent, a Dr. Henderson. He arranged an appointment at the cottage hospital in Grantown but for the time being, Eileen had to wait.

The 'law' which ensured that medical people were always present in the winter sports world ensured that there were several doctors amongst the Struan guests. They heard the consultation arrangements being made and immediately began to discuss the case. As though she were the Queen with a clutch of private physicians, Eileen was soon advised that she was making too much of her injury. All of them were certain that there was no fracture. They suggested that they should examine the limb but Eileen refused to let them touch it. Karl had said 'broken' and her faith was in him rather than the carefree, holiday-making doctors. They teased her, saying that she was probably suffering from a sprain which would clear up during a good night's sleep and that she would be ready in the morning to join them, as she so earnestly wished to do, on the extensive ski tour which was planned for the following day.

Karl drove her to Grantown but had to leave her there in order to rush back to Struan to wait on the diners. Dr. Henderson took one look at the leg and made the arrangements for an X-ray. When the picture was produced there was no longer any uncertainty. The fibula was clearly fractured several inches above the ankle.

Karl telephoned and learned that a lower leg plaster was being applied. He promised to get back to Grantown as soon as he could and rushed about his chores. Eileen waited patiently for him. Now that the diagnosis was made, and the extent of the damage known, she felt better. At least she would be able to get about without too much difficulty.

Karl arrived. She had expected him to be solicitous but the degree of his distress astonished her. He looked anxious in the extreme. In fact, he seemed so upset that the anticipated roles were reversed. The one who should have been cared for became the carer. She started to paint the positive picture; the pain was not acute, she would be able to hobble, the plaster would soon be off.

It was only when they reached the car that there was the dawn of understanding. Eileen could not help but gasp. Their beloved Lea Francis, their first car, was a crumpled parody of itself. All four wings were very badly dented. The exhaust pipe was hanging loose, almost touching the ground.

Ruefully, Karl explained. In his haste he had skidded uncontrollably on black ice at Dulnain Bridge. The car had swirled from wall to wall, bouncing destructively. In the nightmare process he had banged his head quite violently. He, too, was an invalid.

It was a tribute to the Lea Francis engineers that their product was still viable. The stricken couple bellowed their way back to Carrbridge, alarming such animals as were still out in the wintry weather and, in the village, causing a number of alarmed shoppers to run for cover. It was a negative moment, with Eileen facing weeks of impediment and the business losing money for the repair of the car, but there was some satisfaction to be gathered from the expressions of the once confident doctors as the plastered patient swung into the hotel. She had known and they had not and they were suitably contrite.

Getting used to the impediment of crutches, Eileen went immediately in search of Peter who was being cared for by one of the part time workers. The infant seemed totally content which was in one way a relief but in another a disappointment. Had he not missed her? She made some jocular remark about not being needed and the carer looked her squarely in the eye. 'I wouldn't exactly say that, Mrs. Fuchs,' she answered in the drawn out style of Inverness speech, 'he was screaming the place down. The only thing that would quieten him was custard.'

*'Now they believe me!'*

Dr. Henderson visited the next day to check on his patient and found Eileen reclining on the couch giving her son a more conventional feed. He laughed at the story of Bird's best as a sedative. He contemplated Eileen and her child for a while and congratulated her on being so resilient. He might, he announced, even take a picture for the local paper. 'Brave Ski Mother Carries on Regardless' was one of several suggested captions. Eileen, just getting on with the business of being a mother and keeping the hotel going, laughed dismissively. Who would be interested?

The truth was that plenty of people were interested. Eileen and Karl did not at that stage fully realise the extent of their impact. When Jock Kerr Hunter and Donnaie McKenzie appeared at Struan, not long after the double accident, the couple were flattered to be asked to a meeting which had been convened by the Scottish Council for Physical Recreation. The only item on the agenda was the development of Cairngorm as a skiing area. The Struan owners were even more gratified when it was made clear that Karl's presence was considered essential.

The gathering was to be held on March 30th at the Nethybridge Hotel. The Fuchs were told that most of the people who had an interest in the development of the region would be present and that not all of the invitees would necessarily be positive. There was speculation that the landowner, Colonel Grant, might very well take the view that roads and ski-lifts would be a desecration.

Because of the cumbersome plaster, and the need to look after Peter, Eileen decided that she would not attend but nothing short of a cataclysm would keep Karl away. Full of excitement at the prospect of major works on the mountain, he drove to Nethybridge.

The room was crowded. The Provost of Inverness, Robert Wotherspoon, who was also vice-chairman of the Scottish Tourist Board, had been appointed to control the proceedings. It soon emerged that almost everybody at the meeting was in favour of the development of a ski industry in the area. Frequently, attention turned to Karl. Even though his English was still very limited he seemed to dominate the proceedings. His charismatic confidence filled the space. Through an interpreter he communicated boundless optimism.

The snowball of enthusiasm began to roll. There was animated talk of extending the road and of installing high level lifts, not just one Poma but substantial chairs. Had Karl understood more of what was going on he would doubtless have strongly argued the case for a funicular railway from Aviemore. Yet there was someone in the room who, with a few words, could blow all the dreams to pieces. Colonel Grant, the landowner, was keeping his counsel until he had heard all the arguments. At last, Robert Wotherspoon asked for his comments.

The good gentleman rose to his feet. His speech was clearly well thought out. He listed the positive aspects of the proposal which, he thought, were three-fold. Firstly, the development would bring a great enhancement of social life to the area. Secondly, it would extend the season, thus bringing great economic benefits. The third positive comment was in fact a correction of a negative. Colonel Grant announced that, contrary to the rumours, he did not believe that the creation of a ski facility would conflict with other uses of the land.

The reservations were doubtless coming next. The pessimists assumed that he had rehearsed the benefits only to make himself appear reasonable. He would, they thought, go on to talk about the desecration of unspoilt beauty, the irreparable damage to the environment, the threat to endangered species and a host of other negatives.

Instead, the Colonel uttered just one cautionary note. It must, he said, somehow be ensured that skiers did not deposit litter,. disfiguring the beauty of the hills. Provided that this stricture was observed, the landowner declared that he had no objections whatsoever. With that, he sat down and the enthusiasts inwardly rejoiced.

It was decided that a new organisation, the Strathspey Winter Sports Development Board, should be established. Robert Wotherspoon applauded the move but reminded the founders that the District Council, although in favour of development, had no available funds. He declared firmly that the new organisation would have to find its own finance.

Immediately a person, an older man with silver hair, a bristling moustache and a leg that stuck out at an unusual angle, was on his feet waving a five pound note, a not inconsiderable sum in those days. Maurice Knowles, Karl's interpreter for the occasion, who just chanced to be on one of his frequent Struan holidays, proffered the money to the Provost who graciously accepted it, declaring that this act of generosity marked the first token of public confidence in the new Association.

Whilst making his donation speech, Maurice waxed lyrical on the likely profits to be made by a chairlift during the summer months. His Austrian experience showed that tourists who were too lazy or incapacitated to ascend on foot would queue to use mechanical uplift. Far from adding to the enthusiasm, this caused concern. Nobody wanted to think of the broader effects of the new infrastructure. It was ruled, most undemocratically, that there should be no reference to summer trade in the minutes.

Officers were then elected. It was obvious to everyone that Colonel Grant should be in the chair. He graciously accepted the honour and the process of turning part of Cairngorm from wilderness into ski playground had formally begun.

Soon afterwards the scope of the new body was increased to embrace more hotels. Another new organisation, the Strathspey and Badenoch

Hotel and Boarding Keepers' Association was established. An initial funding target of £6000 was set for the new bodies. Colonel Grant was given £168 to pay for a survey of the route of the proposed mountain road.

Myrtle Simpson notes that there was immediate hostility from some skiers to the shape the Cairngorm development was taking. Mocking comparisons were made with St. Moritz. Philip Rankin suggested that an invocation of the ghost of the road-building soldier, General Wade, might be advisable. There was, it seems, an understandable hint of jealousy from those who had struggled, with minimum resources, to make progress at Glencoe.

The new Development Board, disregarding the doubters, began to be active. As though woken up from a long hibernation, hotels and guest houses in the area entered into the spirit of change. Establishments which had routinely closed in winter stayed open. The Craiglynne in Grantown decided to develop some apres-ski in the hope of luring hesitant customers. For their first Saturday evening dance they had but two guests and, in mild desperation, Colin Sutton rang Struan asking them to decamp en masse. There was no needless rivalry. Gladly most of Struan's clientele went then and for many weekends thereafter.

In fact, the Grantown hoteliers quickly realised that winter sports offered a major opportunity and began to think about setting up their own teaching venture. Through contacts established during the war, they came to hear of a Scandinavian called Odd Gulbrandson and offered him a pioneering post which he accepted. A 'Scottish-Norwegian' school, companion to the Austrian one, would be established in time for the Fuchs third season. The initiative, according to Myrtle Simpson, soon received official backing. She writes;

'Karl's activities in Scotland drew the attention of other continentals to the area. The Norwegian Tourist Board wanted to link their name with winter sports in Scotland and backed the "Scotland/Norway Ski School" that was set up in Grantown-on-Spey. This was at the suggestion of Colonel Sandvik, who thought that the Scots should adopt the Norwegian method of instruction and also cement the friendship that was forged during the war.'

A more negative couple than Karl and Eileen might have seen this as threatening but they strongly welcomed the move. Relationships with their Grantown friends remained highly cordial. With the proposed construction on Cairngorm it seemed that there would soon be almost unlimited trade. They took the view that any initiative which strengthened the ski base in the Cairngorm area would be ultimately beneficial for everybody.

The speed and scope of the changes swept Karl and Eileen along. They found themselves talking about new roads, chairlifts, mountain restaurants and a ski school in Grantown when it was not so very long ago that they had met on a misty mountain in Austria. In that short time they had married, bought a hotel, started a ski school and successfully run their pioneering establishment for two seasons.

It was a time for boldness. Throughout the second season they had averaged over twenty students in the school. They had coped with these by employing their part time assistants and by very frequent use of Eileen. Even so, the classes had often been too large. In the immediate future, the part timers would not be sufficiently available to deal with the anticipated surge in clientele and Eileen, who would have a growing infant to look after, would often be otherwise occupied. Clearly, they needed to recruit a full time instructor.

The first instinct was to turn to Austria for the recruit but this would take time and there would certainly be problems with acquiring a work permit. Karl declared that he would look locally.

He had, in fact, noticed that there were one or two people on the hill who had clearly been taught abroad. There were others who, through watching Karl and by virtue of great natural ability, had reached a point where they were potentially good demonstrators. Such a person would need training, of course, but they would be immediately available without complicated bureaucratic negotiations.

Even though the official skiing season was over, there was still snow trapped in thin strips down the middle of some of the colder corries. The true ski fanatics made use of these residual slivers, sometimes until June. Karl knew that if he were to drift over towards Coire na Ciste there would be a good chance of seeing someone with the will, and the technical potential, to become an instructor.

Carrying his skis, on a sunny, warm day, Karl wandered through the heather towards the top of the steep, narrow run. If there chanced to be nobody there he would at least enjoy the opportunity to let his skis fly. He reached the top of a rise and saw, to his surprise, that there was a small tent pitched on the edge of the snow. Just as he reached the temporary residence a figure appeared trudging up the corrie, skis expertly balanced over one shoulder.

Karl judged that the man emerging into view was perhaps in his late thirties but the thinning hair and slightly stooped posture suggested that he might be older. The sinking sun beamed off wire-rimmed glasses. The large, hooked nose on which this instrument was perched glowed red from prolonged exposure to ultra-violet. From the rucksack on the skier's back a head suddenly popped up. A dog looked at Karl and barked once.

The man greeted Karl as though he knew him and declared that his name was Plum. The dog, he said, was Rover. The man confessed that he had been watching Karl's classes, noting, copying. He hoped Karl did not mind and then, perhaps by way of payment for the distance learning, offered his unknowing instructor a cup of tea.

Karl gladly accepted. It had been a dehydrating hike up the mountain. He deposited his skis and made as though to sit beside the tent. Plum, in an accent which Karl later learned was native to Manchester, said that he could brew up where they were but it would be better to go to his other, lower, residence where his wife, Robbie, was already making preparations.

The men then played the 'after you' game. Plum wanted a free lesson, Karl wanted to see how this somewhat portly person with a dog on his back could possibly negotiate the steep, narrow gully which was before them.

Karl graciously set off, skiing quite fast but making sure that his style was exaggerated. At a point just before the run steepened, he stopped. He was extremely surprised to see that Plum was not far behind and was skiing with commendable style. Rover looked Karl in the eye as his master skidded expertly to a halt as if to say, 'That surprised you, didn't it maestro?' Well, it did.

'Gut,' Karl said, referring not to Plum's protuberance but using the German which he guessed the man would understand, 'Serr gut'. Modestly, Plum declared that he had progressed greatly since he had had the advantage of watching Karl.

They skied down, Karl limiting his speed so that Plum could follow his track. Whenever possible he glanced back and yelled encouragement. He knew that this 'find' could be the one he had been looking for.

At the lower tent, Karl was introduced to Robbie, a dark-haired, full faced woman with a ready smile. She seemed delighted to meet the person who had been, up until then, just a distant inspiration. When the tea was delivered, Karl was amused to see that it contained substantial quantities of heather but it tasted none the worse. He found himself warming quickly to the unusual couple. When the tin mugs were drained he innocently suggested to Plum that there was time for one last run. The guest was not altogether surprised when Robbie said that she would come too.

It was a long, very steep climb to the top but the campers were almost as fit as the Austrian. They said that they were planning to spend what promised to be a calm night in their upper residence in order to have a dawn run down the Ciste. Evidently, another walk up the hill was as nothing to them.

Robbie led the way. As soon as he saw her skiing, Karl knew that he had found not one but two recruits. She was, he thought, actually better than her husband, more fluid and graceful. People would learn from her simply through seeing the clarity of her body movements. In spite of this comparison, Plum showed that he too would be an excellent teacher. Half way down the corrie, Karl formulated his plan.

Before parting from the lower tent to make the descent to Glenmore, Karl made his proposal. There were language difficulties but his meaning was abundantly clear. He was offering both of them employment for the following season. The Worrals were flattered and delighted. Their chief ambition was to be amongst the mountains. The prospect of being able to earn a living whilst doing what they loved best was irresistible.

It turned out that the couple had a camper van which would fit without difficulty into the spacious Struan garden. They had been climbers, members of the Karabiner Club, before they discovered skiing and were used to spartan conditions. They had no need of Annexe accommodation. The deal was quickly negotiated and in the autumn months before the start of the 1957 season the new instructors took up residence. The dog lived there too, treated like a child and having its nose wiped with a handkerchief by its doting 'mother'. The new instructors breezed through their pre-season training and became instantly essential to the school.

*Plum and Robbie*

These two, natural eccentrics in the eyes of many, were part of the beginning of Struan's unusual style. Plum, particularly, was a person for whom normal rules did not apply. He saw nothing odd about having tents at the top and bottom of Coire na Ciste, nor in having a dog on his back as he skied. For him it was entirely normal to use the dinner table cutlery for depicting slalom courses and to leap to his feet wherever he might be to demonstrate technique. He knew the mountains better than most and delighted in taking skiers to remote places. Occasionally, as in the time when he contrived to sink a Land Rover up to its axles in a Glen Feshie bog, this led to problems. The hapless guests, who were due to go home that evening, were stuck with him for long, cold hours until a tractor could be found and they all had to stay an extra night. There were, Eileen recalls, no grumbles; the group had come to accept the unexpected as far as Plum was concerned. They understood that if they wanted the rewards of adventure they had to face the risks of inconvenience.

Whilst the new instructors were still settling in, Odd Gulbrandson, the Norwegian who was taking on the task of setting up the Grantown-on-Spey school, arrived. A true man of the mountains, an excellent skier and a speaker of German, Odd became an ally rather than a rival. From the outset he and Karl shared information about snow conditions in the various teaching venues and cooperated in overcoming the frustrations of working in a region which was not properly developed for winter sports.

Encouraged by the Grantown development and anticipating great improvements on the mountain, Karl felt justified in realising one of his plans for Struan. After the first season he had moved the ski shed from the Annexe to one of the outhouses next to the hotel but this was by no means adequate. Something much more spacious was required.

From a man called Jack Drake, who ran a nearby Alpine nursery, he bought a second-hand wooden building. Aided by Sandy Panton he erected this on the planned site at the back of the yard. The two of them worked to install shelving for boots, racks for the skis, a workbench, a counter and seats for those who would be trying on footwear. Smells of leather and wax filled the new space as equipment was installed. Colourful posters decorated the walls.

The third season, embellished with this new professional facility and the comforting presence of the Worralls, was so reassuringly successful that Karl felt able to accept the invitation of the army to go over to Glencoe to set the course for their annual championships. His love of racing had not diminished and, even though he was still debarred from all competitions because of his professional status, he could not resist the chance to set and test a course. Plum and Robbie, supplemented by Eileen if need be, would be able to manage for a while.

Karl drove over to Glencoe full of expectation. Even though he treated the matter of hiking uphill lightly, it would be a real treat to be dragged, to be able to have run after run without the effort of the intervening ascents.

From the moment of his arrival, the visitor was treated royally. The

Poma was made freely available. Though a very modest man, not given to any form of boasting, it was gratifying to Karl to be able to show off his silky skills. Everyone deferred to him, even those whose enterprise and impressive energy had created this first Scottish professional lift. The course-setting was a delight and everyone associated with the event expressed their full satisfaction at the Austrian's contribution.

On the drive back, Karl reflected. The visit had been memorable and his admiration for the pioneers was unbounded. Yet there were negative thoughts. All that was so evidently happening at Glencoe highlighted the lack of development at Cairngorm. True, things were moving but because official bodies were involved, the pace was excruciatingly slow. Badenoch District Council had made no progress whatsoever on the acquisition of finance for the proposed road. Beyond this hurdle was the perhaps higher one of backing for the lift. Who would pay for this?

It was obvious to Karl that there was a massive will in Scotland to take advantage of the winter sports opportunities afforded by the magnificent mountains. It seemed, though, as if most of the energy was being channelled away from Cairngorm. Dundee, supplemented to some extent by Aberdeen, was the Glenshee powerhouse, Glasgow fuelled the Glencoe development. There was no comparable city base for Cairngorm. It was true that the Highland Ski Club had over seven hundred members, one or two of whom were part time instructors for Struan, but the main activity of that organisation seemed to be the provision of a Sunday bus to Garve. The Aberdeeners, when not enjoying Glenshee, were to be found using a portable tow at Abergeldie. There the skiers had become so numerous that a local beginner had written to a newspaper pleading for the police to be called in to control the 'downhill boys' who raced through the pack causing terror. Cairngorm had little to show by comparison.

The contrast between Glencoe and Cairngorm at that time is vividly painted by Frith Finlayson. He tells of a late season visit to Speyside to ski with his friend Bob Clyde who had moved to Inverness to work as an engineer. Since his eastwards migration, Bob had largely missed out on the benefits of the Glencoe lift. He professed himself mightily impressed with the improvement in his friend's skiing which, in part, was obviously due to the greatly increased amount of downhill running.

In foul May weather, they made dogged use of the residual snow until, on a 'last' run down Coire na Ciste, Frith jumped athletically over a gap in the snow only to break through into another part of the icy burn. A bone in his left leg snapped. Instead of falling directly into the water his body turned such that his skis formed a bridge across the hole. Inverted, his head in the water, Frith was in dire danger of drowning. Strong stomach muscles came to his rescue but the pain from the leg made all movement highly unpleasant. In those times skiers did not have instant release bindings. He was stuck.

Frith records how his companions managed to extricate him but the problems were only just beginning. None of them carried first aid equipment. The nearest stretcher was seven miles away at Glenmore. The weather worsened. Many hours passed before the relief party returned and many more as the shivering Frith was carried through the deep heather to the track. Had he not been so fit, had he been skiing alone, the chances are that he would not have survived.

An event such as this highlighted the difference between Cairngorm and the other venues. At Glencoe and Glenshee the public road was close to the ski areas. An injured person could be transferred to hospital relatively quickly. In the Cairngorms, rescue was a tricky business unless expensive helicopters were involved. The simple fact of increasing numbers on the mountain was of no benefit as far as safety was concerned; the logistics of moving a badly injured skier remained the same.

Just when it seemed that, for all the goodwill and enthusiasm, Cairngorm was doomed to be an occasional, arduous and potentially dangerous ski venue, totally unsuitable for the pupils of the Austrian and Norwegian schools, a financial breakthrough raised fresh hopes.

Badenoch District Council, finally despairing of ever raising sufficient capital for the new road without a contribution from the public purse, took the desperate step of applying to Inverness County Council for assistance. Generally such requests for extra funding are not sympathetically received but, to delighted surprise, the Inverness worthies agreed to accept the burden.

There was a proviso, which was that the private road from Coylumbridge to Glenmore should be ceded to the county. This might have been a massive obstacle but such was the will for progress that the transfer of ownership presented no problems.

Another snag appeared. The County Council then declared that before the work could start on the new mountain section, the existing track through Glenmore would have to be brought up to an acceptable standard. The estimated cost of this work was over fifteen thousand pounds. Things were obviously not going to happen in a hurry but at least the officials made budgetary provision.

Karl and Eileen were therefore feeling tolerably confident that they had made the right decision to settle in the area when, to yet more delight, their second child, Lisi, was born in September, 1957. The making good of the existing road would surely take many months, the construction of the mountain route at least a year and the erection of the as yet unfinanced lift probably another but at least by the time Lisi was toddling there would be significant progress.

*Then there were four.*

It was obvious that, with two youngsters to look after, Eileen's time as a ski instructor was temporarily over. With Plum, Robbie and part time help Karl would be able to manage during the quieter times but when demand increased there would be problems. The last thing Karl wanted was for his school to acquire a reputation for over-large classes or unpredictability. In spite of the long time scale of the Cairngorm developments, it seemed that the time was right to risk acquiring another full time instructor.

Eileen imagined that he would repeat the Plum experience. After all, the standard of skiing was improving steadily. There would surely be others who would welcome the chance to become teachers. Karl had other ideas.

He needed an ally, a fellow countryman, someone whose experience was akin to his. He also desperately needed an Austrian friend with whom he could converse freely, who would need nothing explaining, who would respond without thought to a comment about a sporting hero or a development in skiing technique. He would, he declared, make enquiries in Austria.

Eileen reminded him of the likely problems with work permits. The regulations had remained exceedingly tight. Karl was not deterred. The Austrian Ski School, Carrbridge, had to have another Austrian in its ranks. He would accept no other outcome.

## 12. Norbert and the Shift to Gegenschulter

Karl contacted a friend in Bruck and asked him to recruit a suitable instructor. He knew that there would be young people in his native land who, for the minimal rewards of board and lodging and modest pocket money, would snatch at the chance of coming to Britain, if only for the opportunity to learn English and to have a touch of adventure.

Whilst the enquiries were being made, Eileen approached the authorities for a work permit. The response was swift and negative. Doggedly Eileen argued about the economic benefits to the Cairngorm region and pointed out that there were no suitably qualified native workers. Through a long and difficult negotiation, which went to the political heights of the Secretary of State for Scotland, she finally won. Myrtle Simpson, with some inaccuracy as to number, records this significant step:

'Karl Fuchs had been the first continental to have confidence in Scotland as a place to ski. He had been so encouraged by the potential of his ski school that he asked the immigration authorities for permits to bring in five trainers from the Arlberg area of Austria. He was in fact allowed only one permit and this was taken up by a young skier from his own village, Hans Kuwall.'

Hans arrived at the beginning of the 1958 season and settled to the task remarkably well. As Karl had dreamed, the new instructor quickly became a friend as well as a colleague. The sense of isolation and the sadness of cultural deprivation were dramatically relieved. There was a further psychological boost in Hans' swift appreciation of the potential of the area. It was very affirming to have the support of a young, ambitious skier. It made the Struan gamble seem more secure.

Quite soon, Hans began a courtship of Barbara, one of Eileen's domestic workers. This raised the possibility that the newcomer's stay might be for much longer than a season and Karl was utterly delighted. His relationship with the young man deepened. He began to see Hans as a younger brother or even a grown up son. The fact that he seemed bent on marrying a Briton strengthened the bonding.

The positive feeling was given a boost by a steady growth of media interest in the enterprise. When Walter Gunn of the Daily Express called to say that he wanted to write a piece, the Struan proprietors were delighted to cooperate. The ensuing article provided great national publicity for their venture.

'Carrbridge, the little town in the Inverness-shire uplands, soon got used to the mid- winter suntans, the yodelling that floated down from the surrounding mountain tops and the brisk out-of-season trade that came in the wake of its popularity as a skiing centre.

Local people even accepted with amused tolerance the yells of delight in the crowded hotel lounges when the weather forecast was more snow. But even Carrbridge rocked a little when Peter, Plum and Rover hit the ski slopes this year.

Peter is the son of Karl Fuchs, the 'headmaster' of the ski school. Everyone expected him to follow in his father's ski tracks but not at the age he did. For Peter is only two years old. When the snow fell in the Fuchs' garden in January, Peter abandoned his toys and demanded skis. Father sent specially to Austria for a miniature pair and Peter took to the snows. Now, every afternoon, he swishes down the nursery slopes with the boys like a veteran, while distinguished doctors and tight lipped legal men take nose dives into snow drifts not so very much higher up the ski runs.

Peter takes purlers like everyone else but they have not affected his confidence. The biggest moment of the day for Scotland's and probably Britain's youngest skier is when his father holds him firmly between his knees and takes him for 30 mph runs down the hills.

Carrbridge had just recovered from the shock of the ski tot's appearance when Plum and Rover arrived. Plum is a 38 year old bearded giant of a Mancunian. Rover is his dog, a 13 year old terrier going grey of whisker. Everywhere Plum, real name Norman Worrall, goes Rover follows. And that includes going places on skis. Whether it is an overland trek or a 60 mph dash down a mountainside, Rover is tucked into a rucksack on his master's back. Plum - 'I was once a plumber' - claims Rover is Britain's widest travelled dog, either on skis or on foot. He has been up every mountain in England and Wales and every interesting Munro in Scotland. He has also been pot-holing. Said Plum: 'He loves skiing but he does give me a look that is sheer reproach if I fall.'

Plum took to the quiet hills 13 months ago. His wife, known affectionately to everyone as Mrs Plum, was seriously ill. The doctors advised a long holiday, free from worry. Plum sold his business, let his house, converted his van into a caravan - all without telling his wife. Then he drove up to the hospital to collect her. They have been back to Manchester once since. Said Plum: 'The noise and the rush nearly drove us crackers - and Rover didn't fancy the back alleys after the freedom of the hills.'

Plum plans their holiday will end about a year from now. But he is not certain. One thing he is certain of is that Mrs Plum has never been better in her life. 'We don't know what will happen', said Plum, 'but we feel that after it is over we will have kicked life in the pants for two years.'

Carrbridge is proud of Peter, Plum and Rover.

And perhaps a skiing tot and a skiing dog are not such strange sights after all, the badge of the ski school is a white hare that looks surprisingly like Alice in Wonderland's white rabbit.'

Not long after the article appeared, Struan had even greater cause to be proud of its newly famous instructor. He was asleep in the caravan when his generous nose picked up on an alarming scent. Alerting Robbie to fetch Karl, he rushed to the kitchen which was filled with black smoke. He flung himself to the floor and crawled under the cloud, trying to reach the blazing gas cylinder which was the cause of the stench. By the time Karl and Eileen arrived, Plum was unconscious. Karl dragged him out.

Whilst Eileen and Robbie tried to revive Plum, Karl dashed into action. Using techniques learned as a policeman he quickly brought the blaze under control. The next time Eileen was aware of her husband, he was manhandling a red-hot iron cylinder out of the door.

*Peter watching his father do a spectacular 'helicopter' turn*

In the fresh night air Plum recovered quite swiftly and both Karl and Eileen poured out their gratitude. Without his prompt action there could have been a major disaster. Plum was a suitably modest hero and he, in turn, was grateful for Karl's rescue effort.

Apart from this near-disaster, the Austrian Ski School operated satisfyingly smoothly throughout the season. Karl, Hans, Plum and Robbie, instructing full time, were helped by the part timers whose ranks had been swelled by Walter McKinnon, barman at the Inverness Ski Club 'local', and Viva Shepherd, a school teacher from St. Andrews. There were quiet times, of course, but generally the team was kept busy and the hotel was often fully booked.

The body blow came at the end of the season. Myrtle Simpson records a simple fact which, for Karl and Eileen, was devastating. She writes; 'After a successful season Hans married Barbara, a housekeeper at Struan House, and the young couple moved to found another ski school at the Carrbridge Hotel'.

The unexpected loss of Hans' services, and the establishment of another Austrian ski school so close to their own, was not pleasant news for the Struan couple. Myrtle Simpson notes that Karl's organisation had already dealt with something like two thousand students and that there was plenty of scope for others but this, from the Struan perspective, was not entirely the point.

There was also the acute problem of finding a replacement for Hans. It might have been possible to manage with somebody from the locality but there were two powerful reasons why this would not do.

In the first place, if, as seemed highly likely, Hans intended to employ Austrians then Struan would surely have to do so. Potential customers were attracted by the prospect of being taught by someone with Continental experience and it would not do to have their new rival offering what might seem to be a more European service.

The second factor was perhaps more important. Word had come, in letters and through people like Viva Shepherd who had been recently to Austria, of a startling new ski technique known as 'gegenschulter'. The official Austrian body which controlled ski teaching had given 'reverse shoulder' its complete endorsement. No satellite school could truly call itself 'Austrian' if it were not practising and teaching the new methodology. Struan could not dream of being left behind.

What the innovative technique amounted to was this.

Put a beginner on skis on a moderate slope, explain the simple principle of the stem turn, which involves using the edge of an angled ski like the rudder of a boat, and ask them to attempt the manoeuvre. The chances are that the instinct for self-preservation will cause the subject of the experiment to lean back and to bring the leading shoulder round as the turn takes effect. Both of these intuitive moves are inimical to efficient skiing.

Leaning forward had long been acknowledged as a means of controlling speed but relatively little attention had been paid to shoulder position. Good skiers sensed that 'facing down the hill' was a good thing but tentative beginners usually opted for what felt like the safest shape. The new Austrian teaching method was devised to correct this.

It involved extreme exaggeration. Whatever the strain on the muscles which control the torso, the shoulders had to be parallel with the skis except when heading straight downhill. Anyone traversing across a slope should, according to the new orthodoxy, be twisted such that the shoulders followed the direction of the skis.

In essence, the principle was sound. It is still highly inadvisable to ski 'with rotation' but the new teaching method was very extreme and it quickly acquired the status of a religious dogma. It was not sufficient to have shoulders *approximately* in line with skis as is the common, much more comfortable, practice today; the alignment had to be perfect.

Karl imported his disciple of the new technique. The proselyte was a small, cheerful, wiry man of abundant energy called Norbert Uitz. Reassuringly, he was from Aflenz; a fellow Steierer. He had very recently completed his ski instructor's course under the tuition of the famous Professor Kruckenhauser and was, in Eileen's description, a 'red-hot' proponent of the most exaggerated 'gegenschulter'.

Within a few days of Norbert's arrival the entire staff of the Struan House ski school had been converted. 'Get that shoulder back!' became as common an injunction on the slopes as 'bend the knees' or 'lean forward.' For all that it involved mild contortions, the new method produced elegant skiers. In the extreme traverse position, practitioners seemed securely locked onto their line until, with a 'down-up-down' and an unforcing twist, they turned into the opposite trajectory.

*One of Karl's early female instructors demonstrates the approved style*

Norbert entered a world where the Cairngorm development was still in a very early stage and where the initial delight at the construction of a lift in Glencoe had considerably faded. Three seasons of poor snow and inclement weather in the west had dampened enthusiasm. There were debts, with little prospect that the tow would ever earn enough to pay these off. Some felt that trade could be improved by building a chairlift to link the road with the tow. Others favoured the erection of a substantial shelter. Moves were made towards the collection of money but in the inner sanctum of the highly influential Scottish Ski Club the climate of opinion was changing.

Nothing had actually happened in connection with the building of the Cairngorm mountain road but the work to surface the Glenmore track was well under way. It was evident that the public authorities were serious in their determination to develop the area. Cairngorm with a road to two thousand feet was an entirely different proposition to Cairngorm with a tedious footpath. The snow was more reliable in the East. All it would need, after the road was finished, would be a tow to the top of the mountain and Cairngorm would be the place to ski in Scotland.

A proposal was made by leading members of the Scottish Ski Club that all of the resources collected for Glencoe should be channelled into the Cairngorm Winter Sports Development Board. Understandably, the idea met with considerable resistance. Those who had struggled long and hard to build the facilities at Glencoe strongly resented the shift of emphasis. There was a battle which the 'Coe' loyalists lost. In a highly significant move, a substantial sum of money was conveyed to the Cairngorm fund.

Philip Rankin, the main inspiration behind the development at Glencoe, was extremely unhappy. With club funds cut off, he approached the landowner and suggested that private enterprise might be the answer. To general surprise, Major Fleming agreed to inject £12,000 on condition that the existing equipment, and the rights to tenancy, were ceded to a new company. Club members were not wild about handing over the fruits of their hard labour as well as their savings but it had to be agreed that there was no viable alternative. A 'sweetener' of £500 for the erection of a hut helped the process and before long the 'White Corries' company was in sole charge of the Glencoe operation.

Work started immediately on the construction of a new tow which was scheduled to be ready for the 1960 season. It was evident that the Glencoe spirit was not to be crushed by the might of the Cairngorm road rollers.

Norbert Uitz was not the only European to come into this developing world. Odd Gulbrandson had handed over responsibility for the Grantown school to a man called Eilif Moen. Eilif, who still lives in Speyside with his English wife Vivien, recalls the pre-ski road days with affection. He tells that he was 'lured' to Scotland by one of the wartime instructors who warned him about the primitive conditions and the vagaries of the climate. It was the kind of challenge which appealed to him.

Within a very short time of his arrival, Eilif met Karl and the two of them formed a close alliance. They discovered almost immediately that they had very similar ideas about the best places to ski. Continuing the tradition of cooperation, Karl imparted hard-won local knowledge. Between the two ski school leaders there was a mutual respect which transcended commercial rivalry. There were, of course, differences in ethos. Eilif declares that his classes were more fun-based than the efficient 'Germanic' lessons conducted by the Austrians. There was also, in those days of extreme 'reverse shoulder', a contrast of skiing methods but this never led to discord between Austrian and Norwegian. The instructors from the two schools were frequent visitors to each other's establishments. In the absence of specialist shops they cooperated with equipment; Eilif recalls buying ski boots from Karl. He remembers also, with gratitude, how Karl used his considerable connections in Austria to facilitate a meeting with the famous Professor Stefan Kruckenhauser at St. Christoph.

What impressed Eilif most in those early days was the keenness of the students. In the face of appalling weather, people kept on practising and striving to move beyond whatever stage they had reached. Eilif says fondly that it was 'inspiring'. He and his colleagues felt like winners whenever individual ski progress was achieved. This was nothing to do with conquering great heights or breaking speed records but just related to people setting themselves personally challenging targets and sometimes meeting them.

A Norwegian Olympic skier who worked with Eilif for a while, and who might have been expected to be contemptuous of the conditions, wrote from the prestigious American resort to which he moved to say that he greatly missed Scotland. For him, the challenge of overcoming the hardships was more rewarding than the effortless skiing of the well-groomed resorts.

Eilif says that beginners were the 'bread and butter' of the Scottish ski schools in those early days. Instructors needed to have great interpersonal skills rather than brilliant technical ability. The chief challenge was to maintain hope and faith when poor snow conditions and atrocious weather were prompting despair. The process was as much to do with the struggles of life as with the limited business of learning to ski.

Even though Eilif's assessment of the importance of the struggle is doubtless substantially correct, it was still clear to him, as to everyone else involved in the Cairngorm area, that there were limits. A relatively small number of hardy souls would persist against all difficulties but the development of the facilities was a high priority if the more moderate people were to be attracted and retained.

Karl shared this view which was strongly reinforced when he was invited by the Dundee Ski Club to visit Glenshee. The club boarded him with Finlay and Ruth Cameron who lived in the former keeper's cottage at Devil's Elbow. They became immediate friends. Later, Eileen and the children were regular visitors, even after the Camerons split. Finlay was adopted as an uncle by Peter and Lisi. Amongst many admirable attributes, he was an expert piper. Years later, when he lost the end of a finger in an accident, he still managed to play by courtesy of a metal 'thimble'. He was a resourceful man and the children warmed to him.

On that first occasion Karl was mightily impressed with what he saw. Normally be-suited businessmen were in rough clothes, digging out tracks, erecting buildings, even cleaning toilets. Frith Finlayson refers to 'some very strong willed, able men' in charge of the Glenshee development. Karl met David Jamieson who, according to Myrtle Simpson, was the chief amongst these diehards. Karl discovered that the club planned to build two tows and install new huts. The loss of their main base, the Spittal Hotel, through fire had not diminished their enthusiasm.

When he came back, full of praise, he commented to Eileen that if their business were to be entirely safe, they needed their own Glencoe and Glenshee, a place where it was possible to drive up to snow level for most of the season. Until such time, years ahead it seemed, as the Cairngorm road was completed, they should have a high-level venue within reasonable distance.

Very often, Eileen had the radio on as background to her work in the kitchen. She remembered that frequent reference was made in the weather reports to a place called Tomintoul. The road to this village seemed to be blocked by snow more often than any other. There must, she reasonably assumed, be many times when the road was open but with snow piled up on both sides.

There was a guest in the hotel who had been a pre-war skiing champion. With her, Eileen set out one day to investigate. They drove through Tomintoul, seeking the highest point in the road and thereby came to an uninhabited spot which the map recorded as being the Lecht. The women parked and explored. Within moments they were sure that Struan had found its Glenshee equivalent.

It was late by the time the explorers returned. Struan was in full party mode as they relayed the news of their discovery. Karl declared immediately that the next day classes would be at the Lecht. This development obviously necessitated new celebrations. The party intensified. The moment soon arrived when, to most of those assembled, there seemed no point in going to bed. Someone suggested an immediate departure to the new slopes. Another pointed out that they had left the skis at Findhorn. All the more reason, the proposer argued, for setting off instantly. In the end, a degree of sense prevailed. People slept for a couple of hours, ate a hearty Struan breakfast and set off. They all agreed at the end of that first day that The Lecht was an excellent addition to the skiing repertoire.

One who concurred readily with the assessment was Bill Blackwood. At the Lecht he could drive his vehicle to the most convenient spot and set up a tow with the minimum of hauling and lifting. By this time, his satanic devices had significantly improved. The long poles had been replaced with short metal hooks which could be used to grip the rope but generally skiers dispensed with devices and simply grabbed and clung. This eliminated the nuisance of having to carry the implement on the descent but it involved a danger because, for all his ingenuity, Bill Blackwood had been unable to eliminate the peril of the twisting rope.

Presumably as a result of its scheme of construction, the hawser rotated slowly as it travelled. When it was wet, as it most often was, any loose material on the gloves tended to become intimately bonded. The unwary would not notice this until they tried to shift their hands. Then, great was the panic! Ahead was the large return pulley and the charming prospect of being mangled.

Occasionally the bonding between skier and uplift device became more intimate. It was not unknown for other parts of the clothing to become coiled. This produced a different alarm scenario, for as the anorak integrated itself with the rope it threatened to tear. And supposing, having ripped the outer garment, the rope then took it into its devilish mind to do some more undressing? Fanciful, maybe, but in the moment of acute unease the prospect comes into the mind of being systematically stripped and ending naked, but for hat, boots and socks, at the shameful top.

As far as is recorded, nobody suffered this extreme fate, although clothes were certainly damaged. Bill Blackwood had no answer to this but he did install a trip safety device. Anyone with rope-integrated gloves who progressed beyond the scheduled exit point skied into a thin cane which swung on a hinge and, by a miracle of mountain engineering, disengaged the gears. The only suffering for the one who triggered this device was the cursing of those who were left hanging on at an angle of forty five degrees with their arm muscles seizing and their heads full of calculations as to how they could exit without falling over.

There was one day towards the end of that exploratory season when even the Lecht had insufficient snow and Bill had established his tow on the brow of a slope in Coire Cas. The change in angles on the chosen pitch was such that the top wheel was not visible from the lowest one. Customers embarked on the steeper slope and, with fortitude and a measure of luck, were carried over to the final easier section.

A small boy was using the facility. Hanging on was no great problem to him because his body was so light. Doubtless he felt confident in the manner of adventurous children and could hardly wait to start another run but when the time came to peel away, he could not.

Happily the trip switch was just ahead but less welcome was the discovery that the designers had not planned for lightweight folk. The rope rose towards the return wheel and with it rose the child. Like a pantomime fairy, he sailed upwards. His only hope, as he soared ever higher, was that a trailing ski would catch the trip, but it did not. The young hands were destined to be crushed.

Had there been someone immediately behind the child on the rope they could have tripped the safety device but there was not. Had there been anyone skiing at the level of the automatic cut-off they could have rushed over but there was not.

There was, though, a skier coming down the hill, an adventurous soul who had walked up higher and who was enjoying a longer descent. He was a senior local policeman by the name of McGeoch. He had but seconds in which to calculate. It seemed to him, perhaps rightly, that by the time he had skied the distance between the top wheel and the trip device, the boy's fate would be sealed. With instantaneous courage he changed direction and headed straight for the screaming, dangling youth. McGeoch, tall enough to reach the rope, scrabbled frantically at the trapped gloves.

Just in time, his efforts succeeded and the boy dropped free. What McGeoch was unable to do was prevent one of his own hands being dragged in. Immediately most of his bones were broken and the skin ripped off.

And still nobody came up the rope. It was Norbert, taking a class lower down the hill, who heard McGeoch's chilling screams. Calculating instantly, the Austrian realised that it would take too long to climb up. Instead he skied at racing speed down to the bottom of the tow, shouting and waving as he neared the machine. Somebody hit the clutch and the rope stopped. Norbert then shed his skis and ran up the slope, dreading what he would find but determined to do what he could to make the wounded hero comfortable.

By the time Norbert arrived at the top wheel, McGeoch was free but his hand was mangled. The shock and pain had rendered him semi-conscious. Knowing that there would be a long wait before the rescuers arrived, Norbert peeled off his sweater and made a pillow for the sufferer. He stayed there, regardless of the cold, comforting the policeman until the stretcher party took over.

Eilif Moen, who happened to be teaching a class much lower down the hill, was at first unaware of the accident but he remembers vividly hearing the gory news and then seeing the unfortunate policeman being carried down the hill.

*Norbert the Scot!*

Intricate surgery eventually restored McGeoch's hand to the point where it was viable but it remained claw-like. The skin was largely composed of scar tissue and movement of the fingers doubtless often gave him pain.

The mishap, which could perhaps have proved fatal had the boy not been freed, shocked everyone and emphasised the perils of skiing on the undeveloped mountain. Even with the best systems and the most dedicated rescuers, there were always going to be long delays between an accident and relief. It might have been time for a complete re-think of the viability of the area except that, at last, there was news of crucial developments which would change the whole scene. These were reported in many of the weightier newspapers but one down-market sheet, Reveille, which had a reputation for scantily clad pin-ups and scandal, improbably chose to tell the story. They did so, in mid-May 1959, from the Fuchs' perspective and once more Struan received the welcome boost of national publicity. Under the banner headline, 'Skiers get a Highland Fling' the paper reported;

'Because an English girl fell in love with an Austrian policeman, Britain now has her own 'Little Switzerland'- in the Highlands of Scotland.

When she wed, Mrs Eileen Fuchs did not wish to live in Austria, so Karl, her husband, who had trained with the Austrian Olympic ski team in 1947, said: 'We'll go in search of snow in your country.' Eileen was at Vienna University when she met Karl. Now, instead of practising the law she studied, she works in their small guest house at Carrbridge, Inverness-shire.

It was 1954 when Eileen and Karl came to Scotland and took their guest house. Now there are at least six more full-time skiing instructors, including Swiss and Norwegians, in the area, as well as a dozen part-time skiing tutors. From all over Britain, thousands of people go to Inverness-shire's Glenmore Estate skiing grounds every winter.

And the number is increasing. Not long ago, an anonymous donor offered twenty thousand pounds towards the cost of a chairlift for the benefit of skiers. The offer was made subject to the raising of an equal sum locally. 'We are confident we can raise our share', I was told by Colonel J. P. Grant, chairman of the Cairngorm Winter Sports Development Board.

Local hoteliers have promised five thousand pounds towards the building of a new road up to the two-mile Coire Cas ski-run, above the two thousand feet level, where snow lies until June. Work on the new road and the improvement of five miles of existing road, costing thirty-six thousand pounds, is expected to be finished in time for next winter. The chair-lift will go on for nearly two miles beyond the road-head.

As I drove round the area - it is seven miles from Aviemore, twelve from Kingussie, and eighty-four from Perth - I saw dozens of gaily clad skiers on the slopes. Taking advantage of the big fare cuts offered by British Railways, skiers travel at midweek from all over Britain. 'B.E.A. has been investigating the helicopter position, and local air landings may come eventually," I was told.'

The piece contains the usual quota of inaccuracies, including the claim that Eileen was a lawyer and the startling notion of a two mile chairlift, but the word about the astonishing anonymous donation was true, as was the prediction of the completion date for the building of the road. If all went according to this plan, if the matching funding could be raised and there were no unforeseen snags, Cairngorm would be transformed for the new decade. There would be a road to two thousand feet and a substantial car park at that altitude. Skiers would there find not a hazardous Poma but a sit-down-and-rest chairlift to whisk them almost to the summit of the mountain.

It was a most exciting prospect for the two who had started with so little.

## 13. Not A Killer Hotel

A crucial question, which Struan's new proprietors had scarcely thought about in their enthusiasm for setting up the ski school, was how to fill the summer months.

For Karl, the freeing of time gave him the chance to participate in some late and early season games of football for the Carrbridge team. He discovered, also, that it was possible to recreate his Bruck bridge experience. Locals engaged in the hazardous pastime of jumping off the old structure into what was chillingly known as the 'black hole'. This involved courage, a nicety of judgement and a constitution strong enough to withstand sudden immersion in icy water. Karl was ideally qualified.

None of this generated income. As the last of the skiers left, the Fuchs realised that they needed something that would earn money and they had no desire to return to Struan's former line of catering for diabetics, very worthy though this was.

In the very first summer, they confined themselves to the idea of making the hotel attractive to casual callers. They decided that tables and chairs with gay sunshades outside at the front would attract passing motorists just as they often did in Austria. The furniture could easily be made. The collapsible umbrellas were a different matter. In the continuing post-war austerity such items were hard to come by and only someone with the right contacts could hope to meet with success. Happily, Eileen's network of former associates did not let her down.

On an autumn break, she made diplomatic enquiries of an erstwhile colleague, a formidable woman who had been a member of the Price Regulation Committee. This high flyer had moved to work for Gamages, the famous department store, and had become nothing less than the Managing Director. Not long after the tentative request was made, the shades arrived. Gleefully Karl installed them. The Struan proprietors viewed their hotel frontage from every available angle and agreed; it did look most attractive.

*Summer welcome*

A few days later they went out on one of their exploratory expeditions. They took a last admiring glance at their latest acquisitions as they drove towards the hills. The morning was sunny and all seemed right with the world.

They were not to know that it was one of those deceptive Cairngorm days. Halfway through the walk they were buffeted by a strong wind. Soon they were struggling against the mighty force. They hoped that it was one of those frequent mountain storms which left the valley peaceful but as they drove homewards, the trees about them bent and creaked.

They turned the last corner. Ahead was Struan and outside there were no umbrellas.

It was possible, but unlikely, that they had been stolen. More probably, Sandy had heard the wind and removed them as a precaution. Anxious to discover the fate of their high class Gamages furniture, the couple parked the car and hurried in.

A sorry story was revealed. The storm had come just as swiftly in the village as it had on the mountain. Before anyone had had chance to rescue the sunshades, they had taken off. Like a flock of exotic birds they had flown in formation high above the trees. To an unknowing observer the sight must have been astonishing; half a dozen bright arcs of filled, fluttering material with trailing tails, hurtling up and onwards.

They flew to nobody knows where.

As though burying the idea of trying to turn this part of the wild north of Scotland into a European tea garden, Karl soon afterwards knocked down the wall, covered the frontage in tarmac and created a car park. Not surprisingly, this acted quite well as a lure to passing motorists and there was a reasonable amount of casual trade.

There was still, however, a notion that there should be some summer activity to complement the winter one. A consultant, had one been asked, would probably have suggested an appeal to the hunting and fishing confraternity. It was clear that Struan was destined to be no more than a one star establishment in terms of comfort and facilities but there were doubtless people of the 'sporting' interest who needed cheaper accommodation than that provided by the old Victorian hotels.

For Karl, this idea was anathema. He had experienced his share of living off the land but he was constitutionally a conservationist. His delight at hearing the call of a bird or seeing an animal going about its secret business was a joy to behold and an inspiration. The idea of chasing round the countryside with the sole purpose of slaughter was abhorrent.

He expressed this philosophy in one of his pithy, and personally revealing, phrases. To those who enquired about hunting he would say, simply, 'I am not a killer hotel.'

Uttered out of context, which occasionally it was in a general disquisition, this statement could be alarming. It might have been taken to imply that other establishments in the area routinely murdered their guests. Of course, Karl meant no such thing and neither did he intend to imply, by the use of the personal pronoun, that he *was* the hotel. The use of 'I' rather than 'this is not' was a linguistic mistake but it was also significant. It showed that Karl was so emotionally identified with his and Eileen's creation that it seemed to be a part of him.

With the obvious line of trade excluded, a fruitful indecision ruled. Many years after the events, Eileen wrote; 'We wondered what sport to introduce in the summer and seriously thought about pony trekking, discussing with Ewan Ormiston the possibility of exchange trips through the hills to Newtonmore, and about sailing. We even considered bicycle trekking and toured about a great deal on our own bikes. In the end the skiing took on so rapidly that we did nothing.'

There was, as it transpired, sufficient casual tourist trade during the summer to keep the accountant happy. In fact, on at least one occasion there was far too much. The Struan vendors had omitted to warn the new owners about the coaches. Two turned up simultaneously one day and eighty needy passengers were led by the drivers straight to the Annexe tea room.

There was an understandable moment of Struan panic. For a frantic hour the proprietors scampered up and down the garden path, betimes barking at each other through the primitive intercom, until at last the final cup of tea had been delivered. The experience was quite sufficient to convince Karl and Eileen that large scale catering for tourists would not be part of their business plan. Coaches would, in future, be politely discouraged.

There were other alarums but generally Karl had time, in the first summers, to work on the improvements. With Sandy Panton's skilful help he undertook a range of projects which incrementally, and largely unintentionally, transformed the former Scottish village residence into a charming outpost of his native land. Amongst many other touches, the two of them erected large poles. Thereafter flags, which Karl greatly cherished, fluttered along the frontage and at the ski-shed entrance.

This labour of love involved many trips to Grantown and Inverness for materials. An early Struan customer, Kinloch Anderson, whose Edinburgh-based family business supplied kilts to the royal family, remembers the dramatic closing moments of one such expedition.

He chanced to be standing outside the hotel one bright summer evening, taking the air, when he heard, in the far distance, a noise as of the wailing of a hundred devils. Being a brave man, he did not dive for cover but stepped out and peered towards the source which seemed to be located in the distant Monadliath Mountains. Villagers were out, in various states of alarm. The racket worsened; whatever the menace, it was approaching rapidly.

All at once the cause of the dreadful, mournful howling shot into view. It was a vehicle piloted by Karl who appeared to be waving apologetically to the deafened bystanders and somehow conveying that the screaming of his doughty conveyance was not entirely under his control. Impressive billowing blue clouds of pungent smoke issued from the rear. People pressed handkerchiefs to their mouths and coughed wretchedly.

Karl must, Kinloch noted with relief, at least have a measure of control because, with a shuddering crunching of gears, the car slowed a little as it turned sharply into the Struan driveway. Sadly, the degree of control was insufficient to prevent the Lea Francis lurching into the spectator's very own vehicle. There was a painful crunching of metal but at least the dreadful screeching noise ceased immediately as the wheels stopped turning.

Pained slightly, but certain that mine host would not have deliberately rammed his motor car, Kinloch looked for explanation. Karl waved apologetically. 'Accelerator jammed!' he croaked hoarsely and, as he spoke, the errant machine burst spectacularly into flames.

Karl was, as Eileen recalls, in one of his darker moods and he seemed inclined to let the treacherous motor car immolate itself but Kinloch was reluctant to be a witness to waste. In any case, there was the consideration that his own innocent conveyance might be drawn into the conflagration. He braved the flames to extract an extinguisher from his car and resolutely squirted until smoke was replaced by hissing steam.

Whether this dented the passing-motorist trade none could tell but as the first summers ticked by, an unintended Struan speciality developed which soon removed the need for gimmicks.

Guests in those founding days sometimes persuaded Karl to abandon his carpentry and to accompany them on walks. He quickly came to know the area intimately and his detailed knowledge made the excursions especially enjoyable. The visitors found that his enthusiasm for nature fired them. They were treated to informative, intriguing voyages of discovery.

Karl had learned where to find deer and where to see the bumbling capercailzie, the brilliantly plumed oyster-catcher, the charming snow bunting and the croaking ptarmigan. He could show the walkers where the snow hares lived and convey something roughly comprehensible about their clever trick of changing coats from winter white to summer brown, a perfect strategy of camouflage if only the snow had been reliable. On the long, flat walk through Glen Einich to the terrifying cliffs and the deep, long loch he would encourage any flagging hikers with the word that, if they were lucky, they might see a broad-spanned eagle launching itself from a ledge hundreds of feet above them.

Eileen remembers that; 'Karl was always a wildlife enthusiast and he soon found the guests wanted to accompany him bird watching, deer spotting and mushrooming. This developed before too long into a regular programme of hill walking, ranging from local walks around Carrbridge and the Cairngorm foothills to mammoth expeditions.' Apart from being able to identify fungi, Karl was not anywhere near as expert on flora as he was on fauna. He liked things that moved and the intensity of his delight at the doings of animals easily compensated for the lack of knowledge about plants.

Struan's reputation as a hill-walking centre began to match that of the ski school. People returned, and recommended the establishment to friends, because they found Karl's expeditions uniquely enjoyable.

As always, the countryside spoke for itself but Karl's presence amplified the message. Without pretentiousness he would say, 'The mountains are my church'. Newcomers to wild walking were subtly introduced to the rubric of his 'church' as they went along; shut gates, light no fires, take debris home. When his groups had finished eating their alfresco meals he would rigorously check that every scrap of evidence of human presence had been removed. His companions felt as though they had participated in something beyond the ordinary and perhaps it was no exaggeration to suggest that they had been involved in a secular ceremony of praise.

There was a further attraction which brought people back year after year which was simply the force of Karl's personality. He managed that rare feat of charming the women with innocent flirtation without alienating the men. He possessed a charisma which made others want to please him. He engendered trust. On the summits, in the bewildering mists, the hikers followed. With very good reason they believed that the leader would bring them safely home. He was also unusually thoughtful. One young woman who chose to spend her birthday climbing up Ben Macdhui was astonished and delighted when, at the summit, Karl produced bottles of bitter lemon from his capacious rucksack and invited everyone to drink a toast.

The range of walking was almost inexhaustible and certainly more than sufficient to occupy people for a fortnight. There were local expeditions to the nearby gem of Loch Vaa, easy rambles from the Loch an Eilein car park round that exquisite paradigm of a mountain lake and more adventurous treks beyond Carrbridge station towards Dalnahatnaich. Further afield lay Glen Feshie and the Giant's Face, and a host of other intriguing and delightful areas including the remnants of General Wade's astonishing road. On one exploratory occasion Karl followed this military highway all the way to Inverness. 'Never again', was his heartfelt comment, an expression that was to be used more than once in Struan's history of long-distance walking.

Walkers could seek shelter in the riverside bothy known as Bynack Stable or eat lunch in the more substantial, stone-built mountain shelter of Ryvoan. There was the stride through the deep heather to Forest Lodge along the banks of the turbulent River Nethy, or the delight of hiding from the elements beneath the imposing bulk of the Shelter Stone. There were the mountain lochs, Einich, Etchachan and Avon. Then, literally above all, there were the true mountain expeditions to the summits of Cairngorm, Ben Macdhui, Cairntoul and Braeriach; the ancient bastions, the four-square markers of the great, long cleft of the Larig Ghru.

In the earliest years, Karl would prepare a little surprise for the walkers who ventured onto the peaks. As they breasted the summit of Cairngorm and moved down towards the snow-holding steepness of Ciste Meridh he would ask if anyone fancied trying their legs at skiing.

Naturally, his followers thought that he was joking. Where was the equipment?

As though by chance, Karl would then stumble into a particular patch of deep heather and perform his conjuring trick of producing skis. In those days there was no need for special boots; anybody could be strapped to the laths and sent hurtling down the corrie. It was an alarming slope for beginners, none too comforting for the more expert either, but many had their first downhill slide on such a summer's day.

Eileen used to worry that word would go round and that some unscrupulous person would steal the skis. Karl reassured her that anyone capable of doing the walk, and locating the equipment, would be a mountain person and therefore too noble to descend to the depths of petty theft. The skis, he maintained, were safe.

He was right about the skis but one day when he performed his magic trick he discovered that all the bindings had been taken. There was, apparently, no absolute honour amongst hill walkers. It was the end of the surprise skiing.

The grand finale of the walking fortnight was almost always the marathon-length trek through the Larig Ghru. This was managed by hiring a bus to meet the walkers on the other side of the mountains. Although she loved hiking, Eileen always used to feel sorry for the Larig party as it set off. They might have become supremely fit during their stay, they might have coped with Cairngorm and Ben Macdhui but they had no idea, she believed, of what they were about to face, otherwise they probably would not do it.

She had made the trip twice. On the second occasion, in extremely misty conditions, she had struggled along, just keeping sight of the last-but-one person in the group. She was, as she recalls, 'nearly dead' as the group came to the Sinclair Hut, an edifice which in the deep gloom came as a complete surprise to her. Staggering gratefully into its sheltering starkness she saw a graffito which expressed her sentiments precisely. It said 'Never again' and, just like Karl with his General Wade's road walk to Inverness, she repeated the words with firm purpose.

But Karl, who had taken such a dislike to the old Inverness road, had no negative feelings about walking through the mountains. He completed the journey many times, on one occasion with a Frenchwoman who insisted on walking in bare feet. Eileen's empathy with him, and with the others who submitted themselves more or less innocently to the torture, increased whenever the party was late getting back to Struan. As the summers passed, the hour of return got later and later. 'What a terrible time they must have had,' she solicitously thought.

It was only when she discovered that the ever-increasing lateness was caused by stops at virtually every licensed establishment on the long drive back that her feelings changed radically.

There were days, of course, when even the most intrepid were deterred by appalling weather or when aching limbs simply needed a rest. On such occasions, Karl used to take guests on minibus trips, often to the West Coast, with Loch Maree and Inverewe gardens as favourite ports of call. Loch Ness and Urquhart Castle, the exquisite Randolph's Leap where the rivers Findhorn and Divie spectacularly meet, the east coast beaches and many other enticing venues provided alternative excursions. A whole week of vile weather could be fruitfully occupied.

Few of the hikers would spurn the opportunity of at least one recuperative motor trip but generally they braved whatever the Cairngorms could throw at them. Even in the summer months the unwary faced great risks in that broad stretch of wilderness but Karl's expeditions always returned home safely. He knew his 'church' as well as anybody knew it and he knew how to make his congregation sing.

## 14. We'm a Familie

The success of the ski school and the guided walking was very largely secured by Karl's skill and charisma. It is extremely doubtful, though, whether the teaching and trekking venture would have survived without the hotel. Had the enterprising pair simply set themselves up as an outdoor academy, with a small office or perhaps a shop as a base, it is almost certain that they would have been heading south, defeated, after a season or two. The school and the hotel were symbiotically related.

Yet, for the first few years, the establishment scarcely warranted the use of the word 'hotel'. The name 'Struan *House*' was entirely appropriate. The building was essentially a large family home. Guests coming through the front entrance faced no daunting reception suite; they saw just doors off into inviting rooms and a staircase against the left hand wall, curving round to the right, onto a landing which gave access to old-fashioned bedrooms. The house kitchen and bathrooms were on a similar domestic scale. There was a garage, there were outhouses and a garden. It was a country residence.

The setting was homely, and so was the approach of the new couple. They were not trained professionals in the hotel business. They came with no marketing strategy, nor catering concepts such as 'portion control'. They were intent on looking after people. When it came to paying bills at the end of holidays there was no consultation of ledgers nor production of neatly printed slips. Invoices were compiled, as a guest graphically expressed it, 'on a confessional basis'. In the midst of a conversation about the week or fortnight just gone Eileen would ask, 'What did you have?' and the account would be compiled according to the answer. There was total trust and this helped to foster the notion of extended family.

The meals, too, reinforced the feeling of kinship. They were like the home-cooked versions; wholesome food carefully prepared. Just as in a family, there was no menu. 'You'll eat what you're given,' was the unspoken message and most accepted this in good spirit.

A further factor was the relative isolation of the hotel. Virtually all of the normal services available in towns and cities were at a distance. As far as possible, Struan had to become the reliable provider, a safe place of refuge and in this respect, too, it was like a home.

The birth of Peter, in October 1955, and Lisi just under two years later, helped to reinforce the family feeling. Through a series of creative conversions, the outhouses were turned into a residence. Part of the original garage became Peter's bedroom with the residue being made into a small shop; the second of Karl's ski rooms was pressed into service as Lisi's bedroom whilst one of the remaining segments was turned into a bathroom.

*A corner of the dining room*

There was also a long term process of self-selection as far as the guest list was concerned. First-time visitors either loved or loathed the homely style. Those looking for haute cuisine or five star comfort were quickly out of the door never to return. Any who celebrated the fact that Struan was more like a glorified hostel than a hotel came back year after year. Many of the guests liked stacking the dishes in the dining room to help the waiters and welcomed the fact that they could be totally at ease.

In such an atmosphere, new friendships grew very quickly. People who normally lived hundreds of miles from each other would make plans to 'meet at Struan' at the same time next year. The interpersonal bonds spread out in a chaining process as other new friendships were formed and introductions made.

The proprietors unwittingly became mother and father to this accumulating tribe. It was not that they appeared like patriarch and matriarch, far from it. At the outset, Karl was very fit and lithe and Eileen was a fine young woman in her physical prime. A local resident, who was a teenaged schoolgirl at the time of the Fuchs' arrival in Carrbridge, has a vivid early memory which confirms this latter point. She says that on the school bus, all of the lewd, spotty fifteen year old boys would twist round and leer through the windows as the trim newcomer walked through the village in a pretty pink dress. No; age was irrelevant. Karl and Eileen were the providers, the carers and, as far as skiing was concerned, the great fount of desired knowledge. They had parent-like roles.

With different personalities and innate skills in its proprietors, the hotel would not have developed as it did. Eileen was the efficient one, the businesswoman, the controller of the show. Karl was the genial, generous host. They proffered a safe structure allied with a generous giving. As in all families, there were tensions. Karl's urge to give sometimes seemed to extend beyond sensible boundaries. It was Eileen who had to haul on the reins of expenditure. One who knew the couple well at the time recalls that Karl would buy expensive clothes for his wife which she would wear only on very special occasions whilst she, by stark contrast, would darn and mend, making things last.

Few, if any, of the guests were aware of the occasional conflicts and there were overwhelmingly positive factors to mask them. For example, Eileen soon began to reveal an astonishing capacity for recalling not only the faces and names of guests but minute detail about their lives and families. After a gap of years she could greet people with genuine warmth, as though they were the closest of friends. She would ask, 'How's Sandra getting on with the baby?' or, 'Did George pass his exams?' and rare indeed were the mistakes. It was stunningly affirming to be so accurately recalled.

Karl's memory for people was also good but what little he lacked in that department he made up for in a special confidential brand of conviviality. Somehow he compelled people to want to be his acknowledged friend. His achievements in the field of personal relationships are in some respects more astonishing than Eileen's because of his idiosyncratic use of language. Eileen talked like a speeded-up tape player, conveying information at a formidable rate. By contrast, many people had difficulty in understanding what Karl was saying yet they felt valued by him. A word or nod of approval often had as much significance as that of a father to a needy child.

There were those who claimed that Karl's linguistic development was contrived and there is a case to be made in support of this view. He was certainly an intelligent man, he was married to a woman whose verbal skills were outstanding and he was surrounded by English-speakers, yet he spoke in a composite of languages which was uniquely his. What could this be other than an elaborate act?

Those who claim that Karl's speech was a performance further their argument by observing that he was by nature a consummate showman. They suggest that he found, early on, that many people were fascinated by his diction and so he made it a prime part of his repertoire of attractive tricks. If this is so, the strategy certainly worked. His mode of speech became a trademark, friends affectionately imitated it. It was not only the sound which admirers copied, they would attempt to replicate all the facial expressions and gestures which so graphically conveyed the amusement, anger, enthusiasm, bewilderment, sometimes even despair which 'mine host' was so palpably experiencing. Naturally Karl's intonation had Scottish influences so people referred to his mode of speech as 'Scotstrian'.

Scotstrian was akin to pidgin; recognisably based on English but with its own vocabulary and grammar. Karl would use something like, 'I kop sex bindle stick,' to indicate that he had carried six bundles of slalom poles up the mountain. 'We are a family', a favourite expression, emerged as, 'We'm a fameelyi'. Highland cattle became 'kettles'. Names of people invariably had the German definite article before them; Die Mary, Der Tom, although confusingly he would not always match the genders. 'Die Bill' was not intended to cast doubt about Bill's manhood, it was just the way Karl sometimes chose to speak. It was as though 'Die', 'Der', 'Das' and 'The' became fused in Scotstrian to become an indefinite definite article.

To complicate matters further, Karl invented his own linguistic logic to accompany the novel grammar. His juxtaposition of ideas was often powerful and graphic but to the uninitiated, the meaning could be obscure. He would characterise people very accurately, often resorting to comparisons with animals. Those who did not realise, with sufficient alacrity, that they were in the realms of metaphor struggled to understand why Karl was rattling on about elephants or giraffes.

And the form of words and ideas was not the only intriguing thing about Karl's utterances. He talked very quickly with wide variations of pitch and inflexion. Often his speeches were like a racy version of plain chant; not quite songs but nearly so.

Writing presented problems because his preferred method was the elegant Kurserschrift which no untrained person could decipher. Lists and notes to others had therefore to be penned in capital letters, generally with English words but often spelled phonetically in the Austrian fashion. Thus 'rubbish' appeared as 'rabitsch'. As Eileen comments, it was really necessary to know both languages to gain full understanding.

In spite of this partial adherence to his linguistic heritage, Karl found it difficult, on return trips to Austria, to revert immediately to his original language. For two days or so he would bemuse friends and family by continuing to speak a Germanic version of Scotstrian. Then, as though a switch had been thrown, he would recover full fluency and all trace of his invented tongue would vanish.

It is, in fact, highly unlikely that Karl did anything other than what came naturally in the matter of his speech. He was a pragmatist, an instant doer. He needed to communicate so he just pitched in. For as long as his words more or less did their business he had no need for further refinement. It is unimaginable, in any case, that anyone could keep up such an act. He reached a point where he was just about linguistically viable and there he stuck.

This view is strongly supported by Norbert Uitz who knew Karl better than most and who could communicate fluently with him in German and English. Norbert's view is that Karl was very frequently frustrated by his deficiencies in the local language. So often his contributions were misunderstood. Seminal ideas about the development of skiing in Scotland were lost because Karl had failed to get his point across. Norbert sees a sadness in this; it was almost as though his colleague and friend was in a linguistic prison and that sometimes he was lonely as a result.

Lisi, who used sometimes to 'translate' for Karl when she was older, agrees that there were frustrations. She believes that Karl almost never misunderstood what someone was saying but suffered greatly from his inability to convey his own meaning. She says that the irritation was worsened because some of the apparent misuses of words, which people took to be mistakes, were in fact deliberate. It amused Karl to refer to highland cattle as 'kettles' and to speak of the elite of British motor cars as a 'Royals Royce'.

The children, as they grew, picked up some German from their grandparents but Karl did his best to speak English with them because he thought that it would be confusing to subject them to two languages. The wonder is that they did not develop into Scotstrian speakers.

The linguistic ambivalence with which Peter and Lisi grew up was reinforced when their Uncle John, in a neat symmetry with his sister, asked an Austrian to be his bride. This match became possible because Maurice was asked by some Austrian friends to find a placement for their nineteen year old niece, Elfi, who was keen to improve her English. Maurice duly located a family which was looking for a nursemaid. There the young Austrian, according to family legend, spoke not at all for a couple of weeks or so but listened intently. Then, when she was ready, she burst into fluent English.

John met her at the house where she was working. A friendship quickly developed to the extent that he brought Elfi up to Carrbridge. No sooner had they returned from the trip than John telephoned Eileen to say that they had become engaged.

In fact, John and Elfi were too far away, and too busy with their own lives, to be an integral part of the immediate Struan family but they were regular visitors and they joined in the larger network. Maurice was able to travel north more frequently and he became, over the years, something of the silver-haired patriarch. Constantly genial, ever interested in everything around him, he seemed to have no enemies. Once Karl and Eileen's children were born he was 'Grandpa', not just to Peter and Lisi but to almost everyone.

*Oma peels apples for a strudel whilst Opa mows the lawn*

There was also a 'Grandma' who, because she was Austrian, was called 'Oma'. For the first three years or so, Oma was accompanied by Opa, who loved to help Karl with the garden and whatever construction projects the ex-patriate had under way. Until he died in 1958, Opa helped Karl to keep pigs and chickens in the Struan garden. He even built a small smokery which produced delicious joints of smoked ham using herbs and ingredients he had brought from Austria. Eileen remembers that these home-produced foods had absolutely authentic Austrian flavour. Karl and his father also made barrels of sauerkraut in the Annexe and found various sorts of edible mushrooms highly prized on the Continent but then regarded as poisonous toadstools by most British people.

Generally, guests were willing to try new foods but in the 1950's very few British people had been abroad. There was some resistance. Eileen particularly remembers one evening when Oma had exceeded even her own impeccable standards. The resulting Wiener schnitzel and apfelstrudel were almost too preciously tasty to eat.

After the meal, one of the diners knocked on the kitchen door. Anticipating a flood of astonished compliments, Eileen beamed in welcome. The man, backed by his disgruntled family, was not in a positive mood. 'Call that a dinner? Well, you can keep it!' he grumbled, implying, but not saying, 'Bloody foreign muck!' Eileen recalls that Oma eventually gave up making Austrian soups, with all the mouth watering nockerln and knodeln, because people ate the 'background' soup and left the main ingredients.

In the kitchen that evening, learning Oma's cunning culinary tricks, was a woman called Jessie Hewlett who was to play a major part in the development of Struan as an extended family unit.

Jessie hailed from a tiny, beautiful place called Achiltibuie on the West Scottish coast, not far from Ullapool in Wester Ross. She was of an independent nature and when, as a very young woman, she was asked by a locally born doctor who had moved down to Surrey to work for him, she migrated willingly. She would often speak of the terror which London induced from the very moment of arrival at Euston but she overcame the fear and remained away from home until the wartime deaths of two of her brothers, killed on the same day, brought her back to Scotland.

She had not been long home when she met her husband-to-be, Alan Hewlett, a tall, wiry, weathered, blue-eyed Newfoundlander. He had migrated to Scotland to ply his trade of forester although in time he took employment on the railway. It was this work which brought the couple, via a spell in Grantown, to Carrbridge in 1957. They lived in a council house close to Struan, with their two daughters and son. The children were old enough for Jessie to supplement the family income with work in the Fuchs' hotel. Eileen writes of her; 'Jessie was supremely capable, a splendid organiser and, as we subsequently discovered, an excellent cook but to us she was above all a true and utterly loyal family friend and a second mother to our children.'

Physically she was below average in height, perhaps slightly over the weight that doctors would recommend and with a kindly, bespectacled face that sometimes showed that her life had not been entirely easy. The thinning, curly hair was greying. Under the stresses of cooking for large numbers she could let her anxiety show yet generally she was warm and welcoming, ever ready to listen, always solicitous. Her only visible vice was smoking, which she indulged in to excess, the cause perhaps of a persistent wheeze which was particularly evident when she laughed, which she did with great frequency.

Jessie was a 'second mother' to many more than Peter and Lisi.

As Struan developed, it attracted an ever changing band of workers most of whom stayed only for a season or two. There were students on long vacations, travellers earning sufficient money to move on to the next county, country or continent, people in the midst of major career changes, others who were unsure as to what they wanted to do with the rest of their lives and those who simply wanted to jump off the tread-mill for a while. All of these were far from home and for most of them Jessie became a major focus.

Jessie's close friend and near neighbour, Mrs. Taylor, eventually joined the extended family. She too was a mother, strong in spirit but soft of heart, who also became a great befriender to the itinerant workers. The two women were close in very many ways, they could easily have passed for sisters, yet they never referred to each other, in public or in private, as anything other than 'Mrs. Hewlett' and 'Mrs. Taylor'.

Another of Jessie's near neighbours, Evelyn Fleming, was also a Struan recruit. Evelyn was of a different mould from the homely Jessie and 'Mrs. T.' She was slim, smart and with a very visible energy. She worked quickly and efficiently, spicing the days of those around her with bursts of sharp, sardonic humour. Evelyn was a free spirit. The extra money which she earned went, in part, to the purchase of a scooter on which she toured the area, undaunted by steep hills and indifferent road surfaces.

Apparently on a whim Evelyn dyed her hair to a brilliant red, a shocking thing for a Carrbridge resident to do, and declared gleefully that the change had switched her character to an even more extrovert mode. She doted on her dog, a huge, soppy boxer which delighted in cuddling up to alarmed guests of the Fleming residence. The man of the house, Gordon, seemed to observe his wife's doings with highly amused tolerance. Their one son, Colin, who was to become a close friend and ski companion to Struan's Peter, developed his own laconic way of handling his mother's natural ebullience. Evelyn was strong of opinion, sharp of mind and alarmingly witty; the kind of person who is invaluable as a friend and totally terrifying as an enemy.

In complete contrast with Evelyn, in almost every dimension, was an Englishwoman who, for the early Struan workers, will forever be depicted in memory as a forlorn figure flopped over the sink peeling hundreds and hundreds of potatoes. The eventual acquistion of a machine happily removed this chore for her successors. There was also Daisy, a superb cook but very unreliable in timekeeping and temperament. On one occasion she hit the highly benign Jessie on the head with a pan and then contrived to have a fearsome argument with the normally equable Evelyn. She had to go.

If Jessie and 'Mrs T' were mothers in the Struan family, Evelyn and others were perhaps aunts but there were also other 'relatives'. One couple, John and Margot from Glasgow, were for a while so integrated into the kinship that they ran the hotel when the proprietors went on holiday. Very often they were to be found helping out in various ways and for none of this work did they expect to be paid.

Equally integrated into the Struan community, though paid for her contribution, was Rosie Bell who had worked for the Duke of Atholl, managing his ponies, and who made frequent visits to Blair Atholl to keep in touch with friends. Like many of the people associated with the place, Rosie was adaptable. For a number of years she helped Karl with the guided walks but she was just as happy doing domestic or kitchen tasks.

It was Rosie who, on duty late one evening, was alerted to the alarming fact that blue smoke was issuing copiously from the fuse box cupboard on the landing. Acting with her usual good sense and efficiency she called the fire brigade and then warned everyone to evacuate their rooms. All sensibly complied except a couple in a firmly locked Room Four who were on their honeymoon. Just what they were engaged in that took precedence over survival was left to inspired guesswork but not even the full exercise of Rosie's extremely forceful character could shift them.

It would have been easy to abandon them to their fate but Rosie could not bring herself to be an accomplice in the incineration of newly-weds. She elected, instead, to sit on a chair placed tactically by the billowing box. The plan was that as soon as the flames appeared she would update the doting lovers and hope that the actual fact of visible fire might shift their list of priorities.

She was still faithfully keeping her vigil when the 'brigade', in the manly shape of the local representative of the hydro-electricity board, arrived. Not one for standing on ceremony under such circumstances he smote the smoking fuse box with his axe. Sadly it is not recorded how the lovers dealt with this well-intentioned vandalism but neither they, nor any of the other guests, suffered anything other than a temporary inconvenience.

Another 'sister' in the relatively local Struan family was a young woman called Daphne Fausset-Farquhar who, as her name suggests, was not of the peasantry. Whatever her social standing, she was as down-to-earth as any villager but her mother had issued strict instructions that she was not to undertake any 'domestic' work at Struan. She would, however, do what she could and guests from cities were sometimes startled to see teenaged Daphne sitting in the kitchen, her dramatic long black hair flowing, expertly plucking some pot-destined fowl. In spite of the age difference, she related very well to Karl, perhaps because of their shared love of the countryside. It was not unusual for guests on local walks to come across Daphne charging across open territory on her horse, boldly taking gates and burns in its capacious stride and skidding to a halt in streams of heather fragments mixed with mud.

There were also many others in the local community, much closer geographically to Struan than Rosie and Daphne, who played the roles of siblings or cousins or just plain friends in the family. Jessie's two daughters, Miree and Jean often helped with the work, as did Evelyn's Colin as soon as he reached a suitable age.

And then the very success of the venture spread the village net wider.

From the earliest days there were times, particularly on public holidays, when demand for accommodation was too great for Struan to meet. Eileen turned to the local people for help and found several households who were only too willing to absorb the excess. The only practical problem with this was that, for the first few years, and until Eileen used some aristocratic connections to exercise political influence, there was no street lighting in the village. Those returning to their lodgings after an evening's conviviality often had to grope their way.

The nearest of these satellites, the easiest to locate in the gloaming, was the substantial house to the side of Struan on the way towards Aviemore. 'Crannich' was the home of Mrs. Anderson, a tall, slim woman with steel-grey hair and sapphire eyes, the archetype of the older Scottish widow. She looked after her guests devotedly, fed them sumptuously and gave no obvious cause for caution yet there were many who would rather spend a shelterless winter's night on Cairngorm than cross Mrs. Anderson. She was possessed of great natural authority which few dared to challenge.

One of the first to open the doors of her home, Kinchyle, was Mrs. Ferguson. Her husband had been gardener at Struan when it was a private house and he made a point of always presenting the Fuchs with some of the season's first strawberries. There were also two women called Grant who regularly catered for the Struan overspill and these were distinguished not in the Welsh way by occupation but by the names of their houses. 'You're at Mrs Grant Ellanard's' was a declaration which made perfect sense to generations of Struanites. Mrs. Ritchie, singular of designation, needed no such qualification but she, Mrs. Paul and others became favourites to the point where some Struan guests, especially those with young children, booked to be in one of the houses rather than the hotel.

There were, of course, other hotels and guest houses in the village. The number of these expanded steadily as the ski industry developed but Struan, like a tree securing its basis for growth, spread its roots. It was very much a part of the place.

To the regular Struan visitor the perspective on Carrbridge presented by the hotel's interaction with the local community was predominantly female. Jessie and Mrs. Taylor, Evelyn and Mrs. Walker, the Mrs Grants, Anderson, Ferguson, Ritchie and the others; these were the points of immediate contact. For the most part the husbands seemed to keep to themselves.

Soon after Jessie joined the establishment, Struan took another major step forward in the process of forming its own unique familial identity.

Although it was possible to have convivial evenings in the dining room, with drinks brought in, guests who were fond of carousing repeatedly suggested that it would be so much better if Struan had its own bar. With closing time set at nine o'clock, and with dinner at seven, there was very little time to make the daunting, unlighted trek down the village to the Rowanlea or the Carrbridge Hotel. Serious drinkers, of whom there were a few, found it particularly frustrating.

By 1958 there was even no problem as to where the bar could be installed, for the ground floor bedroom, which Karl and Eileen had used initially, was no longer needed because the conversion of the outhouses had been completed.

Application was made for a licence. The official response was as before; that bars could be created only for local convenience. There being two public drinking places already in the village, the authorities argued that there were absolutely no grounds for opening another. The Fuchs vigorously countered that there was a new dimension; the needs of tourists. This was stoutly resisted, especially by Jimmy Ross, the Rowanlea landlord, and Alistair MacIntyre, whose domain was the Carrbridge Hotel.

A campaign was clearly necessary and a vigorous one began. Regular visitors used whatever weight they could bring to bear and many of the villagers joined in. One, Major Caldwell, was particularly active. Usually kilted, often to be seen in his ancient yellow Rolls-Royce with its tiny rear window, he used all his influence. As the possessor of the table at which Bonnie Prince Charlie had allegedly dined before the battle of Culloden, as the custodian of another historic piece of furniture on which the Irish State Treaty had been signed in Inverness in 1922, as the unlikely host to a totem pole presented by Queen Salote of Tonga on an improbable visit to Carrbridge, the retired soldier was not to be brushed aside.

Eileen celebrates the eventual victory; 'Our first real breakthrough came in the autumn of 1958 when, in the teeth of fierce opposition from other local hotels but egged on by our residents, and helped by a number of far-sighted people, we established a precedent by getting a drinks licence for the benefit of tourists. Up until then the criterion had been local need alone and our own very able lawyer, Robin MacEwan, managed to convince both the local licensing court at Kingussie and later the regional court at Inverness that in view of the rapid growth Karli had engendered in the skiing industry the time had come for a change of policy. This he did in a fierce and quite dramatic debate with lawyers from the opposing hotels and the courts had no hesitation in granting our application.'

What Eileen omits to mention, in this particular recollection, was that they had to pay a substantial sum to the Seafield Estate for their 'consideration' of the change but they felt that it was money well spent. Eileen adds; 'And so the Edelweiss bar came into existence, lovingly built in the Austrian style by Karli with the help of Sandy Panton. It was the cosiest and most intimate of bars and became the very heart of Struan with a unique atmosphere of Austrian gemutlichkeit. Karli's mother and my father loved the bar and greatly contributed to its atmosphere and many were the continental sing-songs they initiated.'

The involvement of Sandy Panton in the creation of the Edelweiss was extraordinary in that he was a very dedicated teetotaller, as were not a few in the immediate vicinity. He was also, though, a tolerant man who felt no need to impose his views on others. He was very much a part of the Struan family and was entirely happy to help in whatever way Karl chose.

Soon after the bar's inception, Karl took to sitting alone in the Edelweiss listening to records of Austrian music. It was a place that could induce great tranquillity. Not infrequently, guests would drink there in contemplation or engaging with others in quiet conversation but peace is not the attribute which most Struanites associate with the Edelweiss. Primarily it was the venue for conviviality, a room where high spirits could lead readily to a heady wildness.

The facility deserves, and duly receives later in this book, particular attention. It was, as Eileen claims, Struan's 'very heart' and many were the memorable occasions to which it played glad host.

## 15. The Ski Road

The Scotsman of November 12th 1958 treated its readers to a full page montage of photographs under the heading, 'Route of Cairngorm Motorway'. The caption under the half page main picture, which showed a very peaceful scene where the Coronation footbridge crossed a burn, announced that; 'Work is to begin soon on a road which will provide easier access for skiers and other visitors to the higher slopes of the Cairngorms'. Another picture showed the ski runs which were being brought into the range of the motor car.

*The White Lady and the Coire Cas are the two main ski runs which will be easily reached from the car park. At a short distance is Jean's Hut, used by summer mountaineers and winter skiers.*

The newspaper revealed that the road was to be ten feet wide, with a maximum gradient of 1 in 10 and with thirteen passing places to the mile. The car park, to be constructed on a slightly sloping natural plateau, would have space for two hundred vehicles.

The Strathspey Winter Sports Development Board changed its name, replacing the first word with 'Cairngorm'. At the first meeting under the new title, the County Council representative announced that a start would be made on the mountain road on March 31st 1959. It was estimated that the work would be finished within a year.

Some very encouraging financial news was given to the Board's members. The total projected cost of the highway had risen to over £36,000, a sum far beyond the original estimates, but of this the local council would have to find less than ten per cent. The County Council contribution had been fortuitously supplemented by input from the Forestry Commission, which had a vested interest in the project, and by a government grant. This latter contribution was perhaps not unconnected with the fact that the then Secretary of State for Scotland was a keen member of the Scottish Ski Club.

By these acts of public largesse, most of the money raised by the Development Board was released for other projects. Naturally, thoughts turned immediately to uplift. A chair from near the car park to the summit ridge would begin to turn Cairngorm into a ski area on Alpine lines. Thanks to Philip Rankin's commercial initiative, the dogged developers of Glencoe would have the very first Scottish chairlift, linking the car park with the drag lift, but there was no reason why the ambitious Cairngorm team, late starters in the development race, should not be close behind.

As the road project neared completion, the media activity spread beyond the heavyweight papers. The middle-ranking *News Chronicle* despatched a reporter, John London, northwards in February 1960. He followed the time-honoured journalistic tradition of writing enthusiastically but with an economy of truth. Under the headline, 'Scots strike it rich among the snowfields' he enthused:

'I have just been discovering how to go skiing without a pocketful of travellers' cheques and a wallet loaded with foreign currency. Over the weekend I went to Carrbridge in Inverness-shire, the centre of Scotland's fastest growing industry - winter sports. The Scots call Carrbridge and other towns among the snowy Cairngorms their 'Wee Switzerland'.

'Swap the porridge and oatcakes for schnitzel and strudel and in Carrbridge you might think the term 'Little Austria' more appropriate. Carrbridge boasts its own Austrian ski school. Seven years ago Karl Fuchs, the man who started the school, was a policeman pounding the beat in Vienna. Then he met the Liverpool-born girl Eileen who is now his wife. They decided to start a skiing school in Scotland. After two hard years came the big breakthrough. Now Karl owns a hotel which is fully booked from December until May.

'More than 40,000 visitors come to the Cairngorms for winter sports every year. With more hotel rooms and amenities like an electrically operated chairlift (to be installed next season), the numbers will undoubtedly still grow. The average hotel charges about £2 a day, with free instruction thrown in. Two young London school-teachers I met were taking their half-term holidays in the Cairngorms. "It works out about half the price of an Austrian holiday", said 26 year old Pamela Isaac, who has skied in Austria. "Also I think this is much better for beginners because each person gets more individual attention." '

In spite of the irritating inaccuracies, the publicity was heady material for Karl and Eileen. It was hard to believe that only half a dozen years previously, professional ski activity in the Spey Valley had been their own private dream. But Karl's excitement was not total. In the first place, he had by no means shed his doubts about the wisdom of opting for a road. Having had more day-to-day experience of Cairngorm skiing than almost anybody else, he knew that there would be acute problems in maintaining access at times when it was most needed, that is, when snowfalls were heavy,

Karl's second major worry concerned the proposed line of the new highway. In an article written some years later by Eileen on her husband's behalf he comments; 'The road was to go up to the right of the Sugar Bowl, thus leaving Coire na Ciste, the best of our runs, a long trudge away. I had often urged that the road should cross the first burn higher up than the Bailey bridge, go to the left of the Sugar Bowl, thus starting near the bottom of Coire na Ciste, and then traverse to the right across the top of the Sugar Bowl.'

He was concerned, too, about the proposed chairlift. The suggested pylon route was close to where he and Eileen had been reduced to crawling on all fours. It would certainly be affected badly by high winds on many days of the winter. Much more practical, environmentally friendly and exciting would be a funicular all the way from Aviemore or, even better, from a purpose-built village nestling in the forest on the mountainside shores of Loch Morlich. There would be no smelly exhaust fumes, no great swathe of tar, no unsightly lines of parked cars, just a largely concealed track curving up the hill with discreet stations at the level of the proposed car park and at the summit. The railway would attract summer visitors too; it would be a year-round earner.

Karl's reservations, and his dreams of a truly imaginative development, went unheeded. The idea of a road was fixed firmly in the minds of the planners. It was what they knew, something comfortingly familiar. The route was also a foregone conclusion.

Whatever the detail, the changes presented some dilemmas for Karl and Eileen. Naturally they saw all the activity as a vindication of their brave decision to open a ski school in the area but there were threats. Whilst conditions were primitive it was of no great consequence that Carrbridge was so far from the main slopes. Often Slochd or the Giant's Face were just as attractive as Coire Cas. Once the access was made much easier and the uplift provided, places such as Carrbridge could easily be marginalised. New hotels would surely open in Aviemore and perhaps even on the Glenmore road. Who would then tolerate the daily extra driving from what would become satellite villages?

There were other pressures. It was already obvious that their cosy Struan House was too small. Presumably there would be a massive upsurge in demand once the mountain facilities were built. At the very least it seemed that Karl and Eileen should expand their operation but would it not be altogether more sensible to re-locate to a dream site, close to the Glenmore road, perhaps even, if land and planning permission could be obtained, close to the waters of Loch Morlich?

There were counter-arguments to this enticing notion. However cunningly they designed a new building it would be difficult if not impossible to replicate Struan's style. There was also the consideration that they were firmly rooted in the village; it would be risking death perhaps to transplant so radically. Their most loyal workers were local and few of them had independent transport. To lose Jessie and her colleagues would be a severe blow.

No decisions had been made about Struan's future when, in the 1960 Easter holiday period, it was possible for skiers to walk up the rough-cut road. Some were even lucky enough to hitch precarious lifts on the backs of slow-moving lorries. In the summer, the road was open to motorists. The way was there for the ski lift constructors to drive all their heavy equipment to the site.

Then the Cairngorm climate took a hand. It was as though the ancient, waking giant had decided to shake the irritating excrescence off its back. Eileen writes; 'The summer of 1960 saw the road completed but in August came the dramatic storm which sent torrents of water down the burn, changed its course, hurtled hundreds of large trees and boulders down and completely washed away a long stretch of the new road, stranding a number of pioneer motorists on the wrong side of the flood. The debris is still plainly to be seen where the road starts to climb.'

Myrtle Simpson notes that there was also serious damage higher up, where culverts were blocked by heavy boulders. It might have been a signal that the road was not intended to be but the County Council, having invested so much faith and capital, could not just leave the scarring track as a folly. They dug into the coffers once more and produced another £8,000, sufficient to repair the damage. The ski road was open for the 1961 season but there was no lift.

The lack of a chair was a disappointment but, through Eileen, Karl gave subsequent thanks for what was by no means a small mercy. They declare; 'It was indeed fortunate that the road was ready for the winter of 1960-61, for the snow was scant. We spent most of the winter in the Lurcher's Corrie which held the snow well that year, and were forced to go up to the top of Coire na Ciste only for the last week of the season in April. Fortunately skiers at that time had not developed the aversion they now have to walking and, grateful that they could at any rate drive up to the car park, they accepted cheerfully the half hour cross-country trek to the Lurcher's Coire.'

But, as with most innovations, there were unanticipated drawbacks. Karl remembers; 'The season brought quite new hazards in motoring up the road. Sanding arrangements were at first not at all adequate and day after day I and other unfortunates had to run uphill in front of our buses, shovelling sand onto the icy surface from roadside heaps or, failing that, scattering heather roots and soil as we went. Every so often passengers had to get out of the bus and push or lift it or a passing motorist out of the ditch. One evening, on the way down, our bus skidded at the worst S-bend at the Sugar Bowl and its back tore a few yards out of the outside fencing before it skidded onto its own side of the road.'

Karl's road reminiscence continues; 'Another evening, the driver suddenly came upon a car parked with its back sticking out of a lay-by opposite a sheer drop down to the river. As there was no room for him to pass, he put on his brakes. Unfortunately he skidded straight into the car. His last-minute horror was redoubled when he saw it was a police car. As most of our local police were in it, our dinner was very late that night and our skiers were kept busy afterwards making statements.'

During that lift-less season it turned out that natural hazards were not the only impediments to the installation of the long-awaited chair. Confident that they would be able to raise the required 'matching' £20,000 to secure the generous anonymous donation, the Board had placed a contract with a partnership of Swiss and Scottish companies but the Scottish firm met unexpected practical difficulties and failed to deliver their side of the bargain. There was a legal dispute which precluded alternative action by the Board.

As if this were not sufficient of a headache, it then became clear that the fund-raising effort was falling far short of its target. The potential users of the lift were less generous than had been anticipated. It seemed, for a time, as if the natural disaster had saved the Board from a financial one but then, in a dramatic development, the anonymous donor dropped the condition of a comparable contribution from the public at large. All things became instantly possible. The only proviso finally attached to the gift was that the chair should be a two-seater.

No sooner had the news of this largesse broken than another reticent philanthropist, later revealed to be Boyd Anderson, provided money for the erection of a substantial shelter at the bottom station of the chairlift. The building, to be known as the 'Sheiling', was to be operated by its own board of trustees and to have a resident warden.

Almost from the outset Karl had, only half jokingly, encouraged his skiers to carry suitable stones up the hill so that one day he could build a proper shelter. Jean's Hut, where people used to take refuge during sudden spells of bad weather, was closed on weekdays apart from the small corridor which would hold at most six people in any degree of comfort. Now he could forget about direct action; a very substantial building was in prospect which would make Jean's Hut redundant.

Most people in the area who supported the development of skiing were much relieved when word came that the lift was to be built. The poor snow of the 1961 season had shown that the road without an accompanying lift could ultimately turn out to be a negative factor. It had given access to hundreds of new skiers, those who would never have dreamed of facing a two hour uphill slog to engage in their sport but who were quite happy to walk a short distance from the car park. The newcomers had made the ribbons and patches of white alarmingly crowded. At Easter there were about two thousand people fighting for sliding space with many of these struggling for access to the two Bill Blackwood rope tows. Some, of course, walked up to the higher levels but a chair would have whisked many more to less populated areas and reduced the congestion considerably. Without the lift, and with ever increasing numbers attracted by the road, the scene could become farcical.

The Board, freed at last from legal and financial restraints, negotiated a new contract. Money had to be borrowed but at least there was a good prospect that loans would be paid off quite swiftly from revenue.

Whilst these plans were being laid, the Cairngorm venture received a massive publicity boost when the Duke of Edinburgh, on an official tour of the Highlands, decided to take a look at the development. Volunteers were recruited to shovel snow into the lower reaches of the White Lady run so that the royal visitor could see Scottish skiing without having to hike up several hundred feet. The national press, scenting a good story, were there in force. Some of the headlines probably revealed more about journalists' life styles and levels of fitness than they did about the Duke. 'The Duke marches 'em up to the top of the hill and leaves them all panting,' was a typical effort.

The accompanying articles told the royal story. One reporter wrote; 'The Duke of Edinburgh toured the Spey Valley to see at first hand the many advances in turning the whole area into a winter sports playground. His visit involved a half-mile walk up a steep mountainside in a gale force and icy wind to watch ski-ing demonstrations

'The mild Highland winter has ruined skiing - as the Duke found to his cost yesterday. The snowline has receded so far up the mountains that the Duke had to walk half a mile - and he was certainly not dressed for the part, wearing only ordinary shoes, a light grey suit and heavy brown overcoat.

*Hands in pockets, the Duke watches the skiers from the foot of the slope*

The article continues; 'But undaunted, he struck off up the mountain at a spanking pace to keep his promise to watch skiers in action, leaving behind a trail of stragglers, puffing and blowing trying to keep up with him. The Duke had to trudge through bog and heather and over boulders to get to the ski-run at the White Lady on Cairngorm itself. Bareheaded and with his hands stuffed in his pockets, he never put a foot wrong. But others swithered and slithered and some officials fell trying to get up the steep half-mile walk.

'The Duke was transported up the new ski road and over another rough sand and boulder-strewn track before his half-mile walk. Informality was the keynote of the Duke's stay with the skiers. In their gaily coloured anoraks, berets and other gear, the skiers crowded round the Duke and, as he did throughout the whole tour, the Duke laughed heartily. It was a gay Duke obviously in his element, learning about winter sports in Badenoch.

*Peter and the Duke*

'There were thrills and spills galore as skiers came hurtling down the narrow ski slope, known as the White Lady. The Duke got a great kick when Norwegian skiing instructress Berthe Lien came crashing down not far away from him. Then he laughed and chuckled when he spotted five-year-old Peter Fuchs skiing expertly but cautiously down the same slope.

'Peter is a son of Karl Fuchs, Carrbridge, an Austrian ski instructor and one of the first foreigners to help turn the area into the St. Moritz of Scotland. Peter has been skiing since he was three and the Duke said: "He shows immense courage." '

One of the national newspapers was so taken with Peter's part in the proceedings that it ran the story with the headline; 'Five year old steals show'.

Once the fuss of the royal visit was over, work started in earnest on the installation of the new facilities. Astonishingly, the Board initially thought that it would be possible to complete the operation without employing a general manager. It was not until work was well under way, and suffering from delays and confusions, that an advertisement was placed in the Inverness Courier. It was seen by one Bob Clyde, old friend of Frith Finlayson, relatively new friend of Karl and Eileen Fuchs.

Myrtle Simpson quotes him as saying; 'I answered the advertisement out of curiosity, but after discussion with my climbing friend, Jimmy Hamilton, who was on the technical team for the Board, I became more interested. I was interviewed by Major Scott and his enthusiasm for the scheme took a hold of me and I decided I wanted the job.'

Through Eileen, Karl records the impact made by Bob Clyde. 'During the spring we saw hopeful first signs of the excavations for the chairlift and Sheiling and in the following summer and autumn the electric cables were laid, the buildings were put up and work on the pylons began. The plans had their teething troubles but in the late autumn Bob Clyde arrived to take charge and seemed with his own prodigious physical exertions to cause the work to spurt forward. He was to be seen daily, normally in atrocious weather, slogging alongside the workmen, bounding up and down the White Lady, always determined to be finished by the appointed date just before Christmas. I well remember a couple of days before that date watching the Swiss engineer on a bitterly cold day lying on top of the iced-up pylons, slotting the cable through with his bare hands.'

In urgent need of an assistant, Bob turned to his old associates in the Craig Dhu climbing club. Tommy Paul, recently returned from New Zealand, had all the requisite skills for undertaking engineering tasks whilst perched on top of an icy pylon in blizzard conditions. Not long afterwards, two other former climbers, Bill Smith and Harry McKay, joined the crew. To a considerable extent, Glencoe came to Cairngorm.

Through Bob Clyde's dynamism and willpower, the lift was completed in time for its official opening on the 23rd December 1961. The total cost had risen to £42,000 and the projected ticket prices had to be raised to take account of a heavy repayment schedule. Even though the facility seemed expensive to the economically average skier, the lure of mechanised uplift overcame the reluctance of the majority of people.

For most of the users, the facility was a novel experience. Unlike more modern versions, where the chairs move continuously and the skiers sit facing in the direction of travel with their skis on, the original Cairngorm one had a 'reservoir' of side-facing chairs. Those getting on had chance to arrange themselves and their equipment before being manually propelled onto the upwardly moving cable. Likewise at the top, there was a chance to disembark before an operative pushed the conveyance towards its return trip.

Very soon it emerged that Karl's fears about the wind had been very well founded. On many days, the system could not operate for fear that the chairs would be blown off the cable. There were other worrying scenarios. Beginners started to use the lift to take advantage of the gentle slopes at the top of Coire na Ciste. This was excellent until they found, when they came to make the return journey, that a sudden increase in wind speed had closed the system down. Many were the heather-hopping and slithering descents made because the machine had unexpectedly stopped.

At least, though, the ones abandoned on the top of Cairngorm had their destinies in their own limbs. The ultimate agony of the new facility came when a power failure or a mechanical malfunction stopped the merry-go-round in mid flight. It was not that the chairs were particularly high above the ground, only the most sensitive souls suffered from vertigo, it was that more often than not the discomfort was acute.

Those sitting, trapped for they knew not how long, exposed to the worst the elements could hurl, entered their own private hells. There was some consolation in that the wind was generally not at full Cairngorm force, because otherwise the lift would not have been operating, but even the 'gentler' air currents which were within the permitted safety bands felt violent to the face. And there were those days when much stronger winds were blowing along the line of the chair, rather than across it, which allowed the machine to operate in much worse conditions.

Whether the air currents were only moderate or tending towards the severe, it was certain that they would find their way through any number of layers of clothing. They would also bring with them their close friends; rain, sleet and snow. If hats were not jammed tightly on or tied, the winds would jestingly remove them. They were especially skilled at working their way through gloves, turning fingers to frozen sticks.

Under these circumstances of swaying, icy uncertainty, pioneer lift users discovered a new variety of misery. The stoppages could last for considerable periods. The day, probably already dark from thick, winter cloud, would become blacker. Those lucky enough to have a companion beside them would agree that, yes, there must be some fail-safe system of hand winding to get people down but they would be hard-pressed really to believe this. Privately they were convinced that they were due for a night on a bare mountain which would result in rigor mortis.

Sensible people would have been finally deterred by just five minutes of being stuck on the Cairngorm lift in poor weather but, as the history of skiing in Scotland illustrates, practitioners of the sport are not sensible. When the lift was working it had no shortage of customers.

The intermittently interested media drew attention to the new scope of Scottish skiing. It was inevitable, most thought, that more investment would come. There would be other lifts, hotels, ski schools and shops. The obvious place for most of these new ventures was Aviemore. It was confidently predicted that the once quiet village would turn into a bustling town. Trains from the south would discharge skiers by the hundred. Bars and night clubs would spring into being to cater for their entertainment.

The reporters' predictions reawakened the Fuchs' worries about the location of Struan. They were aware that very often pioneers do not reap the full rewards. It is those who come after, those who can see the early mistakes and the broader possibilities, who are the chief beneficiaries. To an objective observer, Struan might seem too small, too amateurish and too far away. It was surely time, some of the Fuchs' supporters felt, for them to seize the initiative and become the key players in the Aviemore boom, otherwise they would face the inevitability of a swift eclipse.

## 16. Growing Pains

Writing a few years after the road and the lift were opened, Karl and Eileen explain the immediate effects of the installations on the area.

'All these developments gave a tremendous impetus to skiing in the Cairngorms. The Austrian and Norwegian ski schools were soon surrounded by a multitude of others, Scottish, foreign, hybrid, of all sorts and sizes. Hotels eagerly threw open their doors in winter and new boarding houses and private houses took their overflow, while money began to pour out on extensions, central heating, dance floors, bars and the like. Villages like our own had street lighting installed, the police force was considerably augmented, modern snow ploughs began to appear, sports shops sprang up, the young locals wore anoraks and pulled their babies in sledge prams. There were countless other indications that a new large scale industry had moved in. We even had visits from skiing celebrities such as the late Charles Bozon and Christl Haas.'

Conditions were obviously right for Karl and Eileen to become the primary players in the development of the region. They had been first in the field; Karl was seen by very many as a leader. It was his charismatic presence which had persuaded the public authorities to take on the major work of building the ski road. He was still generally thought to be the most accomplished skier and the best demonstrator.

Yet the story does not run in this direction. Karl never became the 'king of the hill' nor the rich executive with an elegant Aviemore office. This is partly because at heart he did not want these trappings. When he said, of Struan, 'We'm a fameelyi', he meant it. For him it would have been an act of abandonment to neglect the immediate demands in pursuit of a broader power.

Nevertheless, an important aspect of the Struan story is the relationship between Karl and the general development of the Speyside winter sports industry. It is a chapter of false starts, of pacts and apparent betrayals, of large egos and lightly concealed competitiveness. The cast of characters is a long one; Jock Kerr Hunter, Alisdair McIntyre, Bob Clyde, Hans Kuwall, Eilif Moen, Jack Thomson, Eric Langmuir and many, many more. There were schemers and peace-makers, the personally ambitious and the publicly far-sighted but the central counterpoint to Karl's particular tune was played by the ebullient Frith.

Frith tells, in his autobiography, that when skiing appeared in his world he fell for the sport as a lover engages with the object of desire. His ambition was to be what he termed 'a good skier', which, in less deliberately understated parlance, means an excellent skier, someone who can cope elegantly with any combination of steepness, narrowness, snow condition and weather.

He did most of his early learning in Glencoe but soon realised that there was nobody on his favoured slopes who could help him to fulfil this burning ambition so he took himself off to Switzerland where his opinion of the ability of the Glencoe skiers was swiftly reinforced. Referring to 'awful body positions', Frith comments that, 'None of us could be compared with the good skiers of the day. We had a very long way to go.' He found himself a teacher and set about unlearning a plethora of bad skiing habits.

At a time when Karl and Eileen were entering their third Scottish season, Frith returned to Glencoe and began to ply his trade as a freelance ski instructor. Through the good offices of Lewis Drysdale, the Scottish Ski Club gave official backing to the teaching venture. Almost simultaneously a Swiss instructor was setting up business in Glenshee. He was authorised to enter his students for the various stages of the Swiss national ski tests and to award certificates. Given that both Glenshee and Glencoe had mechanised uplift in prospect it must have seemed, at that stage, that Cairngorm was the least favourable place to be running a ski school.

By 1961 Frith had acquired his Swiss Ski Instructor's certificate. It was his intention to return to Glencoe to continue with his solo teaching efforts but in February 1962 he paid what he refers to as a 'seminal' visit to Cairngorm. His first crucial experience on that short trip was a tea dance in the Cairngorm Hotel. In his book he refers to a strong feeling of permanence and growth which he attributes to the fact that local people were much involved.

For the night he stayed with his old friend Bob Clyde and for the first time in Scotland experienced the comforts of sleeping and waking in a proper residence close to the slopes. He writes; 'Breakfast was the first I ever had in a house before going skiing in Scotland. I put my ski boots on in the same place where I had slept. It stands out in my mind.'

After that breakfast, Frith was driven up the road for the first time. He had skied on Cairngorm many times and had memories of the unfortunate encounter with a broken snow bridge as a permanent reminder. But things had changed from the days when he had had to wait hours for rescue. There were cars and buses parked at two thousand feet. There was a caravan selling hot drinks. The chairlift was into its second month of operation. There was great activity on the slopes. Frith recalls his great surprise at finding people other than him teaching skiing in Scotland.

The extent of the Cairngorm transformation was captured by the famous climber, Tom Patey, in an article written for the Scottish Mountaineering Club Journal in 1962. Tom modestly described himself as a 'brave' skier who used the planks purely as a form of transport to remote winter climbs. He had no pretensions to be a stylist except when a few well chosen words, un-backed by subsequent action, might impress the novices. With his customary acerbity he describes the scene.

'Ten years ago Coire Cas was as dreich a place as you might find anywhere in the Cairngorms. As a corrie it was wholly devoid of character. At the time of writing it contains one large continental-type chalet (with the hint of more to follow), a chair-lift which works occasionally, and, on an average week-end in February, upwards of a thousand skiers of all shapes and proportions. I must confess that I now find Coire Cas more stimulating. Even for the mediocre skier there is a milk bar selling hot coffee and no lack of gullible young novitiates upon whom to practice one's skimanship. Knowledge of a few basic terms (mambo, wedeln) and a nodding acquaintance with some of the Austrian and Swiss instructors is an undoubted asset. Skis may be carried or occasionally even worn; although in the latter case the least embarrassing course is to continue steadily ascending till out of sight (langlauf). Coire Cas is undoubtedly a colourful scene nowadays, and it owes this to superimposed humanity and not to the landscape.'

Frith movingly describes how he skied early down the mountain from this busy arena and sat in the forest by a workman's fire whilst he pondered. He had a wife and son to consider and the decision was clearly a crucial one for his family's future. It was in that quiet place that he made up his mind to take his chances with the Cairngorm crowds.

It must have been difficult for Frith to transfer allegiance. Glencoe had been his base for many years and there had been some not always friendly rivalry about the developmental priorities. Some people resented the fact that power and influence seemed to have won for Cairngorm the greater share of the available investment. It was also true that at Glencoe Frith was probably the best regular skier whereas, by the early 1960's, there were plenty of excellent practitioners on Cairngorm. There were also rival ski schools. It would have been all too easy to retreat but Frith was never one to duck a challenge. It was obvious that the road and the new lift gave access to slopes considerably higher than the ones at Glencoe; a couple of warm winters had shown how vital those extra hundreds of feet could be.

He describes how, in typical Scottish fashion, the climate lavished heavy snow at Glencoe during that last season, making the leaving all the more difficult but he expresses no doubts about the wisdom of the decision to migrate. What he does attack are some aspects of the way skiing on Cairngorm was developing.

For example, he soon came across a Swiss ski instructor who, against the national stereotype, was poor at time keeping and excessively scruffy in appearance. Frith knew that he could do much better. For another, it was clear that such few races as were then open to 'professionals' were all being won by foreign nationals. A certain nationalistic pride was triggered, perhaps all the more so because the Finlayson's son, Iain, was beginning to be successful as a racer. In a sign of things to come, Frith says of the foreign presence, 'What got up my nose was people coming from Alpine countries and taking on the right to call themselves a national ski school of the country they had come from.' This clearly did not bode well for future relationships with Karl Fuchs.

In the summer of that year, Frith had his lucky break which came through the deep misfortune of another. The man who had been running the Scottish Swiss Ski School from the Cairngorm Hotel in Aviemore died. Jock Kerr Hunter, who was then a leading light in the Scottish Council for Physical Recreation, was anxious to keep the school going. Frith's Swiss connections made him an ideal candidate. Some spoke of him as, 'the most polished indigenous skier of the time'. He clearly had the technical ability and he certainly seemed to have adequate supplies of drive. The resulting appointment did not meet with universal approval. Frith writes;

'Jock arranged for me to meet the hoteliers involved. This turned out to be an enlightening experience for me! As happens in small country type communities, people had preconceived ideas about outsiders. As they still do. There was a crazy notion that men from Glasgow were wild and difficult to get on with. Glasgow's no different from any other big industrial city. No doubt I was on display. Like most developing Highland holiday places, the bulk of the developers were incomers. The dreaded white settlers. This humorous, if inaccurate pseudonym is still in use, sometimes snidely. The meeting was a revelation to a simple wee Glasgow man. I was amazed how few local people were involved. Two of the hoteliers' men seemed to think they were being cajoled into some quick manoeuvre. They became almost hysterical for no reason. Even if something was going on their behaviour was unbelievable. In the outside world they would have lost.'

A touch confusingly, Frith records that the meeting ended 'with total agreement' but whatever the deeper feelings unleashed by his appointment, Frith started the 1963 season as a ski school director. With his wife, Jean, and Bill and Jim Greaves of sports shop fame, Frith established a company. Surprisingly, perhaps, the chosen name, 'Ski School d'Ecosse', had a foreign touch but no doubt it was intended to conjure notions of the Auld Alliance. To prepare himself fully for the new role, he went once more to Switzerland to acquire the prestigious national Ski School Director's Certificate.

One immediate problem was accommodation. There was a general shortage in the area which had been exacerbated by the sudden expansion of the winter sports industry. It was Jack Thomson, the original Glenmore Lodge instructor, who generously came to the rescue. He had a house with a large garden in Aviemore and he offered space for a substantial caravan. The Finlayson presence on the Cairngorm ski scene was thus completely established.

Eilif Moen, Director of the Scottish Norwegian Ski School and a great calming influence in what was destined to become a turbulent chapter of local history, recalls Frith as a fervent Scottish nationalist who was determined to do everything possible to utilise local resources. Frith's own writings confirm this view. His avowed philosophy was; 'If we are going to sell Scotland as a ski country in its entirety, the bulk of the teachers must be Scottish.'

In spite of this, Frith acknowledged that there was a gulf of standards to be bridged. In one of the very few references in his book to the Fuchs' presence in the area he writes; 'The standard of skiing amongst the indigenous skiers was, on average, not up to the standard of qualified European teachers. How could it be? There were two Austrians, Karl Fuchs and Hans Kuwall, who had skied since their childhood. They had settled in the village of Carrbridge, where they fitted in very well.'

He also fully acknowledges the fact that all his own hard-won expertise came from an Alpine source but his view seems to have been that it was then high time to shift the balance, to increase the proportion of natives amongst the ski instructor population.

According to Myrtle Simpson there were plenty of people who disagreed with this philosophy. She comments; 'The foreign instructors in Scotland were hostile, and even scornful of Frith's attempts and many Scottish skiers seemed to prefer to be told to "bend ze knees" in a broken accent than be shouted at by Frith.'

This is, though, misleading. From the very earliest days, the Austrian Ski School had trained and employed local people and Karl had never had any problems with clients demanding to be taught by a foreigner. Indeed, at the very time that the Ski School d'Ecosse was coming into being, the eight full time instructors of the Struan academy were equally divided between Austrians and Britons. Struan's customers generally took the view that if Karl had confidence in a teacher then they did too. The country of origin was not an issue. It is also true that Karl was a great believer in the nurturing of local talent. He gave his time, equipment and expertise unstintingly to the Carrbridge school children.

A prime example of Karl's willingness to utilise local talent is provided by two Glaswegians, men very much of Frith's ilk, who had decided to abandon the drudgery of the factory for the freedom of the hills. Living frugally on savings, and doggedly learning to ski by watching good skiers from a distance, they progressed from beginner to expert in the space of a season. Karl, who saw everything on the hill, watched their progress just as eagerly as they watched his and was impressed. By the end of their sabbatical year, Joe Docherty and Bill Leitch were offered work which freed them from the factory for ever.

Joe and Bill took up residence with the other instructors in the Struan Annexe, becoming part of the extended 'family'. Apart from the usual spats between humans living in close proximity, there was no particular tension. British and Austrian instructors worked well together. For the most part the teachers would take their breakfasts communally in the hotel dining room and would often join in the various evening entertainments. They formed a generally cohesive group.

Nonetheless, there was doubtless some substance to the notion that, at that time, some skiers were more ready to trust teachers with foreign-sounding names and European accents. There was, after all, no British system of instructor training and accreditation whereas several countries on the continent had well-established schemes. It was probably for this reason that when the *Inverness Courier* decided to run a series of 'learn-to-ski' articles it was Karl Fuchs they turned to for the material. The forthcoming publishing event was promoted in grand style. In a 'Meet your Skiing Instructor' preliminary article, the paper boasted; 'Karl Fuchs, one of Scotland's best known ski instructors, is to write a series of articles specially for The Courier'.

The piece told of the sudden boost to skiing provided by the road and the lift. It gave a surprisingly accurate account of Karl's history, making especial mention of his Olympic connection, his two year reign as police ski champion and the fact that he was the twenty-second post-war instructor to gain the Austrian state instructor's qualification.

The lessons covered all the techniques, including the herringbone for uphill progress, coping with falls and the various ways to turn. Naturally, Karl espoused the current 'reverse-shoulder' technique. This was irritating to some who believed in a more moderate style. Frith comments; 'At that time, the Austrian ski schools were, for some reason, teaching a traverse position of leading with their uphill shoulder well in front of the other. Something I did not subscribe to.'

Whether or not this ideological dispute penetrated as far as the headmaster's office at Gordonstoun School or the drawing rooms of Balmoral Castle is imponderable but whilst the argument raged, somebody in royal circles was coming to an informed decision. A teacher was needed for the young Prince Charles. The plan was that he would be conveyed by helicopter from Gordonstoun to Cairngorm. There, under conditions of the utmost secrecy, he would meet the appointed person, have his lesson and depart.

Perhaps it was due to the boy's father, who doubtless remembered seeing the young Peter snowploughing down White Lady, or maybe a researcher decided that Karl was clearly the most skilled instructor, but it was the Austrian Ski School which received the inquiring call.

Karl was delighted, even though the secrecy rule, which he observed scrupulously, meant that no kudos would attach to the business. Struan workers were told that staff of a certain 'Mr. Green', a wealthy private pupil, might occasionally telephone to make arrangements. They were to take messages and pass them to Karl or Eileen immediately.

The system worked very well. Karl would meet his royal client, conduct the lesson and then, sometimes, the young prince would go, incognito in all-enveloping ski wear, to the Sheiling. For the first year or so of that establishment there were resident wardens, a Mr and Mrs. Carter. They would provide tea and warmth until such time as the aerial transport returned to whisk the august visitor back to his school.

When the series of lessons was over, a confidential acknowledgement came in the shape of a letter from the Gordonstoun headmaster. No financial transaction was connected with this service, neither was Struan ever allowed to use the royal accolade for promotional purposes. The arrangement remained almost totally secret for many, many years. Karl, the soldier and the policeman, familiar with discipline, kept his princely story to himself. There are those, however, who claim that even now the Fuchs style is evident in the prince's ski technique.

There were other notables who decided that the Austrian Ski School was pre-eminent, among them Ian Fleming, busy making a fortune from his Bond books. Karl is cited in one of them by the all-conquering James as 'my old ski instructor' although Karl is certainly not to be held responsible for the notion that the agent could leap from a mountain top hotel and ski down vertiginous slopes in the dark, clad in expensive dinner jacket and patent leather shoes.

Maybe the conflict over styles and the attention being paid to Karl acted as irritants. There was a further source of tension.

Frith was, by nature, an absolute disciplinarian, a stickler for time-keeping and proper dress. He claims, for example, that his school was the first to introduce a uniform jacket for the instructors although there are plenty who would dispute this. To him it was infuriating to see what he regarded as scruffy individuals, randomly attired, drifting towards the meeting place where their students would be impatiently waiting.

Karl, with all his history of being in uniform and working within a strict hierarchy, was certainly not overly casual. Indeed, Eilif Moen recalls the contrast between what he called the 'Germanic' style of the Austrians and the more relaxed approach of the Norwegians. But Karl contrived to come somewhere between the extremes. He recognised that learning to ski was supposed to be more of a pleasurable experience than a military exercise. He had rules of conduct but he was flexible when that seemed the more human way to be.

With all this underlying potential for conflict, the honeymoon of peace between the two ski school directors did not last long but troubles between Karl and Frith began to surface only when moves were made to formalise the hitherto largely ad hoc arrangements for the administration of skiing in Scotland.

A meeting was convened in Pitlochry by Jock Kerr Hunter in November 1962. The purpose, according to Frith Finlayson's account, was to, 'discuss the need for setting up a system to be responsible for the conduct and eventual training and grading of ski teachers in our mountains.' Only ten people attended, including Lewis Drysdale, Jack Thomson and Frith. Myrtle Simpson records that the foreign contingent in the industry regarded the move with some suspicion. It was agreed that a formal, formative meeting should be held in Edinburgh. A date was fixed in January.

Karl felt that he had to attend. He had often discussed with Bob Clyde the need for some unifying body in the area. The consensus between them was that there should be one 'Cairngorm' ski school operating as a federation of all the component elements. A ruling council would set standards, establish codes of conduct and appoint representatives to express the views of the Cairngorm school in national forums. With this arrangement, the area would retain the colourful variety, and the several European identities, whilst ensuring that the Cairngorm customers were given an honourable deal. On the vexed question of training, Karl was more circumspect. Having witnessed the emergence of order out of chaos in his native land he felt that Scotland should proceed with caution, learning from, rather than repeating, the mistakes of others.

The proposal to set up an association of instructors rather than a unitary organisation of schools was not, therefore, entirely to Karl's liking. He saw no reason why Scotland should not, eventually, have its own national standards, just as many other countries did, but he felt that this should come about by a considered, lengthy cooperative effort by everybody, not just the teachers.

There were other negatives. Karl was not, by nature, a lover of committees. The language of these formal gatherings was alien to him. Procedural points, quibbles over fine detail, the niceties of protocol; these were of no interest. He was instinctively a 'family' man, a person of very human response rather than a creature of organisations. There was also the very strong likelihood that Hans Kuwall would be vigorously involved in the proposed organisation. As far as possible, Karl avoided contact with his Carrbridge competitor. He would find it difficult to remain civil in the debating chamber if a disagreement between the two of them emerged.

*Karl, Ski School Director*

The meeting duly took place. Frith's summary of the proceedings is that the Scottish Ski Club and Scottish Council for Physical Recreation wanted a big say in the control of instructor training and conduct. He and Jack Thomson argued strongly that instructors should be largely self-regulating. It seems that the practitioners had their way because Frith writes; 'That's the way it's been ever since, for good or bad.' A new organisation, the 'British Association of Professional Ski Instructors' was inaugurated. Soon afterwards the word 'professional' was dropped, on the suggestion of Jock Kerr Hunter, in the hopes that funds might be forthcoming from the Sports Council but none, apparently, did.

A committee of ten founder members was elected. In recognition of his unique standing in the area, Karl was elected to the Chair.

At many levels there was huge potential for conflict. Frith's account is that from the outset there was petty squabbling about style and standards and a large degree of suspicion from the hotel owners. He felt that the new organisation was perceived more as a trade union than a professional association and that the owners anticipated sharp practice and strikes. Neutrals, such as Archie Scott, the Chair of the ski lift company, and Bob Clyde, expressed approval of the new organisation. Many felt there was no harm in having a practitioners' forum *and* a unified ski school; the two bodies could work cooperatively for the development of winter sports in Scotland.

What Frith refers to as a 'ski clinic' was organised for the committee, presumably with the purpose of monitoring standards. It is not recorded whether or not anyone was excluded as a result but Frith remarks that, 'It was apparent from the word go that the total skills and skiing ability of many of the founder members was rudimentary.' Eilif Moen, ski school director and one of the loyal pioneers of the Cairngorm area, chanced to miss the first meeting and was informed that incomers would not be granted the dignity of a 'ski clinic'. He learned that, if he wanted to join, he would have to take a test. Had he been a complete stranger this would have been understandable but Eilif's most excellent skiing had been on very public display for several years.

With this inflexibility, the endless arguments about the 'proper' way to ski and the personal background, there was acute turbulence in the month before the next BASI gathering. It seemed, from Karl's perspective, as though Frith and Hans were in cahoots. Then, from an entirely reliable source, he heard that one of Frith's instructors had been loudly voicing criticism of the Struan school. It was difficult not to conclude that these slanders were, at least in part, echoes of the views of the Ski School d'Ecosse director. It appeared to Karl that Jack Thomson was also associated with the denigration.

Frith's account of the February meeting contains the following; '...our newly appointed chairman started off what was an attack on myself and Jack Thomson. Unfortunately Karl's English was at times difficult to get a grip of. Neither Jack nor myself had any idea of what triggered this outburst, and outburst it was.'

Frith acknowledges that, later, the source of Karl's wrath became known to him. Attempts were made to heal the breach. According to Frith, the debates were so heated that on one occasion he had to intervene in a physical confrontation between Jack Thomson and Karl. The circumstances were obviously intolerable and Karl felt he had no option but to resign.

There are deeper elements to the dispute. According to one reliable observer of the local scene at that time, the verbal conflict became extreme to the point that Frith was heard to describe his rival as a 'Nazi boy'. This, according to some who knew Karl well, was the big unforgivable. All of the upset about skiing styles and organisations could, perhaps, have been quietened by diplomacy but Karl could not get this personal insult out of his mind. It cut too deeply into his memories of the miseries of war.

The anger which had been simmering was out in the open. Karl and Frith, two of the giants of the region, were in public conflict. Eric Langmuir, who became closely involved with BASI, remembers that the antipathy was evident from the earliest moments. He believes that in fact it had almost nothing whatsoever to do with commercial competition. It was something deeply personal. He feels, with the perspective of time, that there was covert admiration between Karl and Frith. This is confirmed by Frith's mature assessment that Karl was a 'magic man'. In many significant ways the two of them were akin. But they were like stags, clashing horns, too intent on the battle to stop and think what it was that had caused their conflict.

With Karl no longer in the frame, Frith was appointed as Director of Training for BASI, with Hans Kuwall as his assistant. There was, Frith recalls, a difficulty concerning the question of shoulder position. The true Austrian Hans favoured the extreme style pioneered in his country. Frith was inclined, in this matter at least, towards moderation. In ways which are not explained, this disagreement was resolved. Systems of tests of competence were agreed. Jack Thomson was delegated to organise the examinations. There were disputes about the marking but the BASI show had most definitely started.

The 'workers' having organised themselves, it was predictable that the employers would soon follow suit. Eilif Moen recalls that Rudi Prohaska, a man who had been in the Free Czech Air Force during the war and who had opened a ski school in Kingussie with his English wife

Barbara, was the main instigator of the Association of Ski Schools of Great Britain. This organisation came into being in 1964 and it was, Eilif asserts, a deliberate counterbalancing agent to BASI.

In this period of intense development there was another diplomatic initiative. It was strongly rumoured that a National Ski Federation of Great Britain was soon to be formed in London. Myrtle Simpson records that Lewis Drysdale was quick to recognise that this new organisation could easily drain power away from Scotland. He called a conference of Scottish ski clubs and at this it was agreed to form a Scottish National Ski Council. This new body took over many of the functions which previously had been valiantly performed by the Scottish Ski Club. The embryonic organisation had a paid secretary, Guy Chilver-Stainer, and was presided over by Lewis Drysdale.

Taking almost instant action, the new Council, which was essentially club based, created a forum, open to all organisations. This new entrant to the complicated drama was called the British Ski Instruction Council. Potentially it could act as a bridge between BASI and the ASSGB. Frith and Jack Thomson became the BASI representatives on the Instruction Council.

At national and local level, ski politics were in a state of ferment. The ASSGB decided to organise a training initiative of its own. A Norwegian, Arni Palm, was invited to direct proceedings. Frith records how he prevailed on Dougie Godlington, an instructor who was also locally famous for his witty posters, cartoons and cards, to ask Arni Palm to withdraw. When this intervention failed, the key members of BASI simply boycotted the venture. Frith's perception is that the alternative training exercise was 'a charade'. He writes; '.....it left no mark apart from a bad taste in some of our mouths....we did not need any of this childish side-tracking of work which had been successfully and officially carried out by the newly mandated BASI.'

The ASSGB involvement in training ended quickly but the organisation continued. Karl almost always attended the meetings and if he could not be there he sent a representative. BASI, too, survived the early storms. Myrtle Simpson gives much of the credit for this to Frith. She believes that through his rigour and determination he forced the other schools to raise their standards.

But all the time, Karl was yearning for unity. He approved of the Scottish National Ski Council in principle but felt that it should be reconstituted as an all-embracing federation as in other countries. If and when a British federation was established, the Scottish body could work through this for affiliation with the Federation International de Ski. He expressed these views to a reporter from *The Scotsman*, John Milne, whose piece appeared on the 19th of November 1965 under the headlines, 'Austrian believes in Scottish skiing - Glorious future possible'.

'Karl Fuchs is an Austrian who has a feeling for Scotland that most Scots develop only after years of exile. The cynical view might be that this is reasonable, for Scotland has provided him with a fat living since he set up the ski school in Carrbridge in 1954, but Mr Fuchs is still attempting to repay what he considers a debt to his adopted land - an offer which Scotland seems curiously reluctant to accept.

'When Karl Fuchs first arrived in this country the Scottish skier was rather a rare bird. Now the species is widespread, and spreading wider. Commerce rushes to ply the skier with comforts; experts hasten into print to speed his progress; and quasi-official bodies vie with each other to administer him in a scramble which defies the understanding of an Austrian.

'To Karl Fuchs, the future of Scottish skiing seems glorious, and the way to it straightforward. The first step must be the formation of a Scottish Ski Federation; the second, affiliation to a supreme British Ski Federation; and from there membership of F.I.S (the World Ski Federation) follows naturally with a consequent rise in British standards of competition. He marvels that New Zealand and the Lebanon have preceded Britain into F.I.S.

'Why the Scottish bodies have so far ignored the path which leads to the first step is beyond his comprehension. They are all 'on the same rope', as he puts it, and from one who puts 40 years of experience behind his pronouncements, such simple arguments are powerful. That a man who has seen the Austrian skiing industry develop from a similarly muddled condition can be optimistic must be encouraging too. All that is needed is for the Government to be firm, spend a little money - and with his 'one step, two step, three step' he predicts success.

'The risk and expenditure involved he accounts worthwhile - indeed, he considers them necessary, and cites the examples of his own expensive Government training and the abandoning of his comfortable Austrian police post in justification. He extends the principle to the training of instructors and sends his protégés to Norway, Austria or France for their. qualifications - excursions involving both risk and expense.

'The fact that he cannot himself appoint instructors (should he assume such powers he would stripped of his Austrian teaching licence) is only one of the obstacles to Scottish advancement which he considers minor. As beginners in the world of skiing, we are obviously not yet ready to teach ourselves anyway, he argues.

'Similarly, he regrets the lack of snow space and the dwindling ranks of the pioneer skiers, both of which make his coaching of promising youth the more difficult. He can see solutions to both problems, however, and names trip off his tongue in explanations - Braeriach and Corrie Gorm; Donnai McKenzie and Lewis Drysdale; Glenfeshie and Drumochter. But he emphasises that such problems must await the realisation of his ideal of a unified movement.

'The Scottish Council for Physical Recreation has invited him to a meeting in Edinburgh in December, and perhaps there he will have the opportunity of outlining his views on the needs of his sport. Perhaps the weight he can bring to bear as a long-term member of the Cairngorms Board will help him to push his ideals through to the planners too.

'When Scotland achieves the glory he has predicted for her, perhaps skiing's overlords will find some way of allowing a little of it to reflect on Karl Fuchs.'

Frith's reaction to this piece, if indeed he read it, is not recorded but the two men went their different ways. Their paths crossed frequently, of course, on the slopes, in the Sheiling, occasionally socially, but they were cool with each other. When Karl started a style competition and Frith bravely entered, there was a heated dispute which ended with Frith's disqualification and with victory for Norbert Uist. At the Winter Sports shows, which took place at Earl's Court and Alexandra Palace in the early and middle sixties, there were demonstrations and races on a plastic slope in which both men participated. It was on one of these occasions that Boyd Anderson approached Hans Kuwall to ask him if he would consider taking charge of a proposed plastic slope in Edinburgh, planned to be the largest in the world. By 1965 Karl's erstwhile protegé was installed as Director of Hillend.

Although Karl's association with BASI was over, many of his instructors enrolled on training courses and became qualified. Indeed, there were several instances of instructors moving from one rival school to the other; the battle lines were by no means absolute. Frith writes scathingly of some who became involved with BASI;

'There were the odd individuals who seemingly adopted a particular Alpine country's skiing technique. Some of them actually copied what they thought were the habits and style of ski teachers of the country to which their alliance had been given. One of these misguided half wits was observed teaching in an English Austrian accent on the White Lady run on Cairngorm. This man ended up on our committee. Democracy is expensive......With the exception of two of these people, they had very limited Alpine skiing experience. Worse, their personal skiing was poor. It took a great deal of forbearance to listen to them.'

Frith attributes much of the argument which attended BASI's work to people who, regardless of country of origin, were not quite up to standard. He writes; 'There developed a "them and us" syndrome between the foreign would-be-ski-teachers and the home-brewed-would-be-ski-teachers. This was started, as I saw it, by those would-be instructors whether they were native born or not. It's always the poorer performers in their own skiing who become involved in this nonsense.'

Against all these difficulties, BASI produced its first ski teacher's licence, based on a Swiss model, in 1964. Later the Official American Teaching Manual was adopted as a basis. Jack Thomson was elected to the Chair and Eric Langmuir was chosen to present the first professional lecture to aspiring instructors. In his capacity as Director of Glenmore Lodge, Eric did much to assist the establishment of BASI.

In spite of all the problems which it engendered, the sudden growth of Cairngorm skiing was generally welcome to the Struan founders. Karl learned to live without direct involvement with BASI and to keep his disagreements within bounds but the skiing part of their enterprise was not the only area where Karl and Eileen faced difficulties as the 1960's began to swing. There were issues at the hotel which urgently needed to be resolved, issues which went to the very heart of Struan as a family.

## 17. Hard Decisions

The Fuchs's dilemmas, as Speyside skiing transformed itself from cottage industry to a fully-fledged commercial operation, related to their families, the immediate one and the extended one which Struan had generated.

On the smaller scale, Eileen was facing all the problems which are familiar to carers with careers, with the added difficulty that there were few if any boundaries between home and working lives. The demands made by the hotel were indefinite; there was always something which ideally should be done yet, naturally, the children had their legitimate claims upon their parents' time.

It did not help matters that the family home, in the wooden buildings by the side of the hotel, was so close to the workplace. Getting completely away from the work pressures was tantamount to impossible and, once the children started to be independently mobile, there was no practicable way of separating them from the buzz of institutional life.

For Peter and Lisi the proximity had benefits and drawbacks. Lisi recalls the great degree of freedom, the high level of sociability and the perpetual excitement of new people but she also remembers the times when work and family needs clashed. Whenever there was a crisis, an unexpected influx of guests, some failure of services or an unmade delivery of goods, it was usually, and necessarily, the visitors who came first. An example, trivial perhaps to an adult but of immense significance to a child, is associated with food. When there was no time to provide a separate meal, the two youngsters would eat in the Struan kitchen, enjoying the same excellently nutritious meals as the guests. Occasionally there would be a problem with supply. Puddings, which were usually prepared earlier in the day, might not be there in sufficient quantities to satisfy customers and kin.

From a grown up perspective, especially that of one running her own catering business, Lisi can easily understand why the customers were favoured but to a child it all seemed so grossly unfair. The protests were often vociferous.

The children were well versed in manners but they became quite boisterous. Lisi feels now that they were naughty in order to make their parents choose between 'outsiders' and them. They were at their happiest when Karl found time to teach them practical skills such as carpentry, gardening, cement-making and, of course, skiing. They had, Lisi remembers, absolute faith in their instructor just as the ski school patrons did.

*Peter and Lisi*

On many occasions, the saviour of the potentially fractious dramas when things were not going according to plan was Jessie. The 'second mother', the keeper of the kitchen, could almost always find something in the pantry which was at least equal in attraction to the lost desserts. There were negotiations, of course, some hard bargaining for sure, but the flag of child-centred justice was kept flying and peace was restored.

There were many other instances when Jessie had to fill a gap whilst Eileen dealt with urgent business. It would have been very easy for an unscrupulous person to turn these circumstances to advantage, to gain power over the children. Some would have delighted in depicting the mother as a failure and the rescuer as a saint. Jessie scorned such underhand manoeuvres. For her, Peter and Lisi were always Eileen's and she did her best to explain, as the two got older, why certain apparently hard decisions had to be taken.

Eileen was all too aware of the difficulties of raising a family under such circumstances. She was worried, too, about the future schooling of her children. Several decades after the events she wrote:

'My real troubles began as the children were becoming old enough for school. Peter had a couple of terms at the local school but I felt that this was limiting as Carrbridge was very isolated and with their European mother and father we wanted the children to come into contact with children from as wide a background as possible. They were technically not allowed in Grantown Grammar School until they had passed the eleven plus examination (if they passed it) and the rules could not be bent. What was more, I could not help being preoccupied with the hotel when at home and we had only our bedroom in the cottage separate from the hotel so there was no privacy.'

There was, when the difficulty had been discussed over and over again, only one drastic solution. Eileen tells of the decision; 'So, after making many enquiries, we decided, on the recommendation of some of our customers, to send the children to the Rudolf Steiner school in Edinburgh. Many of the parents and teachers there came from the Continent and all sorts of Continental customs were observed and languages taught from the kindergarten upwards; also, in present day language, it was a green school. What was more, Edinburgh offered a mixture of city and country and facilities for swimming, tennis, libraries, shops, theatres and cinemas which did not at that time exist in this area within our reach.

'We took a tiny flat and I used to go down on Sunday night or very early Monday morning and back on Friday evening thereby meeting the departing Struan residents on Saturday when I did the bills, helped with the changeover and met the new residents. I took the ironing, mending, correspondence, bookkeeping and shopping back with me. Without Jessie this would have been impossible but with her it worked very well.

'We had longer than average holidays, about four months in all. Karli used to come down for school concerts and the odd weekend and for October and November when there was nothing doing at Struan and he would run dry ski classes at Lillywhites and then at Kinloch Anderson's. The great disadvantage was the travelling and I have vivid memories of the old A9, especially the Drumochter Pass in winter when the road was seldom ploughed and of the ferry queues at Queensferry before the Forth Road Bridge was built. But we enjoyed watching the bridge being built from the start and walking over the bridge the day after it was opened'.

From the early 1960's onwards until the children left school, Struan was thus deprived of the weekday presence of its chief executive. As Eileen notes, Jessie was effectively in charge, being a hotel manageress in all but title. For the children, the move to Edinburgh had mixed consequences. Lisi vividly remembers the homesickness for Carrbridge but recalls also the delight at escaping the tension of hotel life. At least, in the city flat, they knew exactly where they stood.

Although Karl agreed completely with the scheme to secure the best schooling for the children, the enforced separation was perhaps not entirely in his best interests. He was in many ways a very domestic man and a devoted father. Even though the hotel offered unlimited company he must have missed his immediate family acutely.

Whether as a consequence of the separation or because of more complex factors in his make-up, Karl sometimes turned to the anaesthesia of alcohol. It was all too easy, after a day on the slopes, to slip into the Edelweiss bar and treat the instructors to a warming brew of 'rum tea', one of Karl's favourite beverages at that time. Very often, 'the boss' would not change out of his ski wear, declaring that his boots were as comfortable as slippers. Sometimes, in his wife's absence, he would neglect to eat properly. He would either retire very early to bed or, perhaps two or three nights per week, continue drinking.

The effect on his physique was noticeable. The once trim belly bulged although happily this enlargement of girth had no deleterious effect on his skiing whatsoever. His mind must have made minute adjustments to 'centre of gravity' calculations and adjusted his body position automatically.

There were, however, serious consequences in other departments. His general health began to deteriorate. There were long term problems relating to the frostbite suffered during the war. No doubt the general austerity which he endured in those stark years had also had an undermining effect. The 'iron man' of the mountains, in his forties and having to face the inevitability of physical decline, was beginning to show a degree of frailty.

This, too, must have been difficult to accept. All of Karl's previous life had been centred round physical prowess. He was, above all, an athlete and so many of that ilk find it hard to cope with the loss of their special powers. In addition to the drinking, Karl occasionally found other diversions.

Sometimes, when the weather was too poor for skiing and one or two of the instructors had been detailed to look after the customers, Karl would gather others of his colleagues for expeditions. Most famously he would declare that he was going to Inverness 'for a haircut' or to the shores of Loch Ness to cut slalom poles. Sometimes these things would actually happen but whether they did or not, there would be visits to various hostelries.

Someone who knew Karl well at the time recalls 'lock ins' at establishments where Karl was well known. Favourite places were the Dores Hotel, the Tryst Restaurant, the Eagle public house and the bar at the Carlton Hotel. Karl was warmly welcomed into these and many other places, including a wide variety of shops. As always, people were proud to be associated with him. This interest in Karl Fuchs extended to more than one female. Even though his physique was expanding and his face showing signs of the effects of weather and alcohol he was still capable of exerting massive charm.

The expeditions became notorious amongst the Struan workers. Those who experienced them still shake their heads in wonder at the memory of the zany exploits and in wonder that they all survived. On some occasions not all of the party managed to return to Struan until the following morning. Luckily, ski instruction does not require a very high level of mental acuity. Most of Karl's staff could perform very adequately on automatic pilot.

On top of the problems associated with having to split the family for large periods of time, a further difficulty arose as the 1960's got into their free-swinging stride. It had been abundantly obvious for some time that everything around Karl and Eileen was changing with alarming speed. There were so many new and rich opportunities. How should they react?

There were three obvious courses. They could opt to stay exactly where and how they were, they could expand on the site or they could move the entire enterprise to somewhere nearer to the centre of activity.

As hundreds of Struan guests knew, Karl had long cherished the dream of a new building close to his beloved mountains. He often spoke of a possible move. The hotel would have everything requisite for a skiing establishment; easy access to the slopes, extensive facilities for equipment storage and servicing, a spacious dining area, a vast drying room, places for quiet relaxation and others for social mayhem, comfortable bedrooms with en suite bathrooms and limitless volumes of steamy hot water.

Yet, as the years had passed, the urge to move had decreased in potency. For all its unpretentiousness, Carrbridge had become 'home'. The people had become kin; it would be hard to leave them all behind. And beyond this simple, compelling loyalty was a taxing question; would a new Struan be able to replicate the magic of the original or would it just be another anonymous modern establishment of the type which people with money to spare were planning for Aviemore? When viewed in this light, the very drawbacks of Struan could be seen as advantages. This positive angle could be extended even to the fact of the hotel's distance from the slopes.

Once the number of customers had reached suitable levels, a deal was negotiated with the Highland bus company to provide transport. The hotel acquired its own hired vehicles, growling, grimy single-deckers, and a small band of regular drivers who, for some of the time at least, would also reside in the Annexe ready for the post breakfast start. The journeys to and from the slopes were very much part of the adventure

Frith Finlayson graphically describes his first experience of a ski road conveyance;'....the bus was not the latest model. The driver wore an old, torn tweed coat that went down to his ankles, and he got into the cab through a window that had been removed inside the bus. It would appear the driver's door did not open. The heating system was an open gas fire, with the gas bottle standing next to the fire. Even back in 1962, I'm sure the access to the driver's seat and the heating arrangements would have failed to pass the then rudimentary requirements of the law.'

*'Im bus please!'*

The Struan buses were not quite so dilapidated but they were characterful and they became a major part of the Struan culture, as did the drivers, some of whom were not averse to developing relationships with guests which resulted in transports of a different kind from that associated with their daytime labours. In the mornings Karl or one of his instructors would wander round the hotel, urging people to get on board. 'Im bus please!' was a Karl cry that many people affectionately imitated. Once the travellers were assembled, the boss would ask, of all and sundry, 'You haf efferythink?' and even the most seasoned skiers would, in mild panic, go through the checklist; skis, sticks, boots, gloves, hat, goggles, wax, lift pass, lip salve, skin protection cream, money, packed lunch. Quite often someone had forgotten an essential item.

More or less on time the vehicle would roar off and within it an atmosphere compounded variously of anticipation, hope, fear and determination would develop. If the previous night had been a heavy one the mood might be painfully quiet as hangovers were nursed. Otherwise there would be banter and, very often, displays of spontaneous wit. Not infrequently there would be flirtations, covert or brazen, within that travelling society. Against this background, instructors would make the arrangements for the forthcoming classes such that, by the time the bus lurched into the high level car park, everyone knew what it was they had to do.

The return journey, in the evening, had a different mix, with elation, despair, exhaustion, well-being and comradeship being the chief ingredients. As the bus tipped into the descent, people knew that they had three quarters of an hour or more of being cocooned. The drift along the shores of Loch Morlich could be dreamy with heads full of the intoxicating endorphins generated by exercise. The anticipation of afternoon tea, a bath, a refreshing snooze, an excellent dinner and a sociable evening enhanced hugely the quality of the time. Would it, in fact, be a gain to eradicate this interlude, which could be social or solitary but almost always enjoyable?

In so many other areas, the apparent drawbacks of Struan could be seen as advantages. Could a large, comfortable bar ever generate the gemutlichkeit of the Edelweiss? Would people inter-relate as they did at Struan if the dining room tables were small and spaced far apart and uniformed staff served all the diners? About what would people gossip and grumble and laugh if everything worked perfectly?

The truth was obvious. Struan had developed through adaptation and spontaneity. The renowned richness of its social life came not from architect-designed facilities and the work of an entertainments manager but from the creativity of individuals given freedom of self-expression. It was hard to imagine this spirit surviving a transplantation however carefully the operation was managed.

Yet it seemed folly just to stay as they were. Through a great deal of uncertainty and self-sacrifice they had been leading agents in the development of the winter sports industry in the region. They had taken the initial risk of creating the business, surely they could venture a moderate expansion? There was the danger, of course, that *any* change would upset the highly successful formula, that stalwarts would object to the alteration of long familiar patterns but this was a gamble which, the Fuchs felt, would have to be taken.

Plans were drawn up for a new wing of two stories. An enlarged kitchen was incorporated into the drawings, as was a bigger dining room with an integral bar to be created by installing a hatch from a small storeroom. The extension would more than double Struan's capacity but all of it was kept within scale. Money would have to be borrowed to finance the development but all the indications were that the debt would be repaid very quickly.

Struan's gamble was greatly boosted by the winter of 1963 which, though causing massive disruption with its severity, made it seem as though Scotland would never again have any problems with the quantity of snow. At the Easter of that year all of the slopes around the new chair lift were deeply covered. The sun shone mightily. The builders were primed to start as soon as the weather permitted. By the following season Struan would be a much-changed institution and none could predict whether the magic would live on or die.

## 18. Winter of '64

Immodestly, I introduce myself at this stage in the Struan story. I trust that this chapter, and the later one about the bars, will provide sufficient justification for what otherwise might seem to be a writer's self-indulgence.

I first heard of Struan when I was twenty-three. An adventurous aunt of mine, who had come across the place on a summer motoring holiday, loudly sang its praises. Dorothy was the kind of woman who could get away with leaving her modest old runabout in the House of Commons car park ('It's all right Officer, really!'), a benign Mrs. Thatcher with a much softer handbag technique and a giggle to disarm a psychopath. Politically we were across the chamber from each other but I admired her greatly. When Dorothy heard I was interested in skiing, and suggested Struan, I took her recommendation seriously.

One of my friends owned a much-travelled green Hillman saloon. Easter 1963 saw five of us overloading the conveyance and setting off optimistically up the A1 to the romantically but misleadingly entitled Scotch Corner, thence via the A68 towards the exciting bounds of Caledonia. We miscalculated the length of the journey. Over the steep, blind crests of the ruler-straight old Roman route we were often terrifyingly airborne but we did not reach Aviemore until the darkness of the small hours. Parking where we could, we spent the remaining pre-dawn time jammed unhygienically one against other, sleeping fitfully.

When light came, we burst out and it is no exaggeration to say that we were awed. Tetchiness was immediately banished by the grandeur before us. Luck rather than navigation had brought us to a halt on the Glenmore road. We had Loch Morlich and we had the humpy cake of the snow-covered Cairngorms. The glassy black waters reflected all the majesty.

The five of us had seen plenty of hills, in the Dales, the Lake District and in Wales. In that worst of all winters we had also seen plenty of snow. Yet we were reduced to astonished silence as we gazed at the mountains and their inverted image. What I could not say to my companions, for reasons of bravado, was that staining my reaction of profound admiration was a shadow of fear. Yes, I wanted to try skiing but to a complete beginner the supposed slopes looked suspiciously like cliffs.

After a cafe breakfast in Aviemore we found our way to Struan and discovered that my aunt's 'unknown gem', in its last season before expansion, was booked to the limit. Directed to Crannich, we braved the dour-seeming Mrs. Anderson and crammed into her last remaining spaces. We were acutely sleep-deprived but we hired equipment from Karl. His genial offer of reasonably-priced tuition we declined on economic grounds but also because our youthful arrogance led us to believe that skiing must be intrinsically simple.

There could hardly have been a more deceptively alluring introduction to the Scottish version of the sport. The sun shone brilliantly every single day. There was universal snow. The new chairlift conveyed us, at ruinous expense, almost to the Cairngorm summit. Naively, dangerously, we careered down. Because the piste was so forgiving, and because there was always a safe line of escape, we suffered no injuries.

One late afternoon, when exhaustion had stilled most of us, an endlessly energetic member of our party, David, announced that he was going for a last run before the lift closed. The rest of us sat with the happy herd in the Sheiling and gazed through the huge picture window at the framed White Lady slope.

David appeared, proceeding cautiously as befitted a beginner on a steep run, skiing quite well. He seemed to be the only creature on the piste until, to general merriment, another form appeared. It took the unmistakable shape of large, looming reindeer.

These magnificent beasts had been reintroduced to Scotland as an experiment and they had prospered. Under the watchful eye of a Finnish gentleman called Mr. Utsi, generally known as 'The Reindeer Man', they foraged within the huge area which had been fenced off for the purpose. Occasionally they appeared in the car park, lumbering slowly along, probably looking for discarded buns.

Suddenly aware of another presence, David looked sideways. More in astonishment than disequilibrium, he fell. Maybe seeing a possible source of buns, the sure-footed beast broke into an ungainly trot towards the collapsed skier. People around us cheered encouragingly. They were clearly on the side of the predator.

David scrambled to his feet. Fortuitously, neither of his skis had come adrift so he set off, immediately breaking all personal and group speed records. His friends were impressed and maybe just a touch jealous. The reindeer, inevitably christened Rudolph by the rapidly growing audience, took the *diretissima* whilst his quarry zig-zagged. David was indubitably going the faster of the two but he was travelling a much greater distance. The contest was just about equal.

Rudolph stopped for a moment, perhaps thinking that his cause was lost. The crowd cried its disappointment. David heard nothing but he renewed the excitement by staging another fall, this one more spectacular than the last. Momentum carried him down the slope but when he resumed the vertical position, it was clear to the watchers that some adjustment to one of the skis was needed. Rudolph, apparently playfully, lurched once more into his downward trot.

Nobody had the least idea what the skittish beast might do. Could David expect to be prodded? Worse, would he be pierced? Did reindeer bite? Most people were sure that they were never carnivorous but was it possible, some wretch asked, that its intentions were amorous? Most laughed heartily at this wicked suggestion but those of us who knew David shuddered in horror.

It was a tense moment. Just as Rudolph came within poking distance, David finished his frantic fumblings and pushed off. He took a long traverse, managing to stay upright, and then accomplished an admirable if wobbly, self-taught stem turn. He set off in the opposite traverse but had gone so far across the slope that he all but collided with the straight-running creature. There were great cheers, many now on David's side, as he whizzed in very evident alarm past the outstretched horns. He gained ground, fell again, gained more ground, fell. For ten minutes or more the outcome of the contest was uncertain but in the end, victory went to our gallant friend. Rudolph strode off in search of succulent heather sprigs and we were proud of our companion.

That evening we went, as did most of Mrs. Anderson's clientele, to the Edelweiss bar which bulged and creaked under the strain of its popularity. We had a reason to celebrate. Humans 1, Reindeer 0 was our view of things. After ten minutes or so, we managed to acquire beer which, perforce, we drank out of the bottles. We stood in the shoulder-to-shoulder press, taking it all in.

For reasons which have no relevance here I was, at that time, an extremely naive, somewhat dysfunctional person. Struan fascinated and appalled me in equal measure. The place had an unsettling vibrancy. The deep-tanned ski instructors, British and European, male and female, were like minor gods. Many of the guests appeared to me to be august persons, perhaps true deities. When guitars and accordions appeared and people began to perform, I felt privileged. For the price of a simple drink I was being entertained by all these kings of the wilderness, these titans of the cliffs, these survivors of untold, self-engendered hardships.

Tucked into a corner, completely hemmed in, was a silver-haired gentleman who knew all the British songs and a whole lot more in German. I fancied that through his bushy eyebrows he beamed benign energy into the heaving room.

*'Grandpa'*

The morning after, whilst we were tucking into Mrs. Anderson's excellent porridge and eagerly anticipating one of her cholesterol-packed breakfasts, we were treated to the sight of a tall, ramshackle man wandering about with tears coursing down his weathered cheeks. Never having seen a crying man before, I was shocked but impressed. Here was one of those heroes of the hills, a manifestly hard nut, who was showing emotion. It was said softly, after his departure, that his name was Plum and that his wife, Robbie, also a ski instructor, had just died. Reason enough to cry, of course, but in public? Was there no limit to the freedoms associated with Struan House?

We were seduced by almost every moment of that unprecedented week, even the amazing event of Plum's public grief, and vowed that we would return to Scotland again and again.

It so happened that as the Christmas of 1963 approached I was at a loose end. With a place at Ruskin College allocated for the following October, and being thoroughly bored with my work as a Sales Engineer, I wanted to fill the time with something more rewarding than selling dryers to the paper industry. The summer months would be spent hitch-hiking abroad but there was a winter to pass profitably.

Left to myself I would never have dreamed of writing to Struan but David of reindeer fame suggested that I had nothing to lose. A reply appeared with impressive rapidity. It seemed at first to be written in Gaelic, so incomprehensible to my untutored eye was the scrawl. Being highly motivated, I persisted and slowly learned, over a period of hours and after many consultations with siblings, that Karl and Eileen had greatly enlarged their establishment during the summer and were desperately in need of a barman.

I responded at once, confessing that I had no experience of dispensing drinks and that I was the owner of a relatively new beard. I later learned that mine hosts had had a debate about the facial hair but not about the lack of expertise. They asked for references but before I could supply them, another missive appeared telling me to turn up anyway.

Duty as Best Man at reindeer-David's wedding kept me in Yorkshire until late in December so I arrived at Struan between Christmas and New Year. I was accommodated, along with the ski instructors, in the single-storey Annexe whose well-weathered wood shone silver. We were at the front of the ramshackle building in the small monkish cells. Our cubby-holes had no-nonsense iron bedsteads, rickety cupboards, a quarter-kilowatt electric heater and little else.

The interior of the Annexe was given over to double-bunked dormitories for the budget-conscious visitors. These, along with us, had to make do with sanitary facilities that were limited to lavatories and wash basins. Living conditions were spartan but nobody seemed to mind this in the slightest. For near neighbours I had two young, mischievous Austrians, Franzi and Hannes in their first season as Struan instructors, and the older Glaswegians Joe and Bill, then a few years away from starting their own ski school. Plum, I learned, had been lured to a job with the Youth Hostels Association but he was, apparently, a regular visitor. There were other instructors, some of them part time and temporary, recruited to cope with the expanded state of Struan.

There was also a small corps of domestic staff. The new wing, two storied, projecting from the rear of the house, generated plenty of work. Two young women from Nottingham, Margaret and Kryska, helped the locally based Evelyn with the housework whilst in the much enhanced kitchen Jessie had Miranda. She was the daughter of a cattle breeder who had produced a new, hardy strain of cow called 'Luing' after the family-owned island off the Scottish west coast.

New Year was a madness to be described later. After it there was almost total tranquillity, apart from Peter and Lisi who often were pests, especially to the poor barman who had been charged with not doling out Coca Cola and crisps. The tedium of uttering repeated refusals soon ended when Eileen and the children departed for Edinburgh. The workers were then left largely to their own devices.

In one of the early January weeks, the newly enlarged Struan had a grand total of six guests. Staff outnumbered them easily. Bookings for later in the season were much healthier but for a time we had plenty of opportunity for getting to know each other and the ways of our temporary home.

There being no bar-keeping precedent, and no job description, I muddled along. Karl clearly saw no need to act as supervisor. Through sheer thoughtlessness, I neglected to clean my tiny enclosure. Rather than utter a reprimand, Karl chose to 'show' me by starting to wipe the shelves and bottles himself. I took the hint.

Eileen had given me instructions about how and when to order supplies but, in my initial disarray, I had failed to take the information to heart. It was similarly with the disposal of empties. I struggled to learn my new trade. Because the bar seemed always to be open until two or three in the morning, and because I had clearing and re-stocking to do during the day, I did not open for trade at lunchtime. This seemed to be acceptable but there was no directive.

In that first, gentle, fortnight we all slotted into an easy domesticity. Often, people brought tasks such as letter-writing or sewing into the bar. The few guests went along with the mood and much enjoyed the opportunity to grab the attention of instructors for long periods. Early in the evenings the talk was almost invariably about ski technique or the incidents of the day. Later on, the discourse ranged more widely except that then, and thereafter, politics seemed to be unconsciously taboo.

The paucity of paying customers did not excuse idleness. Instructors still had to work even though they might have only one or two to teach. The house staff, once they had put all the occupied rooms to rights, were kept busy with a time-hallowed Struan occupation; sheet-sewing.

Struan bed linen had a tough time. Perhaps because of her period with the British Travel and Holidays Association, and her role as controller of the supply of sheets and pillow cases to hotels, Eileen was very particular about such items. Waste of any kind was anathema. The laundry items were washed very frequently, a process that involved mangling.

The mangle was ancient and it was hand driven. Anybody, passing ski instructor, bleary-eyed barman, family member or even familiar guest, was in danger of being dragged into the laundry room and put to pressing service. When Eileen was in charge of the process, escape was almost impossible. Her polite invitations were as commands. In the Turkish bath atmosphere, the co-opted mangler would twine and twiddle as the folded sheets were fed. While breath and strength still permitted, the recruit was expected to maintain a decent standard of conversation, generally in the realms of the humanities and the arts.

Understandably, the sheets eventually started to collapse. The feet of skiers seemed to be particularly abrasive. Some were convinced that half of the hotel's clientele went to bed in their boots, a practice which Karl proudly claimed for himself. The middle sections of the clean but fading linen would grow thin. Time for them to be thrown away? Not a bit of it. Cut and sew, sides to middle, hem the edges, voila! - almost as good as new, although significantly smaller. The re-constituted items would be used as under-sheets. Any that needed patching were diverted for use by staff.

More turbulent cycles in the machine, more mangling, more erosion by night-ski feet booted or otherwise; of course they collapsed again but this was still not the moment to consign them to the waste pile, not at all. There was more snipping, further sewing, until they were converted into under-pillow cases. Heads dreaming of stem christies or the charms of ski instructors bore down upon them night after night until even the rescued bits were fraying. The end? Oh no! Smaller than pillow cases are handkerchiefs, dusters, dishcloths and, more glamorously, slalom flags. Karl was the agent of this operation, cutting and dying to his own satisfaction. Many is the Struan sheet fragment which has tugged, fluttered, flapped and cracked in the Cairngorm winds. So few of the keen racers, brushing the supporting sticks with their curving shoulders, had the least inkling that they were dashing past the distributed remnants of Struan's linen store. If sheets could speak!

The days of peace were soon over. The bar closing time drifted later and later. Dreams I had had of occasionally hitching a ride up the mountain for an afternoon's skiing were dismissed. Bed at four, sometimes five in the morning, up at eight for breakfast, cleaning, stocking, ordering; all I wanted by the afternoon was sleep. Like the others, I mainly confined my ski activities to the greatly treasured 'day off', the weekly opportunity to join the fun.

It will come as no surprise to those who know the Scottish climate well that the ferocious winter of 1963 was followed by something close to drought conditions in 1964. For much of the season there was little but thin ribbons of hard-packed snow and ice tucked into the centres of the corries. Every one of Struan's non-instructing staff prayed to their various gods that their day off would be blessed with a huge fresh snowfall and idyllic weather. Not one of these prayers was answered; evidence of the indifference of gods.

Nonetheless we took our opportunities and became, for those precious free days, just like hotel guests. We got up later than usual, had a leisurely breakfast, negotiated with the instructors and made plans to meet the one who was willing to take us.

At around nine o'clock the deep red, ageing 'Highland' single decker omnibus would growl to a halt outside the hotel. The black-coated driver, usually a portly, long-vowelled Invernesian, known for no obvious reason as 'Brem', would stroll into the kitchen to be greeted laconically by Jessie and a cup of strong tea. Karl would finish off dispensing equipment and begin his sheep-dog gathering of ski school patrons calling out his familiar 'Im bus please!'. Our employer, becoming orotund by this stage of his career, red of face and jersey and wearing a pixie hat, was a man-sized, genial gnome. Obediently people would emerge from the drying room or down the carpeted stairs with rucksacks and gloves, boots and hats, goggles and bum bags.

Old Struan hands told me that we were lucky to have Karl as the whipper-in. For a time, it was said, an army officer by the name of Anthony Forbes used to gather the skiing clan by wandering through the hotel playing the pipes, a most reliable way to replace the pain of hangover with a stronger one. When the company was assembled, the said military man would betimes retire to the woods across the road from the hotel and play such frothy masterpieces as the then very popular Eurovision Song Contest winner 'Puppet on a String'. It is reported that traffic used to come to a stop, the drivers congregating to listen in rapt admiration.

Had he been of a sadistic turn of mind, Brem the driver could have replaced Anthony Forbes as the morning enforcer but his delight was to save the demonstration of his skill on the pipes until the evenings. He would warm up the multi-legged beastie in the gentlemen's lavatory and then stride into the Edelweiss bar, blasting the chatterers to shocked silence. Since Struanites at this time of the day were generally just drunk rather than hung over, they adjusted quickly to the noise and sang along lustily.

*Author, a guest (Jean), Brem, Margaret and the back of the bus.*

In the morning routine, instructors would emerge from all quarters, one from the little wooden shop at the front of the hotel, others from the ski shed, some, the bad boys perhaps, blinking blearily on their way from the Annexe. Gradually Brem's bus would fill. Karl would ask his 'You haf efferythink?' and then enquire if everybody was present, knowing that anyone missing would be noticed by somebody. Brem would climb lazily in.

The first reliable sign of the conditions to come was on the road between Carrbridge and Aviemore. For part of the way the mountains are spectacularly visible unless, as is often the case, they are shrouded in mist. The keen ones would look eagerly. Could it have snowed or was that just a mocking frost, sugar-dusting the heather? Was that blue sky in the distance or was it a storm cloud so foul that it was beyond black? How was the wind, the wind, the wind?

The wind! It could be as still as a vacuum at the level of Loch Morlich and storming at fifty by the height of the car park. Nobody could tell for certain how the wind would be but there were ominous signs. A stream of downward-bound vehicles with skis on their roof racks was sure to suggest that conditions were bad. But sometimes people had been up to drop others off, or some had forgotten items of equipment and were returning for those. Nothing was certain.

In the car park, we knew! Were children being blown over? Were the adults bent double? Were hats and gravel hurtling through the air? Was the lift operating?

In 1964 there was still the walk from the car park up to the Sheiling. This was the first physical test; skis over the shoulder, pointed ends facing safely forwards, both sticks held in one hand. A moderately fit person completed the journey in less than fifteen minutes, a trudger took twenty. Then, for most, it was into the warmth of the Sheiling for a hot drink before the morning classes began. Instructors would have determined their strategy; which area, which patch of snow was most suitable for the lesson they were to give. They were usually keen to set off because they wanted to make territorial claims before some rival teacher took up residence. There had, on occasions, been battles. In poor visibility instructors had to ensure that the class followed as closely as ducklings follow their mothers, otherwise the prime place might be lost.

Then came the learning. Karl was as steady as a tower, full of teaching ideas and encouragement, always keen to see progress. Joe and Bill, themselves late learners, were acutely aware of the problems faced by adult beginners. Hannes and Franzi were a-bubble with energy, always alert to the potentially comic. Ho, ho! the barman's first ski-split, nose-dive attempt at a parallel turn, ('Ha, ha, ha, ha, haaaaa Der Rickart! What 'appen? to which I would bitterly reply, through the snowball in my mouth, 'You tell me, you're the instructor.'). Ho, ho! a housemaid going involuntarily backwards, her face showing a mixture of supplication, fatalism and terror. The guests were, of course, treated entirely differently.

Lunch in the Sheiling, afternoon learning, then, if the snow cover was adequate, picking a way down on skis to the car park, otherwise walking, limbs aching, mental state delirious or suicidal depending on how the day had gone. The bus was the rendezvous and people limped, lurched or strode to its decaying interior. 'Good day?' was the invariable question. Wet clothes started to steam. Late returners were silently cursed.

*Karl, Franzi, Hannes*

Staff members on their days off were entirely welcome to join the guests for afternoon tea. Often they did so but usually with a feeling of unease. Great though the lure of Jessie's baking was, and stimulating though the dissection of the day's ski exploits might be, the prospect of a hot bath was a powerful counter-attraction. And what staff knew, and some of the guests did not, was that there was a problem with baths. The business of post-ski ablution was competitive.

In the first instance there was an insufficiency of bathrooms. The bedrooms had wash basins but nothing more. Lingering too long over tea could entail joining a queue of oddly attired, toilet-bag-clutching aspirants. But the problem did not end with the gaining of entry. Once inside, door firmly locked, there was the secondary worry of the water.

Carrbridge's water was a thing in itself. In very small quantities it looked comparatively clear but fill a jug to the top what had one got? Soup! a murky consommé with added attractions such as fragments of heather and what looked like struggling newts. First time guests in the dining room cried out in horror and asked politely for replacement with something fresh from the tap. The truth had gently to be revealed. This was fresh from the tap, this was the best Carrbridge could do. There were assurances from an assortment of experts that absolutely no harm could come from drinking the water. It was, they declared, purer than most.

Some never trusted this but those who were brave declared the liquid to be delicious.

In the bath, the sight was initially alarming. People christened the stuff 'Carrbridge Brown' as though it were ale from the north east of England. Sometimes the bottom of the tub would be completely invisible.

But the feel of it and the silken, caressing, self-indulgent stroking that the water bestowed were wonderful compensations for the turgidity. It was, some said, the softest possible, the least sharpened by chalk. Those who dared to wash their hair in it could not credit how the coarsest of manes was turned into shimmering tresses. A tiny dab of shampoo was converted by the Carrbridge water into mountains of foam. It seemed like a chemical miracle. After a tough physical day there was no pleasure like a long soak in such warm liquid satin.

The problem, though, more often than not, lay with the 'warm'. The process of discovery in this respect could, for some, be traumatic.

The Struan tyro, having triumphantly gained possession of a bathroom, would gleefully turn on the taps. Usually, just to mislead, there would be a surge of piping hot soup and a few boiled twigs of heather. Excellent! Time to take off the clothes.

Struan bathrooms were, like the rest of the establishment, very far from being luxurious. They had heaters of sorts, wall-mounted with pull-switches, the kind that sends all the warmth to the ceiling. The floors were clad in freezing linoleum. The first to take possession in the evening had the bliss of a dry mat as part insulation, the successors had a dire clammy wetness. Whatever the mat state, the need to get into the cosseting water was always primary, so people would step into the accumulated half inch, naked and shivering but still beaming with pleasure. As the liquid accumulated there would be gathering bliss.

At this stage there was no point in not sitting down. The more of the body in warmth the better, yet it was vital to keep the back well away from the tub end. One contact with that and it might be death from sheer shock or, at best, frost adhesion. Once the bath was half full, *then* one could lean back. Ah! the wonder to come!

It was then that the hot water would stop. It would apologise, perhaps, by being hesitant and tentative but, with a few dribbles and spurts to generate false hope, it would utterly cease.

The cold flow had to be turned very rapidly off, otherwise all heat gains would be squandered. The shivering bather then had little option but to stay put, staring resentfully at the treacherous faucet. All smugness about being in possession of the bathroom would transform into hatred and jealousy. There were people in other bathrooms, complacent sophisticates, who were stealing the water. It was obvious that they were filling their baths right to the brim regardless of others. They would be soaking and sighing, perhaps even singing. It was all right for them! And doubtless there were people in the kitchen thoughtlessly draining the system.

Then the hot tap would speak. According to the sound it was not attempting to deliver heated water, no! it was sucking, trying to draw back what it had meagrely delivered. The gurgling, roaring, hollow noise suggested avarice. The dastards in the other bathrooms were not content with having it all already, they wanted more so that it could splosh out onto the lino, later to freeze.

It was only when this kind of pernicious thought was in the bather's mind that the explosions started. 'Explosion' is not too strong a word. *Crack! Splattt! Gup, gup gup! Whareeeeeee! Chap, chap!* The bather, once recovered from the shock of thinking that a military bombardment had begun, would become excited. Something was obviously happening! Maybe an air lock which had caused the hiatus was resolving itself?

In the hope of maximising warmth, the bather's legs would be stretched out, the upper segment blue, the submerged half inch a delicate pink causing the unfortunate to resemble a part cooked lobster. It is because of this elongation that one foot would be carelessly underneath the errant tap. When one of the most devastating shell sounds was accompanied by a spurt, the superheated fluid landed without concern for human comfort, on frost-bitten toes.

Under such circumstances it is impossible, even for nuns and priests, though none of these ever had a skiing holiday at Struan as far as is known, to suppress imprecations. Shouting, the bather would naturally retreat as rapidly as possible, bringing the hitherto protected back into contact with the ice wall. More loud cursing was inevitable, as was a self-preservational lurch forward which would invariably coincide with another vicious spit from the tap. Ceaseless oscillation would be in prospect but the quivering bather usually found salvation by curling up into a foetal ball. There was at least the comfort that the water supply was being restored.

Such naiveté! such unfounded optimism! Yes, there would be trickles, thin and intermittent like an old man's urination, but there would be no flood. The very patient, the ones with strong resistance to frostbite, could outlast the system and eventually enjoy a few inches of water, diluted with cold to increase the volume and so only just at a reasonable temperature for comfort.

Emerging, shivering, thinking only of the warmth of bed, the bather would be greeted by the sour looks of the queuers who could not be expected to hide their contempt for someone selfish enough to soak for so long whilst so many were waiting. There would be further opprobrium from these Struan neophytes when they discovered that the languishing egotist had used up all the hot water.

It could have been that it was this kind of occasional privation which contributed to the development of Struan. In a process akin to natural selection, only those who were stoical by nature, and equipped with a strong sense of humour, survived. Had everything worked perfectly all of the time the 'weak' would have remained to dilute the population pool. Occasional rigours, such as malfunctioning bathrooms, were socially healthy.

By February the hotel was busy and some of the staff were tempted to spend their days off recovering rather than continuing their progress or otherwise on skis. A long sleep in the morning, a drift into Grantown by bus, maybe even a train to Inverness where there was a range of quaintly old-fashioned shops, could provide almost forgotten pleasures. Some of us would sometimes elect to walk rather than ski. We had huge tracts of countryside entirely to ourselves and, perhaps better still, we could ensure that we got back to base before the skiers returned so that bathing was bliss.

The build up in trade increased everyone's work load. In my domain, there were always a few who kept the bar open until well into the small hours, whilst in the house, more rooms had to be serviced and there were more pots to be washed. Amongst the staff, a culture of cooperation developed. Instructors would do stints serving drinks, house staff would help in the kitchen, especially if an evening expedition or in-house event was in prospect and the staff wanted more time to prepare. For the busiest times, temporary help was recruited and, with very few exceptions, these went along with the prevailing mutuality principle. Jessie's eldest daughter, Miree, was away doing hotel work elsewhere but the younger one, Jean, soon to be married, often came in to give unpaid help to her mother.

The wages, for those who were paid, were modest, little more than generous pocket money on top of free food and accommodation, but few worried about this. Ski instruction and use of equipment also came as part of the deal and if all the 'perks' were properly costed, the pay could be seen as more than adequate. Entertainment came at little expense. Those who wanted to could save most of the cash which Eileen presented in small brown envelopes every Saturday.

At the very busiest times, Eileen was available. School holidays ensured that Struan was full beyond its nominal capacity but they also allowed the proprietress the freedom to add her considerable weight to the effort.

It must have been difficult for her to come back to the mayhem after the relative peace of the Edinburgh life. It was also strange for the staff. In her absence, people developed their own ways of working but she, of course, had the most extensive experience. She was an extremely hard worker who knew every aspect of Struan better than anyone yet sometimes people felt that her return was almost an intrusion. Even though Eileen was perfectly amenable it was as though they were being seen as being incapable of managing.

There was another factor which caused initial difficulties whenever Eileen returned.

Karl was generous to excess. Left entirely to himself he would have given until the business collapsed. It was Eileen who had to keep a rein on expenditure. She was not at all mean-spirited but by contrast with her husband's unthinking largesse she could sometimes appear to be pettily restrictive. Most Struan workers understood this difficult dynamic and judged Eileen accordingly, a few did not. The weekends were the most testing because there was insufficient time to adjust. Generally, though, during the school holidays, new patterns quickly established themselves and any resentment faded.

Those of the staff who enjoyed stimulating conversation and diverting company on afternoon walks, always welcomed the times when Eileen was in residence. Whether helping with the laundry or sipping tea in the afternoon quiet of the kitchen whilst the hostess baked scones for the returning skiers, there was always a mind-stretching topic. During the daily ritual of making the sandwiches for the next-day's packed lunches there was often the addition of music. Eileen recalls a quartet singing excerpts from the *Messiah* in full harmony whilst cheese was being spiced up with pickle and boiled egg being bound with rich mayonnaise.

In 1964, Peter was eight and Lisi six. For them the returns to Struan must have been like the release from a cage. In Edinburgh they lived an orderly life, attending their Rudolf Steiner school and being looked after by their mother. Once they tumbled out of the car at the hotel, most elements of order vanished. Eileen was instantly busy, Karl was there, ready to indulge. Jessie lavished affection, staff and guests were available in large numbers for providing attention and being the focus of teasing. The children ran wild. Accompanied by Evelyn's son, Colin, generally called 'Moggs', they plagued almost everyone, especially the barman.

About half way through the season a combination of tiredness, White Lady ice, a stuck stick, ski incompetence and downward momentum yanked my right shoulder from its socket. A mis-directed jab in the hand with an ampoule of morphine, provided by the staff in the Sheiling, compounded the pain. It was only some hours later when Dr. Henderson, the Grantown-on-Spey general practitioner, gave up trying to 'reduce' the injury without chemical and administered a jab of pethidene that I found blessed relief.

I missed one night's bar-tending but thereafter managed to work one-handed. Obviously, skiing was out of the question for several weeks so I extended the range of my walking. As the days lengthened and the light intensified I became bewitched by the natural canvas. No doubt the occasional ecstasies and the sensations of mystical unification with the environment were entirely the product of youthful exuberance combined with monkish repression but they forced me to acknowledge the potency of the place.

Karl very generously made his beloved, venerable Triumph Mayflower saloon car, which he delighted in calling his 'Silver Cloud', available to me whenever he could and so I was able to explore more distant territory. On one expedition, when I was driving up the Dalnahatnich road, I saw a horse and rider hurtling across the rough ground to my left. I stopped to watch and the duo changed direction. As they approached I could see a mud-spattered Daphne. She brought the trembling, snorting, sweat-lathered beast to a halt. It was clear that she was surprised, and perhaps disappointed, to see me at the wheel rather than Karl. As far as her breathlessness permitted we had a brief conversation then she rode off, cantering into the wilderness whilst I continued on my sedate solo drive.

Whilst I was still one-armed, Eileen kindly invited me to join her and the children on an expedition to the famed bucket bridge. A friend and her children came too.

Bucket bridges, mercifully rare phenomena, involve a wire suspended at height. From the wire the 'bucket' dangles although it is usually more like a cart than a water container. A complex system of wires, pulleys and gears enables the bucket to be wound across. This is best done from one of the terminals on the ground but a smaller device 'on-board' allows a lone traveller to make a laborious but unaided crossing.

I was in the bucket with Eileen's friend and her children. Beneath us the broad river sparkled. The surrounding scenery was exemplary in its lushness. The young Peter was on the bank winding us across. Then, for devilment, he stopped, leaving us suspended half way. The children expressed fear, probably fraudulently. With my weak left hand I began to wind the small on-board handle. The gearing was heavily in Peter's favour. He easily stopped the movement. Cunningly I switched the orientation of my efforts and we shot a few yards in the opposite direction.

Relentlessly, Peter used his greater mechanical advantage to return us to the middle. The children started to cry. Our shouts were greeted with hoots of boyish laughter. Eileen was somewhere in the distance, exploring the environment with Lisi. The foolish thought occurred to me that I might have more success in ending the marooning by taking hold of the heavy steel rope above our heads and hauling on it. I reached up.

At that precise moment Peter, not knowing what I was doing, decided that the game was over and began to wind as only a strong, energised young lad can. Unfortunately he chose the direction which I had selected and the pulley, on which the weight of the bucket rested, impinged at some speed upon my hand. It was my turn to scream but Peter thought that it was just part of the game. He tried to overcome what he thought was my playful resistance. It was only when Eileen's friend added her urgent voice that I was able to free my mangled hand. The little finger and the one next to it felt to be badly damaged. I was convinced that all bones were crushed into uselessness. Eileen, alarmed that her first, and at that stage only, barman was being progressively disabled limb by limb, insisted that we once more avail ourselves of the services of the versatile Dr. Henderson.

He wiggled the digits a bit, watched me manfully wince and declared that all the structure was intact. Bruised but otherwise undamaged, I worked as a three-fingered barman for a couple of days and then quickly recovered.

As the Easter of my departure drew near I was able to move right arm and left hand with enough fluency to enable me to take up where I had left off on the ski learning curve. Karl, with absolutely characteristic generosity, gave all staff members brand new equipment as a reward for a season's hard work. My skis were wooden, Kneissl Riesenslalom all of two metres twenty and horrendously heavy. The state-of-the-art bindings allowed release for a sideways twist but not for a forward fall. I took them up to the top of Coire na Ciste where some late snow provided broad, gentle slopes and practised alone until I felt ready to show my ski self in public.

Although I had enjoyed my season immensely and benefited beyond measure I was, for the final few weeks, keen to get away. This, I think, was just a young person's impatience for the new. I wanted to be on the road south eastwards. It was evident that the desire to be moving on had nothing to do with Struan because I made sure, long before leaving, that I was the leading candidate for the post of bar assistant for all the New Years and Easters for all my forthcoming student years.

As the numbers at Struan dwindled, Karl invited me to accompany him, Bill Leitch and Joe Docherty on a trip to see the famous climber, Tom Patey, in Ullapool. I was flattered to be asked but also apprehensive. Accounts of Karl's jaunts had alarmed me and I was sure that a naive character such as me would quickly be embarrassed.

I need not have worried. The 'Silver Cloud' trundled slowly along the narrow roads. In that ninety mile journey we stopped a dozen or more times, to look at a waterfall, to climb a small hill, to examine some rocks, to have coffee, to say 'hello' to someone Karl knew, to admire a peerless view, to talk to some 'kettles' or for no reason at all. As a young man who was always keen to move on, to complete whatever journey I had undertaken, the process was initially frustrating then intensely educative. There was no hurry and at every stop I benefited from Karl's great knowledge of his adopted country.

In Ullapool, Tom and Betty were extremely hospitable. Their extensive garden boasted a replica of a mountain bothy with bunks. Unlike the more remote versions, it had electricity and proper sanitary facilities. Rather than, as I had anticipated, embarking on an orgiastic spree, we spent much of the time in serious conversation. Tom told us of the financial difficulties of his patients who often had to travel the hundred or so miles to Inverness to obtain essential services such as an eye test. The 'system' offered no compensation to most of his flock for the costs of these journeys.

Later the drink flowed more copiously and the talk became lighter but it was all entirely proper. Much of the time, Tom regaled us with fascinating tales of climbing exploits. When we clambered into our respective bunks we were all mood-altered but not to the point of misbehaviour. For reasons which were never manifest, Karl found our accommodation limitlessly funny. He said over and over, perhaps all night because his lullaby eventually sent me to sleep, 'Ha ha ha ha ha, we sleep in de bothy, ha ha ha ha ha.'

Soon after we returned from our west coast trip the last guests departed and the period of spring cleaning began. When I had deconstructed the bars, washed everything washable and reassembled, I was drafted into the house-cleaning team with special responsibility for moving anything that was heavy or stuck.

Had anyone asked me, as I struggled to lift the stair carpet without doing it damage, whether Struan had changed me I would have strongly denied any permanent influence. It was only much later, when I was further down the path of personal development, that I could see how important the experience had been. The place had given me a chance to try out new freedoms in a zone of safety. It was as though I had been moved from a small container into a much bigger one where I felt safe but significantly liberated. The Struan 'family' was so very different from my own.

A simple event on one of the last few mornings illustrates the change.

*Author, Miranda, Jessie, Margaret and Krysksa in the Struan kitchen*

I was having a hard-earned coffee break. It was sunny and the hatch between the kitchen and the dining room was open. The bunched curtains fluttered softly by the distant windows. Across the interior space and through the sparkling glass, the road with its occasional passing traffic was visible. I had been engrossed in the simple work and thinking about trivia but all at once I was filled with a strong sense of opening; the entire world seemed to be making itself available, beckoning, advertising that there was huge enjoyment available for those bold enough to venture out. The feeling was exciting but with it came a large element of fear and, paradoxically, depression. It felt as though all the proffered joy was for others, not for me. They would be having a wonderful time in the coming months whereas I would miss out, unequipped as I was to seize the opportunities.

The only other person in the room was Miranda whom I had come to know quite well. We had said very little but she seemed to pick up on my mood. She smiled and, to my dismay, an inner voice urged me to tell her about how I was feeling. This was by no means my usual practice and it was without consciously intending to do so that I started to speak. Miranda listened patiently, nodding affirmatively then, to my astonishment, she revealed not only that she understood what I was talking about but that she experienced similar conflicts in herself.

It was, I suppose, a small scale event by the standards of many but for me it was a revelation. I discovered that my insecurities were not unique and that I could acknowledge them without being ridiculed or rejected. More importantly, I could talk to a female of the species about a non-trivial matter without being dropped into a deep crevasse.

Miranda was one of the quartet who, in keeping with what had become a Struan tradition, embarked on the end-of-season staff outing. Normally Karl or Eileen would have been present but at the last moment events conspired to prevent them coming. Instead I was delegated to drive the 'Silver Cloud'. Sitting in regal splendour I drove Miranda, Margaret and Kryska along the loch shores and the single track roads. We took the ferry to Skye. The weather was magnificent and the scenery incomparable. We had the best of times.

On my last day, the preparations for Jean Hewlett's wedding were at an advanced stage. The other itinerant workers had gone. Jessie was very keen for me to stay for the ceremony and, in truth, I could have lingered for the remaining few days but I made what I hoped were compelling excuses. The paradoxical need to get away was very strong.

There was some essential nuptial item that was missing. I offered to go to Grantown to remedy the deficiency. As ever, Karl freely made his car available. Mission accomplished, I drove back the longer route via Loch Indorb and the Giant's Face. Speyside was at its sparkling best and I felt dreadful pangs at the imminent parting.

When I returned, there was an impromptu party in progress. A dozen or more people were working hard to set things up for the wedding. There was laughter and much friendly banter. Excited children rushed in and out of the building. The Struan family was in full voice.

I felt a reinforcement of the sadness but the coward in me was still glad that I was fleeing.

Two or three weeks later I was visiting my mother who was in hospital in York. The May sun was unusually strong and the Minster bells rang forcefully. Unbidden, that 'other family' came intensely into my mind and I felt the pricking of tears which, unlike Plum, I would never dare to let free in the company of others. It is likely that my mother noticed but she said nothing. I am sure, though, that I had poured out enough about Struan for her to guess the cause of my distress.

At home I wrote a poem, trite in its imagery and probably mawkish in sentiment, but the process released some feeling and I felt much better. Already I was looking forward to the time of going back.

## 19. Racer Boy

Karl Fuchs was a competitor. He and Eileen would probably not have met had he not been a well known racer in post-war Austria. He knew, when he arrived in Scotland, that his days as a potential international champion were over but the urge to compete was still extremely strong. As a man in his early thirties he could still anticipate some local and regional success. The problem was that he was debarred from Scottish events because they were all for amateurs and he was deemed to be a professional.

It was his love of the race that induced him to leave Eileen, on that afternoon early in her career as a ski instructor, to cope alone with a huge class in the Sugar Bowl whilst he went off to act as vorlaufer on the White Lady. Even though the standard of that race was abysmally low, the simple thrills of being amongst competitors and overcoming the course were sufficient to draw him. It must, though, have been a frustrating experience, akin to a Wimbledon tennis champion having a short knock up with intermediates from a small club.

The frustration of being unable to race did not deter Karl from involvement with Scottish ski competitions. Myrtle Simpson tells that he simply 'decided' that ski races should be held and that he set a course on Coire na Ciste with the same pattern as the 1948 Olympic St. Moritz course. It was at Whitsuntide, when the only snow was in the form of narrow ribbons in the sunless depths of north-facing corries. The event was a success and it became annual. Often the weather was hot. Whitsuntide can fall as late as the first week in June. Competitors became used to perspiring as they toiled uphill and then basking in the sun as they awaited their turn for the downward plunge on the sugary spring snow.

Karl willingly involved himself also in club races, setting courses and helping with the organisation. An indication of the level of racing skill at that time is given by a retrospective piece which appeared in *Ski Magazine*. Through Eileen, Karl says;

'I well remember one incident in a Scottish Ski Club race, for which I set the course down the White Lady and Coire Cas burn. Two brothers turned up from London and decided to enter. One of them took 12 minutes to cover the one-minute course, finishing with one of his new metal skis bent up at right angles by a fall. The other took 15 minutes as he had lost the way and had come down (or rather down and up) by way of Jean's hut. We had to put back the last gate for them as we had removed the flags thinking that there was no-one else to come.'

There was another outlet for Karl's racing enthusiasms, one that quickly came to play a large part in his life. In one of Eileen's memoirs she records that;

'Karli from early on in his life here always got on excellently with the services. After the Marines left, the Navy used to come up for training for their championships and every year in December Karli used to train instructors for the army, with whom as an ex-soldier only too used to snow warfare he had a tremendous rapport. Once enough instructors were trained, the army set up their own centre in Kingussie (now the Joint Services Training Centre). Karli also for many years set the course for the Army championships in the Cairngorms, his best and most original being a two mile one from the top of Fiacaill Ridge to the car park. Some teams, especially the Junior Leaders and our own pet team, the 2nd Battalion Scots Guards, used to stay with us. We used to go to the very enjoyable prize givings and made many friends.'

Until other foreign skiers arrived in sufficient numbers there was little else Karl could do other than play a non-competitive role. The loss of his personal ski racing satisfaction was just one of the sacrifices which he had to make in order to establish Struan. But with the opening of the Norwegian school in Grantown and then the Swiss one in Aviemore, there were eventually sufficient professionals in the area to warrant the creation of a separate event. An annual race for ski instructors was instigated on Cairngorm.

By the time of the first event there were young, keen men in the area. Karl's chances of winning the competition were extremely small. It was true that some of the upstarts would go too fast and crash but there would always be one or two whose luck would hold or who were exceptionally skilful. The 'old man' was realistic enough to acknowledge this but rational conclusions rarely ever extinguish desire. Eilif Moen recalls that so great was Karl's longing to triumph against all reasonable expectations that he finished one Instructors' Race on one ski. Eilif remembers, too, the gloom that descended on Struan in the year when the event was won by the Carrbridge rival, Hans Kuwall. The depression was deepened by the fact that a member of the royal family had agreed, on that occasion, to present the prizes.

It would have been entirely natural, under such circumstances, for a racer whose chances of major competitive honours had been taken away by war and injury, to begin to dream of secondary fulfilment through the success of children. Peter and Lisi had started to ski almost as soon as they could stand and they clearly had better prospects than most people of becoming highly competent. No doubt there were times when Karl did entertain such dreams but he was sufficiently respectful of individuals, and sufficiently wise, not to apply the slightest pressure. The parental policy was to give the children the maximum in the way of opportunity but it was made clear that if they chose other sports, or no sport at all, then there would be absolutely no recriminations.

As toddlers and young children, Peter and Lisi skied quite frequently but they showed not the least interest in being formally competitive. It seemed that if Karl wanted to achieve some final honour for the Fuchs family in ski racing he would have to conjure a miracle by himself but with escalating weight and girth, and with health problems that were beginning to be persistent, he had no apparent chances.

This sad circumstance continued to trouble Karl, but not by any means excessively, and his personal loss was undoubtedly Scotland's gain. He channelled a great deal of his competitive energy into creating the infrastructure of ski racing in Scotland. There had, of course, been local races long before Karl arrived and indeed Scottish-born skiers had distinguished themselves in the pioneering Alpine events, but Continental standards had improved vastly by the end of the 1950's and Scottish skiers had not kept pace. The presence of a well-known, Olympic-standard Continental was just the stimulus that the country needed.

By 1961, enthusiasm for racing was such that the first separate competitive organisation was formed, the Glencoe Ski Club. With very limited resources, the fifty or so activists built their own clubhouse and devoted all their efforts to the training of ski racers. It was at about this time that the Scottish National Ski Council was inaugurated and this, through the National Ski Federation of Great Britain, began to have a voice in the international arena.

The SNSC decided that, since Scotland was short of experience in race organisation, its first training initiative should be for time keepers. Myrtle Simpson recounts the story of how the first willing band of recruits was sent, one October, to the hills around Pitlochry. There was, naturally, no snow but the trainers had thought about this. Motorists, locals going about their business, late-season tourists, ambitious salesmen in their company cars, were startled to see furtive folk hidden in the roadside heather. Many must have checked their speedometers in alarm and looked wildly about them for evidence of a speed restriction on the open country road. Some parts of Scotland were notorious, in those days, for high levels of police activity in the implementation of traffic regulations. The enhancement of Scottish ski racing was doubtless achieved against an unintended raising of stress amongst the innocent.

Recognising that the 'amateurs only' rule was severely limiting the prospects of Scottish ski racing, the SNSC set about removing the restriction. This crucial change came too late for Karl to make a competitive impact. With the demands of his business and the inescapable fact of his gradual physical decline he was not in a position to enter the newly opened lists. However, he was delighted that the teachers which he was regularly importing from Europe would be able to continue their racing careers whilst they were in Britain.

According to the account in 'Skisters', the standard of racing in Scotland improved instantly. Amateurs who had felt themselves to be doing quite nicely were all at once up against people of a different pedigree. Far from discouraging entrants, the new challenge proved galvanizing. The SNSC decided that it should appoint a part time coach to capitalise on the fresh enthusiasm. Karl was utterly delighted when they chose his protégé, Norbert Uitz, for the task.

Myrtle Simpson records that Norbert, full of proselytising zeal for his new job, prevailed upon the Council to allocate extra resources to those clubs which ran junior training schemes. The prospects for future success lay, Norbert realised, with the next generation. Karl agreed, even though it seemed that his own two youngsters would not be among the beneficiaries.

The SNSC took over the organisation of all the major races. 'Skisters' has an amusing account of the 1964 Pitman Quaich which was reportedly set with some glee by Hans Kuwall down 'Glencoe ice'. The setter's mirth apparently vanished when he was invited to act as vorlaufer for his creation and he struck terror into the waiting competitors by hurtling off into the rocks at the fifth gate. Some survived, although it is reported that one succeeded in taking the timing equipment with him across the finishing line.

Although Karl had some reservations about the way ski racing was developing in Scotland, he was overall delighted that what had been an entirely amateur and fairly haphazard process was being brought more up-to-date. If his children ever decided that they wanted to compete they would at least have the chance of working in a proper framework, through junior levels, into local senior competition and then, perhaps, progressing to international races.

All that he had left of his once glittering racing career was the instructors' race which, year by year, became ever more competitive. With several flourishing ski schools, most of them using a proportion of foreign teachers, there were always keen youngsters willing to risk all for the chance of adding another trophy to their collections. A forty year old in deteriorating health had little hope.

Against the advice of some, Karl entered the 1964 event as usual. With his pendant belly he looked an unlikely racer, even though he made the fleshy counterweight seem free of gravity as he skied. One or two friends thought that he risked humiliation in the company of the young tigers but Karl could not be dissuaded. He would ski the course steadily, register a very respectable time, enjoy the process immensely and be entirely delighted with a placing in the top twenty.

The race was, as usual, to be held towards the end of the season. On the preceding day, Karl was being filmed for a television advertisement which sought to associate the delights of winter sport with a well known Scottish tipple, McEwan's Export. The campaign was lavishly funded and the film company brought a full team with them, including an Equity-approved actor who, in spite of advice that no Struan barman would dream of wearing a natty white jacket, insisted on looking like an employee of the Ritz. There were the predictable delays in setting everything up, and then dissatisfactions with minor details of the various 'takes'. The result was that, on the morning of the race, Karl still had some work to do.

The sun shone strongly through the Edelweiss windows. The barman's starched apparel gleamed. The technicians insisted on adding lemonade to the brimming half pint to provide an added, if misleading, sparkle. It was Karl's task to pick up the glass, raise it to his lips, take a foamy swig and declare, 'There's nothing like a McEwan's after skiing! Cheers!'

The fact is that he did not have to act. He did indeed drink McEwans quite frequently after skiing. He *believed* there was nothing like it. He could declare it in all sincerity.

The problem was that the director of the show was not persuaded. It was something in the star's Scotstrian style which caused the difficulty. There was take after take. Karl began to get agitated because he was in danger of being late for the race but the commercial imperative kept him captured. 'There's nothing like a McEwans after skiing! Cheers!' Over and over again he sipped and said it.

Karl could drink. Twenty or so gulps of diluted foam should not have affected him greatly but the palpable fact was that as he set off for the slopes he was more than half gone. He giggled like a schoolboy and grinned as though he were about to have a special treat rather than risk life and limb in a race he had once desperately wanted to win. He was a victim of one of those puzzling events when a relatively small amount of alcohol, taken at an unusual time or in an unfamiliar way, can have disproportionate effect.

*Karl at speed*

The world surely still seemed a rosy place to Karl as he pushed himself off down the slope. Skiing was an easy business. He sailed through as though there were no gates. Youngsters before had been faster but they had all crashed or lost their way through the maze. There was a huge cheer as Karl shot between the poles that marked the finish and came to a precise, neat halt. He was sweating profusely with the effort and the effect of the beer. Someone told him that he had posted the fastest time so far. He knew that he had skied well but could not have dreamed of being in the lead, however temporary the advantage.

There were rivals a-plenty still to come. Karl watched them, one by one. A mistake here, a missed gate there, a spectacular tumble; they were all trying to beat his time and they were all running beyond the limits. The main contenders eliminated themselves but there were the later starters, not fancied to win but good skiers, any one of them capable of putting on a freak performance. Down they came, one after another, some failing to finish, others slower than Karl by a margin. The last one was no different; he was no match.

The man who had won national championships in Austria, who had not so very long ago had realistic dreams of Olympic glory, was the winner of the 1964 Cairngorm Ski Instructors Race. In his adopted home, against all the young lions, he had proved himself a winner.

It was a sweet moment.

## 20. A Barman's Tale

Eileen once wrote that the bar was the 'heart' of Struan. It was this, and a whole heap of other body parts too, most of them visceral. The freedom of the 1960's found full scope in the cosy Edelweiss.

In the original house, the space must have been intended for reception but prior to conversion it was Karl and Eileen's bedroom. It had a bay window and two doors, one giving access from the entrance hall, the other from the dining room. Karl and Sandy Panton 'Austrianised' it totally.

The tiny bar, just large enough to accommodate two with difficulty, was formed by a quarter circle of rough-cut wood, like a palisade, with a corresponding ceiling-mounted 'fringe'. I was quickly to discover that these cowboy 'shoot-out' accoutrements were entirely appropriate.

The bar top was covered with dark red formica and beneath it, at inconvenient height for all but the smaller human beings, was a sink. Between bar and the upper structure was a flimsy green concertina shutter, later decorated with paintings of pretty Edelweiss flowers by Peter at his parents' request. There were shelves, of course, above and below, and a few holders for inverted bottles with their 'optics'. Staff gained access via a lift-up section of the bar and a half door, both of which were usually left open to minimise the risk of claustrophobia. There was, for many years, no supply of draught liquids. Beer was brought in by the crate and stacked on the floor, reducing manoeuvring space even further. During the frequent busy times the fetching of fresh supplies and the removal of empties was a torture.

The remainder of the room, including the bay window, had pine-clad, built-in seating, topped with thin strips of red-covered cushion. There were three or four small, formica-surfaced, circular tables made from barrels and a few nondescript chairs. On the nicotine-stained walls were old skis, snow shoes, crampons and photographs of mountain scenes.

To Karl's great delight there were also small regimental shields. Military men, including General Leathes, the head of the Marines, were regular visitors to Struan and Karl always seized the opportunity to acquire another trophy for his collection. The soldiers took their opportunities too. One of them, attending one of the famous Junior Scottish Skiing Championship prize-givings which were often held at Struan, was presented with a Struan tie, designed by Karl and incorporating the skiing snow hare. The distinguished guest was so delighted with his gift that he tore off his regimental neckwear and donned the Struan one. Eileen's only concern in this, as in many other things, was that Karl's natural generosity sometimes went beyond the bounds of good economic sense.

It mattered not to these senior soldiers that the Fuchs' residence boasted a portrait of their host in German uniform adorned with the Iron Cross. In fact, one Major declared himself to be mightily impressed with the image and gladly supplied another shield to be mounted on the wall.

In time, Karl supplemented the Edelweiss decoration by inscribing, on a strip of wood above the seats, the names of all the instructors. On a shelf in the corner opposite the bar, mounted just above the door into the dining room, were a few tarnished ski race trophies and a small accordion.

From its inception, the Edelweiss was successful. For the bone-weary skier, bathed and fed, there could be nothing more enticing than a cosy bar on the premises; no need to face the exterior cold, no worry about finding the way home when suffering from alcohol-reduced acuity.

Some of the villagers were attracted too and most of them treated the new facility with respect. There were, though, one or two who made a habit of drifting in on Sundays. Nowadays this would present no problems but then there was the curse of the six day licence. On the Sabbath, only bona-fide travellers and hotel guests could buy drinks. To fit the 'traveller' criterion, a drinker had to be at least three miles from home and, supposedly, en route for somewhere further. The fact that this blatantly encouraged the dangerous practice of drinking and driving seemed to have no influence on the killjoy regulation-makers.

*Bartenders*

A couple of wily locals quickly saw that Karl's generosity was almost reflex. It was well known that Struan's ever genial host would greet any local caller warmly with the expression, 'You haf a drink?' It was an invitation to be answered with, 'Why, thank ye Karl, that's very kind, I'll have a hauf and a hauf.' Beer and whisky, the lethal 'chaser' syndrome. On weekdays there was a social obligation to offer to return the compliment but on Sundays the few freeloaders could not pay without breaking the law. Naturally they were so sad about this that they had to have another 'on the house' offering, and then others, to anaesthetise their feelings.

For a while after this practice started, Eileen would stoically tolerate the abuse of her husband's nature, hoping that the process would be short-lived, but eventually she could stand it no more. She took to leaving the bar in a theatrically pointed fashion, trusting that the guilty would take the hint. Instead they usually took more drink and when Eileen returned they would respond to her hostile stare with mock-incredulous 'what's troubling you?' looks of their own.

There were no regular bar workers in the years before the hotel expanded. Karl, Eileen and the ski instructors would take turns at serving drinks. Pricing was based on the advice of Walter McKinnon, bartender at the Carlton Hotel in Inverness. A young man called Hugh Hunter-Gordon, who was later to play a prominent part in the development of Scottish skiing, was one of the most frequent 'instructor-barmen' in the Edelweiss. None of them, however, felt able to restrict Karl's largesse. If mine host ordered free drinks for everyone in the bar, the goods were duly delivered and no record was kept.

Commercially this was not good practice but it was probably through such informality that the Edelweiss became an unconventional place. There were many evenings when nothing much happened beyond quiet conversation but there were plenty of others when, without any individual acting as orchestrator, the social temperature would rise. Very often it was self-made music which started the escalation but it could also be simply a combination of strong characters with a taste for the comic and a desire for the unusual. Impromptu dances, crazy games, story-telling; there were many ways an Edelweiss evening could develop.

It was not for everyone, of course but in this, as in other aspects of Struan life, the clientele was largely self-selecting. Those who were appalled by uninhibited behaviour did not return. Those who loved the prospect of the unexpected came back year after year.

Yet it was not just a case of crude 'natural selection'. What Struan seemed to be able to do was provide people with free space. There are very many who deeply want to be frivolous, or who would love to indulge in extravagant display, but who are constrained by inhibitions. With its rare atmosphere of freedom, Struan seemed to take away the worries about looking silly. It was totally acceptable to do the outrageous.

Once word went round that Struan was the place to be then, naturally, free spirits were attracted. One of the first of the wild was Tom Patey, doctor, climber, 'brave skier' and enthusiast for the Cairngorm ski development.

Tom was born in 1932 in a village called Ellon in Aberdeenshire. His father was an Episcopalian minister and it was the entirely respectable

Boy Scout movement which introduced the clergyman's son to the outdoor life. By the time he was an eighteen year old medical student in Aberdeen, Tom was, according to Chris Brasher, making 'epic' first ascents of ferociously difficult climbs, mainly in winter. In his autobiography 'One Man's Mountains', Tom declares that; 'Winter mountaineering, as currently defined in Scotland, only began as late as the thirties.' He gives full credit for this development to the Glasgow climbers but there is no doubt that he quickly became a central figure in the sport.

Tom chanced upon Struan when he was doing national military service. His Marines regiment was temporarily based in the Cairngorms, practising snow and ice climbing and winter warfare techniques. When he had completed his period of conscription, Tom became a General Practitioner in the west coast town of Ullapool where he and his wife, Betty, had three children. Although ninety miles from Struan, and linked by roads that in many places were wide enough for only one vehicle, he was a regular visitor. Eric Langmuir, a great friend of Tom's and a fellow climber, recalls the 'primitive' Skoda car, to which Tom was devoted, which carried him faithfully on his rounds, climbing expeditions and nocturnal excursions to Carrbridge. Eileen describes the Patey impact.

'Tom was a brilliant accordionist and used to play for hours on end, everything that was suggested from Scottish dance music to bothy ballads to continental folk music. He and his Marine friends particularly liked to tempt Karli into singing German war songs and on many evenings the rafters rang with the Horst Wessel Lied and Wir Fahren Gegen England with a spirited accompaniment and a sonorous male voice chorus. Our Austrian instructors used to slink out in horror when this happened for these songs were still banned in Austria.

'Tom brought his climbing friends, service and civilian and sometimes all the officers from the Colonel downwards would appear. Joe Brown, Graham Nicol, Dougal Haston, Chris Bonington are some of the climbers' names I remember. It was not uncommon to find two eightsome reels being danced simultaneously in our tiny bar. On one of these occasions some of our residents had gone out for a drink and I shall never forget their look of delighted incredulity on returning home as they plunged into one of these Edelweiss parties. Tom would also tour the landings serenading those guests who had gone to bed too early and Norbert and Karli would give the false alarm "In bus please" at 4 am when they got up to make the sandwiches. Skiing holidays at Struan required stamina. The first year Tom ended up in hospital with nervous exhaustion and totally lost his voice while I moved in a daze for weeks after sitting up night after night, cooking in the morning and skiing for the rest of the day.

'We did have some quiet evenings when a local couple who were great Scottish dancing enthusiasts came to teach the guests. The proceedings were too solemn for some and one man danced for a whole evening in a tartan towel for a kilt and a camera case for a sporran without apparently being noticed by the teachers.'

A short way down the road towards the centre of the village was another small hotel which, under the enthusiastic direction of its owner, Jimmy Ross, began to have musical evenings. Eventually even the august Carrbridge Hotel provided organised 'folk nights' but Struan was the place for spontaneity. Tom Patey would sometimes take his talents to the Rowanlea which, one Carrbridge veteran recalls, was the venue for 'serious' music. A young Scottish politician called Winnie Ewing was allegedly once asked to leave the bar because she persisted in talking whilst people were singing. At Struan there were no overbearing rules. The singing was, in any case, usually loud enough to drown out any chatter.

Clive Freshwater, who was based at Glenmore but who, much later, established a very successful water sports business on the shores of Loch Insh, remembers meeting Tom Patey at the Rowanlea. Clive was sufficiently skilled as a musician to perform professionally. He already knew Karl because the Carrbridge Austrian Ski School offered free tuition to Glenmore staff and he had taken full advantage of this. On the evenings when a touch of anarchy seemed inviting, it took little persuasion to get him to give a free demonstration of his troubadour talents in the Edelweiss.

There were other musicians who joined the band. George McLeod who had been working at Glenmore Lodge when Struan started, and returned from the first of his spells in the Antarctic just after the bar was opened, was a singer and guitarist whom Karl particularly welcomed. He had been Tom Patey's associate in Aberdeen climbing days so they were well used to each other's repertoire. As soon as his face appeared in the bar Karl would cry, 'A King George for King George!' and the specially procured bottle of royally-named whisky would be taken down from the shelf. Augmented by Jimmy Hutchinson, Eric Beard and others, these maestros would set the Edelweiss rocking. Sometimes the music would go on for hours, sometimes the entertainment would develop in other directions; always the revelries would persist until the winter dawn was close.

*Tom Patey on Rakaposhi - frostbite no barrier to music!*

Eileen remembers hearing that, the morning after one such evening, a General of the British Army was to be seen wandering around Glenmore in his socks, cursing some devil who had purloined his climbing boots from the drying room. His anticipated day in the wilderness was ruined. It was reported that in the evening, the frustrated General spluttered, turned several shades of purple and pointed accusatorially with shaking index finger as Tom returned from a good day's climbing. Thinking that he was faced with a rare case of ague, the doctor began to rack his brains for ideas for appropriate treatment. There was a moment's total confusion before the good soldier managed to squeak, 'My boots!'

Tom looked down in horror. From being the saving angel he was suddenly the thieving devil. So other-worldly had he been as a result of the Struan night that he had absent-mindedly mistaken the footwear for his. It was only the promise of another good Struan entertainment which eventually placated the furious soldier.

The regular musicians were important to Struan but there were many, many others who just wandered in or who heard of the reputation of the place and made a point of seeking it out. The combination of instruments varied indefinitely. Usually there would be two or three six stringed guitars, at least one twelve stringed version and the accordion but these could be augmented by recorders, whistles, flutes, percussion instruments, banjos, ukuleles, concertinas, Irish pipes, Northumberland pipes and many others.

Karl, with some experience on the mandolin to draw on, acquired his own version of Tom Patey's machine and learned to pick out a few Austrian tunes. His technique, it has to be admitted, was predominantly *glissando*. The seeking fingers, fixed to play in thirds, slid up and down the keyboard until they found the note, whereupon he belted the sound out fortissimo. It was not highly aesthetic but it worked. Those doting guests, many of them female, who deified Karl thought that the performances were wonderful. When the wheezy, sliding sound was accompanied by little bursts of yodelling, the worshippers were in raptures.

But in fact a 'good night' could develop without a single instrumentalist in the house. If 'Grandpa' was in residence, as he quite often was, he could galvanise guests into giving voice. A broad repertoire became known to many people and there were always volunteers who joined the impromptu choir. Other than the all-action Austrian drinking songs, Maurice had a few reliable show-starters. One of his 'standards' was 'Goliath of Gath', a thong to be thung with copiuth lithping. Perhaps his favourite rabble rouser was 'Oh Sir Jasper' which had a lyric not noted for its subtlety:

*Oh Sir Jasper do not touch me (repeated three times)*
*As she lay between the lily white sheets with nothing on at all.*

The delight, if it can be classified as such, was that the song was repeated several times, the first line being reduced by one word with each rendition. 'Oh, Sir Jasper do not touch' was innocuous enough but an inebriated crowd could put all manner of libidinous feeling into, 'Oh Sir Jasper do not. ' With Grandpa conducting to make sure that everyone came in after the appropriate number of missed words the, 'Oh Sir Jasper, *doooooo*!' usually rattled the bottles and glasses whilst the 'Oh *Sir*!' threatened to break them. The piece de resistance, of course, was the final '*Ohhhhhhhh*', which gave every evidence of communal bliss.

*Karl in mellow mood entertains ski instructors in the Edelweiss*

Simple fun, perhaps, but the song and similar ones usually shook people out of their inhibitions and helped to set the scene for later mayhem. The proprietors had not, in the staid mid 1950's, anticipated that the social life would develop quite so spectacularly but they were rightly proud of what they had facilitated. Eileen remembers how news of the wildness quite soon reached a wide audience.

'On one of the more hilarious Marines evenings, when many turned up in drag complete with oranges, they brought a crew who were making a film up at Glenmore. I bet these people they would not dare to make a film of a Struan House evening and sure enough they turned up the next year and made a 'Look at Life' picture showing not only the bar and the Scottish dancing but also a great deal of skiing. This was mainly of Karli and our Austrian instructors of that year, Franzi Stock and Ludwig Langreiter doing threefold wedeln and mambo and also of our two children who were already on skis. It was called 'Snow Business' and Karli and I went to the premiere in Glasgow.'

It should not be concluded that the music and the 'boy scout' singsongs, the orange-breasted drag party and the silly games implied a limiting naiveté amongst the Struan guests. The later evening activities were often strictly for adults only. One Struan veteran tells, with a wry smile and a shine in the eyes, of a happening fairly early on in the ski hotel's history.

A young woman, who had no pretensions to classical beauty but who had a power to attract strong men, found the Struan ambience entirely to her liking. She was wilful, unconventional and eager to take the maximum from life. Amongst the instructors and the climbers an intense rivalry for her affections developed. There were assignations and gossip, boastings and apparent betrayals. The talk was often jocular but within themselves the men were serious; they all wanted this woman.

It happened that, late one evening, half a dozen or more of these ardent suitors were with her in the Struan dining room. Everybody else had drifted off to bed. The men, comradely in behaviour but intensely competitive, attempted to outshine each other. She relished her power. A strange dance developed, the entranced men in a circle, the woman at the centre. Teasingly she drifted towards each of them in turn. One, inadvisably, grabbed her and tried to force a kiss. She seemed to tolerate this for a second but then she bit him on the lip, hard enough to draw blood.

The dance continued, the bleeding one still hoping that his boldness would prove decisive but when she was ready, the siren chose another and left.

The rejected ones sat around, drowning their sorrows in a spirit of disconsolate comradeship until, entirely to their surprise, the woman reappeared with an enigmatic smile on her adorable lips. Had she eaten the selected one, tossed him out of the window, flushed him down the sewers? None knew and none cared. The market was open again. The dance resumed.

It is said that weeks subsequently there were unscheduled, embarrassing meetings of Struanites in the northern English city whence this magnetic female came. Her power persisted.

Moralists might look askance at such happenings but in fact there was nothing amiss. Free individuals were doing what they thought was right for them, exploiting nobody. Then, and thereafter, Struan offered freedom of action and this was part of its intense attraction. Guests and staff knew that they could live their lives to a much fuller extent than normally, they could take risks, exercise to the limits, drink to the point of disinhibition, display without fear of ridicule and express aspects of their beings which were normally hidden.

By the time I arrived as Struan's first barman towards the very end of 1963 the tradition of creative anarchy was already very well set although I knew nothing of such lewd shenanigans. Because of the wedding duties, I did not start work until Hogmanay was looming. I arrived to scenes which extravagant Italian film directors would have relished. Knowing nobody, knowing nothing at all about running a bar, I was a lost being.

On my first evening, when mercifully I was not expected to work after the prolonged train journey, almost the first people I saw were clad in sheets. I had no idea then why they were so attired but Eileen says that they were Roman soldiers, part of a fancy dress event. The mystery got me off to a surreal start. Most of the seeming hundreds who milled about were more conventionally attired but they were alarmingly jocular. The bar, my future domain, was almost inaccessible through the human press. In the television lounge, in the dining room, in the inaptly named 'quiet' lounge, people drank and made exceedingly merry.

I did little but exist in the chaos, absorbing, trying to identify key individuals. Karl was unmistakable and, of course, I soon came to recognise Eileen. The remainder defeated my taxonomical skills. Workers and guests were indistinguishable. It seemed that eight or a dozen people were taking turns at doing what, all too terrifyingly soon, would be my job. From some of these I tried to elicit information about measures, glass sizes, prices and other key indicators but the advice was either vague or in total contradiction to what someone else had said. It was not that there actually was no structure, because Walter McKinnon had made his substantial professional input, but the story, like any one that gets passed from person to person, had become distorted.

I spent as much time as possible in the brand new bar facility which was essentially a storeroom with a hatch which opened out onto the dining room. At least some peace could be found there and conversation could be carried on without shouting. The instructor who was dispensing drinks seemed almost as vague as I was about the logistics but he was excellent at reassuring me that precision was not important. As long as the customers got their drinks and some money went into the till everybody would be happy.

From Eileen on the first morning I learned some of the mysteries concerned with ordering supplies. None of it seemed easy. Whether the bottles were coming from Grantown, Inverness or further afield, the response would never be rapid. Great foresight was required and I had not the least idea how many packets of salt and vinegar crisps would be consumed in a fortnight by an unknown number of rampaging skiers.

I practised being in the pen, muttering what I took to be suitable barman phrases. Osmotically, or so it seemed, I learned about the cash till and the closing down routine. Instructors Bill Leitch or Joe Docherty would, I was told, relieve me for half an hour in the evening so that I could eat dinner in the kitchen.

One rule was made very specific. Non-residents could not buy drinks after ten o'clock and at any time on Sundays. If in doubt about a potential customer's status I was to politely challenge. The penalty for failing in this task could be loss of the hard won licence. There were, I gathered, local anti-alcohol fanatics, members of the 'Wee Free' church, who spurred the Carrbridge constabulary into making raids. It was the policemen's charming practice to pick up the register of guests from the hallway and go round the bar, demanding to be shown the signatures of the drinkers. A serious loophole in this ridiculous restriction was that residents could buy drinks for visitors. All it took was a little exercise of creative introductions and everyone could continue drinking.

The following evening I was in charge of the proceedings Drinks were certainly dispensed, money was tossed into the till but how the economic balance of the business worked out I have no idea. It seemed to me that about one third of the transactions were at Karl's behest and there was no cash and no record for these. When my stack of wire crates contained only empties I tried to emerge with two of them in search of replenishments. Even though the people around me had a vested interest in the venture it took me minutes to escape. In the hallway, in the lounges, in the dining room, people milled. Some angel, probably an instructor, said that he would open the other bar. He did so but there was no appreciable drop in the pressure on my services. It was well after midnight when I noticed the first minor lull and near to two in the morning when it felt as though an end might be in sight. Throughout, there was a dreadful problem with the supply of glasses to the point where, for much of the time, those who did not present me with one could not be given a drink. Collecting empties, which then had to be washed and dried by hand, was an ordeal which I faced only a couple of times.

I got to bed at about five o'clock and spent much of the next day restocking the bar and washing the glasses. The following night was even more hectic. By the time Hogmanay arrived I was not far from hysteria.

The mayhem started as soon as the skiers returned. The bar was stocked to its maximum, every glass was clean and in place. By the time the dinner gong sounded, a good half of the Struan clientele was half cut. The meal took large numbers out of my immediate sight but there were plenty who had either decided against eating or who had made other arrangements. They carried on pouring liquid down their throats whilst I did my best to replenish stocks. By the time the diners returned I was as prepared as I could be.

Arrangements had been made for an assortment of instructors and Struan well-wishers to run the dining room bar from about nine o'clock. There were kind folk who promised to help with the collecting of glasses and the fetching of crates. Eileen assured me that at three or four in the morning she would be cooking a full breakfast and that somebody would look after the bar whilst I ate. With this enticing prospect, I prepared for the siege.

The analogy is apt. For long periods the substantial defence built by Karl and Sandy Panton was rocking alarmingly. When one customer ordered fourteen double whiskies and triumphantly planted the empty glasses all in a row I poured the fluid out as though it were British Rail tea slopping over thick mugs. Every transaction had to be shouted at maximum volume. Not normally much of a drinker, and having piously resolved that I would imbibe only sparingly when on duty, I began to behave out of character. 'Have one yersel,' had up to then been politely resisted but I realised that a degree of anaesthesia was essential for survival. Every now and then, I accepted an offer and a fog began to gather where there had been crystal clarity.

I was feeling exceedingly happy when it somehow registered that the clock was past ten. My sense of duty cut through the haze. To the next customer lucky enough to grab my attention I yelled, 'Are you a resident?'

Did I speak English? Was I insane? All around, people were thrusting glasses or holding up money. 'Excuse me, but are you a resident, are you a resident?'

They looked at me with pity, with incomprehension, perhaps with a touch of ill-considered loathing. This was Scotland, this was Hogmanay, my job was to serve alcohol and I was quizzing the customers as to where they were sleeping! Yes, of course they were residents, they would crash in their comas and sleep on the floor.

Utterly defeated, I made the tactical assumption that the police would be mostly off duty in such a rural area, having their own celebrations. I carried on serving.

At a quarter to twelve I thought that the barrier would topple. I had, by this time, had even more of the whisky and about imminent collapse of myself or the structure I did not care too greatly. I poured and I poured, trying desperately to do accurate mental arithmetic. Whatever total I came up with, people paid without question. I'm sure that there were losers and gainers but that, from Struan's point of view, rough economic justice was done.

Then people started counting, ten down to zero. Those who had been yelling orders desisted, to join in the chant. After the last number came the whoops and the screams and the cries of 'Happy New Year!' People began randomly kissing. To an innocent such as me it looked like an orgy. Safe, so I thought, in my enclave, I watched in astonishment. Of the population of characters within my head, half felt glad to be out of it and half felt desperately sad.

Then someone noticed; the solitary barman! My space was invaded. Females flitted into the confined space, filling it with a heady mixture of pheromones and perfumes. Given that nobody took the slightest notice, being engaged on their own osculations, I relaxed a little and allowed myself a hint of enjoyment. One particularly clingy creature, who seemed determined to make up for all the New Years I had missed and to put a few in store for the Hogmanays to come, made particular inroads on my reserve and I was not entirely pleased when a friendly but insistent loud voice called me back to my duties.

To my surprise, large numbers of people then left, clutching bottles. I learned later that they were going 'first footing', visiting village houses to wish the inhabitants a happy new year. Just as I was thinking that this exodus would bring some relief, more people came to replace them. For a couple of hours I worked at full pace. Messages from the other front indicated that the dining room bar was busy too. On the occasions when I had to force my way out with empty crates and return with full ones I saw no vacant spaces. Every public room in the place seemed to be packed.

Eileen came at about three to announce that breakfast was served. One of the instructors guarded the bar whilst I took my break. Having reduced my rate of drinking once the twelve o'clock madness was over

I was comparatively sober but still sufficiently mood-influenced to see the world in a very positive light. I felt that I was experiencing something very unusual and that the position I held, which allowed me to be part of it but with limitations, was ideal for my psychological state.

After breakfast, some of those who were facing a hard day's work within a few hours time managed to drag themselves off to bed but many of the guests were by no means exhausted. Groups drifted back from first footing, evidently having received excellent hospitality. The dining room bar was closed but the Edelweiss continued to do healthy business.

At about six, when few were ordering drinks, I decided to range around the ground floor, collecting glasses from far flung corners. Every person still conscious in my immediate environment was benignly drunk. Some of them conducted foolish conversations across the Edelweiss tables, some smooched floppily to record-player music in the dining room. Others, I soon discovered, were up to other things.

There were dirty glasses on the stairs. As I collected them, a soft noise from above attracted my attention. The light on the landing had been turned out but there was enough illumination for me to see two closely-encountering bodies both of which seemed to have shed a considerable proportion of their clothing. I hastened modestly away, towards the quiet lounge. It seemed to be empty so I snapped on the light, bringing an immediate assault of slurred and muffled curses. There were couples on both couches and, as far as I could tell from the cries of protest, another on the floor close to the window. I gave them back their darkness and rushed nervously away.

As I passed the front door on my way back into the bar, a man entered. He was tall and slim, elderly but seeming fit. He wore a long, green cape and a countryman's hat. His eyes engaged with mine and I found his look disturbing. He followed me silently into the bar. The alarming eyes wandered constantly as though he was looking for someone. He was clearly not a resident but nonetheless I asked what he wanted and he answered, 'A nip'. By that, and his soft accent, I assumed that he was Scottish but I formed the impression that he would have blended in anywhere. As far as I could tell he had no vehicle but when I asked if he had come far he nodded and said, 'Aye, a very long way.' He drank his whisky in small, frequent sips, and wandered about, peering into the dining room at the few remaining revellers and staring out into the hall. When the glass was empty he deposited it carefully on the counter, thanked me politely and quietly departed.

At that time I had no knowledge of Yeats and the 'Wandering Aeongus' and I have little enough now but I think of that man as an exemplar of the eternal seeker of a lost love. His beloved girl had run off decades ago and he was forlornly searching.

The contrast of quietness which came after the New Year guests departed made me feel a little uneasy. There seemed no point in paying a barman to service six guests but Eileen assured me that life would be busy again quite soon enough.

One evening soon after the crowds had started to gather again I was in the bar, enjoying the time when all the guests were at dinner. Except for the rare occasions when outsiders drifted in for a drink, or Mrs. Anderson next door delayed serving the meal because there was a particular television programme which could not be missed, my entire clientele disappeared for an hour. For half of this I washed glasses and restocked the shelves, for the other I ate my own repast in the kitchen. On this particular occasion I was in the first phase of the quiet time and was going to and from the storeroom. As a relief from the general musical diet of Beatles and Stones I had put on a recording of Beethoven's eighth symphony, one of several discs which I had optimistically brought with me and which, when Eileen was in residence, were used as accompaniment to the daily sandwich-making.

When I returned to the bar after an absence of several minutes I saw a man in a shapeless grey sweater, playing the accordion. Note by note, he was going along with the music. The player looked up, smiled engagingly and continued to the end of the movement. I said, 'That's astonishing.' He modestly shrugged. Boldly I tried, 'Tom Patey, I presume,' having heard of his mastery of the instrument but having no idea that it extended to the classical repertoire. 'The very same,' he replied.

When the diners returned I witnessed the other aspects of the Patey brilliance. It seemed there was no song unknown to him, no hummed phrase that he could not pick up and embellish. Being fond of a song or two myself, and seeing no reason why the barman should not join in the choruses I did so and enjoyed the evening just as much as if I had not been working.

Over that winter I came to know the famous climbing doctor quite well. He often appeared when the Struanites were eating and we discoursed privately on a wide range of subjects. He was by no means tall, and markedly rounded in the shoulders, but he exuded a physical power. His speech was soft, with the hint of a lisp, yet he was the kind of talker who commanded attention. His sense of humour was prominent and a trifle macabre. He would describe in great detail how he planned to outdo his rivals, known to the world as his friends. In fact when Joe Brown and the others eventually visited Struan I could see that there was a very strong comradeship but Tom insisted that one day he would purloin Joe Brown's boots and implant tiny, remotely-controlled heating elements into the soles such that when Joe was negotiating a particularly steep and tricky stretch of ice he could, by twiddling knobs at the bottom of the cliff, bring about a mysterious downfall. For all that I kept smiling and looking for the doctor's grin he seemed entirely serious.

Perhaps he was, because he later told me of a time when many of the comrades, all famous climbers, were on a winter jaunt in the Cairngorms. On the way back a blizzard developed until they were literally wading through drifts. 'One would think,' Tom said reflectively, 'that we could have worked cooperatively but the truth is that when personal survival was in question we would have stepped on each other's heads if that had been the route to safety.'

Tom, it seemed to me, was an honest person who was not afraid of the apparent contradiction between friendship and rivalry. Competitiveness was an integral part of their mountaineer's world and he saw no point in denying this.

The only circumstances when I declined to put my trust in the man was when he arrived early in the morning on his way to a climb and suggested that I should go with him. With absolutely no experience in the sport, and an innate terror of heights, the last thing I wanted to do was cling to a cliff by a quarter inch of boot sole and a couple of finger nails. Tom kept assuring me that he would pick something easy but I had been warned. He was not, of course, lying; it's just that what seemed easy to him was utterly impossible for practically everyone else on the planet.

There were times, though, during that season when it was tempting to take up any sport other than skiing. The climate could hardly have been less accommodating. Rarely was there more 'snow' cover than a few slivers of what was truly ice in the very bottom of the corries. Karl used to say, 'Mah! like de bottle. I cannot ski today.' He would pick up an empty McEwan's container and run his work-hardened fingertip over it to illustrate the point. Of course, his 'cannot ski' was based upon criteria nobody else could perceive. Whatever it felt like to Karl, he always looked immaculate and totally solid, whether he was moving over glass or through a frozen representation of some of Jessie's excellent porridge. The acute shortage of snow might have been bearable during the quieter months when there were fewer skiers competing for scarce space had it not been for Scotland's other bugbear; the wind.

There was one week in February when it started to blow on the Saturday as the new batch of guests arrived and continued without abatement for eight entire days. Those who were up for the week were optimistic on the Sunday. Such a gale would surely blow itself out. Seventy two hours later there were no cheerful smiles. By the Friday, when the air was whistling over the mountain tops faster than ever and there had been no skiing whatsoever, the mood was almost ugly. Reason said that it was obviously nobody's fault that the weather was so vile but sorely disappointed people needed somebody to blame.

As part of my effort to circumvent rebellion I kept the bar open constantly. On the gloomy last afternoon of their ruined holiday the guests were packed into the Edelweiss drinking steadily. Karl was sitting in the window seat and, very unusually, was talking about the war. Perhaps he was trying to put temporary difficulties into perspective. He was certainly succeeding in making hitherto disgruntled people laugh. Those not in Karl's immediate circle were not amused. Mostly they were looking gloomily into their glasses and wondering whether they should once more get mind-numbingly drunk.

Some ski instructors entered, amongst them a young Austrian, one of Hans Kuwall's staff, called Ricky. His eyes were amongst the bluest. He was classically handsome, very athletic. He ordered a beer which I poured into a thin, stemmed glass. We knew each other a little and he made polite conversation as he leaned against the bar. It was very evident that he had been drinking for some time. His companions drifted away. Ricky supped steadily. There was something in his manner which caused me concern and I watched him, wondering if he were more inebriated than I thought. He saw me looking. I thought that maybe the attention was unwelcome but after he had sipped the last of the liquid he treated me to a mirthless smile. Then, to my horrified astonishment, he bit a large chunk out of the glass.

As though everyone had seen or sensed, the noise in the bar stopped instantly. All that could be heard was the crunch, crunch, crunch of Ricky's mad munching. I thought it might be a suicide attempt; the boy had perhaps been unblanced by the wind and was trying to perforate his organs. I saw his perfect, pearly teeth breaking up the shards. He said, appreciatively, 'Mmm, not bad!' as though he were eating a new type of bar snack. He took another substantial bite. Everyone was watching. Fully aware of this he turned slowly round and treated the assembled company to the sight of his unconventional re-cycling factory. One or two called out that he would kill himself but Ricky kept right on, coolly chewing.

Being a polite person, and not wanting to speak with his mouth full, he waited until he had ingested about half of his glass before he asked for another drink, with a fresh container of course, and a packet of crisps. I obliged and watched as potato and booze mixed with the splinters. It was not a conjuring trick; he really was swallowing the stuff!

When the original glass was reduced to the unbiteable stem Ricky put the remnants down, thanked me politely and declared that he was going to the toilet. He never came back.

In the morning, as I was vacuuming the carpet, I came across numberless tiny glass fragments which, presumably, Ricky had exhaled. When Tom Patey next visited I called upon his medical expertise. He assured me that, provided it was chewed very thoroughly, there should be no deleterious effects from eating glass. He also was acquainted with Ricky and knew that the shrewd lad used to make money out of his weird skill by persuading people to place bets. I learned also that Ricky's failure to return that afternoon was not caused by gastric collapse but by the fact that, in his cups, he had forgotten to hold onto the sprung door which led to the Struan toilets. He had walked into the swinging frame and dislocated a shoulder.

Ricky was not by any means the only Continental instructor to import strange habits along with skiing skills. Perhaps the most bizarre of all was one who became popularly known as 'Animal.'

It was said that he had once held the world ski speed record, something well in excess of one hundred miles per hour. It was also claimed that on a subsequent attempt to beat a new best mark he had caught a ski stick in a snow fence straining wire and fallen, dislocating both hips. Reconstructed by the medical profession, he showed no signs of disability. Whereas most of those who skied in Scotland made a practice of avoiding, as far as possible, the patches of heather, Animal scorched through them. His body simply absorbed the stresses and his momentum carried him through. He was like a high speed harvester, sending twigs and fear-crazed birds zooming into the atmosphere. In spring he probably produced instant ptarmigan-egg omelettes.

I saw him once coming down the mountain as darkness descended. Everywhere in the piste were scarcely covered rocks, the terror of mere mortals, the cause of many a painful accident. They were to be spotted and avoided by all except this giant who coursed across them, generating huge trails of sparks from the skis' metal edges. Fast, curving and spectacular were the arcs, making the Animal seem like a travelling steel works.

Having bullied his way through every kind of hazard on the slopes, Animal would return to eat a meal fit for three normal persons and to drink on a similar scale. His thoughts would then turn to women. They were to him something like slalom gates, a series of delightful challenges to be worked through as rapidly as possible.

It might be thought that his potential prey would have grown wary but there were two significant factors strongly in Animal's favour. In the first place, there was a preponderance of women in the ski hotels in those days, not a few of whom came quite determined to have a good time in as many aspects of life as possible. The other positive for the predator was a factor which I christened 'SISP'.

The 'Ski Instructor Seduction Phenomenon', which operates almost universally, reduces intelligent, normally self-controlled women to slavering helplessness. The personal qualities of the instructor are irrelevant to this syndrome. All that matters is that there should be a reasonably expert male skier, preferably with a brightly coloured sweater with a few impressive badges, and a female ski beginner. (The phenomenon seems to be unknown, or certainly very uncommon, with a reversal of gender). The progression from ski, to aprés-ski, to aprés-aprés-ski is almost totally guaranteed under these fertile conditions.

For the most part I saw only the ski and après-ski phases, the chat-ups and the flirtings. All-conquering instructors generally did the decent thing and took their willing captives to the Annexe which, according to the highly amused and well-behaved Hannes and Franzi, was, 'all the time shaking' However, there was one occasion where Animal came close to overstepping the mark.

When he ambled into the dining room at about three o'clock one morning and came up to the bar for a spot of refreshment I assumed that hunting was over for the night but his eyes were still roving voraciously. An object of desire came into his purview. It is obviously impossible that eyes literally 'light up'. None of us has bulbs with batteries hidden in our *aqueous humor*, but this wolf's orbs seemingly sent out invisible laser rays. The beams crossed accurately on their target.

Regardless of the fact that the desired one was with someone else, SISP worked to the utmost. Within moments the two were dancing intimately. The discarded male looked on disconsolately for a while, then slunk away, too sensible it seemed to challenge the hulk.

Once he had gone, Animal and his admirer became ever more bold in their amorousness. In fact, they were soon in dire danger of broaching not a few of the rules of public decency. I had begun a desperate mental search for modes of intervention that would not result in a haymaker punch when, to my relief, another SISP practitioner appeared at the bar with a grinning follower. Any distraction was welcome. 'Rum and black, please, Richard,' the woman said, music to my ears.

I had already served this blithe person with at least seven such concoctions but I poured another and prayed that Animal and Co. would make their exit whilst I was otherwise engaged. The new customer thanked me, picked up the drink, and downed it in one swig.

She then looked at me with a quizzical look which had an accusatory edge, suggesting perhaps that I might have given her strychnine It seemed that she had been overwhelmed with sudden mystification. Her eyes clouded a little. She replaced the glass on the counter, dropped her arms to her sides as though commanded to stand to attention and then fell stiffly backwards, instantly out. There was a noise as of drumming as her body hit the floor.

Her companion seemed more disappointed than alarmed. Luckily one of the residual smoochers was a nurse and the sight of a casualty brought instant sobriety. The lights snapped on. Animal cursed and promptly steered his latest conquest towards the outer darkness. Whilst the rescuer deftly dealt with the patient, I took the opportunity to close the shutters on the bar. For that evening, at least, I had had quite enough.

Happily for my equilibrium, such episodes were not a regular part of the routine. Much more usually the bar would be rocking to the sound of music and on the quieter nights, when the hotel was only partially occupied or when some of the guests had gone on expeditions to Aviemore or Grantown, there developed an odd tradition for playing games. These were not the usual public house pursuits of darts and dominoes but spontaneous inventions. A regular favourite was 'bottle placing' in which competitors had to keep the tips of their footwear on a particular line, bend over with two empty McEwan's bottles in their hands and 'walk' forwards on the bases of the glass containers. The object of the game was to place one of the bottles as far away from the datum line as possible and then 'hop' back on the remaining one. It was, I suppose, potentially dangerous. With the weight of a large human pressing on it the neck of one of the bottles could have broken but none did.

It was after one such evening, when a particularly rich mix of imaginations had produced friendly competitions which had kept people innocently amused for hours, that the perils of not staying in were brought home to everyone. I was just on my way down to the Annexe at about three in the morning when two vehicles drove very quickly up to the front of Struan and skidded to a stop. Improbably large numbers of people emerged. I guessed that they were in search of drink and I blessed the fact that I had closed the bar but then I heard the screams.

I rushed back to find two people whom I knew to be doctors carrying a young soldier into the hotel. One half of his body was badly burned. Although apparently doing his best to be stoical it was impossible for him not to yell occasionally as the movement rubbed charred clothing against the exposed flesh. I could see also that others were wounded, though less seriously.

The lounge was converted into a private place for the badly injured soldier. The doctors did what they could to make him comfortable until the ambulance completed its long journey from Inverness. Everybody else crammed into the kitchen. One of the women had a large wound on her forehead. She seemed extremely calm, probably through shock. One of the doctors hurried in from the lounge to fetch water. He took a quick look at the damage. 'That'll need stitching,' he said to me as though I were a medical orderly, 'shave half an inch or so around it and I'll do it as soon as I can.'

Of course, doctor, just like that.

One of the guests rushed off to get a razor. My 'patient' told me what had happened. The young soldier, a driver in his military career, had offered a lift to several Struanites coming back from Grantown. They had gladly accepted, not knowing that the youth had very recently been warned by one of the officers for driving too near to the edge of the road. On a narrow bridge, which had protruding stones at the base of the walls, the wheels of the Land Rover had struck the impediment. The vehicle had overturned, tossing out most of those who were crammed in the back, and then burst into flames. By great good fortune most people had escaped serious injury.

To my regret the guest returned with the razor. Water was already boiling for its sterilisation. I looked dubiously at the wound and tentatively touched the hair at some distance from the hole. The thatch was very thick and beautiful. The asphalt on the road had already taken a great tuft, but if I were to take even more away it would look much, much worse. The woman read my thoughts and assured me that she understood what had to be done. She must have been in considerable pain but she gave no sign of it. I was still deeply reluctant, not because of squeamishness but because I did not want to be an accomplice in disfigurement however noble the cause.

The dashing doctor rushed in and made a noise of disapproval that the patient was not ready. My prevarication had saved me. He snatched up the razor and began swift, incisive sweeps, working away from the periphery of the wound. Unable to face what was to come, I escaped to the lounge. Something, morphine I supposed, had taken the edge off the burned soldier's agony but he was evidently still very uncomfortable. He seemed to want to talk so I stayed with him until the ambulance arrived.

I blessed, that night and on several other occasions, the peculiar circumstance which seems to link the medical profession with skiing. There seemed always to be a doctor or two and a few nurses amongst Struan's guests. Happily, their services were not often required but it was reassuring to know that they were there.

Apart from Tom Patey, the most reliable in this respect, there was a young nurse called Libby Smith who, with her two close friends, Isabel and Nancy, came up from Glasgow at every opportunity. They were a classic trio with Libby's hair almost blonde, Issy's dark and Nancy's flaming red. Libby was the kind of person who would cope brilliantly with any crisis but this did not get in the way of her ability to enjoy life to the full.

In the most charming manner she and her sharp friends would tease me without mercy. When trade was quiet they would sit on stools pulled up to the bar and engage in banter. Bubble, Toil and Trouble were my private names for them. I liked to think that I had their measure. One evening, in amused desperation during a weighty debate, I responded to Libby's challenging, 'Just a wee minute!' with, 'How many seconds in a wee minute, Libby?' I thought that the diversion might give me time to think. Without even the merest hint of hesitation she said, 'Sixty wee seconds' and went on to make the devastating point which I had been trying to scupper. I knew then that I was lost.

There were many others who regularly parked themselves close to the bar and engaged in frequently interrupted conversation. Rare indeed were the times of boredom. When trade was brisk, the time flew pleasantly by, when things were quiet there was usually somebody who was looking for company. The only hazard in this respect came in the dark hours of the night when those who had had too much to drink imagined themselves to be wittier than they were.

There was one other late phenomenon which for a while I dreaded but which I learned to deal with and which, in retrospect, has a good measure of humour.

Generally Karl did his drinking early, immediately after skiing. He would then have something to eat and go off to the house where, I imagined, since he always got up so early, he slept from mid-evening. Occasionally, though, he would either remain in the bar, or return after his meal break. I came to learn that it was inevitable, then, that he would get drunk.

At some stage of the night he would come to the bar and engage me in conversation. When Karl was sober I understood about eighty per cent of what he was saying, when he was drunk the comprehensibility quotient dropped to about one word in ten. It was not a serious problem, in that what he sought was simply an audience for his monologue. I tried very hard to pick out key words and phrases and to make appropriate noises but I must often have got the interventions wrong.

The first time he attacked, it shocked me considerably. He had been silent for a while, slumped against the bar. His eyes were almost closed, he could have been sleeping, but all at once he looked at me directly and said, with unmistakable clarity; 'You'm rubbish!' Later I learned to say, inwardly only, a jocular; 'Thank you, Karl!' because I came to understand that the insult had no substance but on that first occasion I was shocked. 'Rubbish!' Karl repeated, still fixing me with his penetrating look. In later years, when he got to know others of my kin he would add; 'The Broon family am rubbish!' It was good to know that the insult was not entirely personal!

Without alcohol Karl was a seeker of peace but, as with many another drinker, the booze could turn him into a belligerent. Over the season I gathered that not a few people had been seriously offended. One or two, including the erstwhile very good friends John and Margot from Glasgow, had been driven away. It was a down side of Karl's generally positive character. Stalwart as a friend, he was unrelenting as an enemy and it was necessary to understand that in drink he was not himself

Happily the occasions of rancour were infrequent and experience quickly showed me that on the following mornings Karl would be as charming as always. Probably he had no recollection of saying anything untoward.

Occasionally the anger which showed when he was the worse for alcohol emerged as irritation at times when he was completely sober. Once he marched into a completely full dining room and strode towards the record player innocently doing its job in the corner. It was burbling out the most recent Beatles number which, for no obvious reason, drove Karl towards apoplexy. 'Bloody Beatles!' he exclaimed, 'bloody Beatles! We have Austrian Beatles!'

With that he whisked off the piece of modernity and replaced it with a scratchy disc of folk music from his native land. The diners dared utter no word of protest; the Master had decreed and that, until he had gone, was the end of it.

Perhaps this particular outburst was simply an expression of Karl's chronic deprivation of Austrian culture. He would persuade his young fellow countrymen, Franzi and Hannes, to dress up in lederhosen and all the ancillaries so that they could mount schuplattler displays in the dining room for the entertainment of the guests.

These were, in fact, rather alarming in that the slapping and kicking often seemed to get entirely out of control. Hannes was impish by nature, Franzi more solemn. The live wire would appear to be goading his dance partner and often it looked as though a real fight could break out. Hannes would probably have loved every moment had Franz lost control, which happily he did not. The tormentor would do almost anything for excitement. On one explosive occasion he fiercely squeezed the air bag of a kilted piper who was blasting everyone's ears in the dining room. There was almost a war.

As Easter approached and the hotel, in spite of the very poor snow conditions, filled up to its limits, the bar became almost as mad as it had been during my very first week. There was no focus, of course, like that provided by Hogmanay but it felt as though all of that year-end energy was available for ten crazy days. The bar rarely closed before three or four in the morning and for most of the time it was open there were happenings a-plenty.

Then, as at New Year, the end was sudden. The Easter holiday period came to a close and the crowd vanished almost as one. I was glad of the rest but sad at the departure of many who had become friends. The unhappiness was, however, tempered because most of the partings were not permanent. I knew that I would be returning as would almost all of the regulars, the members of the club that was Struan.

## 21. More Aviemore

There was reason for optimism as the 1965 season approached. The first winter with the enlarged hotel had been encouraging, despite the disappointing weather. Occupancy had met expectations and there was a good chance that the bank loan would be paid off quite quickly. Crucially, far from losing some of its magic Struan seemed to have gained. With more people in residence, and the extra facility of the dining room bar, the nightlife had increased in vibrancy.

There was another hugely positive factor in Karl's world. Norbert had agreed to return for a further spell of work, this time as ski school director and business partner. His good sense, optimism and resilience would be very welcome. Eilif Moen remembers that others were also delighted at the wanderer's return. Norbert's gentle, teasing style appealed greatly to the Norwegians and they had missed the daily banter.

There were, however, worrying developments for hotels such as Struan which were a long way from the slopes.

On the Glenmore road, a very few miles away from the Cairngorm car park, the Coylumbridge Hotel had opened in October, 1964, the first establishment in the area to be built specifically for skiers. Amongst many attractive facilities it boasted a partially covered skating rink, and a 'Woodshed' log cabin bar with an open fire. It also had its own ski school. Dougie Godlington, of local cartoon and postcard fame, had been appointed to supervise eight Swiss instructors.

A significant shift of geographical emphasis was beginning. There was confident talk of a major development in Aviemore with hotels, restaurants, a huge indoor skating rink, squash courts, a cinema and a theatre. The proposed scheme would become the epicentre of skiing in

Speyside. With such a major increase in accommodation so relatively close to the slopes, how could the small, isolated businesses expect to survive?

There was, at the same time, a new installation on the mountain, suggesting that the era of the improvising pioneer was coming to a rapid end. The facility, to the right of the chairlift and at an angle to it, was a T-bar lift which took skiers up the shoulder of Coire Cas. It provided immediate access to an intermediate slope and it would be certain to attract many more skiers to the area.

Happily these devices have largely vanished except at extremely poor resorts in Eastern Europe which bought them second hand from trend-setting French ski centres. They have all the hazards previously listed for the single 'Poma' tows except that the sacrificial victims are not alone. Two skiers stand side by side and wait, in varying degrees of terror, for the conveyor-belt operative to slot a T-shaped bar between them. If all goes well, two pairs of buttocks plump more or less comfortably onto the arms of the T. The bar between preserves the normal decencies like a bolster in a double bed. With a hand each on the stem for steadying purposes, the duo is ready to withstand the initial jerk and to sail upwards.

Chances are, though, that one person is two feet taller than the other. Result; bar heading for the knees of one and the mid-back of the other. The only option is for the taller one to adopt an uncomfortable crouch. Chances are, also, that at least one of the pair has not mastered the technique sufficiently. The initial impetus starts an inelegant pas-de-deux which, quite likely, will result in spillage of both parties. But not always, of course. It is possible to get going and to feel quite complacent until, for reasons which are never clear, the two inner skis become fatally attracted to each other. There is one rule under such circumstances; this phenomenon is always the other person's fault. They are too tense or they are not standing properly or they just have no idea how to control their equipment.

Naturally, the skis don't always press in this way but what they can do for a variation is bump about on an icy, rutted track and quite easily the inner skis can cross, slapping into each other like boats in choppy waters.

From this unhappy coincidence there is usually no dignified escape.

There are occasions, of course, when the upward path runs smoothly but the T-bar causes another hazard unrelated to the techniques of skiing. The sport is essentially sociable but because it is not a team activity it attracts its share of loners. So; to talk or not to talk? The person beside you may be wrestling with a dozen demons, including those called fear and anger. Is it safe to speak? The person might also misinterpret. A friendly, 'Foul weather, what?' could be taken as the skiing equivalent of an invitation to view one's etchings. Trapped on a T-bar there is no honourable exit, until the end of the line appears. Which leads to other problems.

In said foul weather, the point of disembarkation may be invisible until the very last moment but visible or not, there has to be a negotiation because one skier has to peel away first whilst the other 'takes the bar' and releases it gently for its return journey. So often could this little diplomatic discussion go wrong. Fated pairs continued upwards, linked by the bit of wood. They wobbled as disaster loomed and inevitably tumbled into heaps into which the following couples, unless they were sickeningly expert, crashed.

Sometimes pairs escaped such a fate by twisting the bar from its position between their bodies but then it has been known for them to set off downhill, totally unprepared, linked by a magnetism which the upward journey has mysteriously generated. Especially when it is misty, such that the betrothed duo swiftly disappears, it is side-achingly comic to see such a perverted form of parallel skiing.

The worst hazard of all with T-bars, a truly serious one, is the propensity of the wooden arms to become caught in clothing. It is no joke whatsoever to be unable to let go and to be dragged towards perdition.

In spite of the hazards, the new facility vastly improved the Cairngorm scene. Unlike the chairlift, the T-bar could be used without having to remove skis. Continuous ascent and descent was possible. The narrow gully turned into a highway with no traffic rules. Bodies, under highly varying degrees of control, shot across the corrie; up one side, turn, down, up the other. There were collisions a-plenty and involuntary embraces, which were usually passionate in a negative sense, but the increased mileage meant that people could make mistakes and recover. Intermediates could discover what it felt like to link a few successful turns. The general standard of skiing improved quite rapidly. Whereas it had been rare to see competent skiers on the Scottish slopes, it became almost commonplace. In keeping with this new expertise, clothing changed. The anonymous, khaki, string-dangling anoraks with stuffed pockets gave way to sleek, colourful garb. Instead of looking like lost gamekeepers or mad marksmen hunting grouse, the Cairngorm skiers came to resemble the followers of fashion from St. Mortiz or Val d'Isere.

The new lift threatened to end the days of amateur tow operators such as Bill Blackwood. When it was possible, with a competent partner, to half-sit in comparative comfort on the uphill journey, why bother to cling on to a wet, twisting hawser with arms in danger of being yanked out of their sockets?

It is true that probably no skier would willingly have chosen the rope but there was a factor in Bill Blackwood's favour which was depicted brilliantly in one of Dougie Godlington's cartoon postcards. It shows a lift with a queue so long that skiers join it as soon as they reach the top.

The queues for the Cairngorm lifts were not, of course, on the piste but on the busy days they were very extensive. The wait could be half an hour or more. With typically British organisation they were self-marshalled. When the first waiting line reached an unspecified length, some bold souls would start another line behind it. It was understood that newcomers would join this second file and for the most part, people did. Sometimes there would be four or five long lines, all moving forward as a military body when the last of the first file went onto the lift.

This was preferable to the Alpine system, which involved a random crowd all edging, barging and muscling. Skis crossed over skis, sticks were deployed to bar the way. If one fell over, dozens were knocked off balance. At least the Scottish system had order but it required huge patience and there were, of course, unscrupulous practitioners. With seeming innocence, these would swish to the disappearing tail of the first line, ignoring the serried ranks of those behind, or pretend not to notice that a second line was starting. There was usually a degree of shouting and occasionally there was a threat of violence.

*Classes were large*

Because of the queues, there was still scope for the portable tow but its days were numbered. There had been several accidents and there were searching questions about safety. In any case, plans were being discussed to install further T-bars. After his gruesome experience with the police inspector and the hand-grinding, it must have seemed odd to the returning Norbert that the rope tows were still permitted.

In his own country skiing was becoming a highly mechanised activity and it was tempting to make mocking comparisons. But he could see how, in the short time he had been away, facilities had improved on Cairngorm and how rapidly the scene was still changing. There were even some youngsters who, with the right level of training and commitment, might reasonably expect to make their way in the field of international racing. The Jamieson sisters, Frith's son, Iain, Bob Clyde's boy, Fraser, and many others had great potential. During the season he taught a family called Bell whose two little boys, had they been Austrian, would already have been entering the grooming process. When Norbert proved his own racing pedigree, by winning the North of Scotland Championships on Cairngorm in March, there were juniors watching his every move, wanting to learn.

Unbeknownst to Norbert there was yet another keen young racer in the vicinity as his second Struan season came to an end. A family by the name of Bartelski, British nationals but based in Europe, tried to check into Struan for the Easter holiday but found it to be fully booked. The eleven year old boy, Konrad, wrote in his autobiography many years later about the unavoidable disappointment;

'At Easter my mother took me, along with my brother and grandfather, to Scotland for a week's skiing. I was really excited. The prospect of skiing in my own country was very heady and I looked forward with relish to getting the feel of the Scottish hills. We had planned to stay in the Struan House hotel of the Fuchs family in Carrbridge because Karl Fuchs also ran the Austrian ski school of the area and we were keen to benefit from their instruction. Unfortunately Struan House was full and we had to find accommodation elsewhere.'

Konrad already had a strong taste for ski competition. He was, like Peter, of mixed cultural origins. His father had escaped from Poland just before the onset of the Second World War and had joined the Royal Air Force as a pilot, flying Wellington anti-submarine aircraft for Coastal Command. After the hostilities, Jan Bartelski worked for a while ferrying people and goods from Blackpool to the Isle of Man and through this he met, and married, Pamela Vickers, the daughter of a Blackpool civil engineer. He took British nationality and sought to improve the family prospects by applying for work with the British Overseas Airways Corporation but hundreds of ex-RAF pilots were pursuing the same jobs and Jan was forced to look further afield. When the Dutch airline, KLM, offered a pilot's berth he and Pamela moved to Amsterdam. It was there that Konrad was born in May 1954.

The Bartelski family took an annual ski holiday in Kitzbuhel and Konrad, who had an unsettling winter sports start as a three year old, became ever more enthusiastic. He was fired to succeed as a racer by the mockery which was directed at the British skiers by the Austrians. He was determined that the Alpinists could be beaten at their own game. Although that Easter break in Scotland was primarily recreational, the young boy skied hard, always pushing himself to the limits.

It is entirely possible that, on one or several days during that stay, Konrad's path crossed that of Peter. It is by no means unlikely that the nine year old tried to keep up with the older boy for a while but if he did so, his competitive spirit still stayed largely dormant. Konrad continued to develop his ski racing interest, Peter simply got on with the life of a growing child.

Norbert had not long departed from this rapidly developing scene when there were other events which suggested that Karl and Eileen might sensibly move their business nearer to the mountains. The Norwegian school, which had been based in Grantown for ten years, decamped to Aviemore. At more or less the same time, Joe Docherty and Bill Leitch left Struan to start up their own venture there. This posed no ethical dilemmas. Karl was delighted that the two men he had espied on the mountain were furthering their careers but their departure added to the feeling that everything was being sucked in by the gravitational pull of the new centre. There was a real risk that, left isolated from the new glamour, the Austrian Ski School would wither and die.

The Aviemore Centre duly opened with a flourish. The project, with a huge car park at its heart, was ill-conceived in many ways but the facilities were immensely attractive to holiday makers. Visitors could choose between well-appointed hotels and self-catering chalets, they could while away non-skiing days with skating, squash or swimming, they could fill the evenings with a film or show or a meal in a cosy restaurant. For the children there were go-karts and trampolines, play areas and enticing slot machines. There was even a permanent Father Christmas and children began to believe that the benign old gentleman was resident in Aviemore.

As with the Coylumbridge development, the new Aviemore Centre opening was accompanied by an improvement in the Cairngorm skiing facilities. A long-promised chairlift was constructed to link the car park with the two other lifts. The conversion of Cairngorm into a modern ski resort was complete.

The new lift quickly showed how easily people are seduced by convenience and comfort. Ever since the car park chair was mooted, many of those on the residual fifteen minutes of the hike that once took hours had vociferously declared that they would not use the new facility. It was, they assured each other, excellent to have a brisk walk in the morning. It stretched the legs, loosened the muscles, raised the heart-lung rate.

For a week or two after the new lift was opened, a few people walked. Soon thereafter it was a rarity to see people slogging up the track. Cairngorm had become fully mechanised.

Not everyone enjoyed untroubled uplift, however. There is a story, perhaps apocryphal, of a teenage schoolgirl on her first trip. Next to her was a young male teacher who, distantly but passionately, she admired. Blessing the fate which had brought them together on that short journey, she chatted nervously, probably inanely. He responded, when she occasionally paused to draw breath, in his customary kindly manner.

Like its upper counterpart, the lift was a simple side-facing affair where the chairs stopped briefly to allow people to get on and off. The schoolgirl had managed the embarkation but she began to panic about how she would disembark. She made enquiries of her hero and he, driven to distraction by her chatter, made up an improbable story.

They were approaching the point where the lift crossed over the last part of the road. There was netting which protected those who were walking beneath from the hazard of dropped objects. The teacher said that the way to get off the chair was to throw skis and sticks onto this netting and then leap after them.

She did.

Luckily, the net sustained the assault and, with great difficulty, the girl was rescued. She might have been given a medal for heroism but all she got was mocking laughter so it is said.

Whether or not this episode actually happened, it is sure that the elimination of the hike encouraged even more people to join the skiing confraternity. The almost effortless sequence of the drive up the hill, the short ride in a chair, the pre-ski hot chocolate in the Sheiling and then the White Lady lift or the Coire Cas T-bar tempted a new breed of skier. Coach parties came from far afield. The mountain became even busier. It was a whole new world and it was very tempting to conclude that Struan must either move into it or perish, yet it did neither.

Eric Langmuir, whose Glenmore Lodge was closer to the slopes than any other institution, agrees that it seemed a risky strategy for Struan to stay loyal to Carrbridge but he is clear that the normal rules of logic and business planning did not apply to the Fuchs' venture. It was not as though it was the cheapest option; greater comfort could be acquired elsewhere at more or less the same cost. Neither was it, Eric claims, that the ski school was pre-eminent. According to him, although others strongly dispute the assessment, Hans Kuwall's operation was dominant in terms of the quality of instructor and others say that Frith's Ski School d'Ecosse was the sharpest in terms of time-keeping and sartorial standards. But Eric remembers Struan as being unique. He says, 'Karl always had his following. Everyone had a huge respect for him but he tended to keep his school separate. Struan had a homely atmosphere but it encouraged people to do adventurous things.'

This comment summarises very succinctly the reasons why Struan did not collapse under the pressure from Aviemore. Virtually everyone, including those who were openly hostile to him, respected Karl. In part, this derived from his skiing which Eric describes as 'regal'. Although very fast and fluent he seemed always solid on his skis. The idea that he might fall was untenable. Over terrible terrain, in weather which brought despair to many, Karl glided reliably. His example was literally inspiring. He was a constant paradigm, a vivid reminder that excellence was attainable. Given that most of the people then involved in the development of Speyside aspired to being good at skiing it is unsurprising that someone so manifestly excellent at it should be something of a hero.

*Mine host*

Karl's charisma was doubtless crucial but Eric's second point, about Struan being homely, is also very apposite. Most other establishments treated their clients as customers. If the weather was too bad for skiing on the hill they would, for the most part, apologetically leave the frustrated skiers to their own devices. Invariably Karl would go to other venues where conditions were viable or, if this was not possible, he would organise a diversion, usually a very informative and interesting ramble. A favourite was the circuit round Loch an Eilein, always sheltered from the worst of the weather. On hundreds of occasions when most had abandoned all hope of skiing, Karl would conduct his pupils on such a tour in the morning and then take them skiing in the afternoon when the worst of the storm had abated.

Equally important is the third ingredient of adventurousness. An atmosphere which was homely and nothing else would not have appealed to the youngsters who wanted to excel at winter sports; the hotel would have attracted only those who were looking for a large measure of safety. Struan certainly had an air of adventure yet it is too simplistic to suggest that it merely encouraged people to take calculated risks. It went further, it was capable of investing a degree of romantic excitement into events which normally seem commonplace. Karl's love of life was so strong that he filled the space around him with an exported energy. He could turn the most mundane chores or journeys into enjoyable episodes where the only predictable quality was unexpectedness.

Within the hotel he presided, not in any way demanding deference but accruing it just by the force of his personality. The post-skiing gatherings of instructors at Struan were like kingly courts. Beverages such as 'rum-tea' would be consumed in royal quantities. The two or three hours before the evening meal were usually given over to these impromptu parties which were filled with laughter or strong debate. The events were occasions, not just something routine.

The ski shed was another venue where the ordinary was turned into the extraordinary. Karl would work as hard as anybody, dealing with the customers, patiently helping with the trying on of boots, adjusting bindings, selecting sticks. Beginners and experts, children and adults; all were given their proper ration of attention and for the moments that Karl focused on their needs they felt special. He seemed, and indeed was, acutely interested in their progress. He understood that the skills of skiing were, for some, hard won but he wanted everyone to enjoy a measure of the sense of freedom which the sport gave to him. He was an evangelist, offering his message and support to anyone who showed interest.

It was these factors which enabled Struan to resist the power of Aviemore. They generated a profound loyalty from customers and staff. Iain Watson, a young skier from Inverness who used to supplement the earnings from his full time employment by teaching for Karl at the weekends, tells an illustrative tale.

One weekend he called in at Struan as usual and found that there was no class for him to take. The agreement was that if Karl had promised work and none materialised he would pay but on this occasion, no prior arrangement had been made, there was no obligation on either side. Iain decided to go skiing anyway and on the slopes he was approached, entirely legitimately, by Joe and Bill. They had more pupils than they could cope with. Delighted with his good fortune, Iain took a class.

He was surprised, at the end of the day, when Karl, who saw almost everything that happened on the hill, approached him. The message was friendly but simple. Even though there had been no work for Iain he was expected to be available. This precluded taking work with others. A Struan instructor, whether full or part time, was a Struan instructor. Karl spelled out the simple, unthreatening option. Iain could either be on Karl's reserve list or work for others.

In some ways the directive seemed unfair. There could surely be no problem with a system whereby Karl had first call but where Iain was free to seek other work if none were available at Struan. This was not what 'The Boss' wanted. In spite of the slight resentment and the prospect of his earnings being reduced, Iain did not hesitate. Above all he wanted to work for Karl and if that was the price which had to be paid, he would meet it.

As the 1960's progressed, the powerful Struan pull dragged Norbert back whenever he could escape from his duties in Austria. The visits were usually at the busy times of public holidays and Karl's closest skiing friend would, if asked, take a class of two to help out.

This loyalty to Karl led poor Norbert to a brief spell in custody. He arrived at Dover with skis strapped to his car and wary customs officials refused to believe that his primary purpose for coming to Britain was recreation. Why on earth would anyone come willingly from Austria to ski in Scotland? It was as likely as someone from St Tropez travelling to Aberdeen for a beach holiday. They allowed him to call Struan but they insisted on locking him up until the matter was sorted out. It was, Eileen recognised immediately, clearly a case for her redoubtable father.

Always delighted to be of service to the business, Maurice set off immediately on the journey from Purley to the south coast. There is no record of what he said, nor what charm he brought to bear, but Norbert was swiftly released and allowed to carry on with his journey. Although he has no proof, Norbert is convinced that somewhere in the negotiations a certain senior Scottish police officer by the name of McGeoch played his part, perhaps signing some crucial paper with a damaged hand.

The impressive expansion of Cairngorm facilities made it possible for Donnai McKenzie, when he was organising the 1967 Instructors' race, to issue an invitation to the reigning world champion, one Charlot Bozon. To the astonishment of everyone, the great Frenchman accepted.

A frenzy followed the confirmation of the news of the Frenchman's participation. All of the ski schools arranged extra race training. There was a Canadian at the Badenoch school who fancied a crack at the world leader, a Swiss man with similar ambitions and several hopeful Austrians all dreaming of moments of glory. The Norwegians sent for reinforcements.

Eilif Moen wryly confirms that his school exchanged top secret communiqués with colleagues in Oslo. An imported race expert was instantly enrolled as an 'instructor'. According to 'Skisters', the only brave Briton to enter the fray was Plum Worral. Karl might perhaps have talked him out of this, because the man might make himself look ridiculous, but this was never part of Karl's approach. Eileen thinks that sometimes her husband was too easy-going. In later years he would, regardless of the hopelessness of the case, refuse to stand in the way of any of his instructors who wanted to race. Eileen thinks that sometimes this was to the detriment of the school.

The long anticipated day came and the multinational brigade scorched sequentially down White Lady. The snow was fortuitously good, the weather kindly. The Frenchman held his own, but not by much. Eilif's secret weapon was but two tenths of a second off the pace. Karl, twenty years older than the champion, came a very creditable ninth, beating his arch rival Hans Kuwall who finished three places behind. Plum, even older than Karl and without all the advantages enjoyed by the native-born Alpine skiers, distinguished himself by finishing a most respectable twentieth.

Everyone wondered if Bozon, who seemed to enjoy the experience, would return to defend his proud title of 'Scottish Ski Instructors Champion 1967' but the possibility never arose. The following season he was tipped by a Chamonix avalanche over a three thousand foot cliff. He and a number of others were killed.

The race against the World Champion, even though it was only for that one occasion, heightened the competition between ski schools. Most of the bigger organisations tended to hire at least one instructor from their 'home' country who would make a good showing in the races. Norbert was, of course, one of the ones who flew the racing flag for Struan as, some years later, was a man called Sepp Gufler who achieved considerable success. There was also, in the intervening years between these two, a small, dark, lithe young skier called Karli Haas who had the unusual habit of putting his hand on the snow as he turned. As a result he had broken most of his fingers. He treated these recurring injuries as others would a minor cut. He applied a bandage for a while and avoided using the damaged digit as far as possible but otherwise got on with his life.

Although a very different character from Norbert, Karli Haas fulfilled a similar role in Karl's life. He was the son of the man (also Karl Haas) who had been Karl Fuchs' instructor when he was qualifying as a teacher. Karl Haas senior had a small hotel at Lachtal and Karl felt honoured that the son of the house had been released from duties there for the season. The boy was first and foremost a skier, a man who knew mountains and who understood many subtle things without the need for wearisome explanations. He was a kindred spirit. An example of their ski comradeship is provided by one of Eileen's memoirs.

'Karli Haas, who now has not only a ski school but two enormous hotels in Austria, tells the story of how he and the other Austrians were being driven by Karli to Glenshee when, in Drumochter Pass at about 7am, they ran out of petrol. Karli Fuchs was unperturbed and they all got out and waxed their skis until they could get to an open petrol station. When they eventually arrived in Glenshee they had barely time to snatch their race numbers and look at the course on the way up the lift. Karli Haas got off the lift and was immediately pushed out of the start gate to ski down a virtually unseen course. But he won the race.'

Perhaps the most obvious quality which was common to the two Karls and Norbert was a manifest kindliness. In spite of their high level of skill, which might have made them aloof, they were totally egalitarian. They seemed to like people, regardless of their origins or abilities. They helped greatly to generate the warmth and homeliness which made Struan so attractive.

The nurturing, family-like nature of the place, which these three exemplified, is vividly illustrated by a chilling event which happened towards the end of the 1960's.

Stan Davies was a regular winter and summer guest. Usually he camped in the garden with his wife and four teenage children, the products of a previous marriage. With his new partner he had another boy and they decided, for the sake of the infant, to stay at Glenmore Lodge rather than face the rigours of the tent. The youngest of the four adolescents opted to stay at Struan as usual. He was very much a part of the hotel's extended family and Karl and Eileen had no hesitation in agreeing to the arrangement.

One day, Stan set off to ski on his own, leaving his wife to look after the baby. The weather was not good but the lifts were working and, probably because of the poor conditions, the slopes were less crowded than usual.

At the end of the day, he went for a last run. In thick mist, with the light already poor, Stan worked his way down. Towards the bottom of Coire Cas his heart malfunctioned and he collapsed. In his desperation, he must have thought that it was only a matter of moments before someone would come by to give help, but nobody did.

Darkness came very quickly. Presumably he shouted but in a fierce Cairngorm blizzard sound is whipped randomly. Being an experienced mountaineer, the partially crippled man decided that he had to dig a snow hole. Death from hypothermia was a real prospect unless he could create some shelter. It must have been sickeningly difficult, scrabbling in the snow, but he managed to create a hollow. All he could do was curl up and wait for the morning.

It snowed all night and it snowed for a long time thereafter. Naturally, his wife raised the alarm when it was certain that Stan was not coming back but the rescue team could do nothing in the pitch blackness and the raging storm. They went out at first light but everything was covered. There were no tracks, no tell tale signs, no pieces of abandoned equipment. The missing man could have been anywhere in the vast area. After the most exhaustive searches, the team eventually abandoned hope. Stan's disappearance was one of those weird Cairngorm mysteries which might never be solved.

Stan's boy, Paul, obviously in deep shock, chose to stay at Struan. It was, it seemed, the closest he had to a home in that terrible time. Eileen happened to be away at the time, and heard about the disappearance on the car radio, but the Struan staff informally adopted Paul. It was, they thought, the least they could do, a decision which Eileen heartily endorsed once she returned.

It was only when the accumulated snow began to melt, weeks later, that the ghastly truth emerged. People had been blithely skiing over Stan's temporary tomb, laughing, tumbling, having not the least idea of what lay beneath the hard packed surface.

The tale, though ghastly, illustrates the special nature of the Struan force. There were very few, if any, hotels in the area which would have had the same relationship with poor Stan's boy. He was, in fact, just a customer but he was treated, in his time of need, like a son.

Struan's lure emanated from the human bonding, from a loyalty which was close to love. This easily transcended trivial considerations such as degrees of comfort and it allowed the Austrian Ski School to look confidently towards the 1970's even though their skiing world was surely set for even greater change.

## 22. Dez Barnes and the Kiwis

Struan survived the shift of emphasis towards Aviemore by being true to itself but it did not by any means stagnate. The first major change was structural and it came about through necessity.

Not long after I left in 1964 to embark on a summer of impecunious travelling, the Fuchs' family lawyer visited the hotel to see at first hand the delights of the new wing. After making all the right comments he politely pointed out that the bar, formed from the storeroom hatch into the dining space, was illegal. There were, apparently, rules about selling alcohol in places where people took their meals and it was astonishing that the architects had not known about them. There was no option but to close the facility immediately.

It was obviously unthinkable that the larger Struan could cope with just the tiny Edelweiss. Plans were hastily made. The room which the Fuchs family had been using as a lounge, across the entrance hall from the Edelweiss, would have to be sacrificed. There would be advantages. Direct access could be made from the hallway to the behind-the-bar space, thereby greatly easing the problems of re-stocking. There would also be the opportunity to install one or two outlets for draught beer.

When I arrived for the Christmas and New Year busy period, the conversion work was already done. Proudly, I was introduced to the Enzian bar. Even though I had an affectionate loyalty to the Edelweiss, I was impressed. A copper-topped sales counter ran down the full length of the room. The style echoed that of the Edelweiss but the new space had its own character. A rafted false ceiling had been installed with semi-concealed lighting. The Enzian would, I guessed, never be as cosy as its predecessor but it was very welcoming and significantly more professional in aspect.

Presiding over this splendid new facility was a man called Dez Barnes. I knew him slightly because he was one of a large crowd of cyclists from Manchester who were Struan loyalists. Big Jim, Little Jim, Sleepy Col, Pete Street and a dozen or so more had taken up skiing as a way of keeping fit for their summer sport but for many the new activity had become primary. Dez was one such who, ultimately, would become Chief Instructor for Karl but who was starting his winter sports career as a barman.

He invited his temporary assistant into the inner sanctum. I followed through the space which used to house the public telephone but which had been opened up to make a doorway. The trouble, as I emphatically discovered, was that the entrance was only about four feet high.

'Mind yer 'ed,' Dez said, too late but not unkindly. To one who was wondering whether he was suffering from short term concussion or permanent brain damage the bar tender's grin was surprisingly acceptable. 'You get used to it after a while,' he added comfortingly, 'ere, look at these ridges.'

Dez was one of those men who, having lost most of the hair on the top of their heads at an early age, seem never to grow older once the pattern of baldness is set. Perhaps to show that the loss was localised, he had a bushy moustache. His manner was overtly melancholy but I quickly discovered that the facade covered a rich inner store of fun. He was a strong character with firm convictions, a natural democrat.

As far as it was possible to tell with one so laconic, he was enjoying his new role, although he seemed to have quickly progressed to a state of war with Peter and Lisi. Early on, they had ambushed him with a spraying hose. He had responded by tipping an entire bucket of water over Lisi's head. Anxious to win the propaganda war, he told me that the two of them, with selected friends, had taken to hiding in the upper sections of the linen cupboards on the corridors and moaning like spooks as guests passed by. Not a few yelps of alarm had been heard. Worse, Lisi had somehow acquired, one early evening, a small glass of Babycham and had been seen giggling in the bar! I formed the impression that Dez was of the Victorian school as far as children were concerned.

*Dez, in the Struan garden with trophies won at another sporting love of his; golf*

I discovered, on my first duty, that it was not only the Fuchs' lawyer who had been active in my absence. The hotel's accountant had pointed out that it was not entirely proper for Karl to dispense hospitality without keeping a record. Calculations showed that, for all my endeavours, the bar had recorded an operating loss. A little book had been installed for listing the free issues. Staff members were rationed to one complementary drink per night. This did not, of course, stop Karl giving unstintingly. Fred Foxon, who worked for a while behind the copper counter, recalls an Austrian tourist bus passing by and screeching to a halt when the party realised that they had chanced upon a national outpost. Karl rushed out, invited everybody in and ordered forty three drinks on the house.

One of the new staff members, entitled to a free nightly drink, albeit officially a non-alcoholic one, was my youngest brother, Charles, a shy teenager who had decided to drop out of education for a while. Eileen had kindly agreed to take him on for the season, and thereafter if he chose, to help Jessie in the kitchen. He was one of a steady stream of young men nurtured by Jessie. One of them, Stephen Markwick, the son of one of Eileen's Board of Trade bosses, went on to a career in catering and eventually established a very prestigious restaurant in Bristol. Charles' eventual profession was not to be related to his Struan work but, as will be revealed, a very significant part of his personal life most certainly was.

The festivities developed as before and the welcome for 1965 was probably more abandoned than the previous one. There seemed to be even more benign 'gangs' from various parts of Britain. The Enzian bar showed that it could rock just as readily as its older neighbour. I saw very little of my brother. He was often getting up for work as I was going to bed. In the evenings, life was so hectic that we had little time for chat.

Some at home had questioned the wisdom of leaving one so young to cope with the Struan semi-anarchy but I had reassured the worriers that Karl, Eileen and Jessie would act as protectors if need be. As the two weeks or so of the busy period passed, I began to have my own doubts. I had the asylum of the bar and my role as a worker. Innocent Charles, in the evenings, would be a free agent. Without my 'big brother' presence, and with no other constraints, he might be quickly corrupted. Booze, sex; the high life awaited.

Repressing mild anxiety, I left him as planned and went for my second term at college. When I returned to Struan at Easter my expectations of drastic change in my brother were dramatically realised.

I was working in the Edelweiss on the first evening. Because I had arrived late the previous night, and Charles had been working during the day, we had had little time for conversation. When he strolled confidently into the bar he was to me as a stranger. His body seemed to have developed considerably, his manner was completely calm. He joked easily with two or three young women who, as far as I could see, were worshippers. When prompted, he lightly picked up a parked guitar and began to play and sing. My brother! What had Struan done? Having just celebrated his eighteenth birthday he was legally entitled to drink alcohol and he took the proffered whiskies like a veteran toper.

That summer, Charles stayed and I went off on my travels. I learned from him, when I returned, that the hill-walking season had brought near tragedy and what was to prove to be a historic development.

The alarming event happened one night when Struanites, apart from a few late drinkers in the Enzian, were asleep. One of the guests, tucked up cosily between some of Eileen's re-cycled sheets, woke to see a strange mist rising from the floor. The grey fumes, he soon discovered, were disgustingly pungent. Struan, not for the first time, was on fire!

The smoke sniffer resolutely smashed the nearest alarm. Guests, in various garb and mood, appeared and hurried through the smoke to the safety of the garden. The boozers, determinedly clutching glasses, joined them. In their bungalow the Fuchs heard the commotion and instantly responded.

Karl rushed into the kitchen where he found that the rubber pipe which supplied gas to the small stove was ablaze. Decisively, he turned the tap on top of the cylinder, snatched up an extinguisher and doused the flames. He could see, when the fumes cleared, that one of the electric sockets had exploded and, presumably, poured fat sparks onto the connection.

Mercifully the damage was very localised and it was clear that there was no further risk. Leaving Eileen to clear up the minor mess, Karl went back to bed. All seemed well but then the fire brigade arrived. The men declared that nobody should enter the main building until they had made their investigation. Eileen tried the ploy of thanking them for attending and assuring them that everything was under control but there were, she was told, proper procedures which could not be circumvented.

Procedure number one was to break down the ceiling with flailing axes. Eileen stared in dismay as the tumbling plasterboard precipitated jars, tins, pots and pans over the floor. Procedure number two was to splash quantities of water onto the exposed joists. Having made a dismaying mess, the brigade finally desisted from smashing up the kitchen. They then graciously accepted the offer of a cup of tea accompanied by a 'nip' from the bar prior to roaring triumphantly off in their engine.

The garden party guests were just filtering back into the hotel when, on cue it seemed to Eileen, a party of late-nighters from the Carrbridge Hotel, led by Cathy McIntyre, arrived. They had heard the noise and had come to help. One of the Struan guests thought it only proper to provide tea, so the urn was pressed into service. For the remainder of that troubled night, Eileen was washing cups as well as clearing debris. She had only just succeeded in making the kitchen usable when Jessie and Charles, who had heard nothing in their remote sleeping places, arrived to overcome all the difficulties caused by the wrecking and prepare full breakfasts as usual.

The historic development came whilst another of the Manchester cyclists, Colin Whiteside, was looking after the bar whilst Dez was away. Like his companion, Colin had totally taken to skiing and had very quickly progressed to the point where he could instruct for Karl. Also like Dez, though sooner, he eventually became Chief Instructor. The summer bar work was just a means of survival until the snows came again.

Colin had introduced the novelty of selling Austrian-style snacks and was busy serving his customers when four young women came into the Enzian. As soon as he had a quiet moment, Colin struck up a conversation. The casual visitors were, he discovered, from New Zealand.

The talk developed. One of the quartet mentioned that when they had finished 'doing' bits of Europe in the summer months they would be looking for work. They particularly wanted to stay in the Highlands if they could because it reminded them in so many ways of home. On his next visit to the kitchen, Colin spoke to Eileen about these potential employees. She said that there were no vacancies but her barman was not easily diverted. 'Really,' he said, 'you should take a look. They seem very special.'

More out of curiosity than firm intention, Eileen abandoned her cookery and went into the bar. Colin introduced her to Kathy, Ronnie, Lynn and Alison. There was an immediate rapport and she began to calculate. Charles was planning to resume his studies and would be available only at holiday times, so there would be a kitchen vacancy. Normally there would be only two housemaids but perhaps, under the circumstances, a point could be stretched. She thought for a moment or two longer then, to yelps of delight, told the New Zealanders that their winter employment and accommodation problems were solved.

It was the auspicious start of a solid tradition. The first four fitted so completely into the Struan family, and were so excellent as workers, that thereafter the hotel was never without a complement of New Zealand staff, female and male. Generally word of mouth provided sufficient advertisement but some years Eileen arranged for a notice to be posted in New Zealand House.

With very few exceptions they were excellent workers. They also had a strong impact on the development of Struan's social life by cunningly contriving to introduce an element of order without detracting from the spontaneity. They would decide themes for parties, enthuse the guests and creatively set up the venue. They generated a momentum which ensured success.

When the *Guardian* chanced upon Struan in 1965, their reporter, Hilary Haywood, picked up on the atmosphere which had so readily absorbed the New Zealanders. Under the heading 'Father and Mother of skiing' the article contained the familiar potted histories of the proprietors and then waxed lyrical:

'Physically, Karl looks the part of the father, being paternally large in all directions, he blames it on Eileen's good cooking, but she looks more like a sister than a mother, being lively, agile and beautiful. His hands are sensitive and long fingered, hers are practical and there is obviously no job that they don't tackle successfully between them.

'They both adore the beautiful Scottish countryside. Sweeping off his Styrian hat laden with international ski trophy badges, Karl, whose English is idiosyncratic but ever hopeful, almost chokes as he says, "Here is a paradise - a paradise for everyone who loves nature." And he puts his hat on again, sighs with pleasure and grasps his wife's hand. Jolly and practical in a bright dirndl, she grins back and goes off to make coffee for everyone in her large, hospitable kitchen.'

It is not entirely certain that the many people who patronised Struan during the late 1960's would have used the word 'paradise' to describe their place of stay but they would have certainly agreed that the hotel generated sufficiently large quantities of pleasure and excitement to counteract the occasional frustrations. The New Zealanders were very much instrumental in creating this positive atmosphere. Although they worked hard between bouts of travelling they were essentially on an extended holiday and the mood was generally light. Eileen recalls their impact:

'They fitted in at once and in their spare time organised dances and evening activities in general. One I well remember had the theme of the South Sea Islands. Dez took a party to Nairn to collect stones, shells, seaweed and sand which together with bits of net were made into a wonderful backcloth while others produced the most beautiful leys to hang round the girls' necks. Many were the hat dances and pyjama parties, the sing songs and Maori war dances and the barbeques down the garden.'

The various 'gangs' joined in with these activities vigorously. Not a few of the 'Manchester Boys' had made the transition from guest to worker but this did not prevent their participation whenever they were off duty. The 'Dundee Boys', a smaller group from Sheffield, the 'Barnsley Boys', some dentists from the Midlands, the 'Glasgow Boys' and the 'Glasgow Girls'; these and many others were regulars. The mix of regional styles made for great inventiveness and a rich variety of humour.

One of the dentists, an antipodean who was based in Wolverhampton, was the prime instigator of a simple game called Australian dominoes which became a regular early evening pastime for twenty or thirty people.

The players would congregate in the dining room and sit round a couple of contiguous large tables. One person placed a domino vertically on its end. The next player put another beside it, the third placed a bridge across the two. Thereafter the structure grew vertically. The one who finally caused the collapse had to buy an entire round of booze. They also had to down their own drink in one. The problem for the regular losers was that they became inebriated faster than the others and thereby more clumsy. A few became quite quickly drunk whilst the others ended up with a long line of charged glasses.

For the bar staff the game was a pain. Most players chose, for tactical reasons, to drink half pints of lager or beer. The stock of suitable receptacles dwindled very quickly and the table on which the game was played became a shallow lake. But the devotees loved every moment.

They cheered and they jeered and they laughed until the room shook. After the game there was always some other diversion, something creative perhaps or just dancing to records. Australian dominoes was always a prelude to a good Struan night.

The perpetrator of this activity was one of the handful of leading spirits who pushed back the boundaries. He was doubtless a dedicated and highly competent dentist but at Struan he seemed to have few limits. One evening he and Alex Newton, one of the several Manchester men who were on their way to becoming instructors, decided that they would drink a full measure from every bottled alcoholic beverage on display in the Enzian bar.

Given that there were fourteen varieties of malt whisky alone, many blended versions, a dozen or so liqueurs, gins, brandies, vermouths, ports, sherries and many more, this looked more like a suicide attempt than a night's entertainment. It happened that it was Dez's night off and sober observers, concerned for the safety of the two, urged me to stop serving them.

When Alex dropped out after achieving just over half of the target I felt that the problem would quickly resolve itself. Jim was showing clear signs of unsteadiness. The usual Struan night life buzzed on around him but he was not to be diverted. He appeared across the counter every few minutes and fixed his unfocussed vision on the next in the line. As the bar emptied and night shaded towards morning, some concerned friends of the fanatic urged me to cheat. He would, they said, have no idea where he was up to. I should skip half a dozen of the malts and tell him that he was two drinks away from the end.

Now, it was true that by this time Jim had no idea where he was staying, no notion of which country he was living in and only the vaguest recollection of his personal identity but what he *did* know, with absolute accuracy, was how many bottles were left. I suppose that I should have simply refused to serve him but a confused mixture of libertarianism and fear closed this as an option. He was causing no trouble for as long as he got what he wanted, he showed every sign of exercising free choice. On the other hand, at the slightest hint of frustration he was suggesting aggression. It seemed simplest just to allow him his will.

At about five in the morning, Jim made his one concession. The four remaining liqueurs he allowed me to mix. He downed the sticky cocktail and stood, grinning inanely. His Everest had been climbed and it did not matter if he perished on the descent. Two of his minders were committed to staying with him just in case he collapsed. One went with him to the toilet where, probably life-savingly, he was sick. I closed the bar and went to snatch a few hours sleep. When I arrived in the kitchen for breakfast I enquired anxiously about Jim. He had, I learned, gone out skiing.

There were not a few who felt that for once the Struan licence had been taken too far. Jim had risked his life although, it had to be admitted, he had survived the ordeal extremely well. Apart from this one lapse into introverted lunacy, Jim was a highly sociable being who would join in with whatever the general will declared should happen. He was one of those, like Tom Patey, who seemed to hum with energy.

His more circumspect drinking partner, Alex, eventually became ski school manager for a season. He also took on the summer hill walking where, amongst his several comic tricks, he horrified the children by swooping on what he declared to be grouse droppings deep in the heather and eating them with manifest relish. The black stuff was, in fact, liquorice which he had previously planted but the 'eeeearrrrghhhhh'-ing youngsters were not to know that. Alex was a natural entertainer. His impersonations of Karl were impeccable. Often he would pretend to *be* Karl to the confusion of the uninitiated.

The luck of the draw which had given me the late duty for Jim's drinking marathon had me on my own in the Enzian not long afterwards when there was a different kind of test. The place had been rocking but as the clock approached two, things had quietened a little. Dez had exercised his option for an 'early' night.

Unusually, the people in the room above the bar had been complaining about the noise so it was a relief that there was just a general buzz of conversation rather than singing and loud bursts of laughter. I was in the midst of serving a large round of drinks when the lights failed. The screams of delight and horror were loud enough to waken the village and the subsequent yellings as people groped mischievously about were at a very high volume.

Such failures in the power supply were by no means uncommon and I knew roughly what to do. There was a fuse box on the landing and wire for repairs. All I had to do was locate the element that had blown and all would be well.

There were also candles and matches strategically placed. I produced illumination, to the pleasure of some and the dismay of others, and deployed candles all round the bar space. It looked very pretty. Those with a romantic bent duly uttered their 'aaahhhs'. Announcing that I was going off to be an electrician I finished serving the round and then left the customers to their own devices knowing that I could trust every one of them to steal neither the stock nor the takings.

Locating the blown fuse took me longer than I had anticipated. I had just plucked out the relevant one when I heard a fantastic explosion. Someone, it seemed, had burst into the bar with a gun and was shooting the bottles. Dropping the element in sheer shock I picked up my candle and hurried downstairs. There was another shattering bang and the crashing of glass. People were screaming hysterically. I entered my claustrophobic enclave expecting to see blood. I looked about wildly. Most of the wretched inebriates, far from being terrified and grieving for their lost ones, were doubled treacherously in laughter. 'The shelves!' one managed to splutter, 'the candles are exploding the shelves!'

Well, who would have thought? The tiny flames, not by any means close to the glass, had caused differential expansion. Three of the shelves and maybe two dozen glasses, were in bits on the floor.

Not entirely as amused as the customers, I dealt with any residual danger and went back to my box. With the lights restored and the clientele calmed, I set about clearing the mess. I was on my hands and knees, gathering some of the larger shards, when I heard the bar door burst open and then a female voice screaming, 'There's a mouse!' Her accent was heavily north-western English. The name of the animal came out as though it had been squashed.

I rose wearily to my feet. The woman, one of the complainers from the room above the bar, was clad, not entirely decorously, in her holiday nightie. Under the cloth clamped close to her head were old-fashioned rollers. Some customers, still tickled by the memory of the exploding shelves, renewed their guffaws. The complainant made it very clear that the encounter with the creature had been naught of a joke. People sobered and debated. Some were in favour of hunting with staves and broom handles, others, the humanitarians, proposed the notion of empathetic counselling; for the woman, they explained, not the mouse. I think the guest believed that I, as the only available employee, should work some kind of miracle. Happily the woman's husband was one of the revellers and gallantly he bore his wife off, promising unspecified action.

In the bar on that chaotic night was a senior policeman, not one of local ones, who posed an occasional dilemma. He knew Karl and Eileen well but he was certainly not their guest. Should I refuse to serve him after the official closing time? On one after-hours occasion he watched me tending to customers and muttered, 'It's better to lose a bit of custom now than to lose your licence.' At the time he was sipping his own illegally acquired drink.

Dez was much bolder in these matters than I was. When, in later times, the son of a local very high dignitary attempted to use his father's status to buy drinks after hours Dez was adamant; the rule covered all. Similarly, when a prominent ski worthy arrived after closing time with an entourage of hardy mountain men, Dez stood up to the lot of them. He had, for his courage, a cigar stubbed out on his forehead but he was not too disconcerted; right had been done.

Maybe it was the senior policeman who sometimes prompted the local force into raiding the bar although the word was that they were galvanised mainly by the religious Wee Frees. Their most unwelcome visits put me in mind of films of the French Resistance where gestapo raids on quaint little bars wrecked everyone's meagre ration of wartime fun.

In fact, the Carrbridge policeman, Hugh McLennan, never harassed the Struan drinkers. His line was that as long as there was no trouble outside there was no need to intervene. It was when the Boat of Garten men covered the local man's days off that there was a raid although there was a sticky period, just prior to the opening of Aviemore centre, when an augmented police contingent had to fill their time. The Sergeant, called McClean, was publicly vilified for damaging the tourist trade through too much diligence but he quickly became Karl's friend on the hill. He always supported Eileen at the licensing court and remained very approachable even when he achieved the exalted rank of Chief Inspector.

Naturally, the bar staff had mixed feelings about the police but were not averse to calling on their services when needed. They were my first thought on the evening when a man called Pete Street, yet another of the Manchester crowd who was making a career for himself in the skiing world, announced that he had just seen two young men rolling a barrel down the road towards Aviemore. It was a reasonable conclusion that they had purloined it from the Struan yard. Pete, contrary to my plan, thought direct action might be preferable. He asked me to join him. I was exceedingly averse to doing so but in order not to seem cowardly in the macho skiing world, I agreed.

Pete drove in the direction of the miscreants. For a mile or two I wondered, optimistically, whether he had been hallucinating but then we saw them, dramatically caught in the glare of the headlights against the darkness of the forest. They were like children playing hoop-la. The stolen property rolled merrily along as they took turns to kick it.

My leader knew already what he would do. He stopped in front of the trio and wound down the window. Shouting in his matiest conspiratorial voice he asked them if they wanted a lift. They most certainly did. Within a moment the barrel was lifted into the boot of the car and the lads were huddled on the back seat.

Driving slowly, Pete introduced the topic of the barrel. So skilled was he at winning their confidence that they quite readily revealed its provenance. Pete pretended to get excited. 'Are there any more?' he enquired with every evidence of greed. 'Aye!' they replied, 'dozens'.

It was a small step for Pete to suggest that we should go back for as much free beer as would fit into the boot and the lads therefore had no qualms as we turned and headed back towards Carrbridge. As we approached Struan the youths gleefully pointed out the source of limitless intoxication.

Pete stopped the car close to the hotel. Quietly, without sounding in any way judgmental, he explained that we were from Struan and that, if they simply disappeared, we would treat the theft as a youthful escapade. I was mightily impressed and waited for the grateful chorus of, 'Thanks mister', but this was not the way the script was written. Presumably it was because they had been so easily duped that the culprits became blinded to good sense. They insisted that because the barrel was openly on display in the Struan yard they had every right to take it. It was their barrel and it was we who were the thieves.

With an air of bemusement, Pete and I soon found ourselves driving, at the behest of the felons, to the house where the Carrbridge constable lived. He was not too delighted to be knocked up towards the end of what had been a quiet evening but it was immediately evident that the youths were not unknown to him. He took us into the room which served as a station and explained to the bad lads that it was not acceptable to lift items from other people's property no matter how openly displayed or inviting. Still they would not budge.

Wearily the constable began to take statements. The barrel was impounded as evidence. It was with considerable sadness that Pete and I left the station about an hour later and we made sure that thereafter the Struan stock was locked within a shed.

Happily, police involvement of whatever variety was a relatively rare event and as the 1960's approached their end, the social base continued to strengthen. Although no particular evening was predictable, there were certain loose and informal conventions which almost guaranteed conviviality. Some of the New Zealanders stayed for more than one season and these 'veterans' passed on knowledge to the incomers. And the 'gangs', although they sometimes changed in composition, had hard cores of members who knew what to do.

In the spirit of those times, individuals became more daring. The fancy dress and 'theme' parties provided the opportunity for great inventiveness and exhibitionism. Dez, when he was not working the bar, was a most creative fancy-dresser as was Tony Rice, one of two brothers who found skiing taking over their lives and who now works in a New Zealand ski resort. A talented artist, he appeared one evening with elaborate make-up and tennis balls in the knees of his trousers. One glimpse of him reduced everyone to helpless merriment. With just a few clown-like gestures and absurd facial expressions he made people collapse. The absence of obvious boundaries between the staff and the guests opened up many opportunities.

For the most part, Karl and Eileen stayed away from these happenings, although they would occasionally linger long enough to admire the costumes and enjoy the pre-inebriate fun. With increasing health problems, Karl was making sterling efforts to limit his drinking. It became very rare for his early visits to the bar to extend into prolonged sessions. He would appear, chat gaily with his legion of admirers and then depart for his meal and go early to bed. Though still a relatively young man he seemed to be preparing himself for partial retirement. His dream, and Eileen's too, was that one day the children would take over the business.

There were still, though, many examples of his resilient spirit. Whatever he was suffering in the way of medical difficulties he could still charm the customers and generate high levels of respect. Some of the regulars seemed to perceive him as a minor deity. I watched two women, sitting side by side on one of the short Edelweiss seats, following their host's every move as he did his sociable rounds. When his glance lit on them they beamed with unbridled pleasure. I saw, also, that Karl knew precisely what to do.

Both of the women were of above average girth. In fact, an objective observer would have said that they entirely filled the seat they were occupying. When Karl, no sylph himself at that stage of his life, wiggled mischievously and made as if to sit down between them I thought that this was an unachievable goal. But Karl sat, at first on the two customers, and then gradually insinuated. Certain it seemed that the ends of the seat, which Karl had installed many years ago with the craftsman Sandy Panton, would not stand the strain. They creaked very audibly and shifted a fraction but they stayed firm as Karl sank into the flesh sea. Everyone in the bar was watching and laughing and the squashed ones beamed as though they had just won a trophy. There was a worry for some that the three might be stuck inextricably but they just laughed uproariously until the whole room seemed to shake.

There was, I am sure, nothing prurient in Karl's action on that occasion and probably none when he sat next to Rosie Bell on the very same seat but attitudes were, quite rightly, changing. What once passed as innocent amusement was being re-categorised as harassment and Rosie, though no belligerent feminist, was in this respect properly modern.

A Struan stalwart from the earliest days, a hill-walking leader who knew Karl better than most, Rosie took up less than half of the available space on that seat so when her employer sidled jocularly up to her, she knew that it was not because of physical constriction. He began his flirtatious banter and Rosie responded, more than a match. With words proving ineffectual he began to tap one of her knees with his fingers.

Rosie looked for all the world as though she might swat the invader but instead she looked Karl directly in the face and said, for all present to hear, 'Unhand me, sir, or I'll cut off your antler'. Everyone, Karl included, burst into laughter.

It was a rebuke but a mild one and Rosie knew, as everyone did, that Karl was no crude molester. In fact his behaviour towards others was always respectful, he took the slight risks only with those he was sure would join in the fun. He had a habit, which Eileen declares she both liked and disliked, of taking new staff members straight to the bar but this was purely in the way of making them feel welcome. He was a natural giver and the bar was the place where he could lavish unstinted hospitality.

Although most of the New Zealanders travelled during the summers, some lingered. This factor helped to ensure that the development of Struan's social life was by no means limited to the winter. My brother recalls his warm weather spells of duty with affection.

'I probably worked there during the summer almost as much as anyone else except the locals and Dez, three years worth of holidays at least. I guess the summers were rather tame compared to the winters, but they were still great fun; very hard work, but lots of good times swimming in Loch Vaa playing tennis and golf at Boat of Garten, quoits on the lawn and of course walking in the hills. We still had some great sing songs in the bar but never quite as good as the winter ones! The Glasgow Boys (mostly university students) first came in the summer. They were great singers and sports. They subsequently became regular visitors in the summer and the winter. Some of the construction workers from the

Aviemore centre used to come regularly to drink. They were real hard-case Glaswegians, not your usual Struanites. We also did some skiing right through the summer, mostly over the back in Ciste Meridh. We used to walk up which was really hard work in the hot weather; the fit ones straight up the White Lady, others up the Coire Cas track.'

It was on one of these summer skiing exercises that Karl provided yet another demonstration of what made the hotel so special.

Amongst the guests was a family in which the father, a relatively young man, had generally to use a wheelchair. He had broken his back in a fall from an apple tree and was partially paralysed for the remainder of his life. His wife and children were keen skiers and when the prospect of an unexpected few runs on Ciste Meridh was presented, they were eager to take advantage. They were also, however, unwilling to leave their disabled relative behind.

Karl sprang into action. He made enquiries of the chairlift operators and recruited Angus Carlyle, a greatly valued, all-seasons Struan worker, as assistant. In ways which defy easy imagination the wheelchair was fixed to the White Lady chairlift and taken to the top. There, Karl and Angus fixed ropes to the conveyance and dragged it, steadied by the devoted family, across the heather. The ride must have been at times alarming for the occupant of the chair but he made no complaints. With great cooperation and large portions of laughter, the gang succeeded in bringing the man to the top of the Ciste. There he was able to bask in the sun and watch his loved ones enjoying their sport. It is hard to imagine that any of the other local hotel owners would have taken such trouble.

It was humane touches such as this which induced the far-from-home New Zealand staff to adopt Karl as a favourite uncle. For a surrogate 'grandpa' they always had Maurice who had had professional links with their country and knew it well. He loved the bubbling energy which the ex-patriates brought to Struan and was for ever encouraging them to join in with his sing-songs. Though no longer a youngster, Maurice showed no signs of a dwindling appetite for fun. He declined to join in most of the organised games but where spontaneous singing and dancing were the order of the evening, Maurice was your man.

He was at his best at New Year. On the rare occasions where there was no instant spark, Maurice would get people going even though they might have at first groaned to hear the first bars of 'Oh, Sir Jasper' or one of the favourite Austrian drinking songs bursting out of the old man's white-moustached mouth. Later, Maurice would be standing and shouting and embracing along with people just a fraction of his age. When, mysteriously, a piper in full regalia appeared just after midnight one Hogmanay and led everyone down the snow-covered A9 road for first footing, Maurice was there. He was also present when some Dutch visitors introduced their delightful custom of letting off fireworks to welcome the new year. And he was there too, eyes sparkling, face displaying huge enjoyment as it mischievously did, when one of the male New Zealanders, a Maori, enlivened one end of year party by performing the 'haka' wearing, as became evident, only a kilt.

It seemed, as the end of the Fuchs' first full decade approached, that their enterprise was as solidly grounded socially as it was in the skiing domain. The 'gangs' appeared to be self-perpetuating, the supply of New Zealanders looked constant and Dez would surely continue to rule over his domain. Individuals would of course move on but they would always be replaced by other outstanding characters. There would be constant 'refreshment' to ensure that there would be no staleness. Whatever the moneyed moguls of Aviemore might contrive, the bright future of Struan could surely not be in doubt.

## 23. Like Father...

In the final year of the 1960's, a series of articles appeared in the Glasgow Herald. It was focused on a new Cairngorm Winter Festival which had been organised in Aviemore. The February the 29th piece was headlined with; 'Scottish skiing has come a long way from the nursery slopes' and promoted with a reader-enticing paragraph:

'Once skiing was a sport enjoyed by the favoured few - those who could afford the time and money to go to Switzerland, Austria or Norway for a winter sports holiday. Now the picture has changed; every weekend in winter busloads of young people from Glasgow and Edinburgh head north for the Spey Valley, and visitors from the south come to ski in Scotland, saving their foreign currency for summer holidays. This week the first Cairngorm Winter Festival is in full swing, and Jean Nicol has been up there talking to some of the people who have helped to put Scotland on the skiing map.'

The 'people' were Karl Fuchs and Frith Finlayson but the reporter chose to obtain the story from their wives, one of whom she persistently refers to, perhaps with a touch of national bias, as 'Aileen'.

'The Cairngorm Winter Festival, now in its second day, promises to be the start of a new era for snow sports in Scotland. And yet if it hadn't been for the hard work and determination of a small group of men, who realised the potential of skiing in Scotland as far back as 1954, there might only be deep silent corries instead of crowded ski slopes and the cries of enthusiastic skiers.

'Austrian-born Karl Fuchs, owner of the Struan House Hotel and ski school in Carrbridge, and Frith Finlayson, born in Glasgow and now owner of the Ski School d'Ecosse in Aviemore, are two of those pioneers who will be remembered as being responsible for the development of the Cairngorms. Last week, as preparations for the festival were being completed, I spoke to Mrs Aileen Fuchs and Frith Finlayson's wife, Jean, who like her husband is a Glaswegian.

'Both women are obviously delighted at the way the big gamble of 15 years ago has turned out. I spoke to English-born Mrs Fuchs at Struan House which she and her husband took over a few months after they were married in 1954.

' "Karl was determined to start a ski school", Mrs Fuchs explained. "He was in the police force in Austria, which is rather like our armed services in that he was able to go on courses where he learned to ski and became an instructor. We looked at various spots for the ski school before finally deciding on Scotland. Part of the reason was that I liked Struan House at once. It was the first time either of us had been in Scotland."

'There are now 12 instructors in the ski school, including Karl. The most recent change is that now 10 of the instructors are British whereas most of them used to be Austrian, but they are sent to Austria to take special examinations and courses.

' "There is a lot of controversy about the various methods of skiing," Mrs Fuchs explained. "People have even been suggesting that a Scottish method should be introduced, but I think we have a tremendous lot to learn from the Continentals before we can introduce our own method."

'Mrs Fuchs admits that she herself has never been a very keen skier. "It was always just a good way of getting fresh air. I'd no idea that I'd be in the business professionally, or be a hotelier." '

The familiar biographical background is covered before the report returns to contemporary matters.

'The new Aviemore centre is the perfect place for children, according to Mrs Fuchs. "You can just drop the children off at the centre for a day and they are quite happy. And of course it's marvellous for the tourists too. In the fine weather we can look after them, skiing or climbing, or walking, but the centre provides entertainment. There is even a babysitting service in the mornings."

'One complaint that Mrs Fuchs did have is that there is no bus service between Carrbridge and Aviemore. "The only way to get to Aviemore is by car. To start with, the railway station was going to be closed and buses were going to be laid on but the station has been kept open and there is no bus service. Some of the trains don't even stop here now." '

The focus shifts to Frith's wife, telling the story of how the Finlaysons came to be in Aviemore and giving details of the running of the Ski School d'Ecosse, before turning to a negative aspect of the development.

'Of course there are a few things about the developments in the valley that both Mrs Finlayson and Mrs Fuchs feel could be improved. One of the most important is the development of the ski slopes. Since the Aviemore Centre was opened the ski road has certainly been greatly improved, and there is a new restaurant, although this benefits summer visitors more than skiers, who don't really want a large meal at lunchtime.

'Plans that were made for new chair lifts and T-bar tows have not been put into action. There was also talk of developing new areas of snow for skiing. Mrs Fuchs pointed out, "We will be devoid of skiers in a few years' time if they are made to swarm about the slopes like ants. There are a few good areas of snow with corries coming down which are perfect for skiing but at the moment they are practically inaccessible." '

Perhaps pursuing Eileen's remark about controversy over styles of skiing, the reporter sought opinions. Dougie Godlington is reported as saying, 'Methods of skiing have become more simple. People used to think if you twisted your body around and waved your arms around, this was the way to ski. Gradually it has come down to the feet which is really all that matters. But you must keep to a good technique in Scottish snow, as it is more necessary to keep your skis under control all the time here.'

Great skier though Dougie was, there are many who would have argued, then and now, that this approach is a touch simplistic. Without a considerable flexibility in the body and a subtle shifting of weight no amount of feet arrangement can produce a good skier.

Had the journalist really seized upon the issue of style, and talked to Karl and Frith as well as Dougie, an entire further article might have been generated but there was another controversy which grabbed the reporter's attention. One of the articles begins, 'Although there is no denying that the Aviemore Centre has brought more prosperity to the area some of the hoteliers in neighbouring villages are noticing a drop in the number of visitors.' The strong inference is that it might have been better if the Centre had not been built at all.

Nobody is quoted and there are no statistics. In pursuit of a story, the reporter expressed the dismay, real or imagined, of non-Aviemore hoteliers to Derek Brightman, director of 'Cairdsport' a shop which sold and hired ski equipment. His response, suitably vague under the circumstances, was optimistic in the extreme. He is reported as saying, 'Although it may seem that the centre is attracting people who might have gone to hotels in the other villages, I think the whole thing will expand so much that people will have to go to the surrounding district.'

In the absence of a sociological survey there is no knowing the full impact of the new facility. Perhaps some of the guest houses did suffer a drop in trade and maybe some of the casual bed-and-breakfast customers swapped allegiance to be nearer to Aviemore. Whatever, the important truth for Karl and Eileen was that the special pull of Struan was easily powerful enough to retain their loyal clientele.

Their commercial confidence was high enough, in this uncertain phase, for them to undertake another building project although it was not, on this occasion, with a view to increasing the capacity of the hotel.

It had been obvious for some time, at the weekends and during the long school holidays, that Peter and Lisi were at an age where they needed more living space. The bungalow was just not adequate for two lively youngsters. It was decided that resources had to be devoted to remedying this problem and, in a remarkably short time, a new residence was erected at the rear of the hotel, physically attached to the main building but with no directly connecting door. It was the first proper home that Karl and Eileen had had in the fifteen years of their marriage.

The new building might, perhaps, have not been so urgent had both of the children shown signs of wanting to pursue their studies. If Edinburgh were to be their main base, and Struan just a short term holiday home, then some cheaper way of providing them with more room could probably have been found but it was obvious by this time that Peter was no academic. His energies were largely physical. Like Karl, he enjoyed practical pursuits, making and mending, improving and extending. He had also, from his mother, acquired a drive to get things done although Eileen claims that, unlike her, he was never ready to compromise on standards.

Peter's practicality suggests that he was ideally constituted to achieve what his parents earnestly desired, that is, his gradual taking over of the running of Struan but in fact he showed no especial interest in skiing. He enjoyed charging down the slopes but whereas his local contemporaries were entering junior races and gaining crucial experience, Peter spurned such competition. The fact that Frith's son Iain, a couple of years older, was already being spoken of as a likely candidate for the British Olympic team in 1972 apparently provided no incentive. Excellent though he was at the discipline, Peter seemed destined to be a recreational skier.

As ever, Karl and Eileen applied no pressure. If their son wanted to return to Carrbridge and work in forestry or on the railways, that would be acceptable to them. They would continue to provide a home for him until such time as he was ready to move on.

The same, of course, applied to Lisi whose academic achievements were greater and who, taking after her father, was beginning to display considerable talent as an artist. Her teachers felt that her ability was such that she could consider applying to art colleges when the time came. With this prospect, she too would be unlikely ever to want to take over the running of Struan. She seemed to have inherited her father's perfectionism and would surely want to follow a career with less day to day pressure than running a hotel.

It was too soon for Karl and Eileen to worry seriously about the long term future. There were always the options, eventually, of finding a trustworthy manager or of a straight, sad sale. In the meantime they needed to make proper provision for their children. The new residence achieved this goal. All that was certain in connection with the two youngsters was that they loved their Scottish home. Peter was already an accomplished countryman, very familiar with the hills and all the territory around them whilst Lisi's enthusiasm for the locale shines through a postcard which she sent in June 1969 from a school trip.

*The picture of Peter, Eileen and Lisi which accompanied the Glasgow Herald articles*

'Dear Daddy,

We had a great time at the Youth Hostel last weekend. I swam in Loch Tay it was good but cold. We had very good food all the meals were hot. We went on one walk through Glen Lion. It rained heavily but we liked it. On Sunday we walked up a big hill which was covered in pine trees.

We walked almost right up until we could see Loch Tay and about seven of us ran down to the beach which was private but there was no notice. We all swam in our pants and vests. I wore my climbing boots every day and they were very comfy. The whole of the class spent all their money and we wanted to buy things. How is Bimbo? - quite well I hope. See you on Friday. It is our long weekend we have the whole of Monday too.

Love from Lisi.'

It was typical of Lisi that her thoughts included concern for Bimbo. Her first cat-love had been Sandy, a stray which had been found in Inverness and brought to Struan. Bimbo had started his life with the Fuchs family in the Edinburgh flat and when he moved north Sandy, tending towards old age, felt most discomfited. Like most of his kind, he found a second home with the Grants who had taken over the Panton cottage. With a daily dose of porridge and a place by the fire, Sandy had in some respects become the Grants' animal but, so the Fuchs family believed, he still regarded Struan as his primary home.

Towards the end of 1969, Karl took the children to the Alps for their regular early season holiday. With them was Colin, 'Moggs', Fleming, son of Struan's Evelyn. He had become Peter's close friend even though he was a year or two younger. Lisi wrote a pencilled post-Christmas letter to her mother.

'Hotel Garni, 28/12/69.

Dear Mum,

I hope you got the first letter. Sorry but I can't find a pen. I am getting on with parallel turns very well. Today we had 2 runs right up to the top of the Valuga and Dad and me found a bunch of great tee-bars and we were on them nearly all day. Yesterday and today I had spaghetti for lunch at the top station. The spaghetti is great. I'm glad to hear that Sandy and Bimbo are OK.

We met 2 of Hans instructors here. Girl & boy, they are very nice. Trains come and go here all the time. This morning we saw two very dark red squirrels outside. Gunter is great fun. Last night Peter and me soaked him. I was throwing snowballs & Peter was shovelling snow down his neck. Ask Jessie if they liked their present from me. Did you? Peter's instructor 'Ernst' is the best I have seen on the hill. We got your letter this morning. Oma helped me wash my hair the other day.

Love from Lisi.'

Soon after this lively communication, Eileen received a postcard from Lisi, the great communicator. It is a typical adolescent communication, indicating how much of the child there still was in thirteen year old Peter. It gave no indication of the momentous event which was just about to happen. She wrote, 'Peter is the maddest twit I've ever seen. My anorak is broken (the zip). Peter is reading my Famous Five book which I'm halfway through and he won't let me read it. It's not fair because there's about six other books.'

A day or two after this missive was posted, the 'maddest twit' made an announcement which delighted and amazed his father. For no obvious reason, Peter declared that he wanted to enter the weekly visitors' race. Most of the competitors would be competent adults. One or two of them would be excellent skiers. Nevertheless, the youth had decided that he wanted to test himself against them through the gates.

Treading warily, not making too much of the matter but with his heart racing with gladness, Karl gave his son a few general hints. He probably knew that Peter, with the impetuosity of his age, would ignore any strictures to ski steadily but the words were worth saying. On the appointed afternoon he stood at the bottom of the course with Lisi and Moggs, barely able to breathe.

One by one the visitors came down, some of them just scraping through the gates, some tumbling but several mimicking the professional racers. Then it was Peter's turn. The boy, a very long way from full growth, looked tiny. In gravitational terms alone he was at a distinct disadvantage but even at that stage Karl could see that he was of a different class. He flowed through the gates, making them seem an irrelevance. When the times were compared it emerged that the boy amongst the men had come a brilliant second. For Peter it was a life-determining event. He came back to Scotland bent on entering the racing fray. Karl was more delighted than he could say.

In order to start his competitive career, Peter had to acquire a start licence which, in turn, entailed entering a qualifying race. There would have been no problem with this but for the vagaries of the weather. All of the early season suitable events were cancelled. For the first of many times Peter came up against the ski racing bureaucracy. Because of his unusual start to life he was clearly far ahead of his contemporaries but nobody had the courage to waive the regulation. Nonetheless, Karl used his contacts in Austria to find race trainers. Eventually the precious license was obtained.

For Eileen, her son's conversion into a racer was a mixed blessing. There was a constant worry about injury and there were supportive duties to be performed. At Glencoe, for example, where father and son were to ski the same course, there was a bitter wind, a steep climb in thick mist and a long cold wait by one of the gates. Karl, racing in the veteran's class, sailed majestically by, crying out, 'Luffly!' and jokingly wagging an upraised finger as he skied to indicate to the more amateur older racers that a lesson was being given. He easily won his category. By contrast, a fast and furious Peter shot into view with a bent stick. He had fallen higher up the course and was raging against himself. In the presentation ceremony the boy got nothing whilst part of Karl's reward was to drink a pint of beer quickly which, to the amusement of those who knew him, he achieved with great difficulty.

Peter's failure in that particular race did nothing to detract from his growing reputation. A letter arrived, suggesting that he should join the elite Kandahar Club. Through this, he began to go for spells in the Alps for specialist training and to participate in suitable competitions. Galvanized by her brother's success, Lisi began to race on the Scottish circuit whilst he was away. Karl went with her to the various race meetings. On their return, Eileen always asked how they had fared and Karl would routinely say, in Scotstrian, 'Lisi won, of kurs.' In some respects the girl was showing more potential than her brother.

The children became so competent that Karl used them as fore-runners for the army championship course. The Duke of Kent made an appearance and Karl, confident of his son's ability, delegated him to wax the royal skis. When asked if the equipment had been satisfactory the

Duke laughed and said that it had indeed and added that, 'At least the skis didn't fall orf'. Eileen practiced the difficult skill of curtseying in ski trousers and was told that her effort was the most graceful of all those presented.

This event passed off successfully but Karl was not so pleased on a subsequent occasion, when Peter and Moggs, in an effort to impress, came down a competition course at top speed and took out several of the gates. Forerunners are supposed to ski decorously and set a guiding track. It was Lisi who performed the business properly, gliding down the restored course without an error.

Despite the over-eagerness which caused the partial demolition of the army course, Karl had no hesitation in allowing Peter to enter the 1970 British Junior Championships, to be held on Cairngorm. He knew that the boy had no realistic chances of winning. The idea was simply for him to gain experience and, ideally, to complete the courses in respectable times. Amongst the several who would surely beat him was a slightly older youth called Konrad Bartelski, who had extensive Alpine experience.

In fact, since the family holiday when they had failed to find a place at Struan, Konrad had pursued his chosen sport with as much determination as the demands made by his schooling would allow. He was especially fired up to win this particular race because he knew that very soon afterwards, the selection would be made for the team to attend the Sapporo Olympics. Although still very young, he had an outside chance of representing his country.

It would have been easy for Konrad to dismiss the Scottish challenge for the title but he was all too aware that any one of the leading youths could, on a good day for them and a bad one for him, win by a margin. There was also another rival who happened to be a friend. Konrad had met him a couple of years earlier on a British junior training event in the Alps. In his book, Konrad describes meeting, 'a midget with bottle glasses who didn't look as though he could ski the nursery slopes let alone the downhill'. The midget's name was Willy Bailey.

Frith Finlayson was appointed Chief of the Courses for the championships. The competition consisted of a slalom and a giant slalom. To win either would be excellent but the champion would be the one with the best combined results.

Willy, something of a slalom specialist, posted an excellent time in that discipline but Konrad, at the peak of his form, skied superbly and outpaced everyone. The margin was such that to win the overall championship, all Konrad had to do was finish reasonably high up the giant slalom order of merit. He could not, of course, afford to fall or miss a gate. If he were to be disqualified in the second event, Willy or any one of a handful of Scots would take the title.

On the day, the gods of form did not desert him. Konrad was the second on the start list and recorded a time which all the assembled pundits agreed would be extremely difficult to beat. The young man, reasonably confident that he was the British junior champion-elect, stayed at the bottom of the slope watching his rivals come down. The system was such that all the main contenders had the earlier start numbers. It soon became very clear that Konrad had succeeded. In his book he recalls the glorious moment and then adds, 'As I had gone at number two I was able to watch the other skiers from the bottom. Among the later starters a young skier caught my eye. He was not amongst the leaders but his skiing had a touch of class about it and I was impressed. His name was Peter Fuchs.'

In spite of his youth and inexperience, Peter came tenth overall. He had proved that, at the age of fourteen, he could hold his own against the older boys.

Peter's new enthusiasm for the sport was such that when the family went for the usual summer holiday with Oma, he abandoned the normal pleasures to do some training on the glacier at Kaprun. Lisi's diary shows that, for all their minor disagreements about the rights to certain books, she was delighted to visit the young racer and sad when they had to leave him behind. Doubtless she taxed him with the idea that he was missing a coveted visit to the ski school and hotel which Karli Haas had created at Lachtal. Since his season at Struan, Karli had expanded his father's business and, in typical Struan networking fashion, had lured Miranda Cadzow, formerly Jessie's helpmate, over to work for him. Peter would have welcomed seeing these people but race training had to take priority.

The new interest was strong enough to take Peter and his friend Moggs away from the usual Christmas delights. At the time in 1970 when he should have been exchanging presents and eating traditional fare, Peter was in Switzerland, training for the Kandahar junior races and the British Alpine Junior Championships. Eileen wrote, saying that conditions on Cairngorm were not very good and hoping that he was having better luck. She reported that Lisi and friends had been up the hill with Dieter Bartsch, Karl's latest Austrian recruit who, all agreed, was an excellent instructor. With strong messages that he was very much missed, Eileen reassured her son that she had sent in his Scottish National Ski Club registration form and found his start licence for the coming season; he would not be cut off from his obsession.

Lisi missed her brother too. The two of them had for so long been good companions when their parents were busy dealing with Struan visitors. One of her letters begins with the story of an unfortunate accident in which one of the Struanites broke a leg but then relieves the gloom with some typical Cairngorm hilarity.

'The BBC were up today and you know what Karen did? We were walking down and she swung her skis round and they hit the BBC van's window and it cracked. Dieter hurt his leg just slightly today by running smack into a snow fence on the White Lady after bombing through a slalom. The other day up skiing we were going up that T- bar at the top of Coire na Ciste and it stopped and started running backwards and then after about 10 seconds Dad shouted to us to get off and move and sure enough just as he was saying it the whole lot fell down. What a crack.'

The Kandahar was held at Les Collons. In the giant slalom for the John Black Trophy, Peter finished fourth, three seconds behind another promising youngster, Piers Iliffe. Moggs, still only thirteen years old, finished fifteenth out of a field of forty. In the slalom the younger Carrbridge boy missed a gate but Peter came third and when the combined times were calculated he found that he was second, just behind the more experienced Stuart Fitzsimmons.

The 1971 ski season, which in Scotland was the mildest for fourteen years and which did nothing to enhance Aviemore's pretensions to be a serious ski resort, was a spectacularly successful one for Peter. He won the Greaves Cup and in the West of Scotland Championships, where two good Austrians were racing as well as top local seniors, he came fifth overall. In April he took the Scottish Junior crown with ease. Competing for the Coronation Cup he and Stuart Fitzsimmons tied for first place and had to share the trophy but it was still an excellent result. At the end of the season he was awarded a modest, but very useful, training grant. Eileen remembers, 'Karli fetched over some first class Austrians to train him and Lisi and to act as instructors in the school and there was no stopping Peter.'

Karl's determination to provide trainers knew no bounds. On one occasion when Franzi Stock, who was due to fill the role, broke his arm Karl immediately called his friend Gustav Fischaller at Glenshee. Gustav had employed a good, young racer called Fredi Krauer for the season. As it happened, Fredi was just on the point of point of climbing into his battered Volkswagen to start the long drive back to Switzerland when the call came. After a moment for consideration he diverted and stayed at Struan for a while. The contact proved fruitful because Fredi and his sister Edith returned the following season to work as Struan instructors. They fitted in excellently, getting on particularly well with the New Zealanders and becoming very much a part of the extended family.

Spurred on by her brother's success, Lisi achieved some very creditable placings. In one of the events she almost beat Moggs but he then showed his true potential by finishing fifth in the Scottish Juniors even though he was still younger than most of the entrants.

The British Junior Championships were held that year at Brand in Austria. Peter was fourth overall, Moggs thirteenth with only three boys of his age or younger ahead of him. Given that they had started competing relatively late, the Carrbridge friends had performed excellently.

The National Ski Federation of Great Britain had decided that anyone who had achieved a set standard in the races would be granted their coveted 'Three Star' award. Although Peter did not win any of the silverware he did meet this criterion and was handed a letter saying that he was entitled to wear the badge, either metal or cloth or both, at a cost of six shillings per item. He did not get round to responding to this until March but Ian Graeme, the Federation secretary, responded positively.

'Dear Peter,

Here are the 3 star badges you asked for. Thank you for your postal order.

Congratulations on your efforts at the Austrian Junior Championships. Splendid. Your father must be truly delighted. Please give him my regards. John Shedden also gave me news of you.'

John Shedden was a lithe, jokey Liverpudlian with a passion for skiing who had been Struan's Chief Instructor for several seasons. He was on his way to making a significant career for himself in the winter sports industry.

As soon as he could legally do so, Peter left school. His one academic achievement was the gaining of an 'O' level in German which he easily acquired at the expense of about one hour in the examination room. The lack of qualifications did not matter; all he wanted to do was race.

It would have been possible for Peter to return to Struan, leaving Eileen and Lisi to the Edinburgh flat, but neither of the Fuchs females wanted this. Lisi let it be known that she would be entirely happy to finish her schooling at Grantown Grammar if a place could be negotiated. This was done and the apartment vacated. The separated Fuchs came home.

After all the years of dislocation, of hazardous journeys up and down the primitive A9, of repeated greetings and farewells, the family was once more united. A new Struan era was beginning. With Peter at last showing a massive interest in racing, with Lisi also beginning to take the sport seriously, the venture seemed set for a long and glorious history.

## 24. Only the Good...

Peter's first golden year of serious ski competition was only just over when news came of an event which shook Struan.

Tom Patey went out climbing in May 1971. He was with inexperienced friends, introducing them to the delights of abseiling from a sea stack off the northern Scottish coast. It was a manoeuvre he had performed many, many times before. Some of Tom's climbing friends had often chided him for his persistence in using an old-fashioned knot. Some said that it was unsafe. The veteran always lightly waved aside their worries. What had always worked would continue to work, he said.

He whipped the rope through its usual contortions, checked it swiftly and launched himself over the edge. If the knot held at all it did so only briefly. That brave, brilliantly talented musician, that innovatory climber, that healer of people and father of three, plummeted to instant death.

The many national news items recorded his age, 38, and credited him with the origination of televised climbing with the dramatic assault on the Old Man of Hoy. Chris Brasher wrote a moving tribute to his erstwhile climbing companion in The Observer:

'If he had been born at the right time he would have reached the summit of one of the highest peaks in the world, perhaps Everest or Kanchenjunga. Tom was always prepared to commit himself to anything which intrigued him. He was, for instance, utterly committed to freedom of action. The material things of the world were of no interest to him except as tools to enable him to explore the hills or to visit a friend. He was prepared to go anywhere at a moment's notice if there was a good climb or a good sing-song at the end of the journey.

'He was, naturally, a master climber, one of the supreme exponents of moving fast over difficult ground and at his best on mixed routes of rock, ice and snow. The most impressive thing was not his style, which was fierce and ungainly, but his speed and judgement of line. These are not unique qualities, yet Tom was unique. No other man, surely, has combined his talents as a serious mountaineer and a ribald entertainer. He was the greatest entertainer in the climbing world - a maker of ballads about the Alpine Club or about his friends Joe Brown and Christian Bonington. His writings in prose and verse will be remembered and sung as long as there is climbing.'

For many at Struan it seemed impossible, in spite of the certainty of the news, that the scruffy Skoda would no longer grind to a halt outside the hotel, that the ambling, shy-smile figure would not come quietly into the Edelweiss, that the accordion, moulded by him after so many million key-pressings, would no longer sound like an orchestra, that the snowy hills would never again see the strong, dogged figure battling up towards a terrifying solo climb, that the ski classes would no more take cover as the triumphant wanderer hurtled erratically towards the valley.

Tom Patey's spirit had permeated the wood of Struan's cosy bar. He had been there from the earliest days, had seen the fire of its spirit splutter into tiny flames then burst into glorious conflagration. So much of his repertoire, musical and spiritual, was recorded in the fabric so lovingly installed by Karl and Sandy Panton. It was unimaginable that such a colossus had been wasted.

Because of Tom's death, it was into a slightly subdued Struan atmosphere that another giant wandered, although the newcomer would have no pretensions to deeds of derring-do or international fame.

Charlie Walpole had been working in his native Hertfordshire and came to Struan through a trip organised by his local Young Farmers' Club. Instantly at home in the Annexe bunks, he made the transition from guest to worker very smoothly. Karl recognised immediately the big man's ability to tackle any practical task. Ski fitting and servicing, boot mending, stick straightening, wood chopping, carpentry, electrical repairs, plumbing, drain clearing; Charlie was designed to be Struan's jack of all trades. Karl, able to do fewer of the maintenance tasks because of the success of the ski school and indifferent health, grabbed onto Charlie. He realised, also, that once the new man came to know the area he would be an excellent leader of the summer walks. Above all, he sensed that Charlie would be utterly loyal, a 'Struan' man through and through, part of the family.

Charlie had huge, work-hardened hands and a large-framed body which might have been frightening but for the fact that he was the exemplar of the gentle giant. He had been born prematurely but the tiny infant had grown to well beyond average proportions. As a child he had started to learn to play the violin but had to give it up when his hands grew to double-bass size. His warm rural burr and his deep, slow smile quickly banished any anxiety that he might use his physical power to ill effect yet there was also an unspoken assurance that, if a friend were in need, Charlie would do everything he could to provide assistance.

With the handyman came an accoutrement, a medium-sized, broad-backed, amiable, shaggy dog called Ricky whose copious, multi-coloured silky coat demanded to be stroked. Within days of his introduction to the place, Ricky was lying contentedly in the ski shed, soaking up the perpetual attention, or ambling with wafting, long-haired tail into the bar to see who would win the prize of being allowed to bury hands in the lush, soft neck fur.

Although he was highly competent and experienced, Charlie's introduction to the Struan services was not without complications. He had a great deal to learn. The electrical system was the most puzzling aspect because it seemed to have no regard whatsoever for the laws of physics. Fuses blew for fun, entire circuits failed without obvious cause.

Water was hardly any better. Charlie tells, with a customary eye twinkle and total and refreshing lack of concern for his reputation, of how one day he cut through a rising main with a chainsaw. A geyser of Icelandic magnitude was his instant evidence of disaster. The pipe had no right to be where it was but the spout shooting up to the Scottish sky proved incontrovertibly its existence. Charlie remembers, also, sitting up all night priming the failing Struan boiler so that there would be hot water for the guests and spending hours, with his impressive set of rods and plungers, trying to clear accumulated sewage. He seemed not to mind doing these things and he certainly enjoyed relaying all the odiferous details to anyone foolish enough to give him half an opportunity in one of the bars.

As anticipated, Charlie soon became a leader of the summer excursions, taking over from Rosie Bell, sometimes working in concert with Karl, sometimes alone. The hill-walking programme had become solidly established, with an Edinburgh-based travel agent supplying groups of immaculate Alpine Germans. With Karl, and often Maurice, in the party those who spoke little English did not miss out on the constant flow of information. There were also regular visits from American schoolchildren who held summer camps in the Annexe, with daily flag ceremonies and a mock Burns night in the unseasonable month of June.

There was a regular programme of ten itineraries which Charlie quickly learned. This started with a circuit of Loch an Eilein and ended with a major hike, often through the Larig Ghru. At the busiest times, when there were enough walkers for two parties, Charlie and Karl would drive to opposite ends of the trek and meet for lunch at a prearranged spot where vehicle keys were exchanged. Karl's long-nurtured friendships with gamekeepers came in useful in this respect because he was allowed access to normally private roads. He was trusted with a key to a gate on the track at Derry Lodge. Through this, many a Struan long-haul hiker was spared five miles of flat, featureless trudging.

*Summer walking party with Karl*

Generally, the people who signed up for the expeditions were amenable and sensible but there were hazardous moments. One woman, with a covert programme of her own, could not be persuaded to follow. Having no knowledge of the area, with neither map nor compass, her chances of solo survival were extremely slim. Like a sheep dog, Karl kept her with the party until they reached the flanks of Ben MacDhui. Thinking that the woman had learned her lesson by this stage, Karl relaxed a little. It was only when he turned to make one of his regular checks on the group that he saw a determined figure scrambling up a very steep slope intent, it seemed, on claiming the mountain's scalp ahead of all her companions. Shouts failed to divert her so Karl had to set off at a pace to head the rebel off. Thereafter he kept as close to her as though they were linked by felon's chains.

Charlie quickly learned to deal with these hazards and all the other ones of blisters, extreme fatigue, general disaffection, intra-group disagreements, disorientation and despair against the climate. He also took over much of Karl's role of evening entertainer. There were hundreds of yards of film, shot by Karl, of previous expeditions. As with the winter skiers, there seemed to be no problem with people watching others do what they had been doing all day. Regular visitors always had the potential thrill of seeing themselves and of pointing out their starring roles to others.

On Fridays, at the end of the walking week, Charlie would join the ramblers in the Edelweiss where, instead of doing the activity or looking at it, they would talk, remembering the high and low points, reliving their life-enhancing experiences.

Charlie was just approaching his first winter season at Struan when another blow, much greater to the establishment than the shocking death of Tom Patey, landed viciously.

Jessie, the seemingly unshakeable rock, the one who had sustained Struan through all the years that Eileen was spending her weekdays in Edinburgh, collapsed. When the diagnosis came it was devastating. The surrogate mother to so many far-from-home people had an inoperable brain tumour. Her working days were over and in weeks or months she would surely die.

There was no point in keeping her in hospital, nothing could be done. She returned to Ellanwood Road, within hailing distance of her Struan kitchen, to be nursed by her shocked, doting family.

For Karl and Eileen. Jessie had been as near to being kin as anyone can be who is not physically related. The prospect of losing her for ever was an appalling one yet they had learned, through all their setbacks, that the hotel business is unrelenting. No matter what personal feelings are paining, distracting and numbing the spirit, the guests must not be inconvenienced. Whatever the problem, it is not theirs.

Even though she, too, was crippled by the imminent loss of her closest friend, Mrs. Taylor took over Jessie's role. It was not easy for anyone who had known and loved the Struan stalwart to keep the hotel running when, only a short distance away, their treasured companion was stoically waiting for the end but they did so because they had to.

Peter went to the Alps early in the Autumn for a prolonged spell of race training. Struggling to deal with the nightmare of Jessie's illness, Eileen was glad that an unusually busy bed-and-breakfast trade in October kept her fully occupied. Then, in November, the customary lull came. Eileen wrote to her son, telling how the New Zealanders were sheet-sewing, Karl painting windows and Dez putting up bunks whilst she organised a large-scale mailing of brochures. Lisi, she reported, was 'busy at school' whilst Moggs was, not for the first time, having much trouble with one of his knees.

Soon after that letter was sent there was some positive news for Struan, although in the context of Jessie's illness it seemed trivial.

For some time it had been obvious that, even with the Enzian in full swing, the bar provision was inadequate. On the busier nights both bars would be densely packed and there would be huge overspills in the dining room. At peak times it was frustratingly difficult for customers to obtain service no matter how frantically the bar staff worked.

Karl and Eileen had concocted a plan to knock through from the Enzian to the lounge, thereby creating an L-shaped bar with windows to the front and side of the hotel and a real, live fire. The line of the counter would follow that of the room and new, full-height access would be provided for the head-bruised staff. Better still, a door would be created from the space occupied by one of the lounge windows. Supplies could then be brought in directly from the yard.

Eileen's good news was that the application for permission to extend the bar had met with approval. She tells Peter, 'so we can do it when we can afford it'.

Whenever she. could, Eileen carved a few hours out of the day to enjoy a walk. The excursions were especially welcome at that time of Jessie's illness. Sometimes there were guests or staff members whose timing coincided and Eileen had company but quite often everyone had gone about their business by the time she was setting out. On such occasions she would, if the creature were available, borrow Ricky. Charlie would usually be occupied with maintenance or manufacture and was delighted that his dog would be getting extra exercise.

Ricky was an excellent walking companion. Presumably because of Hertfordshire farming experience he knew perfectly well that sheep and cows were to be left entirely alone. He could trot happily across fields full of these beasts without even a glance in their direction. He had, though, a problem with goats. Perhaps he had not come across them before, or maybe one had irritated him enormously in the past but no threat or inducement could keep Ricky grounded when a goat hove into view. The first Eileen knew of this was on a day when the two of them were walking far up the Findhorn valley. Some keepers in a Jeep saw that the dog was not on a lead and drove over to remind Eileen to keep him under control. Diplomatically, she clipped a lead to the dog's collar but as soon as the keepers were out of sight she took it off. Almost at once the dog hurtled ahead, scampered round a corner and a most dreadful primal commotion started. Thinking that a deer was under attack, although she had seen none and Ricky usually left them alone, Eileen ran.

Ricky was in the middle of the river, on an island. With him was a wild goat. The dog was being heavily buffeted by the horns which, happily, are tilted backwards on that species and were thus being used as a battering device rather than as piercers of canine skin. It seemed likely that the local resident would win over the invader but doggy honour was at stake. It took all of Eileen's shouted authority to persuade Ricky to concede.

Happily there were few of Ricky's hated species in the area and for the most part Eileen could allow him to wander free. Every now and then he would make a completely forlorn foray in the direction of a snow hare. He was on one such chase one day on Bynack Mhor when he contrived to slip between two rocks and became completely stuck. Left to his own devices he would surely have perished and it took all of Eileen's strength to lift the poor creature out. Those who knew Ricky well were fairly sure that, as an essentially pacific canine, he would have been utterly horrified had one of the flop-eared creatures jumped into his jaws.

Jessie was still clinging on to life when, early one afternoon, Eileen drove with her delightful, tail-wafting companion to Glen Feshie. They set off across the boggy moorland high above that most exquisite of valleys. It was an area that she knew well. The two of them trekked the nine miles to the top of the glen, where the river does a U-turn and then made a turn of their own, back towards the car. Eileen had timed the walk to finish at dusk but some exceptionally heavy clouds gathered. The residual daylight was stolen. She began to worry that, with several streams to cross and narrow bridges to find, the growing gloom might make navigation difficult. She discussed the situation with Ricky. His amused, slightly sardonic glance indicated, 'What problem?'

Quite quickly the lack of light became acute. Trusting Ricky absolutely, because it seemed she had little choice, Eileen followed. The route was complicated and there were several points where critical decisions had to be taken. Always slightly ahead, Ricky waited patiently at each junction. He was not hesitating, merely making sure that Eileen was within sight. More than once she was convinced that her supposed guide had his mind more on hare-hunting than on life saving but she ploughed faithfully on.

It was almost totally dark when she recognised where they were. Ricky, a few yards ahead, the white bits of his coat the only visible sign of his presence, stopped and sat, waiting for her to catch up. His expression, when she could see it through the gloom, said, 'There!' Eileen burst into her effusive, doggy-speak torrent of thanks. To her amazement, Ricky did an uncharacteristic thing. He reared on his hind legs, put his paws reassuringly on his companion's shoulders and came as close as any 'dumb' creature can do to saying, 'Not at all, Eileen, glad to have been of service.'

The 1972 winter season began and Eileen found time, once the Hogmanay mayhem had ended, to write to Peter at one of his Alpine retreats, telling how greatly she missed him and Edinburgh. 'There is nothing to do here but work,' she told him, 'and the work is too hard without Jessie.' Eileen's unhappiness at the loss of her most reliable stalwart was not helped by the worry that Karl's health was deteriorating. In spite of the facts that he was, for once, taking the prescribed pills and making an effort to slim by reducing his usual intake of beer, his blood pressure continued to rise.

Throughout that winter and the following summer, Jessie clung to life. Her death, still deeply shocking even though long anticipated, did not come until the September.

For the Fuchs family, for numberless dozens of workers and for literally hundreds of guests, she had been an elemental part of Struan's character. It was difficult to believe that the venture could survive without her and absolutely certain that things would never entirely be the same.

## 25. The Show Goes On

Jessie's imminent death was as distressing for Peter as for anyone else not of the immediate family. So often she had dried his tears and mediated in disputes but as the first horrifying diagnosis was made he was mercifully distracted from the worst of the grief by exciting developments in his ski racing career. His 1971 success had not gone unnoticed. The National Ski Federation of Great Britain, preparing for the Sapporo Olympics, was forming a training squad. At the end of September, Karl received a letter from the manager of the men's Alpine team, Richard Berry. It began;

'Dear Karl,

'David Freeth has asked me to write to you concerning the training this winter.

'At his recent visit to the Aberdovey Outward Bound Training School he finalised the arrangements for physical training this October. He has asked me to invite your son to join the National Training Programme at this time, and to go to Aberdovey with the other boys. The trainees are due to arrive on the 12th October, ready to start preliminary tests at 13.45. The training will finish on the 23rd October at midday. I hope Peter will be able to attend this training. Naturally we have taken into consideration all the details and discussed it with Gordon Richards who runs the School, and we feel it would be very beneficial to him.

'Snow training will start on the 26th October in the Lotschental. I have made no arrangements as yet for the journey out, but I will probably be travelling by car and Peter could meet me in London and travel out with me.'

The letter went on to say that equipment could be bought at a discount and that a uniform for the hopefuls, the 'Espoirs', was on the way. It was stressed that Peter must have insurance up to £1,000, a crash helmet 'as used by motor-cyclists' and a certificate as to blood group. Richard Berry went on, perhaps superfluously in Karl's case, to note that Peter's clothing should be suitable for temperatures down to minus thirty degrees Celsius and to advise that the Federation could act as informal banker to save Peter having to carry large amounts of cash.

From being just a junior with great promise, Peter was all at once in the national frame. Everyone knew that his chances of being amongst the chosen four were slight but he was at least being considered as a future representative of his country. The Kandahar Club recognised his new status by presenting him with a 'special gold' award accompanied by a personal letter from Sir Arnold Lunn. For good measure, Lisi was granted silver status.

When Peter arrived at Aberdovey he quickly discovered that the programme for the course was physically daunting in the extreme. It included swimming, stamina training, rock climbing, canoeing, sailing, road running, cross-country running, weight training and something just loosely called 'PE'.

A young boy, closeted for a fortnight with people he barely knew, might have been lonely and afraid but almost from the first moment Peter established contact with Konrad Bartelski. It was kinship at first sight. Konrad writes of that meeting, 'We hit it off immediately.'

In direct contrast to his new friend, Konrad had had a disappointing 1971 season. In his book he has harsh words to say about his coach of the time, Michel Rudigoz, who seemed to be incapable of offering proper encouragement to the keen young skiers under his care. This verdict is reinforced by Frith Finlayson whose son, Iain, was under the same practitioner. Frith remembers that, 'There was, however, a big problem. The morale of the team was non-existent.'

According to Frith's account, Iain and his companions suffered from slack management by people who could not even keep time discipline. Iain had reported to his father that the transport arrangements were chaotic, the food poor and the trainers indifferent. In the racing there had been major setbacks. In one slalom, Konrad and Iain had finished second to last and last in times which Konrad had found humiliating. Then, in a late season race, an extremely drunken Austrian, who had had to be held up on the course inspection, swanned into fourth place. The gulf between the British and rest had been all too evident. Konrad was absolutely certain that the chasm could be crossed and it was exciting for him to meet Peter whose skiing he had admired and whose enthusiasm seemed to match his own.

The two of them used their immediate rapport to outwit the Outward Bound instructors who, towards the end of the fortnight, dumped the trainees twenty miles from base with equipment but no money and left them to navigate their way back across open country. Through cunning, and coded communication, Konrad and Peter had contrived to take 'three green handkerchiefs' of the paper variety with them, sufficient to hire a taxi for most of the journey. The instructors were astonished to see them back so early and only temporarily annoyed when the ruse was revealed. The fact that Peter had come out top of all the fitness tests indicated that he was no slacker and the escapade was treated with good spirit.

Immediately after the course, Peter and his new companions set off for the Alps. Eileen wrote a 'wherever you are' letter, congratulating her son on being the fittest person on the Aberdovey course. She told Peter that his progress was giving Karl the most immense happiness. She says, also, that Lisi and Moggs were missing him 'terribly'.

Peter's unexpected addition to the national training squad increased the Scottish element and even though it was as near certain as could be that he would not be amongst those going to Japan, the local excitement rose. In the *Press and Journal* of 30th October Ed Rattray commented;

'The Scottish club skiers at this time are looking ahead to the Games in Japan, in February 1972. Looking ahead of course because for the first time Scotland has a strong representation in the British teams in training. The Ski Council and its many clubs have been working all year to raise sufficient funds to support the Scots in training and to send the chosen team to Japan. The fund target has not yet been reached but as ski fever begins to mount, so the money begins to roll in.'

Later in the same piece the writer celebrates the fact that 'ski fever' had led to the creation of a new race track on Cairngorm ready for the following year's British Championships. It was not, however, just another piste but a course which had been fully approved by the international authorities. For the first time, leading foreign skiers would be attracted to the event because 'FIS' points would be there for the winning. Rattray reveals that;

'The Cairngorm Board have not been daunted by a whacking trading loss incurred last winter, for they have gone ahead and constructed an international size Giant Slalom race course on Cairngorm.

'All being well, this will have its first full use in April when the British Senior championships come to Scotland. This improved course will have two immediate benefits - our racers will be able to race for international points where previously they have had to travel to Europe to do so, and the new course should take some of the congestion problems off the heavily-used White Lady slope.'

The reporter strikes a note of caution, recalling the mildness of the 1971 winter but for Peter, particularly, the prospect of racing against top opposition on home territory was intensely exciting. Even though the event was months away, and the vastly more important Olympics were to take place sooner, he and Konrad determined that they would make the best possible showing in front of the home crowd in April 1972. Their resolve was made all the stronger when the British national press added its push to the bandwagon.

The *Guardian* of the 3rd of November told a wider audience of the developments on Cairngorm and not long afterwards *The Scotsman* added its voice to the clamour. Under the headline, 'Top World Skiers to Race on Cairngorm in April' the article quoted the chair of the organising committee, the former Struanite, Hugh Hunter Gordon, as saying that the race would enhance the skiing prestige of Britain and establish Speyside and Cairngorm as the undisputed centre of the sport in Britain. He drew attention to the benefits of segregating the racers from the recreational skiers but noted that the new slope would be available to all when no racing was taking place. A spokesman for the Highlands and Islands Development Board is quoted as saying that, 'This event, a major one in the international calendar, is recognition that the Spey

Valley is without doubt the United Kingdom's premier winter sports resort. Achievement of international status is a tribute to the immense amount of work done by all the organisations and individuals involved in establishing the Valley's facilities over the past 15 years.'

Surprisingly, as the *Guardian* article reported, the British Junior Championships, which Lisi and Moggs were due to enter, were not scheduled to follow the senior event's lead. As usual they were to be held in the Alps, at Les Collons-Thyon in early January. Maybe the decision to hold the Junior event abroad was simply to do with the unreliability of early season snow, especially after such a disappointing winter as the one that had gone before. If so, the Cairngorm climate was soon in its most mocking mood. Lisi wrote to her brother on the 20th of November;

'Dear Peter,

'By gee what snow there is down here, real deep powder. Moggs, me and that daft little bugger Alwyn Murray went down to the hall with the snow bike. What a laugh. Peter Rice and that lot were just leaving tonight and we soaked them completely. We went up skiing today and all the chairlift was working as well as the Ptarmigan T.

'(The flakes falling outside just now are about an inch in size. Hang on, I'll just go out and measure it, about four inches rapidly getting on for five of pure dry powder snow.)

'We went to school yesterday and Lewy sent us all home in case the road got blocked. Anyway he was a fool because it was great sunshine afterwards. I went 20 miles on skis yesterday. We tied a rope to the minibus and went round the car park about one hundred times then dad drove us up to Dalnahaitnich and up and down the road. 4 times. It was great, the fastest I went was 36 miles per hour.

'It's half to eleven now and the snow is falling and lying like hell.'

The letter relates some local gossip and gives news of Lisi's beloved cats, Sandy and Bimbo before returning to ski-related themes.

'There's no sign of Frith up there. Dieter's a nut case because he was supposed to have been in London a couple of weeks back with Judy and he never rang up but when he got back to Austria he rang up. Marie says he's madly in love with Judy, almost in despair.'

'Dieter' was Dieter Bartsch, one of the Austrian instructors whom Karl had brought over primarily as race trainers. As Lisi's gossip suggests, he had fallen heavily for one of the Struan New Zealanders. Lisi goes on, 'Mogg's knee was so bad sometimes that he could hardly walk and it was hell of a swollen but he's got pills and it's getting a bit better, poor thing.'

In her next letter, written a few days afterwards, Lisi laments the deaths of the schoolchildren in the mountains. The tragedy was very immediate to her because Karl and Eileen had seen the party as they ascended. Sensing a coming storm, Karl had said to his wife, 'We go down now'. From the chairlift they had noticed that some of Cathy Davidson's party were wearing jeans. They remarked on this to the chairlift staff who said that they had warned the young group leader of the dangers, to no avail.

The tone of Lisi's communication is understandably more sombre than that of the previous one and she concentrates mainly on ski business. She writes that, even though it was still only November, both Willy McConville, one of Karl's long-serving instructors, and Moggs were instructing. She also tells Peter that another Struan regular, Alex Newton, was due to start work soon with two fresh Austrians and a new British instructor called Don Rumbold. The Carrbridge Austrian Ski School was preparing for a new, busy season.

Maybe as a way of countering the image created by the poor snow of the previous year, the Highlands and Islands Development Board did its best to ensure that Struan and all the other establishments had the best prospects. It produced a glossy colour brochure extolling the delights of Speyside winter sports. It presents the area in a very glamorous light and, for all that it has to be judged as a piece of publicity rather than an objective picture, it vividly illustrates how much the Cairngorms had developed in time since Karl and Eileen settled there. Hotels by the dozen, an extensive system of lifts, varied apres-ski facilities; the potential customer is easily persuaded that here is a winter sports resort of significance. The back page was used to show the extent of the skiing.

In the brochure, the ski schools were carefully listed in alphabetical order which conveniently put the 'Austrian Ski School' in pole position.

The accompanying text read, 'Karl Fuchs introduced the Austrian style of skiing to Spey Valley. All his instructors are trained in the Austrian method and have reached high standards of ski teaching, imparting a controlled and elegant style to their pupils.' Struan also had a quarter page advertisement, with a colour photograph of the hotel, offering full board and ski instruction for £15 or £20 per week depending on the season.

*The Cairngorm skiing area*

The brochure did not, of course, allude to the unpredictable snow conditions, the wild weather, nor to the fact that success had brought serious problems of overcrowding on the slopes. Beginners and intermediates were faced not only with the challenges of balance and posture, they had always to be on the alert for other moving bodies, some of them out of control. In the narrow confines of Coire Cas people stopped to gather breath and courage. Others skidded to a halt because the stationary forms below blocked the natural line of descent. One moderately sized ski class could provide a mobile barrier. The need for expansion of the facilities was acute.

Whilst the Cairngorms prepared for the new season, Peter and Konrad stayed in the Alps, training hard and gaining as much race experience as possible. Their immediate aim was to be chosen for an elite squad from which the final Olympic four would be selected. At the age of sixteen, Peter's chances of the ultimate honour were minuscule and he knew that he would be lucky even to jump the first hurdle. Konrad, by contrast, had real prospects of going all the way to Sapporo.

The friendship between the two of them deepened day by day and through this Peter came to know 'the midget with the bottle glasses,' Willy Bailey. The three of them found themselves forming a sub group within the training squad. They perceived themselves as the keen ones, the true competitors. They were dissatisfied with what they thought to be the lack of full commitment of the others and began to doubt the wisdom of the Ski Federation officials who seemed to be more concerned with diplomacy and the trappings of their office than the true imperatives of ski racing. Even though the Olympics were their main preoccupation, they began to talk about how essential it would be for them to show everybody that their approach was the right one by conquering all in April's British Championships.

When the time came for the announcement of the names for intensive pre-Olympic training, neither Peter's nor Willy's was on the list. There was also disappointment for Konrad for, although he was to continue with the squad, he would be only the reserve. His race results put him fourth in the national rankings but it had been decided that, regardless of ability, there had to be a Scot in the team.

It would have been easy for Peter, a young man far from home, to retreat and lick his wounds after this rejection but there was no diverting him from ski racing. With his parent's full consent he decided to remain on the Continent to gain as much race experience as possible.

Eileen wrote to him at the beginning of December with detailed advice about who to contact in various parts of the Alps, where he might find free or cheap accommodation with friends and discussing the best strategy for future training. It was written before the official decision was made public so there is advice from Karl about correct behaviour; 'If, of course, the British Men's Team invited you back you would have to cancel everything else - you never know what your luck might be! Daddy says the selection will be announced soon so behave. beautifully and modestly as always.'

The letter has further advice about equipment, money and insurance but also, and as always, it contains earnest reassurances that the boy is greatly missed by everyone. There is news that Moggs, whose persistent knee problems had kept him off the slopes, was beginning to ski again and that he and Lisi were greatly looking forward to going to Les Collons-Thyon for the British Junior Championships.

Just after this letter was sent, news came through to Struan that Peter was, after all, to continue training with the national squad as an official reserve. Eileen wrote immediately, expressing delight. She conveyed Lisi's profound hope that her brother would be able to get across to see her at Les Collons. There was domestic news; Jessie's illness, Mrs. Taylor's stalwart support, Moggs' hard work in the kitchen for pocket money and a description of the fickle Cairngorm conditions where the massive November accumulation had melted to leave snow only at the summit. To add to the woe, Eileen reported, the chairlift was often closed because of wind.

The selection of Peter as a reserve had repercussions for Konrad and their friendship. The men in charge made it clear that the 'mandatory Scot' rule still applied, such that if Iain Finlayson were to be injured then Peter would take that place. Konrad's hopes rested on an injury occurring to one of the three non-Scottish squad members. Inadvertently, Peter had significantly diminished his chances.

They talked, as good friends should, about the possibilities and manfully decided that they would accept whatever fate delivered. Their negative feelings were turned not inward on their relationship but towards the administrators of their sport. They reinforced their view that something radical would have to be done if they were to have any chance of succeeding against the properly organised Alpine countries.

Lisi and Moggs travelled to the Alps for the British Junior Championships. Lisi wrote home with a list of people she knew who were there and expressing very genuine sadness that one of her contemporaries, Piers Iliffe, had broken his leg whilst training. Moggs, who had been skiing well in Scotland, found that the intensive pre-race training had exacerbated his chronic knee problems. He knew, before the forerunner blazed the trail, that his chances of success were much reduced.

The slalom was a disappointment to Lisi. She fell half way down the course and had to withdraw. The giant slalom was a different matter. Running fluently she came a very creditable second and, in so doing, made her breakthrough in junior racing.

Immediately after the national races there was more extensive competition billed as the International Inter Club Junior, a giant slalom event. Moggs' injuries were too severe for him to compete but Lisi represented the Struan interest. Stuart Fitzsimmons, who had won the national junior title, again triumphed but the *Scotsman*, in its report of the event, noted that, 'The next Scots placed were Carrbridge pair, Duncan Riley (14), eighth and Lisi Fuchs (14) ninth, giving Scotland for the first time three places in the first ten of an international event.'

Ahead of Lisi, in second place, was fourteen year old Lucinda Iliffe, the sister of the boy who had broken his leg. Lucinda had won the girls' title at the national championships and she was clearly the one for Lisi to beat in the future if she were to win the prestigious prizes. The next immediate opportunity would be the European Junior Championships, open to all under-18 year olds, to be held a few days later at Madonna di Campiglio in Italy. Peter wrote on the 3rd of January and mentioned the prospects of his sister.

'Dear Dad and Mum,

'We're leaving Meribel this morning to go to Val d'Isere for the Lowlanders' race. I'm having trouble with my legs, my right one is a bit better now because I've been resting it for about a week but my other one's getting bad in the same place as I hurt it in Kaprun. I did one day's downhill training here only in the morning after not skiing for a week and beat all of the Espoirs by quite a bit.

'The skis I've got are great and I get them free now. Me and Willy aren't going to the Olympics although we beat all the rest of the team by quite a lot.'

'Lisi might be going to Madonna di Campiglio as well as me. I don't know if I'll be alright though because of my legs. But Dieter and Peter Lorenz reckon that Lisi will be in the B team if she skis as well as she's doing now. She's skiing just as I was this time last year.

'Moggs has got both cartileges bad and he can hardly bend his legs. It's a pity because I think he could have won the British Juniors.'

The references to injuries were worrying for Peter's parents. Ski racing was evidently a hazardous business but there was always the danger with keen young competitors that they would dare too much or not allow the proper time for healing. It might have been preferable if Peter's stresses and strains had prevented him racing in the Lowlanders race but in fact he did well in the slalom and was far ahead of the field in the downhill when he fell at the last gate.

Nursing his pain and his pride, Peter moved on to Italy where, sadly, he did not see his sister because she had had to return home to resume her schooling. Eileen wrote once more to her son on the eleventh of January.

'Dear Peter,

'We have been hoping for a 'phone call from you in Val d'Isere and I have been eagerly scanning the papers. There was a very nice bit in the Telegraph which said you had been "cruelly robbed of victory" in the downhill by somersaulting near the last gate and losing your skis. It talked about you and Willy having inquests after each race and drawing diagrams in the snow. You must have been frightfully disappointed. But we were pleased to see you came fifth in the slalom. Well done indeed. The downhill reminded me somehow of that first race of yours at Hillend when you knocked down a pole in the very last gate - what a long time ago that was!

'Lisi and Colin arrived at Waverley and Lisi is very sick at being back at school as you can imagine. She did very well in the races, didn't she? Lisi tells me you are really enjoying yourself and I am so glad.'

Whilst Lisi and Colin returned to their mundane schooling, Konrad and Peter kept on with the training in the hope that luck would swing in their direction. Naturally, they stopped short of hoping that both a Scot and a non-Scot would be injured but could not help anticipating how exciting it would be if fate took them both to Japan. They travelled from venue to venue, entering the races which had been deemed suitable by their trainer, striving always to improve. They were always at a disadvantage compared to the well-funded, technically advanced Alpine and Nordic skiers but they were not by any means disgraced. Peter's injuries gave him constant trouble. When Eileen wrote towards the end of January she hinted that he was not skiing flat out.

'Dear Peter,

'I do hope this letter gets to you before you move on. I'm glad you managed the downhill at Madonna - I expect you went carefully, as Stuart and Co weren't far behind you. We saw no mention of you at all in the slalom. Daddy thinks Richard Berry has other plans for you! We shall hear all about you from Dieter when he comes. I am so glad the winter is passing so that you will be home in a couple of months or so. We all miss you terribly.'

The letter goes on to report, with mild surprise, that Eileen had just heard a report on Radio Four which ended with predictions about the likely winners at the forthcoming East of Scotland Junior Championships. The commentator had cited Colin Fleming as an excellent prospect amongst the boys and Lisi Fuchs as the likely winner in the girls' competition. Eileen reports wryly, 'Poor Moggs can't ski anyway because of his bad knee.' She tells Peter also that the *Scotsman* had recently mentioned Lisi as the 'sister of the Scottish Junior champion, Peter Fuchs' and delights in the reflected glory. Referring to plans for Easter, when the long-anticipated British Championships would be held on Cairngorm, she goes on to say, 'I am very much looking forward to having your friends Willy, Konrad and Co. to stay here with you.'

Although taking her schooling seriously, and making no grand plans about a future in ski racing, Lisi trained as and when she could for the East of Scotland junior championships to be held at Glenshee. After the event, the local press reported that, 'The deceptively graceful skiing of Lisi Fuchs (14) of Carrbridge, who was best girl, gave her third overall and second place in the slalom. Her continuing improvement could embarrass the boys later in the season.'

Peter heard the news of his sister's progress and was suitably proud. He and Konrad had more or less resigned themselves to the idea that they would not be making the trip to Japan and, although they gave of their best in the Alpine races for which they were entered, much of their thought was on the British Championships. Konrad, significantly older and much more experienced than his friend, was insistent that only if they proved themselves in that arena would they be in a position to exercise the essential influence for change.

They were engrossed in these prospects when something happened which switched Konrad's attention totally. Julian Vasey, an Englishman, suffered a terrible accident. All of them were very genuinely sorry for him and truly wished that it had not happened but the outcome was that Konrad was suddenly in the squad for Sapporo.

The trip for the seventeen year old was a revelation. He sensed that his keenness was not matched by the others in the party. In the downhill he managed a very respectable forty-second, achieved without the massive technical support and general back-up available to the major teams. He was particularly pleased that he finished all of two seconds ahead of Iain Finlayson because this amply justified his place in the squad. Iain did better in the slalom, finishing twenty third. Overall, though, the performance of the British team was disappointing and very quickly the rumblings of discontent were made public by John Samuel in *The Guardian* of the 24th February 1972. As part of a lengthy piece he wrote;

'The attempt to keep a British senior men's team in top world ski-racing is almost certain to be abandoned next season. Only Iain Finlayson of the Olympic team will again be available. Alex Mapelli-Mozzi and Royston Varley told me in Hong Kong, where the residue of the British Olympic team have been staying this week, that they were giving up because they could see no chance of success with the existing set-up.

'It is a sad blow for those who have argued for a British presence in the most popular of Continental winter activities outside of football, but the increasing professionalism of the circuit has made the men's withdrawal inevitable. At one time it was hoped that Scotland would produce good enough skiers to keep Britain in with a respectable chance, but progress has been slow while the Scottish have built from grass roots, if that is not too severe a metaphor for Scottish snow, and the success of the World Cup circuit has meant an ever-increasing gap.

'A policy study made by Major General Reginald Leathes, chairman of the National Ski Federation before the Games, states categorically that Britain lacks the resources in money and administrative manpower to support national teams in the semi-professional World Cup series and World Championship competition of today, and a reduction in the national effort at this level is inevitable. It is hardly likely to be disputed when the Federation considers future racing policy in May, following the British championships in the Cairngorms.'

John Samuel goes on to point out that modern ski racers have to devote ten years to the sport, something which General Leathes reportedly saw as being well beyond the resources of the British. The soldier's view was that scarce money should be devoted to the development of club racing, not to the support of an elite. He reinforced his argument by agreeing that the administration of skiing, dependant as it was on volunteers, was not geared to the modern Alpine scene.

The piece made gloomy reading for the young hopefuls. At the very start of their sporting careers the leaders seemed to be saying that nothing could be done to help them. When Konrad returned, he, Peter and Willy Bailey met at the Swiss mountain resort of Lotschental. After the disappointment about attitudes at Sapporo, Konrad found it exhilarating to be with such keen skiers. The boys recognised that unless they took an initiative little would be likely to come out of the May meeting to which John Samuel had referred. The disbanding of the Olympic squad meant that there was no longer any focus. The youths decided that, without making too much of an issue of the matter, they would provide their own focus. There *would* be a British 'team' and they would be the core of it.

They continued to race on the Europa Cup circuit as and when they could, surviving on parental largesse and living very frugally. As Eileen recalls, they often ended up sleeping rough in places such as railway stations. The families did what they could to support from afar.

To the youngsters the privations were not important. What mattered was that they were rubbing shoulders with the likes of Franz Klammer and Piero Gross. Naturally they were not winning against these giants of the sport but neither were they being totally disgraced.

Eileen wrote to Peter on the 26th February, telling of her efforts to have him and Willy entered for the Austrian championships and then again on the 4th March, welcoming the fact that he would soon be coming home with his two ski companions in tow. She noted, too, that General Leathes, who had stayed at Struan a few years before, had asked for accommodation for the duration of the British Championships. As on the previous occasion, she planned to board him out with Moggs' parents in nearby Ellanwood Road.

In spite of the official gloom about the prospects for British ski racers, there was great optimism at Struan in that post-Olympic period. It was true that the embryonic nucleus of Konrad, Peter and Willy would be chronically under-resourced, and would therefore be unlikely to cause the Alpine giants much anxiety, but it was felt that energy and enthusiasm would compensate to a very large degree for the lack of financial backing.

The positive feelings were greatly boosted by Lisi's racing exploits. To her East of Scotland junior title she added that of the North. The local press treated her to headlines trumpeting her victory. In all of her races she was beating many of the ambitious boys. If she could avoid injury and continue to develop as she was doing, there was every likelihood that she would join the dynamic trio and one day win real ski-racing glory for her family and her country.

In all of the Scottish racing excursions, Karl would drive Lisi and Moggs to the various destinations. For Lisi particularly the sight of him standing rock-like by a crucial gate was always vastly encouraging. Sometimes he would bring any available Struan instructors with him to act as extra support. At Glenshee they invariably stayed with Finlay Cameron who would cook enthusiastically but not especially well. Lisi's fond memory is of seeing a row of burnt Heinz treacle puddings outside Finlay's back door but no culinary disaster could detract from the homeliness and warmth of welcome.

For Peter and Lisi's parents, but particularly for the ski racer Karl, it was a heady time. How thrilling was the prospect of the forthcoming British Championships to be held on home territory, with distinguished foreigners competing for the first time and with the Struan family primed to prove that the British racing spirit was very much alive.

## 26. The Three Musketeers

Peter was home for the West of Scotland championships in mid-March. The race promised to be an ideal warm-up for the big event. At Glencoe he had the honour of first place in the start list. Perhaps trying too hard, he missed a gate and was disqualified. It was not, after all, quite the perfect platform.

The gang of three gathered two weeks before the all-important races were due to begin. Struan accommodated them and some of the other young racers. Karl used all his experience to reduce tension. Trips to the cinema and liberal quantities of Coca Cola seemed to help with fraying nerves. There was rigorous training with Dieter Bartsch, otherwise the three companions talked tirelessly, making plans, mapping out the future improvements to the status of British skiing. John Samuel's article had provided the young men with what seemed to them like a mandate to take direct action.

The Scottish National Ski Council produced a special issue of their '*Scotskinews*' to mark the racing occasion. In an introductory piece it was noted that a milestone in Scottish skiing history was being passed. 'Who would have predicted 10 years ago,' the magazine asked, 'that we would have Olympic medal winners skiing in races in Scotland?' The publication was packed with detail about the seeding process, the names of officials, the various prizes and many other matters. What must have been of greater interest, and perhaps alarm, to the determined trio was the strength of the home challenge. Making their mark on the slopes, the essential preliminary to their campaign, was going to be very far from easy.

*Konrad, Dieter, Peter, Willy, Lisi outside the Struan ski shed*

The start lists excluded the foreigners because only a British national could be declared champion. Top of the rankings for the first phase, the Giant Slalom, were two British Olympic skiers. Konrad held third spot, Peter and Willy were placed sixth and seventh. Ahead of them were Frith Finlayson's boy, Iain, another Olympic performer, and Fraser, the son of the 'King of the Hill', Bob Clyde. There were dangers beneath them as well as above, keen competitors such as Stuart Fitzsimmons and Duncan Riley. Any one of two dozen or more could beat the trio.

Howard Bass, in *The Daily Telegraph* of 15th April, celebrated the forthcoming event. After explaining the formidable European challenge, the writer added that, 'The British Olympic skiers, Iain Finlayson and Konrad Bartelski should be conspicuous among the home entries which number 54 men and 22 women.'

Whatever the secret dreams of the young British skiers, there was no prospect that they would beat the world-class performers catalogued by

Howard Bass. At that stage of their careers an outright win would have been akin to a good club runner defeating half a dozen Olympic champions in a one hundred meters dash. What mattered was the performance against the domestic rivals.

Frith Finlayson organised the courses for the great showdown under the overall supervision of the Chief of Championships, Hugh Hunter-Gordon. In his autobiography, Frith recalls how, in those days before mechanised piste-preparation was available in Scotland, they had to recruit an army of volunteers to trample up and down the slopes on skis, making the surface as flat as possible. Happily there was no shortage of willing feet and the course was stamped into excellent condition.

At last, the great day dawned. To the astonishment and delight of those who knew the Cairngorms well, the sun shone. The giant slalom element was the first phase. As ever, there were two runs, with the aggregate times as the significant measure.

Older, more experienced, visitors hurtled down the White Lady. As expected, the foreign stars recorded excellent times as did the two Britons who were seeded above Konrad. When he pushed off he knew that he had to ski to his limits and that consequently the risk of making a fatal mistake was high. Happily his technique did not let him down. His time was very competitive.

Inspired by this example, both Peter and Willy had excellent runs. The first quarter of their self-appointed task was done. The next goal was to complete the second leg in even better style and thereby ensure that their aggregate times were lower than those of their domestic rivals.

As before, the visitors showed the way, then the two British Olympians threw themselves down the steep slope. It was obvious that nothing was going to be given away. Konrad, running third of the indigenous skiers, again focused his mind and put his young body into action. There were turns which could have been tighter, lines of descent which might have been faster but as he skidded to a spectacular halt the cheers of his supporters told him that he had achieved his goal. The two Olympians who had gone before him had been beaten. All that remained was the anxious wait whilst the others, knowing what they had to achieve, came hurtling through the gates.

At the top, Peter waited his turn. In spite of Karl's best efforts, the tension was almost unbearable. For his family, for his new ski-racing companions and above all for himself he yearned to do well. Iain Finlayson pushed off then when he had gone, Fraser Clyde departed in a flurry of sticks and swirls of kicked-up snow. Neither of them beat Konrad's time. Provided that the racers yet to come did not produce something special, the trio had at least proved part of their point. Peter was desperate to reinforce the message.

He pushed and the pent-up forces inside him were released. The racing track was well-marked by those who had gone before. The gates, far apart to an observer, came quickly one after the other to the speeding runner. There were moments when all seemed in control, other terrifying ones when disaster seemed possible but he was pushing himself, wanting to excel.

At the bottom he learned the thrilling truth; he had beaten Konrad by a tiny fraction.

His friend might have been dismayed but if so, he showed nothing of it. The shared excitement overwhelmed them. There were some excellent racers to come and the first and second spots could still be snatched but the only one who would be welcome as a usurper was the third member of their trio, Willy.

Coming immediately after Peter, he posted a very commendable time but he was behind both of his companions. Stuart Fitzsimmons had his tilt at the leaders, as did Duncan Riley and the others. None could make up the deficit. The three rejoiced; even if they crashed out of the slalom they had most definitely made their mark.

*The Scotsman* of Monday April 17th carried an article by Harry Reid which reported that French skiers had dominated the first phase but also devoted plenty of space to the local interest. In part the piece read;

'Right on cue, at 11 a.m. precisely, the sun starts shining (it is already shining down below, in the valley, shining on the distant white hotels of Aviemore in anticipation of the coming delights of apres-ski). Right on cue, at 11.1. a.m. precisely, the first skier appears on the skyline - Max Renner of Austria, zig-zagging down the White Lady. The British Alpine Ski Championships, the first international competition to be held in

Britain, have begun. On this April Saturday morning, on the flanks of Cairngorm, history is being made.

'The top Briton was 16-year-old Peter Fuchs (Carrbridge), who was eighth, a performance which must have delighted his father, Karl Fuchs, who did so much to pioneer skiing in the Cairngorms.'

The reporter also recorded that two of Britain's finest female skiers, Davina Galica and Gina Hathorn, came second and third in the women's event. Reid quoted Davina Galica as saying, 'Nowhere on the Continent would you get so much snow in April, except possibly Italy,' whilst Gina Hathorn recalled that when she started, she had to walk up Cairngorm. 'Changed days,' Reid noted.

Changed days indeed for Karl and Eileen, with the mountain which they had chosen showing off gloriously to the world and their sixteen year old son in the lead of the national championships!

As the slalom phase began, it was clear that Willy, even though he was something of a specialist with a seventh ranking amongst the contenders, could not realistically hope to win the overall title. The gap between him and the others after the first phase of the championships was too great.

The case was very different with Konrad. The older boy, with only a marginally worse record in the short race discipline, was ranked fourth of the Britons behind three Olympians. They might well pip him to first place but they would have to win by a large margin to counteract Konrad's lead from the first phase.

Peter, in spite of his brilliant showing in the giant slalom, was much less secure. He was scheduled to start in fourteenth place. He would have to ski well above normal expectations if he were to keep some of the others from pushing him down the overall rankings.

Exerting admirable self-control for ones so young, focusing totally on the task, the two skated fluently through the gates. Neither of them fell, neither missed a gate. Konrad was more or less true to his ranking, Peter pushed beyond his usual level of performance. When the times for all four runs were aggregated, Konrad was fractionally ahead of Peter but, more importantly, they were both faster than any of the other Britons. Konrad was British ski champion, Peter the runner-up.

Recalling the euphoria which came from these races, Konrad wrote many years later, 'When the three of us met up in the piano room of the Fuchs' home after the races we knew we were on the right track. All we needed was the money.' They began to plan.

John Samuel was very taken with the talk of a bold initiatives. On the 19th April 1972 he wrote a piece in the *Guardian* which Konrad marks as the true launching of their venture. It bore the striking headline; 'Ski youngsters in revolt'. Whilst not neglecting to report all the other news of the championships, Samuel wrote;

'The British champion over the last four days has been Konrad Bartelski, but in spite of a foreign sounding name and an address of Duinvoetlaan, Wassenaar, near the Hague, Holland, his instincts are entirely British. He is a moving spirit in a youngsters' revolt which is aimed at putting Britain rather more firmly on the ski-racing map.

'Bartelski feels that the British capacity for the sport is not being adequately represented; nor does he feel that the training regime is adequate for the purpose. So does Peter Fuchs, aged 16, the son of Karl Fuchs, an Austrian who more than most has helped to establish Scottish ski-ing.

'All the three young racers - Bartelski is 17, Fuchs is 16 and Bailey 17 - have been members of the official British Espoir Group, but reckon that their training has not been adequate. "We are not trying to win races but to get fit for the job", said Bartelski. "Nothing we have had in training so far has put the proper priority on things. We all hope to join individual national teams after our own training programme. Peter can go to the Austrians, myself to the Poles and Bill will, we hope, find another national team to accommodate him. It is a do-it-yourself programme, but we feel far better than anything we have had officially. At the end of it, we hope to be in condition to think about racing and gaining handicap points."'

This strategy of separatism soon changed. When the three met once more at Struan a month later and talked exhaustively they decided to stay together and to organise themselves into an embryonic British racing team. They chose a name, 'The Three Musketeers', which, they felt conveyed the idea of tough, resourceful, well-intentioned winners.

Willy was given responsibility for equipment, Konrad took charge of finance and public relations whilst Peter concentrated on the racing programme. They all quickly delivered. Konrad persuaded his parents to provide a second-hand Volkswagen minibus. The three of them converted this, creating sleeping space for three and room for luggage and equipment. Willy somehow arranged the production of distinctive jerseys whilst Peter prevailed on Karl to make Dieter Bartsch available as trainer. Joining in the spirit of things, Dieter agreed to work for a mere £11 per day and gladly wore the 'uniform' jersey of the group.

Peter and Konrad, joined later by Willy, spent a summer month at Dieter's house in St. Johann am Tauern, on a rigorous fitness training programme. As this was coming to an end, news came of an offer from the Australian Ski Federation of two training places for British athletes. The British authorities decided that Bob Clyde's son, Fraser, should be one of the chosen. They offered the other place to one of the Three Musketeers. On the ranking established by the British Championships, Konrad should have been the nominee but the ever-resourceful racer had an alternative plan. Through his father's connections in the aviation world he could obtain a very cheap flight. Once in Australia he could live as they did in the Alps, on very little indeed. It was Peter who took the official place.

An Australian newspaper covered the visit of the three Britons. It reported that Konrad and Peter looked to be in good form at Falls Creek but then, a little later, under the headline, 'Unsuccessful Week in Australia', it recorded that, in conditions reminiscent of Scotland at its worst, all three missed gates in the giant slalom on Mount Buller. The correspondent noted that Peter had had the handicap of an injury but added, 'the fact that Fuchs is racing again indicates that he has recovered from the bruised calf muscle which kept him out of the second race at Falls Creek.'

Truly believing that the worst he was suffering from was severe bruising, Peter flew back to Europe. He intended to spend a brief recuperative spell at home before meeting Konrad in Munich. The two of them planned to drive to Dieter's house, where Lisi was benefiting from some individual coaching, before going to Dachstein to train with the Austrian juniors. Whilst waiting for her brother to arrive, Lisi wrote one of her entertaining letters to her parents.

'Dear Mum and Dad,

'Thanks for the two letters, just got one from Shena today. Yesterday and today were the first two days with good weather but today the snow was a bit soggy and dangerous so we stopped slalom training and continued free skiing. I got through the first gate of the slalom but the ruts were so big I couldn't go further.

'We've got a race on Sunday and I'm skiing not very well at all, can't even do the gates of a wide slalom. Peter's coming tomorrow. I'm much fatter now since I came. I'm arriving back on the 4th so school on the 5th, tell Shena why the hell is she going on the day before I get back when she doesn't even start school? Tell her to go on the night of the 4th. She's only written me one letter! We're going training in a few minutes.

'Paula hurt her ankle yesterday but not too bad. There's this stupid boy who's in my group, he's got all the pattery clothes etc and always tries to go in front of me but when he does I nearly run into him 'cause he's so slow. I'm going shopping with Jane Allison and a girl called Carolyne (she came out with her own car so we drove up to the cable car with her today). I'm most friendly with Jane I think. I'm so stiff from training now. Piers just can't wait till Peter gets here. Lucy Molineux is here, she's got a big metal plate in her leg but she's skiing really good I think. She's not allowed to train slalom or anything yet cause she's got to get another operation still. Patsy's getting Kastingers with me as well. My Humanics are really hurting me now, my ankles are rubbed a bit. I can't be bothered washing any clothes so they're dirty.

'How's Sandy and Bimbo? We never got Kandahar jumpers this year but I get hot anyway. You know unless I get any better than what I'm skiing now it's no point going on when I see the kids over here, even the rest of Kandahar are better now. There's a whole lot of Americans here just now like last year. A girl hurt her leg today, don't know if it broke or not, no wonder in all that snow.

'My lips are all cracked up so I'm going to buy some lip stuff, really good stuff, makes yer lips all white, my face's caught the sun too, just beginning to get goggle marks. I'm going to try and get overtrousers too and see how much those ski trousers with zips are, doubt if I'll get them tho. We're going training in about half an hour, Toni Wimmer's lot are gone now, not that I saw them train at all.

*Lisi on the patchy Cairngorm slopes*

'The food's not bad at all. Nearly all of us sleep in the building with the swimming pool in so it's handy. The bus never came to take us up today so we were late.

'Well I want to go and post this now, we're back from training now and I had a swim. I thought it was really tiring training today.

'Looking forward to seeing P & K tomorrow. Maria just arrived this afternoon, chattering away as usual. Hans Bosch has just got back from the Blizzard factory with new skis for Stuart and Andi Fitz. I should be getting my boots soon and skis I hope.

'Anyway cheerio.

'Love Lisi'

At that time, as the letter suggests, Lisi was ambivalent about her future as a ski racer but she was, in any case, too young to leave school. As soon as the training session was over she would have to return home. All that she could do as far as racing was concerned was keep fit and enter as many of the Scottish races as she could. If, later, she chose to follow in her brother's footsteps she would not be too far behind the Austrian girls with whom she had been training.

After a joyous but brief reunion with Lisi, Peter went with Konrad to Kaprun for a training stint and then to Lausanne where Willy was finishing his schooling. Arrangements had been made for the three to train with the Austrian 'C' team and, on the strength of this, two ski manufacturers, Kneissl and Kästle, provided free equipment. Salomon gave bindings and money in return for advertising space on the van. Clothing and accessory manufacturers were equally generous. The show was, literally, on the road.

Konrad recalls that the experience with the Austrians seemed to benefit Peter more than it did him. There could easily have been tension but happily the two of them were able to continue their close friendship even though they were in fierce competition on the slopes. They used the tension positively; when one was lagging the other fought to catch up. Because Willy was still at school, the two wanderers spent great swathes of time in each other's company. There were difficult moments, naturally, but overall the bond between them strengthened.

The pre-season training over, they began to race, aided by Dieter and joined by Willy. They were not expecting miracles and neither were there any. There were some modest successes, there was a sense of progress and the other teams began to acknowledge that there was a meaningful British presence on the circuit. Worryingly for the rebels, the British Ski Federation also began to take notice.

The circumstances were odd. Officially there was no British ski racing team. The entirely volunteer officials of the Federation, which had minuscule financial resources, were faced with the fact of a trio of very young skiers, aided by a trainer, who were entering races and being seen by others as the national representatives. They felt that they had to take action.

It was decided that money must be found and offered to the gang but, in order to avoid giving the impression that the tail was wagging the dog, there would be conditions. The three would have to become five, with Stuart Fitzsimmons and Alan Stewart joining the training group. This would then become the official British presence on the ski racing circuit.

Long and repetitive were the arguments between the three. The money was very desperately needed but they were in danger of slipping back into the confusion and indeterminacy from which they had so recently escaped. After much agonising, economic pressures prevailed. It was, after all, possible to believe that things would be entirely different. The balance of power had definitely been shifted and the Federation would not be able to dominate as they had done in the past. Dieter's group duly expanded but at its heart the seminal trio retained their own bonding and their own identity.

*Peter, the young racer boy*

The newly official team of British racers moved from one Alpine venue to another in a nomadic existence that was entirely acceptable to ones so young. There was always fresh interest, new excitements, the challenge of the races and, above all, the desperate desire to improve to the point where they could rival the elite. When the wanderers saw what depth of resources and public support the other teams had, it was easy to slip into pessimism but when one of the group was despondent the others had the energy to provide the necessary lift. With many set-backs and a few minor triumphs they kept going. Peter's 'bruised calf' gave him much trouble, Konrad had pain from his knees but their youthful determination took them through the agony.

Whilst the males were struggling against the might of Europe, Lisi showed her calibre amongst the local worthies. In February she entered the North of Scotland Championships, held on Cairngorm and, even though she was still very much a junior, she raced against all-comers and finished equal nineteenth in the giant slalom. She out-paced many of the seniors and not a few of the, doubtless dismayed, boys. The only female to finish ahead of her was Helen Carmichael, the reigning British Ladies' champion who had been gaining very useful experience in America. In the slalom, Lisi did even better, being the first female and thirteenth overall in a strong field. When the results were combined, the younger of the Fuchs children emerged as the North of Scotland Ladies Champion.

Some began to speak of Lisi as a potentially brighter prospect than her brother. In the marginally less competitive world of women's ski racing she could have chances to reach the highest levels. The attention was flattering but still she was unsure. There was so much about skiing that she loved but she was of a different nature from her brother and she did not share his fanaticism for the sport.

Luckily the head of her school was a skiing devotee who was utterly delighted when Lisi, along with fellow pupils Douglas McDonald, Duncan Riley and others, won the school ski championships in Glenshee. He did not resist unduly when his female star skier demanded to drop the hated mathematics. It was evident, in any case, that Lisi's true academic talent lay in the arts. Neither did he demur when she needed time for training or racing.

Like her parents, Lisi longed for the time when Peter would return, as promised, to participate in the Scottish national championships but he could not leave the Alps until he had shown off his skills in the British event to be held at Flaine in France. It was widely assumed that the three rebels would sweep the board.

What the watching ski world did not know, what even Peter did not fully realise, was that his 'bruised muscle' would never heal without resting. As the British championships approached, he experienced considerable anguish. He bravely took part, but only tentatively and came nowhere. The other two Musketeers, perhaps imbued with over-confidence, crashed out of the slalom. The only success the trio registered was when Konrad took the giant slalom but the coveted combined crown went to their coopted rival, Stuart Fitzsimmons.

For the first time since their venture started, the three felt a sagging of morale. Willy decided that he should concentrate on slalom, Peter kept his promise to return home. Only Konrad remained in Europe, taking part in the end of season races.

Though disconsolate about the British championships and dismayed by the refusal of his mysterious injury to clear up, Peter was heartened as he returned to Struan by exciting news of yet further development of the Cairngorm facilities. His father's early vision of a road to the base of Coire na Ciste and an associated lift was about to be realised. Avidly he read the piece in *The Press and Journal* of March 26, 1973 which had the headline; 'A scheme to spend £200,000 opening up a classic Cairngorm ski run, Coire na Ciste, has just been announced'. The subheading for the article, by Peter Mitchell, claimed that; 'There's plenty of snow in the Corrie of the Coffins'. The piece began;

'There's no business like snow business, they tell you in the Spey Valley. People like Austrian Karl Fuchs and his wife Eileen started a residential ski school in Carrbridge in 1954 and are still excited about the Cairngorms. They've seen the sport, like Topsy, just grow and grow. In their pioneering days it was much harder work to go skiing. There were no lifts and tows, no fancy road-clearing vehicles, no restaurants at 4000 feet.'

The reporter then spelled out the problem which the new road and ski lifts were intended to solve. Up to four thousand skiers had been packing onto the slopes at weekends, causing desperate overcrowding, especially when the snow was sparse. The new access would open up the Coire na Ciste run with its gentle upper slopes and taxing lower reaches through the steep, sheltered gully. Astonishingly, an anonymous donor had provided £100,000 of the cost, with the remainder coming from the Highlands and Islands Development Board and the Cairngorm Winter Sports Development Board.

The article quoted many delighted people, including Frith Finlayson, but there was a note of dissent from campaigners for ski development on Ben Wyvis in Ross-shire. They felt that the Cairngorms were at saturation point and that the money would be largely wasted. Karl could not agree.

There was also an overwhelming mountain of ski political gossip for Peter to absorb. The British Ski Instruction Council, which had been formed in an attempt to bring rival factions together and which was being chaired by Clive Freshwater, was in trouble. The Scottish National Ski Council, the National Ski Federation of Great Britain and the Association of Ski Schools of Great Britain had all pulled out in what looked like a concerted move. In his version of the events, Frith Finlayson depicts a tangled mesh of dispute and double-dealing. The withdrawals were, he suggests, disgraceful acts of vindictive politics. The word around the valley, which Peter absorbed with all the other tales, was that things were not going too well for Frith within his own organisation, the British Association of Ski Instructors. Spey Valley turbulence was never just the prerogative of the weather.

A few days of home comfort were sufficient to restore Peter's enthusiasm. He knew that the break from Konrad would be short-lived. Even though his calf was still sore, he entered the Hird Trophy, the first leg of Scottish Ski Club championships.

It was not destined to be an easy race. The new British champion, Stuart Fitzsimmons, was amongst the entrants as were all the usual local rivals. Any one of them could win. Indeed, it was not by any means impossible that Moggs might spring a surprise. For once in his short life he had some respite from his enduring knee problems and he was skiing very well.

A local newspaper carried the results of the race; 'In the Scottish Ski Club Hird Trophy slalom yesterday, held in Coire na Ciste, Peter Fuchs (17), of Carrbridge, won with a two-second margin over Stuart Fitzsimmons, the reigning British champion. Peter was appearing in his first event in Scotland since his return last week from training and racing in the Alps as a member of the British Men's Team. His sister, Lisi (15), took seventh place (first girl) in a field of 43 skiers. Other places were also taken by Colin Fleming also of Carrbridge, third; Alistair McKinlay, fourth; and Douglas McDonald, fifth'.

The outcome for the Struanites could not have been better. Peter's two second margin was emphatic, Lisi's 'first female' was an astonishing confirmation of her potential and Moggs' third place suggested that in a year or two he might also be of a standard to compete regularly in Europe.

This club competition was followed, soon afterwards, by the Scottish national event, open to a much wider range of competitors. Amongst them would be Sepp Guffler, an Austrian who had been training Lisi, and another Austrian, George Gstrein who, in Peter's absence, had won all three of the Scottish regional championships. Stuart Fitzsimmons was also racing. There was even more for Peter to prove. For Lisi there was a big opportunity to demonstrate that she was no longer just an outstanding junior but a leading contender on the national scene.

With the headline, 'Holiday Romance Bears Fruit' John Samuel told the story in *The Guardian*.

'The changes in British ski racing continue apace. The Scottish ski championships this weekend were a triumph for a brother and sister pair and a younger generation who could come to dominate the British scene in the next few years. Peter Fuchs, aged 17, won both the men's slalom on Saturday and the giant slalom yesterday, and his 15-year-old sister Lisi, took the women's slalom and with third place in the giant slalom, the combined championship like her brother.

'Some may have seen this coming for a time. The Fuchs family have been a major force in the rise of the Scottish ski industry. After Eileen Fuchs, an English girl, married Karl Fuchs, an Austrian Olympic class skier, after meeting him on a ski holiday, they started the Austrian ski school at the Struan Hotel, Carrbridge, 19 years ago. It was the start of the cosmopolitana which can still surprise many first visitors to Cairngorm, many of whom are hardly prepared for the snatches of German and Norwegian on the slopes and the red-and-white insignia of Austria on anoraks, helmets and minibuses.

'This weekend Peter Fuchs beat two Austrians, Josef Gufler, one of his father's star trainers, and Georg Gstrein, winner of all three Scottish area championships this season. These are the sort of young Austrians who come to Scotland for two years or so to work, race and further their experience as instructors and trainers.

'Peter and Lisi Fuchs have absorbed the atmosphere but their father has never attempted to push them. In Peter's case he made up his mind, albeit only in the last two years, to commit himself to ski-racing and Lisi is presently wavering. She is at present concentrating on A levels at Grantown GS and though in physique an absolute natural as a racer- she had the fourth best time of all the 49 men and women starters in the slalom- she wonders whether she will be happy in the sometimes riven atmosphere of Scottish ski racing.

'"I tell them that ski racing is hard. All I ask is that they are happy. If not they should not do it,"' says Karl Fuchs in his fractured German-English.

The local press celebrated. In one journal Peter was described as, 'the brightest star in British ski-racing for many years'. For Karl and Eileen it was thrilling beyond measure to have both their children as national champions.

Konrad, missing his companions, but with his determination restored, rejoiced at the news of Peter's success against the skier who had taken the British Championship from them. He was in a generally positive frame of mind when Dieter suggested that the time might have come for his trainee to enter his very first World Cup downhill.

The world of downhill racing is largely separate from that of the slaloms. Dedicated maniacs hurl themselves down near precipices, largely unencumbered by the 'gates' which keep the slalom skiers turning constantly. Strength and steely nerve are needed to cope with speeds well above fifty miles per hour. Legs have to be like high tensile springs, eyes have to be sharp, the brain has to be calculating rapidly, ordering tiny adjustments to the body position so that balance is maintained and the optimum line of descent chosen. It is a dangerous business. A mistake at sixty or seventy miles per hour can bring very serious injury, even death. It is not for the faint-hearted.

Konrad had little hesitation. It had been clear for some time that slalom was not for him. It would be eminently sensible to step up to the longer, faster race where his clear expertise in giant slalom could be used and developed.

Because he knew the mountain particularly well, Konrad elected to enter the infamous Hahnenkamm race at Kitzbuhel. The regulars declared him to be crazy. Nobody would have a very first downhill race on such a formidable and notorious track. The newcomer was not deterred. All Konrad cared about was reducing his total of 'FIS' points, the measure of his progress. As in golf, beginners start with a fixed maximum of points and then strive, through doing well in the races, to reduce the total. He was sure that his detailed knowledge of the Hahnenkamm run would allow him to record a very respectable result.

The race proved to be a baptism of ice. Konrad managed to finish but sufficiently far down the field as to have no effect on his FIS rating. Nonetheless he was not deterred. On a better track, with improved preparation, with a greater ration of luck, he would do better.

Peter heard of his friend's venture and determined that he, too, would step onto the larger skiing stage once he returned to the Alps. In the meantime he had his attention fixed on the Coronation Cup, the second part of the Scottish Ski Club championships. Having already won the Hird Trophy, the first part, he was well placed to become overall club champion.

The Scottish newspaper headlines told the story. 'Another Cup for Fuchs', 'Peter Fuchs Takes Scottish Ski Club Title, ' and, 'Carrbridge Skier Wins Giant Slalom' were typical examples.

The *Glasgow Herald* noted that Lisi did extremely well to finish twelfth overall, a placing which was good enough to secure for her the women's version of Peter's club title. The brother and sister had a clean sweep of Scottish events. Eileen recalls that there was nobody else at the prize-givings!

Re-energised by his Scottish success, and feeling moderately comfortable with his still undiagnosed injury, Peter returned to the Alps in time to have his downhill baptism at Zell-am-See. Although he was as fearful as anybody would be about testing himself against the heroes, he knew that in fact the physical pressures of the new discipline would be less than those of the slaloms. Without the need to make tight turns, his ever-troublesome knees and the painful calf would have an easier time. On many of the occasions when they had made long downhill runs in training he had been able to relax.

The reunion with Konrad was joyous but sadly the discipline of schooling meant that Willy could not be with them. The two trained hard under Dieter's guidance and felt modestly confident that they would not make fools of themselves on the day of the race.

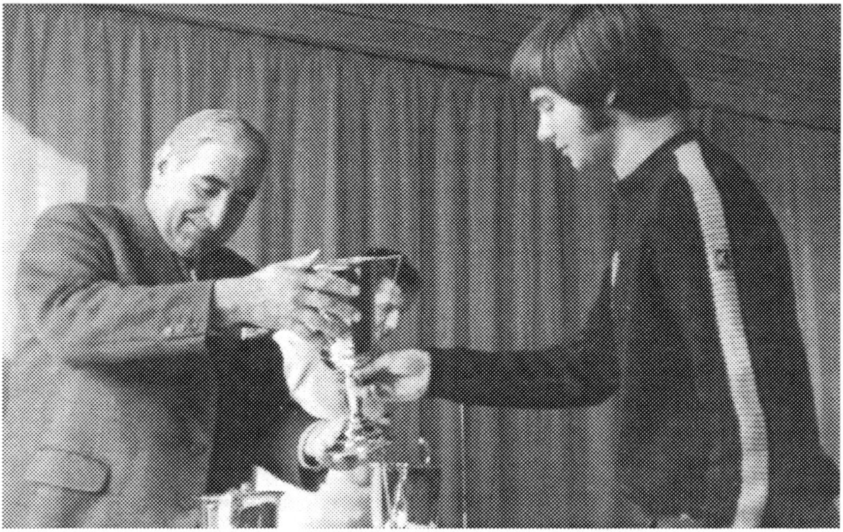

*Another trophy for Peter*

There were two legs to the competition. For a beginner in the discipline Peter did admirably well in the first race whilst Konrad had his moments of comparative glory in the second. The two Musketeers did not frighten any of the established heroes of the downhill but they proved that they could survive in the glamorous world of high-speed, dangerous racing.

After the race, both of them were sure that, in spite of the risks, this was what they wanted to do. Their new dream was that one day one or both of them would stand on the winners' podium at a world class downhill. The immediate target would be one of the European series of races but then, even though it might take years, they would triumph in a World Cup competition. The British flag would flutter proudly against an Alpine blue sky. The crowds would wonder at the impossible achievement and would cheer as though the foreigners were one of their very own.

## 27. Against The World

In July 1973, Dieter's group of five convened at Struan for a spell of pre-season training. *The Strathspey and Badenoch Herald* was impressed. Their reporter, Peter Emslie wrote;

'Over the past few weeks the Spey Valley has been the venue for a highly successful innovation for British skiing. Five young men, with their Austrian trainer, have been using the facilities of the Spey Valley to start their long haul towards the beginning of the international racing season in early December. The skiers, all in their late teens, include Peter Fuchs, Carrbridge, who with fellow Scots Stuart Fitzsimmons and Alan Stewart from Balmore are all members of the British Men's Ski Team. Konrad Bartelski and Willy Bailey, both from towns further south, complete the five-man team. The training programme has encompassed a wide variety of activities, including cross-country running. The boys have also been making full use of the gymnasium and swimming pool at Grantown Grammar School to complete their training.'

What the paper did not report was the problems with a large, grey feral feline which had taken to raiding the Struan rubbish bins. Hearing some squawking in the middle of the night, Peter went out to see Sandy and Bimbo, in single file, advancing on the intruder. Assuming that both the brave Struan cats would be maimed or killed, Peter ran to shoo the enemy away. He aimed a kick, not intending to hit the animal, but it leapt and fastened onto his slippered foot. It took much shaking and shouting to send the creature on its way and the wounds were so extensive that the doctor prescribed antibiotics.

A short time later, Alan Stewart was sleeping peacefully in the Fuchs' piano room. As he dreamed, the bold cat crept in through an open window and, for reasons known only to the animal, it pounced. Alan's unconscious reaction earned him a savage bite on the hand. Peter heard the noise and rushed gallantly to the rescue whereupon he was bitten too. Both suffered swollen hands which made the business of pushing off at the start of a race very painful indeed. *The Scotsman* of the 14th of July also neglected to relate the feline hazards but it did record that the 'boys' had run up and down Ben Macdhui in record time in their bid for super fitness.

Konrad, who had briefly returned to the academic world to take an examination, recalls the agonies of getting back to full fitness but they all worked with total dedication. After a while, they were joined by a young Canadian called Ken Read. Peter had met and instantly liked Ken who had all the support of his national team but who shared the youthful enthusiasm of the young British skiers and wanted to spend time with them. Karl and Eileen welcomed them all unstintingly. Konrad refers gratefully to 'the wonderful facilties that the Fuchs family made available to us'.

It was typical of Karl to do anything he could to support others. And it was not just that his generosity was limited to ski racing. Without being in any way formal in approach, he was a natural supporter of 'career development'. It was said of him, many years later, that virtually every British skier who became well known in the ski world had at least some contact with Karl. Ali Ross, whose books, articles and videos about skiing became famous, was no stranger to Struan and it was no problem to Karl that Ali worked for a time with Frith Finlayson. Relationships between Karl and Ali always remained very cordial. John Shedden was an instructor for several seasons until he too graduated to working in senior positions and writing well-received books about the sport. The 'Don', to whom Lisi had alluded in her letter to Peter, moved on too, as the *Daily Mirror* of September 15, 1973 reported.

'When Don Rumbold was a lad, the folks on his council estate thought skiing was a sport for toffs and foreigners. If they thought about skiing at all. Some of them even muttered darkly that Don was a 'bit soft in th'ead', as he trudged, skis over his shoulders, in search of snow. Any snow would do for Don. A patch of frozen grey slush in a cobbled back-street. A slope in the local park. "I was ski-daft", he says.

'With the aid of text books from the local library, practising by the light of street lamps on misty winter evenings, he taught himself to ski. He saved his cash and took a skiing holiday in the Cairngorms. Within two years he qualified as an instructor. It made him the ideal choice to run Britain's newest ski centre and now Lancashire has the longest artificial ski run in England.'

After giving all the statistics about the facility the reporter returned to Don:

'All he had 15 years ago was a ton of determination. After clocking off from his job as a sheet metal worker he'd scour the streets of Bradford, his home town, for snow. "There's hardly a back street I've not skied down one time or another," he mused.

'His enthusiasm for the new centre is forgivable. He and his small staff have virtually built the ski run themselves. For months they laboured to contour the hillside and lay the £20,000-worth of nylon matting. In March the work fell behind schedule because of a heavy snowfall. Last month, in torrential rain, the top of the slope slid downhill and nearly buried the log cabin restaurant. "We've had setbacks," said Don, "but it's been worthwhile. All we've got to do now is persuade the locals that skiing is not an exclusive sport. I'm after everyone, from all walks of life; universities, factories and especially the schools." He added; "There's nothing to stop anyone skiing. We have boots and skis for hire and you can book an expert instructor." Don confessed; "There's a lot of posh accents in the skiing world. It used to affect me in the Cairngorms. But I said 'blow 'em'- and worked all the harder." '

It would be going too far to suggest that Don and the other Struan 'graduates' owed all of their success to Karl but most very readily acknowledge his major contribution.

The Three Musketeers greatly relished the support given by Karl and Eileen but when the Scottish phase of the preparations was completed they had to tear themselves away from home comforts to go to the glacier at Dachstein. There, the trusty Volkswagen was joined by a rusting old Bedford van acquired by the two newer members of the squad.

Ken Read was an inspiration to them all. He was their type of skier, brave and dedicated. They practised all the disciplines, including downhill on a manufactured track. Parts of this were icy and one high speed mistake by Stuart Fitzsimmons led to a bad fall which cracked one of his vertebrae. The dangers of the sport were once more brought painfully and unavoidably to the attention of the squad but they persisted with the training. For young people an accident, like death, is something which happens to others.

Konrad remembers that Peter was skiing so well that the Austrian juniors would come over to watch him. He writes, 'He was skiing like a dream, sailing through the gates and going really fast with superb style and minimum effort.'

*On the road*

The *Daily Telegraph* got wind of the romance of the operation and in the December 14th 1973 issue of the magazine section the paper ran a major piece with a two page, full colour photograph of Konrad airborne on the glacier. Entitled 'Skiing on a Shoestring' it pointed out that the Austrians had a team of eighty five racers with an entourage of thirty eight. The British had five members and one trainer.

Five pages of text tell the story. Konrad is described as a 'self possessed young man, well grown with brown eyes and hair'. When asked for an assessment of his closest skiing friend, Peter chooses to say that Konrad is not very nationalistic, to which there is no response. Konrad declares that Peter is, 'very open-hearted, generous and helpful' and adds that his friend can also be a touch stubborn. Peter laconically agrees that this is so.

When asked what they would be doing if they were not skiing for ten months of the year, Konrad declares that he would be at university studying business management or economics, Willy says that he would be following a course in commerce whilst Peter says, 'When I'm at home I help my father in the house doing anything, painting or anything like that. I suppose I'd be doing that. I can be quite content doing small things or nothing at all.'

When Dieter is asked to assess his charges he says, 'They're younger than usual, twenty times more willing, and very determined. They take skiing very seriously. Their talents are considerable.' Konrad's best result, eleventh place in the combined results of the Kitzbuhel World Cup event, is proudly mentioned. Suggesting that Willy's main expertise is in slalom, Dieter goes on to say of the third member of the trio, 'Peter is a very good skier. In Austria they would say that you must look for a boy like Peter.'

Soon after this article appeared, Konrad achieved a very respectable twenty-fifth position in a downhill race with seventy-five starters. In the next event, at Schladming, Peter, along with many of the top racers, crashed into the straw bales but Konrad advanced to twenty-second. There were significant successes for both, however, to the point where in the European Cup races they were starting in the first group of fifteen. Willy, whose poor eyesight meant that he had to wear thick lenses and who grew tired of paying for replacements for glasses shattered in downhill falls, returned to his resolve to stick exclusively to the slaloms. Both of the downhill specialists were sorry about their friend's decision but were otherwise pleased with their progress. They knew, though, that they would not be truly satisfied until they started to make an impact in the World Cup series.

So intent were they on pursuing this goal that they had no plans to compete in the British Championships which, that year, were to be held in January in Val d'Isere. It was not that they were denigrating the event. They simply felt that the important task for Britain's top male skiers was to make their mark on the wider stage. They had no longer any need to prove themselves at national level. A World Cup event at Garmisch was far more important in their opinion. One more good result would mean that both young men would no longer have to go through a qualifying process to enter World Cup races. This was the important goal.

The Ski Federation thought differently. In a lengthy piece in *The Guardian* of January 3 1974, John Samuel told the story. He revealed that it was only when an imperious telegram from the British National Ski Federation arrived at Garmisch that Dieter and his team reluctantly travelled to Val d'Isere. Given that the Federation was paying for Dieter's time, the skiers had little option but to obey.

John Samuel assessed the championship prospects in an article published the following day. Konrad was, he said, the clear favourite to take the men's title. The case for this was all the stronger because the injury which Stuart FitzSimmons sustained on the glacier had ended his racing for the season. Samuel argued that Peter would be Konrad's strongest challenger although Willy was judged to be capable of pushing them both to the limits.

The article then turns to doubts about the downhill course, shorter than the one used for World Cup races but nonetheless much longer than anything available in Scotland. Some thought that the younger racers might come to grief on the bumpy, taxing track. There had been a plea that a giant slalom should be substituted but this plan was dropped when the organisers conceded that they would remove some of the obvious hazards.

Focusing on Peter's prospects in yet another article, Samuel revealed that Dieter was experimenting with the Kästle skis to which Peter had remained loyal in spite of evidence that other makes were faster in certain snow conditions. If Peter felt any pressure from all this attention it was increased when one Scottish newspaper headlined its scene-setting piece with, 'Fuchs is Scotland's hope'.

The slalom came first. The course was controversial. The last gate was roughly ten metres offset from the finishing line, which brought the best racing line as close as possible to one of the final poles. This feature was against International Ski Federation Rules which state that difficult figures should not be set at the beginning or end of a course. It was also reported that overall the run did not encourage the rhythm which the rules demand. The head of Val d'Isere's coaching organisation undertook a course inspection. Expert though he was, he hit the finish pole and had to extricate himself from a straw bale.

Both Konrad, who came first, and Peter, who finished just behind his friend, made light of the problems. Willy was placed fourth. A Scottish paper broke the news with, 'Fuchs just fails to take slalom'. The article proudly pointed out that the Scot had missed out by a mere one third of a second. All the papers reported the tearful exit of Valentina Iliffe who failed to negotiate the tricky last gate and who reportedly showed her rage with tears and a stream of curses in fluent Italian.

Buoyed by their shared triumph, the Three Musketeers began preparation for the next phase of the championships in a few days time; the downhill. The headlines subsequently told a sorry story. 'Britain's leading men injured', cried *The Guardian*. 'Bartelski is out of final race', announced the *Daily Telegraph*.

John Samuel wrote that the decision by the National Ski Federation to force the members of the men's team to divert to Val d'Isere looked even more controversial in the light of these injuries, sustained in pre-race training. Both Konrad and Peter, he reported, had run off the downhill course at a 'manifestly dangerous' place where two other skiers had suffered broken legs. Konrad hit a stake holding up safety netting and Peter fell backwards with such violence that he bent the rear metal support of his left boot.

Neither of the main contenders had given up hope of finishing the task they had started so well; both felt that their injuries would allow them to complete a downhill course. But then cruel nature took a hand. A very heavy snowfall prompted the organisers to talk about substituting a giant slalom for the bigger course. Dieter Bartsch is quoted in the newspapers as saying, 'Bartelski has heavy bruising affecting his left kneecap and is doubtful for next weekend's World Cup downhill at Morzine. Fuchs also has a bruised left leg but not in such a bad place. He can just about ski a downhill with his weight mostly on his good leg but he can't do a giant slalom where you need both your legs for the turns.'

John Samuel lamented that the injuries were a great setback because the world championships at St. Moritz were only a month away. He suggests that the National Ski Federation had been caught unawares by the success of the gang of three and comments;

'Largely through self-help and dedication the team has built up a spirit unexampled by any men's group since the war. The contacts with the Austrian racing ski organisations enjoyed by Karl Fuchs of the Austrian Ski School at Carrbridge - he is father of Peter - have meant first that a trainer as talented and devoted as Bartsch is available and then that the facilities of the Austrian national teams are generously given.'

At the last possible moment, the organisers decided that a downhill would, after all, be possible. Peter immediately signalled his intention of racing. Konrad, with heavy bandaging on his knee and pain at every movement, was still very unsure. When the time came for the statutory practice run down the course he plied himself with strong painkillers and pushed off. Half way down the track he decided that he would at least get himself to the starting gate. The final decision would be taken immediately after the bandáges were removed, minutes before he was due to push off.

With yet more analgesics inside him, and with courage and determination pumping up the adrenaline, Konrad made his way to the starting point and threw himself down the slope. Afterwards he joked to the reporters that he could not have let the title go to a Scotsman again. He skied well and set a challenging time.

Peter, fighting his own battle against pain but just as determined, also plunged down the course. He flashed across the line just less than half a second ahead of his close friend. Both of them were well ahead of the other contenders. What nobody knew, as the downhill phase came to an end, was who had won the overall title.

The organisers began their complex calculations There was a lack of clarity about the rules. On one interpretation, Peter was the champion, on another it was Konrad who could wear the British men's skiing crown. Seasoned race organisers declared that they had never seen anything so close. After much deliberation it was decided that Konrad was the winner. If he had been just one hundredth of a second slower over a course of more than a mile, Peter would have pipped him. In the *Daily Telegraph* Konrad is reported as saying, 'What a pity it could not have been a dead heat.'

John Samuel exulted that Konrad and Peter were in a different class to the others and that their performances gave every hope of a significant display in the world championships. Peter and Konrad's delight at the end of the competition was magnified by the fact that Willy had finished third overall. Between them they had swept the board.

Other newspapers carried the story. A Scottish paper led with, 'Skiing Second for Peter'. After making the obligatory reference to Karl, the article recorded the fact that Peter had already taken part in three world cup races that season. There was also special mention for Moggs, Colin Fleming to the journalists, who put in a 'creditable performance' coming ninth in the combined results.

Lisi's story was entirely different. It was not originally intended that one so young should compete in the national championships but she was persuaded, at the last minute, to join the fray. The man who had been acting as her trainer, Sepp Guffler, was unable to be with her and so she was tagged onto the British team. Their trainer made it very clear that Lisi was unwanted.

In the slalom she was going well and the locals, as was their custom, began to shout, encouragingly, 'Hop, hop, hop!' To the inexperienced young Briton this sounded like, 'stop, stop, stop!' so she did. The organisers, seeing that a simple mistake had been made, allowed a re-start but Lisi's concentration had gone. She felt foolish and had lost her sense of purpose. She fell half way down the course and failed to record a time.

The next event was the downhill. Apart from one exploratory run with Sepp Guffler down a course in Obergurgl, which she had enjoyed, Lisi had never skied a downhill course. She joined the other women for the pre-race practice but the trainer virtually ignored her. At the end of one run, Peter happened to be there and he exclaimed, in astonishment, 'It was you!'

Lisi demanded an explanation. Peter told his sister that he had been on a lift and had seen a woman skiing fantastically fast down the practice course. He had commented to Konrad who was sitting beside him and they had both agreed that the female racer must be one of the elite. The fact that Lisi had been wearing an unfamiliar outfit had fooled them both. Lisi was immensely flattered by the implied praise but what she did not reveal was that she had been to a considerable degree out of control on the icy, rutted surface. The mad speed had not been entirely intentional.

She went back up for another practice run. It seemed to her that the course was dangerous but the officials were maintaining that it was suitable for the race. She pushed off and immediately her skis were clattering, lifting at the tips, almost crossing. Control was impossible. She fought the forces as best she could but then the fall began. Sliding, bumping, being thrust into the air, losing equipment, thinking that she would never stop, Lisi careered down. When, at last, she managed to come to a halt she realised two things. The first was that she was extremely lucky to be still in one largely uninjured piece. The second was that she did not want to put herself through that kind of torture ever again.

On the spot, the very young, very talented skier 'retired' from international racing. The loss of her talents could have been avoided with more thoughtful management. After the actual race, during which there were several serious injuries, an enquiry was ordered. The course was, indeed, deemed to be unsafe but the decision was too late for Lisi.

The aftermath of the British Championships gave John Samuel time to reflect on the state of the national ski racing organisation. He used space in *The Guardian* to express his considered views.

'In truth British ski racing is in need of a major reorganisation which should reduce some of its reliance on amateurs. Whatever the rights and wrongs of the dispute whether the top men should have been fighting for FIS points at the Arlberg-Kandahar, or proving themselves to the British at the British championships, there was clearly a lack of co-ordination. The leading racers have out-stripped the organisation behind them. The men's manager, Ian Steven, lives in Dundee and exchanges information with Dieter Bartsch, the men's trainer, via tape recordings. It so happens that Bartsch's recorder has been broken for weeks and Steven is not due on the Continent until the World Cup caravan reaches Kitzbuhel. British racing badly needs a full-time racing secretary to administer both men's and women's teams and perhaps to double as men's manager during the winter.

'Long term, the National Ski Federation have ambitious plans to encourage a home ski industry based on two million holiday skiers and closely linked with the Association of British Travel Agents. It has a target of two hundred artificial slopes, including a number of large ones, like Hillend, Edinburgh, able to stage competitions in dual slalom. It is expected then that the sport will have much to offer sponsors.

'Short term, skiers as good and determined as Konrad Bartelski, Peter Fuchs, Willy Bailey and Alan Stewart, none of them with out of the way private means, need something more than the inconsistent and sometimes out of touch support of an amateur committee. Government support is skimpy, the Sports Council's lowly budget of £6 million is necessarily spread thin. Sustenance rate of £1-50 a day for a competitor engaged in Olympic standard competition abroad is almost derisory by today's standards and still guided by the 90 Day Olympic restriction which has now been waived. In practice each skier has to find about £1500 pounds a year to keep going.'

Of course, nothing changed immediately but the Three Musketeers were still high on the spirit of their adventure. They had not wanted to take unnecessary risks by entering the national championships but they had proved their point. They were the best and they had left nobody in any doubt about that fact.

The team moved on to Europa Cup races in France. Willy, still vacillating, had yet again become despondent about the state of his skiing and he opted out of the downhills. By contrast, Konrad and Peter were relatively high up the start list. This gave them an advantage which, for so much of their racing careers, had belonged to others. They had earned their chance. Peter, still very young to be racing at such a level, finished a highly commendable eighth whilst Konrad, for the first time, was on the podium in third place. Willy, a disconsolate spectator before the race, was instantly reinvigorated by these first top-ten finishes. He rejoined the gang. Maybe one of them would, after all, one day prove that they could beat the best on the world stage.

They had an immediate opportunity to try at the world championships. This was not a part of the World Cup series of races, which is determined by compiling scores over several months of racing, but an event which takes place every four years, separated by two years from the Olympic sequence. The winner wears the sparkling crown of 'World Champion' for the forty eight months until the next competition. It is a much coveted prize.

Konrad, by virtue of his European Cup successes, was in the second ranking of this more exalted company. Peter was further down the list but at least neither of them would be running last down a course which had been rutted by all the earlier racers. In training, both of them crashed, Peter sustaining a bad cut to one of his knees which required nine stitches, Konrad hurting both of his knees. Luckily, the weather deteriorated and the race was postponed, giving them time to recover. They then both began to ski well, Peter particularly so.

The slalom was torture for Peter who kept complaining about the 'bruised muscle' which had troubled him ever since the accident in Australia. The agony was so extreme that he stopped after twelve gates and retired from the race. Konrad and Willy both fell on the first run. Alan Stewart fell on the second, wrenching an ankle and therefore having to scratch from the downhill. All told, the British team was not acquitting itself with much distinction. John Samuel was not too dispirited. He reminded his readers that Konrad and Peter were really downhill specialists and mooted the idea that the two of them could possibly start in the first fifteen at the 1976 Olympic Games in Innsbruck.

Then came the downhill. Recalling the event years later, Konrad writes about the extreme nervous tension at the start of that important race. He says that Dieter had to all but throw him out of the start gate. Fate had delivered him the worst draw from the second group. He was the last of the second fifteen and twenty nine hard driven pairs of skis had scarred the course. He made mistakes and was furious with himself at the finish yet he managed to be fifteenth overall, beating many of the first rank starters. Peter, with even more runnels and ruts to contend with, was nineteenth, showing even more relative improvement over his initial ranking than his friend and rival had done.

John Samuel, excited that Britons had at least proved that they could compete with the best, rushed over to slap both of them on the back in sincere congratulation. He found them not celebrating but raging about the mistakes they had made. Peter was particularly furious with himself because in training he had been consistently out-skiing Konrad. Astonished at their lack of pleasure, Willy pointed out that for the very first time in ski racing history two Britons had finished in the top twenty of a world class race. There were, the third of the 'musketeers' pointed out, some Alpine countries which had not achieved as much. Slowly the young men came to acknowledge what they had done. With ludicrous levels of support, at a very early age, they had proved themselves to be amongst the best skiers in the entire world.

It was a formidable achievement and *The Times* of Feb 10, 1974 was ready to give praise. The article reinforced Willy's point. Two Britons had finished in the top twenty of a World Championship downhill and that, the reporter suggested, was an astonishing outcome, especially in view of the meagre resources available to the team. The writer claimed that British men's skiing was at last on the international map. Jeremy Palmer-Tomkinson, one of Britains' top skiers of former years who watched the race, is reported as exulting that the two had broken through into the top echelons. A subsequent article in the same paper points out that Konrad and Peter were not only the youngest racers in the top twenty but that they both had to contend with serious injuries. In spite of everything, the article points out, the youths had out-skied the entire French team.

Others were impressed. Suddenly, offers of assistance began to flow in. The prospect of riches after the times of hardship was tempting beyond endurance. Konrad records that, 'in our naiveté, we took them all,' but he goes on to express his considered view that most of their subsequent troubles began at that time. He writes; 'From now on we would spend more time competing against our "helpers" than against the other racers.'

The need to adopt a more commercial approach was spelled out in an article by John Samuel which appeared in *The Guardian* of February 12th 1974. With the headline, 'Scotland is base for breakthrough', the reporter told of talking with an international group on the train down from St. Moritz following the world championships. There was an Englishman amongst them called Roy Ferris, who gladly acknowledged that he had come to skiing mainly through Karl Fuchs. He had progressed to the point of running a Canadian ski school with over one hundred instructors who were teaching the sport to 'thousands of Vancouver schoolchildren'. He told Samuel that he was sure that Scotland must soon be the base for a British skiing breakthrough. Others in the group disagreed but all acknowledged that a prerequisite was the discovery of new sources of finance. Had they been on that train, Konrad and Peter, unaware of future problems, would doubtless have agreed.

In his book, Konrad tells the engaging story of how he and Peter treated themselves to the luxury of a good hotel for the occasion of the World Championships. A waiter, whom they took to be a friendly soul, kept encouraging them to have extra servings of the delicious food. As highly active young men with healthy appetites they gladly went along with all the offers and it was only when they were given the bill for their brief stay that they realised that apparent amicability had been cold salesmanship. The final total was far beyond their immediate means.

They were facing the very real prospect of spending time as plongeurs in the hotel kitchen when they should be racing against the best in the world. They were bewildered and angry and feeling distinctly helpless when an Englishman picked up on their plight. As someone with a keen interest in skiing, Robin Bailey knew of the two and, as a very successful businessman, he also had money. It was embarrassing, of course, for the young men to accept largesse but they were deeply grateful to their saviour.

What none of the three actors in this small drama realised was that before long their threads of fate would be tightly entwined. After the singular success of the World Championships, British ski racing needed an organiser, a fund-raiser, a manager with proven ability to take it into the modern age.

It turned out that the Two Musketeer's saviour in that hotel in Pontresina was that very man.

## 28. A Wanderer Returns

After finishing my studies I had two or three years of doing my own thing and then, slightly to my surprise and through relatively little effort of my own, I acquired a proper occupation in the Education Department of London's Holloway Prison. Even more to my astonishment I then teamed up with Jenny, one of my new work colleagues.

Jenny was a South Londoner by birth. Although she was only in her early twenties when we met, the man she thought of as her father was already dead and her mother, tortured by arthritis, had not long to live. When her mother died, Jenny discovered that her natural father was not the late Leslie Herbert Cole but a Basque separatist called Pedro Dominguez.

After being thrown out of home at the age of sixteen by her once doting step-father, for nothing more pernicious than having boy friends, Jenny had made her own way in life and had suffered accordingly. Her spirit was, however, indomitable. She had gained entry to the Hornsey College of Art, acquired a qualification in ceramics and participated fully in the famous 'sit in' which was the precursor of the 1968 student unrest in Europe. Altogether she had what might be termed a colourful background and I had no doubts that Struan would appeal to her. Early in the 1970's we made our first visit, the former employee returning as a paying guest.

Struan suited Jenny extremely well but, alas, the skiing did not. She persisted for a while but even an idyllic Easter akin to my introductory one, with days of warm sunshine and zero winds, failed to captivate her. She was one of those intensely practical people who just could not see the point of spending good money to get up a mountain only to slide down it again at great risk to skeletal integrity. The end came for her one Christmas Day when, in a high velocity blizzard, we were stuck on the White Lady chairlift half way up the mountain. As the flakes insinuated themselves through all our layers of clothing, as the frost bit at our extremities, as we numbly speculated that in the darkness we had been forgotten and were doomed to die, she decided that loyalty to me did not include a suicide pact.

Fair enough. Happily, she enjoyed walking, provided that the conditions were not too extreme, so generally I alternated skiing and hiking day by day. At the times when I was indulging in what she saw as evidence of insanity she would walk alone or, perhaps, stay cosily indoors reading or working on one of the many crafts at which she was effortlessly expert. After a year or two she undertook a part time degree in English and Psychology and then she had studying to keep her gainfully occupied whilst I persisted with my folly.

It was wonderful to renew acquaintanceships. Eileen seemed not to have changed in the slightest but it was obvious that Karl's long term health problems were beginning to take their toll. He was still skiing perfectly, of course, but his girth had considerably expanded and in the evenings he often seemed to prefer the sanctuary of the house to the bustle of the bars. I was pleased to hear, though, that the two of them had been able to start taking substantial pre-season trips abroad. Of all people, they deserved their share of leisure. Karl's incipient infirmities were no barrier to travel, as Eileen relates;

'In the 1970's Karli started taking me for late autumn holidays to Austria. We would just get in the car and drive across. He was a superb driver and never turned a hair on the often snowy, icy and fogbound roads and if he did happen to skid he positively enjoyed getting out of it. We would spend four or five weeks touring the length and breadth of Austria, visiting Oma and many other relations and friends in Steiermark, Salzburg, Tirol and Vienna. We would visit Peter and his friends, watch the training and do a bit of skiing ourselves.'

I used often to wonder, when hearing about these expeditions, whether or not Karl was chronically homesick and all I could discover was that his attitude seemed to be ambivalent. When he was in Scotland he missed his native culture to a great degree but whenever he was in Austria he looked forward keenly to getting back to Struan.

*Karl and Eileen*

After all the catching-up conversations came the first trip up the hill and I was mightily impressed with the developments. There was not just the road I remembered going up the mountain but a junction and a one way system. The car park had been vastly extended. With the luxury of my own rusty but reliable Rover, I was able to explore and came, with more amazement, to the Coire na Ciste development. Like many another, I had always thought of this as the best run available in that part of the mountain. I agreed with Karl that the first lift should have been created in this much more sheltered spot, where snow lingers for weeks after the other slopes have lost their cover.

I discovered, to my alarm, that the new chair up that corrie was of the continuously moving type. Clients kept their skis on and sat gracefully down as the chair reached them. At the top, a prepared, gentle slope allowed a graceful exit. All one had to do, I was assured, was stand up and glide.

The theory! Maybe the lift was a prototype or, more likely, a reject from some richer resort but whatever good qualities it possessed, gentleness was not amongst them.

The first anxiety for the neophyte was the shuffle across from head of the queue to a place in line with the on-coming chairs. There was a supposedly sufficient gap between chairs to allow for this simple journey but with the fear of the unknown, a slippery surface and skis which seemed to want to do anything other than be dangled, it was an undignified scramble.

Once in place, I copied what I had seen others do. The trick was to look backwards, to grasp the thin, metal arm of the chair as it came within reach and to sit quickly. Since that time I have been on many such devices and generally the system works well. What nobody had told me was that this particular beast came with a thoroughly vicious streak. Whether it was going too fast for the good of its clients or whether there just happened to be a particular blip as it picked up passengers I have no idea but far from gracefully lifting, it whacked painfully. Not a few punters, those whose height was not entirely appropriate, were tossed contemptuously aside.

The fact that for me the agonising blow came at knee height ensured that I sat down but I did so with a gasp and a thump and almost with an involuntary shedding of sticks and sundry other items of equipment. I was but half in the seat and wriggled desperately to settle back before the drop beneath the chair increased. Then, breathlessly lowering the safety bar I tried to compose myself for the forthcoming exit. Easy, or so they said. Just stand up and glide.

Later I confided in a couple of the ski instructors at Struan and was delighted to hear that my undignified, bruising ejection by that dastardly piece of machinery was not unusual. There was, they smilingly affirmed, something wrong with it. The causal chain had not been worked out but it was generally acknowledged; the chair tossed as it reached the point of dis-embarkation. Those who had been through the ordeal a couple of times learned to make allowances and most survived. Very many others found themselves hurtling on their backs towards a group, some of whom were laughing, some of whom were in various stages of putting themselves and their disarrayed equipment to rights.

Maybe Jenny was sensible in avoiding such trials. What was happily sure was that the other side of the Struan life was very much to her taste. She loved the Edelweiss and used her sweet, true voice to excellent effect in the sing-songs. Being by nature a gregarious soul she got on well with Karl, Eileen and most of the staff. Sadly she arrived too late to meet Jessie, but she 'knew' her through my fond descriptions and the loving references made so often by guests and workers. Just as Jessie would have done, Struan absorbed Jenny and made her a member of the family. We resolved that every Christmas and Hogmanay would be spent in its welcoming embrace.

It was soon after I renewed my acquaintanceship with the place that Struan had another of its incendiary episodes which, happily, had nothing to do with me nor, directly, with Eileen's erstwhile habit of setting things on fire. She tells the story.

'I returned from an afternoon walk to the Culbin sands to find Lisi and a policeman waiting to lead me gently to the laundry and drying room. They had been completely gutted. Karli had smelled smoke and gone to find a washing machine on fire and flames all around. He had, as usual, tackled the blaze and was getting it under control when he was physically hauled away for his own safety by some of the bar staff. By the time the fire brigade arrived there was nothing more to be done. Lisi and a friend had returned from an outing to find the dining room and the kitchen under (fire brigade) water and had cleared the whole thing up. Thanks to them dinner was as usual though we had no electricity. What was worse, we had no laundry or drying room throughout a very busy period but managed to wash in the kitchen by using Jessie's old twin tub Hoover machine throughout the day and drying in the Edelweiss bar with many extra heaters. Even our dear old vintage mangle, which I always used instead of a rotary iron, had been burnt but villagers came to the rescue with another equally vintage model. Karli was a tower of strength and did all the considerable redecoration himself.'

The event was large enough on the local scale to warrant a report in the *Strathspey and Badenoch Herald*. Their reporter, not too knowledgeable about electricity it seems, wrote: 'Guests at Struan House, Carrbridge dined by candlelight last Friday evening after an outbreak of fire, which gutted the ground floor laundry and drying room, caused an electricity shut-off. Two bedrooms above the laundry were damaged by smoke but Aviemore and Grantown firemen, some wearing breathing apparatus, checked the flames before more extensive damage was caused. Although the 18 bedroomed hotel was fully booked, no-one was injured.'

There was no sign of any damage when Jenny and I arrived for our regular holiday and I was unable to distinguish the substitute mangle from the original one. Regardless of the various crises, Struan seemed to maintain itself, year after year, with reliably cosy Christmases and wild Hogmanays. Of course, the personnel changed incrementally; instructors moved to other schools, generally in the Alps, and the membership of the 'gangs' varied year on year but there was a sufficiently large common core to ensure that traditions remained more or less constant.

The continuing New Zealand involvement was extraordinary. Most of the wanderers stayed for only a season before heading home but others became rooted. Like the various 'Manchester boys' and others, not a few of them progressed from being beginner skiers to instructors. Almost all of them were benignly lured along this path by Karl who had a knack of making learning to ski a highly enjoyable experience. Eileen remembers; 'The staff had their own races and the instructors a style competition arranged by Karli. Later there would be an array of silver cups presented in the dining room with trays of special Austrian open sandwiches all prepared and beautifully garnished by Karli himself.'

As a result of all this encouragement there came one season when four of Karl's team, Shona, Kathy, Lynn and Wendy were all New Zealand 'graduates'. Tragically, two of this gifted quartet met untimely ends, Wendy being killed in a road traffic accident on the way back from the slopes and Lynn dying in a railway accident in her own country. The earlier horrors were compounded when, only a year after Lynn's death, another former instructor, Kim Hansen, drowned in a fishing accident. It became evident to me, though, as the tales of antipodean doings emerged, that these hellish fateful interventions could not take away from the fact that the vast majority of the New Zealanders derived huge benefits from their time at Struan. Many of them would admit to occasional periods of unhappiness. One subsequently wrote, 'The kitchen was the centre of the NZ girls' world, a place where they cried when they were homesick and laughed when they reported catching another in bed with a packet of chocolate biscuits.' But all of them would agree that there was very much more fun than misery.

It was, of course, not only chocolate biscuits which ended up in bed with the New Zealanders. Many were the liaisons, some of them covert. One woman remembers how she would steal from her bed in the 'maids' house, the Fuchs' former residence close to the hotel, and tiptoe down to her ski instructor beau who resided in the Annexe. Early one morning, as she was making the return journey, she noticed that her earlier footprints were unmistakably imprinted in the freshly fallen snow.

*Karl outside the ski shed*

Without, perhaps, thinking her strategy out too carefully, under the intoxication of passion and perhaps other influences, she returned to her lover and borrowed a pair of his size ten gum boots into which her still-shod feet easily fitted. Treading carefully she padded backwards, eliminating her own footprints. She crossed the yard, intent in making it seem as if her lover had strode from the back door whilst she had chastely gone to her own place of rest. All she had to do was take off the boots at the door, carry them to the bungalow and return them later. She had almost completed her trick when she heard a soft, warning cough. Understandably, she froze. When she could bring herself to look it was evident that the ski shed door was open and that Karl, an inveterate early riser, was watching with quizzical interest. What could the miscreant do but laugh? Karl uttered a soft 'Mah', smiled and shook his head. Of one thing the woman was entirely sure. Her secret was safe.

This adventurer was at least in charge of her own destiny. I heard tell of another from that distant country who woke in the black of night to the noise of an intruder. Light revealed an entirely naked man clambering into the vacant bunk above her. The odd thing is that, in reporting the episode, the woman said that she was not afraid because 'she thought the invader might her boyfriend.' *Might* be? Did she not *recognise* him? And what, in any case, was a lover doing sleeping three feet above? There were some, those with suspicious minds, who suspected that the 'sleep - walker' was just a cunning seducer who planned to make everyone feel at ease with his nocturnal nudity before slipping into occupied beds.

No doubt there were many, many interactions that remain secret to the people involved but a goodly number of the partnerships which formed did so openly. Eileen rejoices that there was; 'a high marriage rate between hotel staff, instructors and guests, the first between Richard Brown's brother, Charles and New Zealander, Libby Nolan. There were several weddings from Struan, notably that of Marg Phibbs and one of the Dundee boys, Dave Will for which Karli and I stood in as the bride's parents. Karli looked really splendid for his one and only appearance in a grey topper and tails. Our Lisi was abroad and could not be a bridesmaid so as a consolation prize she became godmother to the first Will baby, Lisi Jane.'

In that 1970's time, Dieter Bartsch, Karl's star Austrian import who was training the racers, was also pursuing his New Zealand Judy and there were many other world-spanning courtships either ongoing or in prospect.

One of the general effects that continued as a result of the constant New Zealand presence was a certain structuring of Struan's night life. A touch of spontaneity was thereby lost but most regulars agreed that the gains were impressive. The organised events were by no means staid. Indeed, they became ever more adventurous.

*A Struan union: Charles and Libby, some years after their marriage, with their daughters Francesca, Danielle and Charlotte*

During one of Jenny's early festive times it was announced that, for one evening's entertainment, the men would be encouraged to don female clothing. It was thus that I learned the essential truths that tights keep legs surprisingly warm, that handbags are useful for the pocketless and that some men will chase anything in a short skirt.

We discovered, also, that there were new delights and hazards associated with the Hogmanay festivities. For one thing, Mrs. Taylor had moved to a house in the middle of the Carrbridge golf course. The place was very comfortable and totally welcoming but getting to it in total darkness whilst completely inebriated was a major challenge. Many a reveller fell into the stream and at least one broke a leg in the non-theatrical sense.

Another of the mixed blessings was the more frequent appearance of pipers whose music sounded delightful from a distance but who could deafen for hours if they played within the confines of the bar.

One year I treated myself to a solo week of dedicated skiing in February. I had expected Struan to be quiet and therefore did not anticipate any risqué social evenings but in fact the place was almost full. Towards the end of my stay, just when I was congratulating myself on having escaped without embarrassment, the informal social committee of domestic workers and ski instructors announced that there was to be a 'panty party' with, in my case at least as an ex-employee, no excuses for non-attendance. Not having had experience of such an event I made discreet enquiries. I learned that revellers had to wear any garment which would reveal that they were wearing evidently feminine underwear. What my informants refrained from telling me was that the cowardly way out was to wear knickers as a hat or, even more pathetically, an arm band.

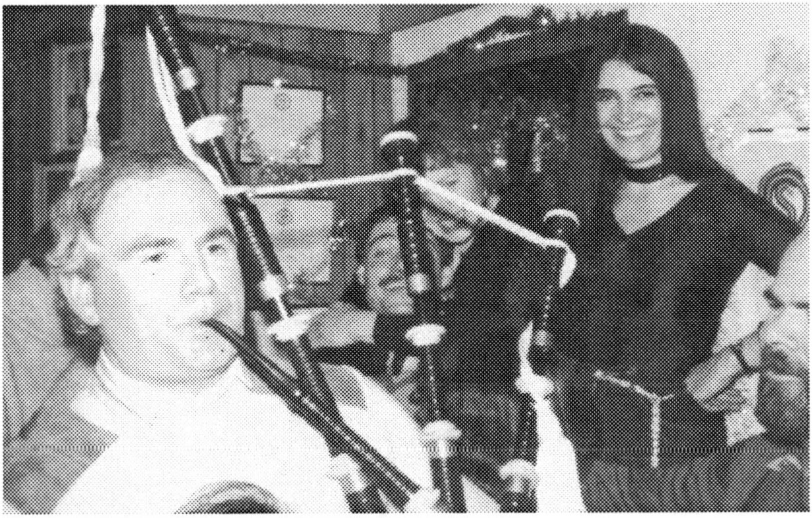

*The piper plays, Jenny bravely grins and her sister Wendy takes refuge.*

Taking the task seriously, I was forced into a red-faced expedition to Grantown. There, to my surprise, I found the courage to purchase a pair of lurid green satin briefs and light brown tights. When I later nervously emerged down the hotel stairs, wearing these with a loose shirt just covering the underwear, there was a girl of maybe ten or eleven in the hallway, watching the proceedings. She had, I gathered, been allowed to stay up long enough to see the start of the show. She solemnly surveyed me and then said, with every indication of seriousness, 'You should always dress like that!'

Given that I was the first to emerge in the approved attire, and that the non-participant drinkers in the Edelweiss gave me jocular hell, I found the innocent encouragement very morale-boosting. When, soon afterwards, that year's riotous gaggle of New Zealanders appeared wearing very little indeed I was no longer dismayed. A generally decorous but wild Struan night ensued and the early mockers doubtless regretted that they had not been bold.

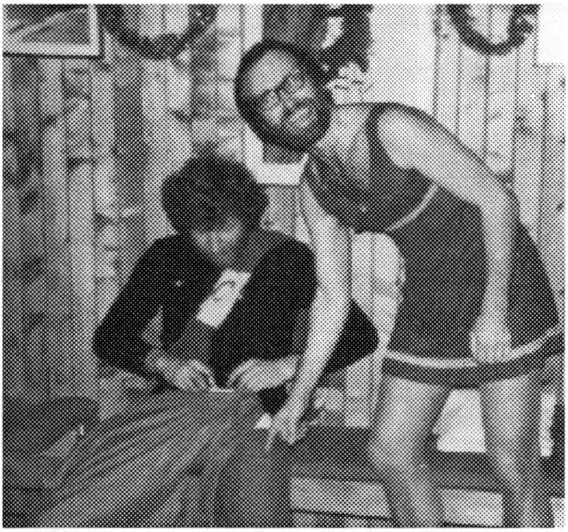

*Boys will be girls: New Zealand barman Larry and the author at a Struan Christmas celebration.*

It was during that week that I found myself one afternoon half way down White Lady in deep slushy piles which reminded me of moist sugar. Turning was taking huge effort and I paused for a rest. Before setting off again, I looked up the slope as one should and there, emerging through the mists, I saw something which brought me, totally unexpectedly, very close to tears.

At first all I knew was that someone was coming down that difficult slope faster than I had ever seen anyone travel before. Then I could see that the person, who was setting up a wake behind him like a speedboat, was completely in control. Then I realised that it was Peter.

Having no idea that he was home I had no anticipation of seeing him. He was past me in a brief moment but I had no doubts as to who it was. We had, occasionally, skied together during my season at Struan when he was but an eight year old boy. Even then he was far too quick for a ditherer to keep up with. His philosophy for dealing with ice, which he attempted to instil in me, was to get over it as quickly as possible to the good snow beyond. The difference between us was that he *believed* in that better patch beyond the limits of immediate vision whereas I did not.

I remembered his childhood courage as the adult form hurtled past me. It seemed impossible to me that anyone could travel so fast in such conditions and not fall over. It was one of the most inspiring sights I have ever seen. Neither television nor the wide screen can even approximately communicate the power of someone skiing extremely fast.

Peter's stay on that occasion was brief and we had only the slightest chance for a talk but for the remainder of that week I had the image of his pell-mell figure in my mind and it helped me to ski with more courage and determination. It still does.

As the seventies progressed, the process of 'professionalisation' of Struan's social life spread gradually. For the first time paid musicians were to be seen with amplifying equipment in the bar. The New Year celebrations involved not just random record-playing for dancing but a small ensemble. Some of the older hands regretted this but most admitted that there were strong compensations. On the occasions when a well-organised event coincided with a burst of the improvisatory spirit then a good time for all was guaranteed.

There were countervailing episodes, however, which would have been unthinkable in former times. Perhaps the two trends were somehow related. Eileen recalls;

'Generally speaking there was harmony throughout the New Zealand period, though there was one dramatic morning when I woke to be told that two of our three New Zealand barmen were in police cells in Aviemore. They had got drunk on their night off and assaulted the duty barman when they returned. This led to a general set-to in the bar when guests and staff joined in to defend the duty barman and someone phoned the police. Needless to say they got their marching orders and I had to face a sorry procession of black-eyed and bloody-nosed guests waiting and some refusing to pay their bills.

'More high drama in the bar involved Willie, a British ski instructor and barman, an ex-soldier in our Scots Guards regiment, who used to ski in the army championships and who had served in Northern Ireland and was very highly strung as a result. On evening he saw some workmen from the new A9 pestering his girlfriend. He leaped over the counter and attacked them whereupon they fled and called the police. Peter and I were fetched out of bed by the police saying, "Your barman's gone berserk." We found general chaos, groaning casualties and bloodstains. The next day the unfortunate barman was charged in Inverness Sheriff Court and I heard from our lawyer, who by chance defended him, that the Sheriff took one look at him and said that he could not try the case as he knew the defendant. In fact the Sheriff was a visitor of ours of many years standing and had been taught skiing by the defendant!'

Charlie Walpole, who saw the various eruptions, estimates that there was, in fact, roughly one fight per month, usually related to the closing of the bars.

Happily for us, Jenny and I never witnessed any of the ructions and we always greatly enjoyed our festive season holidays at Struan. Although the Scottish way is not to make a great deal of fuss over Christmas, the hotel was always attractively adorned. As Eileen remembers; 'Karli never forgot the interesting and beautiful Austrian customs to which he had been brought up. At Christmas he spent many hours decorating the hotel and ski shed and the numerous trees and providing entertainments and special parties for staff and guests. At Easter he bought Easter eggs for the entire staff and distributed to bar guests baskets full of hard boiled eggs which he had dyed in as many colours as he could find.'

The winter visits were literally wonderful. On the days when we had walked, perhaps the fifteen mile or so round trip to Loch Einich or past Bynack Stable and Forest Lodge along the dramatic bank of the River Nethy, or up into the hills, we would rejoice in the glow of healthy tiredness. As Struan veterans we would ensure that the bathing experience was blissful and then, usually, we would sleep, as cosy in our sheets and blankets as any tucked-up child. And then we would awake and drift down to the Enzian for a pre-dinner drink and a chat with an unpredictable combination of good Struan friends, knowing that, after the meal, there would be more talk, singing, or a developing party, that would keep us royally entertained until well into the night.

For all the many, many times we went there, we never grew in the slightest tired of Speyside, of the Struan routine or of the endlessly intriguing people. Day by day we looked forward to all the elements; the good cooked breakfast, the hours enjoying the most magnificent of scenery, the picnic lunch, the returners' tea, the bathing, the dozing, the aperitifs, the excellent dinner, the drinking and talking in one of the bars, the singing, the dancing. We felt that we were very privileged, lucky members of a non-exclusive club.

I suppose we thought, like many others seemed to, that it would never end.

## 29. Olympians

With the advent of Robin Bailey everything changed for the 'Musketeers'.

The press revealed the new skiing messiah as being a former paratrooper with substantial business interests in fruit and vegetable retailing. Physically quite small but large of personality, Bailey described himself as, 'a bit of an opportunist, a bit of a madman and a bit of a perfectionist'.

Robin Bailey began his expenses-only task of managing the British ski team in March 1974. Quite quickly he raised £58,000 to add to the £10,000 provided by the Sports Council. By pointing out that the car company, British Leyland, was sponsoring the Austrian team, another motor giant, Chrysler (UK), provided two Sunbeam Avenger estate cars and a mobile workshop for his skiers.

As often happens, once the money began to flow from one source, other ones opened up. One of the Speyside journals proudly revealed that, 'Peter Fuchs (Carrbridge) has been awarded a grant of £500 by the Scottish International Education Trust, which was set up a few years ago by Sean Connery. The award will help Fuchs defray the cost of being a leading member of the British men's ski team'.

For Willy Bailey, who had in any case been expressing reservations about Dieter's coaching methods, the new regime was not welcome. He took an almost instant dislike to his namesake. When the Spanish national team offered a haven, he quickly accepted the chance to escape.

Peter and Konrad were devastated at the loss of their travelling companion but for Peter especially there was some compensation in that Moggs was drafted into the squad, along with others, to bring the total up to twelve. A rigorous programme of pre-season training was devised for the summer of 1974.

The *Sunday Post* devoted an article to Peter which explained the new arrangements and revealed that Karl and Eileen had spent some £1800 the previous year to help their son's career. The *Press and Journal* of the 15th of July described the training arrangements, although the reference to the Red Devils is a piece of romance on the part of the reporter.

'For the men of the British ski team the serious business of full training began on July 1. Eighteen trainees, including all the top names in Scottish junior and senior circuits, have been living at Carrbridge for two weeks, undergoing a physical training and selection programme supervised by Dieter Bartsch, the British men's team trainer.

'The programme of PT, swimming and mountain running has also included football matches against Grantown-on-Spey and cycle racing against a North of Scotland select. Dieter Bartsch moves now to Aldershot with 12 selected trainees to continue with a 14-day advanced fitness course run in collaboration with the Red Devils parachute unit.

'At Aldershot the team will specialise in circuit training and confidence training, a form of controlled exposure to dangerous situations. The team will also have the use of a wind tunnel where each racer will learn to adopt aerodynamic racing positions, so saving split seconds in downhill racing which is the fastest and most exacting of the three Alpine types of skiing.'

The combination of young ski hopefuls and military training proved attractive to the British national press. The *Daily Express* of July 30, 1974 announced that; 'Britain's ski boys jump to it as Paras roar out the orders'. Their reporter, Christopher Hilton, wrote as part of a long article;

'The assault course - three times round the 200 yards in about six minutes - is only a part of the training which the Paras have been giving them. Consider the Confidence Course. Bars, arranged as scaffolding, reach up like skeletons into the trees with ropes and platforms attached. One training officer stands alone, directing the climbers and swingers with more incisive commands.

'The 12 skiers have not only spent the two weeks living with the Army, they have been given the same treatment, mixing with regular soldiers in training. Now they scale a rope wall, haul themselves over scaffolding to two parallel bars 50ft up with only a platform underneath. Each man in turn stands with a foot on the bars and inches forward over the two metal clips which make him lift his feet and almost lose balance. He stops on the word of command and touches his toes. On the ground, one man who has made a mess of a jump is carried away by two others, his face contorted in pain.

'The highlight of it all is the wind tunnel at the Royal Aircraft Establishment at Farnborough nearby. In it the skier, his skis clamped to the floor, crouches as the wind builds up to 55 miles an hour - what he would expect to encounter coming down a mountain. He watches a metre set into the floor which records his wind resistance so he can find the most streamlined position.

'Peter Fuchs, an 18-year-old from Carrbridge, Inverness, emerged from it and said; 'Here you can really practise racing positions and learn to cope with slipstreams.' The assembled boffins watched with detached interest. The skiers seemed to enjoy it, too - at least it was better than the assault course.'

At the summer training on the Dachstein glacier, Konrad and Peter began to realise that maybe Willy had had a valid point after all. The euphoria generated by the extra money was short lived for the remaining pair. As Konrad puts it, for them it was like being taken out of a small, elite grammar school and pushed into a noisy comprehensive. Attention was significantly diluted. Although the two of them still had faith in Dieter, there were arguments.

As the new season approached, team trials were organised at Zauchensee in Austria. Only the fastest of the gang would qualify for continuing support. Willy came over for the event. He was still very much interested in representing his country in spite of his disaffection. The races began and Willy, in Konrad's words, 'wiped the floor' with all the others.

Peter and Konrad were understandably dismayed by this but their shock at the ski humiliation was as nothing compared to what they felt when Robin Bailey suggested that the two of them had deliberately allowed Willy to win so that he would qualify for support.

Tensions between Peter and Konrad and the officials worsened. There was the usual confusion over the 1975 British Championships held at Val d'Isere. It seemed that, with the new professionalism, the imperative for all British skiers to take part might have been waived but not so. As before, attention had to be diverted from the World series of races to satisfy the officials that the national championships were not being slighted. Peter, at least, was relieved from the immediate dilemma because the 'bruised muscle', which had troubled him ever since the accident in Australia, had at last been properly diagnosed as a partially ruptured Achilles tendon. This, a very serious injury, needed time to heal. *The Scotsman* of the 4th of January looked forward to the championships and made their prediction.

'In the absence of Peter Fuchs, who has pulled an Achilles tendon in training, the British captain, Konrad Bartelski, is an expected winner. His main challengers from Scotland will be Stuart Fitzsimmons (Edinburgh) and Alan Stewart (North Queensferry), both members of the British team who have been having an uphill battle in international races so far. On balance Fitzsimmons should come through in downhill and Stewart in slalom and giant slalom.'

But the 'expected winner', was not at Val d'Isere for the opening slalom. Konrad missed it thanks to what Robin Bailey publicly confessed to be a 'monumental cock-up' on his part. The error was a simple confusion of dates. Instead of competing against Stuart Fitzsimmons and the others, Konrad was racing in a World Cup event at Garmisch. There he had one of his best ever results but he was nonetheless embarrassed to be turning up at Val d'Isere with half of the national competition completed.

Willy, who had crashed badly at Garmisch, and Peter, travelled with him. Dieter, not a party to the administrative error, told the press that everything was geared to the Olympics, only just over a year away, and that the main thing was for his leading men to have as much top downhill experience as possible.

Before the somewhat devalued national Downhill could be staged at Val d'Isere, the process of adjustment to the new system of management of British ski racing claimed another casualty. Hugh Hunter Gordon, chairman of the National Skiing Federation Alpine Committee for several years and the man who established the International Ski Federation system of handicap points, resigned his position, citing pressure of work and what he called 'the crisis of confidence' in ski racing as his reasons.

One of the major points raised by Hunter Gordon was the lack of agreement amongst Scottish skiers. The newspapers quoted him as saying; 'Many Scots feel we should concentrate on home affairs where we've more than enough to do to keep the pace. We also wonder whether the casualty rate for young skiers trying to make the top is too high.'

In the course of an explicatory *Guardian* article on the 8th of January 1975, John Samuel affirms Hunter Gordon's views and makes an oblique reference to what can only be the long-running feud between Frith and Karl. He wrote; 'The divisions within Scottish skiing can be considerably more fraught than those between the Scots and English. If Scotland did present a united front things would be considerably easier. But people running ski schools in the same centre in some instances never speak to each other.'

The three leading men, with the chore of the British Championships out of the way, had to try to ignore the turmoil and return to what they saw as their major task; acquiring FIS points and working towards a level of expertise and fitness where they could mount a realistic challenge in the 1976 Olympics.

Willy, still with the Spanish team, escaped from the pressures within the national camp but his two companions soon faced new difficulties. Their friend's doubts about Dieter's competence as a coach began to influence them. The trust had been absolute but now the skiers began to realise that they generally performed better in the summer than in the winter. There could, of course, be many possible explanations for this but the two started to speculate that their training regime was ill-conceived. Their mood was doubtless influenced by the fact that both of them had injuries which kept them temporarily out of World Cup contention.

At this stage, the media had no hint of the brewing troubles. Walter Gordon, in the *Evening Express*, of January 18 1975, treated his readers to a highly optimistic assessment of the British skiers' prospects. He said that in spite of Konrad's broken wrist and Peter's gradually healing Achilles tendon, there was a real basis for Olympic hopes. Dieter is quoted as believing that a medal was not an impossible aspiration. He was, the article claimed, working to a long term plan with the Innsbruck games as the final goal. Part of Walter Gordon's piece reads;

'Last season the top British pair were sweating to get their FIS points down below 40... and they did. This meant that they moved higher up the starting lists in future races so that they had a better chance of improving their FIS points so that they could move still higher up the list.... For in the topsy-turvy world of ski racing it is the man who has proved himself the fastest in previous races who gets the best chance of winning - by starting first. Basically FIS points are awarded on how close a skier's time is to the winner's. By various magical formulae these allow racers who may never have competed against each other to be put into an 'order of merit' according to their achievements in previous events. In this starting list, the best are at the top with the weakest at the bottom.

'This season Konrad Bartelski's FIS points for downhill are 19, and Peter's in the 20's. Peter already has one period to his credit where he had less than 20. One more good result will give him a FIS rating below the magic figure which will give him free entry to any World Cup downhill event on proven merit. When Iain Finlayson and Fraser Clyde from the Spey Valley were competing in the Olympics at Sapporo in Japan, Scots race officials thought it was wonderful that their points were below 100.

'Dieter is encouraged by the fact that his squad is well disciplined and prepared to carry out his instructions to the letter. There was evidence of this when Peter Fuchs was training at St Moritz. The downhill course there has electronic timing with an intermediate check-point. Up against top opposition, Peter was consistently fastest in the top-half of the course and invariably finished amongst the first four or five for the whole course.

'The British team is not just a two-man team affair. Behind Fuchs and Bartelski are Stuart Fitzsimmons and Willy Bailey, and backing them are half a dozen others. Duncan Riley, Colin Fleming and Sandy Russell included, all of whom are getting the advantage of being part of a squad where the top men are the brightest prospects Britain has ever had.'

There were two heavy blows to the Three Musketeers before the preparation for Innsbruck could go much further. The first was that Willy, who many thought had returned to skiing too soon after the very bad fall at Garmisch, announced yet again that he would enter no more downhill races. So many times he had declared that he had reached the end and so often he had relented. This time Peter and Konrad were convinced that the resolve was permanent. They were deeply dismayed. Years later Konrad wrote; 'Of all the Musketeers, Willy probably had the most natural talent.....If he had had his talent properly nurtured, he had the makings of a real winner. He deserved much more than that exit in a shower of snow.'

The second blow fell upon Konrad.

His wrist injury was sufficiently recovered for him to enter the World Cup Downhill at Megève in France. By this time, Peter's leg was once again giving him severe pain so Konrad was the only representative of the Three Musketeers in the race.

The weather was very poor by Alpine standards. The race organisers struggled with the decision as to whether or not the event should be cancelled. At last they announced that racing could start.

With his wrist heavily bandaged, Konrad took off. His parents were among many millions watching the event on television and, as always, he was desperate to do well. High on his list of anxieties about the course was a jump over a road about halfway down the course. The organisers had altered the configuration of the leap several times so there was no well-established point at which skiers knew they had to take off. Pre-jumping at a point he had identified in practice, Konrad found that he was not clearing the road. The tails of his skis landed on the abrasive surface and then he was over, head first, rolling, flailing, shedding equipment. Commentators later gave him the name '*Chef de la chute*'. It was a fall which looked fatal and when his body came to rest and lay immobile, the watching world could not help but think the worst.

Dieter was at the start area and as soon as news of Konrad's terrifying crash came through, he made as if to ski down. The police, going against their usual practice, refused to allow him through their line. According to a report in the *Evening Press* some time later; 'Dieter, tired of arguing, simply side-stepped up the hill from them. He put his ski stick handles against his chest so that the points were sticking straight ahead and skied at the police line. They took one look at this "knight on skis" and jumped out of the way.'

It took three quarters of an hour for the helicopter to arrive. Happily for Konrad he remembered nothing of the interlude between taking that jump and waking in hospital. Almost his first conscious experience at that moment was seeing Peter and his then girl friend paying a visit. The young woman involuntarily put a hand to her face as she first saw the patient. It was only then that Konrad realised that he was, temporarily as it turned out, badly disfigured. He asked Peter to describe the fall and thereby came to realise how fortunate he had been to survive.

Unlike Willy, who had suffered considerably in his major accident, Konrad had felt nothing at all. Apart from a badly bruised knee, the short-lasting insult to his beauty and the vague after-effects of concussion, he sustained no evil consequences of the fall. Even when shown a video recording of the tumble he saw the cartwheeling body as that of a puppet; he saw no reason to end his chosen career.

One outcome of the episode was a dramatic improvement in his personal fame. His 'recognition-factor' with the public increased exponentially. When the Italian racer, Erwin Stricker, visited Konrad in hospital he said; 'A good crash is better than coming second any day. People won't forget this for many, many years.' He was right.

Robin Bailey, who had witnessed the death of a French skier in the European Junior Downhill, was quoted as saying, 'We are not satisfied that all the safety measures possible are being taken. Konrad certainly misjudged the jump at Megeve, but the bad fall was partly due to a flat landing area. If it had been angled he would not have been thrown forward so severely. I honestly thought he had been killed. It was a dreadful moment.'

In spite of Konrad's ghastly fall, Peter's recurring injury, Willy's retirement and the growing dissatisfaction with their trainer, the two remaining Musketeers were still sufficiently motivated to overcome all the disincentives. In the *Evening Express* of March 8, 1975 Walter Gordon was still intent on talking up their chances. There could, he claimed, be a British world skiing champion within the next two or three years.

Walter Gordon's first contender was, of course, Konrad. An Austrian called George Gstrein, who worked at Glenshee and did some racing in Scotland, was cited in support. Gstrein said, 'In two or three years Konrad Bartelski could be the world champion. He is so good.' The Austrian expressed strong approval of Konrad's rise from the fifth to the second group of starters in downhill races. He commented, 'It's amazing. He is so young and so determined'.

Walter Gordon then turned to Peter's chances and declared that it was only a run of bad luck with injuries which had prevented him being up there with Konrad. George Gstrein's quoted view is that Peter could, with a clear injury-free run, achieve the highest levels.

The Alpine season came to an end with Peter beginning to find his ski legs again and Konrad commendably high in the FIS ratings. After the last race, the Scottish members of the British team faced a rush to get home in time for their national championships. Peter, Moggs, Stuart Fitzsimmons, Alan Stewart and Duncan Riley drove from Austria to take part. They did not arrive until nine in the evening on the day before the races. It was not ideal preparation.

John Samuel previewed the event in *The Guardian* of the 12th April. He judged that Peter was the favourite but declared that Alan Stewart, Colin Fleming, Duncan Riley and Stuart Fitzsimmons would all run him close.

Stuart Fitzsimmons was the first of the eighty racers out of the start gate in the slalom. The Cairngorm cloud swirled around making conditions difficult. Stuart's time of 42.9 seconds impressed the experts but Peter, running second, managed to beat it by a fraction. Alan Stewart was a touch slower whilst the watchers on the finishing line waited in vain for the emergence of Duncan Riley and Moggs, both of whom fell higher up the course.

One the second run, Peter was again the fastest with Stuart and Alan not far behind. The aggregate times were extremely close and any one of them could win the combined title by skiing well in the next day's giant slalom.

The course was set over almost the full length of the White Lady and Peter was the first to test his mettle on it. He had the advantage of there being no racer's ruts but on the other hand he had no target to beat. He had to combine courage and caution in just the right proportions. His time, 64 seconds exactly, set the challenge for the others.

Alan Stewart went second. Peter's performance was put into perspective for, well though Alan raced, he was two seconds slower. Barring a miraculous run by some of the later starters, only Stuart Fitzsimmons could take the championship from Peter. He hurled himself down the course and when the clock stopped he had taken precisely the same time as the leader.

Compared to the World Cup races on the Continent, the event was a minor one yet it meant a very great deal to Peter that, notwithstanding his recent history of injury, he had proved to be the best in Scotland.

With this fillip, the end of the season was welcome to Peter; at last his ever troublesome tendon could be given a chance to heal. Too quickly, though, from that point of view, the pre-season fitness training started and then the squad was back in the Alps, beginning the run-up to the mighty Olympics. No sooner had the process started than Peter's over-worked legs began to give problems. He sent a card from Val d'Isere early in December.

'Dear Mum, Dad and Lisi,

My legs are getting better quite fast so I should be skiing by next week but I've missed 3 races by then. The one at Lienz was a real give-away points race and Stuart got 26 points if you can imagine. I'll be home on the 22nd.'

Olympic fever helped to generate fresh interest. The dedication shown by Peter and his companions was cited in a *Scotsman* article of December 16th 1975. Announcing sponsorship for Scottish skiing by drinks and tobacco companies, the newspaper informed its readers that the winner on a points basis overall in the various Scottish races would become the 'Pernod-Gauloises Cup' holder; so much for the healthy image of skiing!

This commercial initiative was matched by a push from the Scottish

National Ski Council to raise funds from the general public for the Olympic effort. This took the form of a leaflet with photographs and potted biographies of the ten Scots in training. Peter, first in the gallery, was described as; 'Fluent German speaker, raced only from the age of 14 by which time his technique was already excellent. Determined and professional. Scottish champion 1973 and 1975. Member of the British World Championship Team 1974 when he finished 19th in the downhill.' Moggs' paragraph described him as the Carrbridge-based son of a forester, and, 'the youngest of the trainees and least experienced but he possesses an easy temperament and is learning fast.'

The back page of the leaflet appealed to Scottish patriotism. It urged; 'Surely this is a matter of pride for Scotland. Act today! Money is urgently needed to support our teams!' Just how much was raised in this fashion is doubtless recorded somewhere in the annals of the SNSC but it is hard to imagine that many were moved to contribute.

No doubt the squad members were pleased that this effort was being made on their behalf but Peter was not the only one with worrying fitness problems. On a card sent from Austria, addressed to 'Fam Fuchs', Konrad wrote; 'Dear All, Great start to the season - out of the starting gate onto the injury list! I'm at S. Anton at the moment having a broken bone spur removed from my knee. Days in hospital/month out of action. Also with Peter's misfortune we believe somebody doesn't like us here. Have a good season! Happy Christmas, Konrad.'

The selection of the elite group for the Olympics was looming. In earnest discussions with Dieter, Konrad and Peter secured agreement that there would be only four nominated skiers. It was important for morale that every Briton in the race was capable of making a respectable showing. It would be embarrassing to have team members finishing minutes behind the winner. They felt also that with a small group once more they could re-kindle the spirit which had fired the Three Musketeers to such unprecedented success.

It was a bitter shock to the two most experienced men when Robin Bailey and Dieter announced that, in fact, the maximum of six would be in the Olympic downhill. The two leading racers were dumbfounded. It was not that they lacked respect for the newcomers; they would surely make their mark one day, but they were seriously inexperienced and would surely not enhance the reputation of British skiing as the television cameras of the world focused briefly on their failures.

The decline in relationships gathered pace as fast as a skier fresh out of the starting gate. At a downhill at Lienz, which promised well because Konrad in particular had been achieving excellent times in practice, Dieter provided, over the radio, information on the state of the course which, in the skiers' estimation, proved to be dangerously inaccurate. Going too fast as he hit the first truly steep section, Konrad struggled to cope with a track which he describes as being like the surface of the moon. He fell, damaging a knee. Soon afterwards Peter crashed out, though luckily without serious injury.

The damage to Konrad's knee, part of which was historic, caused even further bad business between him and Dieter. In the skiers' perception their trainer was unsympathetic to injury. They felt that he had scorned Willy for complaining about chronic back pain and now he was being dismissive of Konrad's agony. To make matters much worse, Konrad heard from a team mate that Dieter had been maligning him.

Konrad was sufficiently incapacitated to pull out of the Val d'Isere downhill. It was a miserable time. A ski-circuit friend, a Frenchman called Michel Dujon, had been killed whilst preparing for the race and, in the eyes of the two senior British racers, there had been totally insufficient acknowledgement of the young man's death. It seemed that everyone around them was cynical. There was a bitter-sweet element, too, when their close friend and training companion Ken Read won the race, his first downhill victory. It was impossible to resist thinking that it could have been one of them on the top step of the podium.

Konrad's knee required further surgery. The doctor predicted an eight week break from skiing but within just over a quarter of that time Konrad was back with the team. He was upset that nobody had troubled to visit him in hospital, even more angry when he was required to join in a game of football almost immediately after returning. The discontent grew even stronger.

In the last major race before the Olympics, a European Cup event at Haus which took place just four weeks after his operation, Konrad missed his first win by a margin of just two-hundredths of a second. Peter was thirteenth, Stuart Fitzsimmons just one place behind that. All of them finished ahead of the likes of Leonard Stock who went on to win a World Cup and an Olympic gold.

Konrad paid the price for his success. His knee became dreadfully sore and swollen. The doctor, when consulted, would comment only that he was an idiot for skiing on it at all but the disobedient patient felt justified; he had come closer than ever to winning a major race. The doctor was probably right but it would have taken a much greater injury to keep Konrad from the great world stage.

He and Peter shared a fairly frugal Innsbruck apartment for the Olympics. Karl arrived. Eileen remembers that, 'Karli, with memories of 1948, was proudly admitted to the course on the Patscherkofl and to the Olympic Village in Innsbruck.'

The course was a source of great dismay to Konrad. He was a 'glider', a man who liked to float over the snow, making fine adjustments, coaxing his skis into the optimum track. The Innsbruck slope was sheet ice. By day the authorities heated it with reflectors so that the melted surface would freeze hard in the night.

There was almost unbearable tension. Peter and Konrad felt that Dieter had become obsessed with ski preparation, yet the edges of Konrad's skis were comparatively blunt. When a challenge on this matter was made, Dieter replied that his leading contender always skied better with blunt edges, which was perhaps true of snowy courses but, Konrad felt, potentially lethal on ice.

Konrad records that the atmosphere in the camp was poor. In addition to the rows between the skiers and Dieter, Robin Bailey was skirmishing with the journalists. In Konrad's judgement their manager was too abrasive, too ready to give evasive responses for him to be effective at public relations. The reporters seemed to lose enthusiasm for the British cause and this badly affected the morale of the racers. Karl visited Peter regularly and said that he thought practice was going well but when the time to start the real business came, neither Konrad nor Peter felt inspired.

Eileen watched the event on television with her father in Franz Stock's house in Finkenberg. She was shaking with nerves and was plied constantly with steadying coffee. Franz Klammer, the local favourite, set a formidable target. Konrad, the first of the Britons to go, was only a second or so behind the great man for the first quarter of the course but then, in what he describes as an 'idiotic mistake', he fell. Dieter urged Peter, the next of the British, to ski steadily so that at least one of the squad would finish.

He did as he was told and duly completed the course but his time was not good. The Duke of Kent rushed over to clap him on the back and say, 'Well done old chap!' On many occasions Peter had been so upset at doing badly that officials and dignitaries had suffered the backlash. It was no different on this occasion. The well-meaning member of the royal family was treated to some swearing which he seemed to take without flinching.

Alan Stewart and Stuart Fitzsimmons, freed from the imperative to complete the course, were more relaxed and they both finished ahead of Peter.

In the Press conference after the race, Peter was still too upset to contribute. The more phlegmatic Konrad said, 'I was into the compression quicker than I had ever been but suddenly I was upside down, staring at my skis and the sky. I know you can't go on making excuses. I'd really worked for this. Four years.'

His vast disappointment was evident to everyone. He spoke of his operation and the work he had done in an effort to make up for lost time. He said, 'I kept on telling myself, a thousand times, that I had the condition, that I could still do it in spite of all the racing time and experience I had lost.'

Peter recovered sufficiently before the closing ceremony to arrange for Karl to join in the celebration. Eileen remembers that there was much delight but even this aspect was tarnished because the lack of success for the two leading skiers had further soured their relationship with Dieter. As with the previous Olympics, it felt as though a serious eruption was about to ensue.

It was not a particularly happy band which returned to the haven of Struan but as always there was an eye towards the future. There would be other big events and fresh opportunities. The endlessly interesting and challenging life of the skiing world would certainly go on.

## 30. Family Developments

Peter had reached the highest slopes of his chosen mountain and had had his chance to reach the very summit. There were many who thought that his sister, too young for the 1976 Games, might eventually have gone even further in the sport. But whilst Peter was working hard in the build up to Innsbruck, Lisi had not regretted her 1974 Val D'Isere decision to quit.

*Lisi in the forest*

Brother and sister had talked often, when their paths crossed on the Alpine circuit, of what it was that drove them. Peter was very often sick before a race. Sometimes, to Lisi's adolescent shame, he cried but not through fear of physical hurt. What worried him so greatly was the prospect of failure. Yet it was not a young man's pride, nor team spirit, nor nationalism which was the chief consideration; what mattered was his father.

Never, at any stage of his development, had Peter felt the slightest pressure from Karl. When he did well he was lavishly praised, when he had a setback there was uncritical support. At all times it was clear that he should continue racing if and only if he were enjoying it. There was no overt reason as to why he should care so inordinately about his father's approbation. The forces were to do with child-like things and the innate power of Karl's personality.

Lisi understood. She, too, wanted to please Karl and there was for her another, similar, factor. She also wanted to win the approval of her brother. But these combined forces were not sufficient to keep her in the game. She loved skiing and she wanted to do well but for her it was just not worth risking permanent damage, even death, for the sake of prestige. The risks far outweighed the potential rewards. Peter, Konrad, Moggs, Willy Bailey, Stuart Fitzsimmons, Valentina Iliffe; dozens and dozens more had all sustained injuries which would probably affect them for the remainder of their lives. Konrad had been within an ace of paying the ultimate price. Charles Bozon and others had tragically done so.

There was a further consideration. For a significant part of her young life, Lisi had been an unwilling observer of the machinations of ski administration. Most of the disputes with which competitive skiing was riddled seemed absurd and petty. Ego protection was evidently more important than the realities. It was, after all, only a sport.

With ski racing no longer an option, Lisi had faced the open question of what to put in its place. There was ever the prospect that one day she could become involved in the Struan business but in 1974 she was still very young to be thinking along those lines and in any case, Peter's future almost certainly lay in that direction. His thoughts, at that time, were mainly focused on the Olympics but one day, surely, he would want to step into his father's boots.

Lisi decided, instead, to develop the considerable aptitude as an artist which she had shown at school. She applied to art colleges and was offered a place at Dundee. The tutors there advised her to make time to look at the exhibition of work created by the latest batch of graduates. Keen to see what sort of standards she was aspiring to, Lisi went to the display.

These students, it immediately turned out, were in the grip of the early manifestations of minimalism. Single, simple objects and almost blank canvasses were supposed to be invested with huge artistic significance. It was difficult for the bemused applicant not to laugh. Maybe the contrast with the earthy realities of the ski-racing circuit was too stark but, whatever the reason, Lisi made another instant decision. She did not relish the prospect of spending years in training simply to produce such emptiness.

Unsure what to do next, Lisi worked for a while at Struan but then Sepp Guffler offered her a berth as an instructor at Obergurgl. She decided to take it. Skiing was still very attractive to her and, indeed, she still intended to compete, entirely for pleasure, in local races where the pressures were few.

Lisi and her parents travelled together to visit Peter and the team. On the way home, Karl and Eileen deposited their daughter at Obergurgl. They were delighted, soon afterwards, to hear that Lisi had been chosen above all the Austrians to demonstrate good ski technique.

At first, the life was enjoyable. There was a challenge in finding the optimum way to get pupils over their personal skiing barriers. From Karl she had learned a huge array of techniques which had been tested and proven over many years. But then, as the season began to drag, she realised that she had found another potential career which was not for her. A card, sent to her parents in February, tells of an antipathy to certain students and gives strong hints of homesickness.

'Dear Mum and Dad,

I've got beginners this week, it's horrible. I can't stand those brats. Peter was over the other night again (he's not very well). Konrad ok again. Snowing heavily now, wet snow! Send 2 packs Familie cereal please. (Muesli stuff), love, Lisi.'

When the season ended, Lisi came gladly home. She found that Karl's health was visibly deteriorating. He had recently been on a ski tour which had turned into a Struan classic. En route they had come across Plum Worral who, improbably, had been leading a party of skiing nuns across the frozen wastes. Leaving the Mancunian to his own route, they had claimed the scalp of Ben Macdhui but Eileen reported to her daughter that for the first time ever she had been faster on the uphill stretches than her husband. In spite of the fact that he had effortlessly sailed past her on the downhills, it seemed very likely that the trip would be Karl's last long-distance venture on skis. The indications were that he would be less and less able to carry on with the heavier chores of running the ski school.

It would have been easy for Lisi to pitch into the Struan working life, filling some of the gaps caused by Karl's growing incapacity, but she still did not feel that the circumstances were right for such a commitment. More in desperation than desire, she embarked on a secretarial course at a college in Edinburgh. She lodged in the family flat during the week and came home at weekends, an arrangement that was tolerable because the course was only for a year.

In the February of 1976, whilst Peter was still in pursuit of Alpine glory, her parents set off for Innsbruck to watch their son in the Olympics. On the way they stayed with Maurice in Purley. As ever, Lisi put pen to paper to tell Karl and Eileen about her college studies, her health and a host of other topics. Knowing that her father would be especially interested she reported that, 'I saw Peter on T.V. but he was quite slow, it's a shame but never mind. I was racing at Glenshee with Moggs and Werner. Moggs won the first run of the slalom but was second after the two runs. I ran out in the second run. I won the GS on Sunday and Moggs came third in the combined. All I got was a small shield, all the prizes went to the combined results.'

Just as important as the ski trophies, though, were the cats. Lisi added, 'Sandy and Bimbo must be quite lonely because when I go home there's an awful fuss and commotion, even from Bimbo. He gets very nervous when I'm leaving on Sunday. They are always there when I come home, screaming their heads off.'

It quickly became clear to Lisi that, after the uncertainties of ski racing and the transience of the ski instructor's life, it would be difficult to settle to secretarial routine. One by one her options were being eliminated. Needing time to think further about her future, she returned to Struan and earned her living by working in the family business. Whenever Peter was home she eagerly listened to his news of the racing circuit but still felt no regrets about not being part of it. Her brother seemed to recover from his Olympic disappointment but the world he described was not enticing. There remained, of course, the vexed question as to what she would do with her life but she was still only eighteen and there was plenty of time to think about whether she wanted to continue studying or to look for training in some saleable skill.

In this indeterminate state she went, one evening, to a dance in Aviemore. There she noticed a tow-headed, handsome young man who aroused her interest. He was, she learned, called David Sinclair. In the relatively small Speyside community it was not difficult to contrive another crossing of paths and she discovered that David shared her interest in creativity. He was working in a pottery but had a wide range of craft skills. They began to see each other regularly.

Soon David was a frequent visitor to Struan where the only immediate problem was the behaviour of his dog, a creature of the Pyrennean Mountain variety called Risa, which had been abandoned by its former owner. Its new master had done everything to restore the dog to health but it resisted most of the efforts to bring its liveliness under control. At Struan, Risa was a liability and her days of visiting were shortly numbered. Lisi's devotion to the animal and its owner did not diminish.

Replicating her mother's experience almost exactly, albeit at a dozen or so years less of an age, Lisi had a swift courtship. The pair were married in November 1976. One of the local papers previewed the event. The headline was; 'Ski girl Lisi gets set for her big day.' The account ran;

'A young Carrbridge girl who has made her mark in the skiing world, is busy with preparations for the most important date of her life. But thoughts of ski racing will be far from her mind when 19-year-old Lisi Fuchs walks down the aisle at St Columba Church, Rothiemurchus, this

Saturday, for her wedding to Mr David Sinclair, of Kirkcaldy.

'Lisi, a former British junior champion and twice Scottish lady champion, is the daughter of Eileen and Karl Fuchs, of the Struan House Hotel, Carrbridge. She will have her cousin, Barbara Knowles, of Purley, near London, for her bridesmaid, and god-daughter, Lisi Jane Will, of Brechin, as flower-girl. David (23) whose parents, Betty and David Sinclair, live in Kirkcaldy, will have his brother as best man.

'The couple met at a dance when David was working at a pottery in Aviemore.

'And one of the most important guests will be Lisi's brother Peter, home on a flying visit from training with the British team.'

*'Press and Journal' photo of the couple*

The Struan family gathered for the event. Dave Will, one of the earliest of customers, drove the wedding car. He also proposed the toast. He had strong claims to be a member of the Struan clan. Some years previously, he and one of the New Zealanders, Marg, had had their own Struan wedding, with the bride using the hotel as her home for the day. The catering for the reception had been, in Eileen's estimation, 'magnificently done' by Stephen Markwick, the son of her former Board of Trade superior.

The new couple had nowhere of their own to live, so Struan absorbed them. Mrs. Anderson, at the next door property 'Crannich', kindly provided a spot in her garden for a kennel where Risa could safely reside. The pair had little in the way of capital but they found enough to buy a plot of land with a derelict barn. They planned to demolish the structure and to build their own house. David was, like Karl, completely undaunted by any practical task. He began the Herculean work immediately.

With Peter away for most of the time, the Fuchs house was quite adequate for two couples. Given that the four of them were working long hours, and that the Struan bars provided an evening escape, there would probably have been little pressure from the new arrangements. The four would doubtless have co-existed peacefully for an indefinite period had it not been for the circumstance that in fact they were five.

The young couple, in the first flush of love, had acquired a pet, a creature on which they both doted. It was not yet another cat, nor a loveable puppy which chewed everything it could get its jaws onto and got determinedly under busy feet, but a bird, an innocent, safely caged, avian beast. It resembled one which Lisi had seen on a visit to Yorkshire when she was a child. She had cherished the thought of owning one like it ever since.

Karl, especially, loved birds. He was a renowned expert on the local fauna. He would spend hours seeking eagles and ospreys, would talk enthusiastically about the doings of oyster-catchers, capercailzie and ptarmigans. Yet this particular flying friend drove him to distraction. It was a mynah and it talked and talked and talked in an astonishing variety of accents. Lisi and Davie thought it entirely charming that their pet chattered so cleverly. For Karl and Eileen, the incessant squawking was the noise of nightmare.

A crisis developed. It was declared that the bird had to go. Davie suggested, as a compromise, that the bird could reside in the bar. Eileen was convinced that it would quickly drive all the regular customers crazy.

Unwilling to part with their baby, Lisi and Davie decided to try housing it close to Risa's kennel where it could chatter to the other birds in the trees. The problem with this was that the poor dog was also driven to distraction. The newly-weds went down to greet their mini-menagerie one morning to find that Risa had managed to paw the door of the cage open. The bird had flown. In the fashion of all of its kind, the dog looked abjectly guilty.

*The growing family*

If the bird were intent on freedom, it played a foolish hand. Lisi and David went into the woods adjacent to the Crannich garden and it was not long before they heard the random speeches. Their friend eyed them from a high branch and continued to talk. Risking serious injury, David began a cautious climb, all the while engaging the creature in lunatic conversation. It seemed very likely that the mynah would simply take off once he was within grabbing distance but chat was the priority. It seemed surprised and aggrieved when it was grabbed. The squawking and swearing were formidable but the bird was restored to its home.

There seemed no option, then, but to move. Their house was but a few diggings and a dream in their hearts but the plot of land was entirely suitable for a caravan. Living on the site would have great advantages for Davie, who could work on the house as and when he pleased.

Everyone was delighted with the solution. Karl and Eileen had their peace restored and the young couple had their independence. The mynah bird had pride of place in their new abode and talked even more than before.

There are probably not too many people who have experienced life with a garrulous mynah in a caravan. Lisi, a survivor, reports that even with love as strong as hers, the strain quickly becomes insupportable. There was no escape other than to run screaming into the soggy field. Shortly after the move to the temporary home, the mynah returned whence it came; a shop. Peace returned to that particular part of the Spey Valley.

The creature's days with them would probably have been short-numbered in any case because Lisi very soon had a real baby to deal with and then, not long afterwards, another. The couple, with the junior David and Kris, perforce moved into the half-built house but, for the time being at least, Lisi had found her occupation. She was still only 21 but she had what she wanted; a husband, two children and a home of her own.

## 31. Parting

Whilst Lisi's life developed on domestic lines, Peter and his companions continued on their quest for racing glory. There was an understandable despondency after the Olympics. The flow of money almost dried up. Peter and Konrad tortured their brains trying to find ways of keeping going with reduced costs. Eventually they decided that the men's and women's squads would have to be reduced in size and amalgamated under one trainer.

The first chance they had to air this view was during the British Championships of 1976 which were once more being held on Cairngorm. There was a not untypical day when the wind tried to blow everyone off the mountain. Ian Wooldridge amusingly portrayed the scene in a piece written for the *Daily Mail* of March 2nd:

'Britain's version of the Winter Olympics was staged on Sunday on a khaki hillside equidistant between Balmoral Castle and the last rumoured sighting of the Loch Ness Monster. Necessity determined the exact spot since this was one of the few places north of Bournemouth with a slick of snow long enough to slide down. In the circumstances an unexpectedly large crowd turned up to witness the giant slalom. There was Peter Fuchs's dad and mum. There was me. And there were three other people whose names I couldn't catch in the gale.

'We got a super welcome. "Jolly nice of you to come," said Alan Stewart, who won the event by 0.82 of a second from Peter Fuchs, with Stuart Fitzsimmons third. "Anyone who comes up here on a day like this needs his brains testing." Mr Stewart was hardly understating the case. It was less like the Olympics than Scott's second Polar expedition. If it hadn't been for the Pernod man plying us with massive quantities of his company's plasma they'd probably find our bones up there next September.

'For a start the wind speed at the 4,084ft peak of Cairngorm was measured at 70 m.p.h. It cut through a sheepskin, two sweaters and a shirt like cold steel and picked up handfuls of jagged stones and hurled them straight into your face. Because of this the White Lady chair-lift had to be stopped. "Sorry", said Bob Clyde, who won the MBE for developing Aviemore in the Cairngorms into Britain's premier ski resort, "but if I let you use the lift you'd probably be blown out and killed."

'Put like that, we decided to walk. More importantly so did all 72 competitors in the Scottish giant slalom, girls as well as men. They simply hoiked their skis on their shoulders and clumped their way upwards, ever upwards, over 2,000ft of rocky outcrops, mountain streams, and, eventually, the sort of snow you could have sealed up in bottles and sold as glue. At the summit they had to crouch low to prevent being blown off.

'The way down through the 36 slalom gates was at least starkly defined. The piste was about as wide as two lanes of a motorway and if you came off that you were ski-ing on boulders. There were about 15 yards of snow to pull up in after the finishing line. This proved to be insufficient for Miss Anne Robb, one of our Olympic ladies, whose progress towards the valley below was eventually impeded by a bed of dead heather.

'Notable by their absence from this blue riband event of British winter sports were Herr Franz Klammer, the Olympic champion, most of Britain's ski officials, who had such a lovely time in Innsbruck, and the majority of the distinguished critics who concluded at the Olympics that our skiers were a load of rubbish. This is not a view I share.

'For one thing, Stewart, Fuchs and Fitzsimmons confirmed their selections as Britain's best by coming 1-2-3. For another, any skier who goes uphill like a Sherpa and comes down like flesh and blood being bounced over stones is not my idea of a suitable target for gratuitous calumny.

'This is hardly fair to Aviemore and the Cairngorms where, for 30 weekends of the year, upwards of 7,000 ski around in ideal conditions. On the other hand, when you've seen conditions like Sunday's you simply marvel that we finish as high as anywhere between 25th and 60th in the great Olympic events. It is as surprising as good cricketers coming out of Czechoslovakia or champion golfers emerging from the Soviet Union.

'Anyway, our three young lions are completely brassed off as being portrayed as the squares on some snowy hypotenuse. "It was really disappointing to come home and hear suggestions that we weren't really trying", said Stewart. "We've only been knocked by those who don't know what they're talking about", said Fuchs. Fitzsimmons just rolled his eyes.

'As it happens, there is an enormous row going on inside British skiing with the Scots showing disgust at the brass-hat autocracy of London, London telling the Scots to mind their own business, both London and the Scots screaming that the Press and the BBC commentary team are a bunch of ignorant hacks and everyone shrieking that it's absolutely disgusting that the British Government doesn't advance about £1 trillion to keep our skiers in a manner to which they have never been accustomed.

'It's all nonsense, really. We should all stop screaming and shrieking and realise that what we saw on the freezing upper flanks of Cairngorm on Sunday was the true spirit of the Olympic Games. It was about 72 kids going up and down a mountain on a bad day because they wanted to.'

After this wild day, all the skiers and officials were sheltering in the splendid surroundings of the Coylumbridge Hotel. George Stewart, the chairman of the British Ski Federation's Alpine Committee, was persuaded by Konrad to hold an impromptu general meeting, open to all including the journalists.

The battle between the purse-string controllers and the would-be spenders was joined. The Federation officials maintained that there was no money for the following year. The *Guardian*'s John Samuel urged them strongly to reconsider. There was no concession but at least the idea of combining the sexes for training purposes was agreed. There was a chance, at that juncture, for Konrad and Peter to suggest that Dieter might be replaced but, in the event, loyalty prevailed to a man who was, in spite of the disagreements, still their friend. The meeting dispersed without truly resolving the underlying problems.

Peter's thoughts were, in any case, diverted. He had at long last found a doctor who thought that remedial surgery could be performed on the troubling Achilles tendon and was due to go into hospital in Surrey for an operation that would rule him out of racing for at least six months.

Whilst his companion was incapacitated Konrad went, at Dieter's suggestion, to Argentina for a FIS downhill. This might not have been possible but for the cheap travel arrangements enjoyed by Bartelski senior but this was the way things were at the time.

Once in Argentina Konrad met up with some young Americans and, so he notes, 'found out what real training was all about.' By the time of the race he was feeling extremely fit but sadly he fell whilst flying along. Not too dismayed, he made his way back to the team which was based at Hintertux and there the stark contrast between the ebullience of the young Americans he had just left and the apparent deadness of his team mates struck Konrad forcefully. It seemed to him that Dieter was uninterested in his Argentinian experience and that, in fact, the returning traveller was not really welcome in the group.

Konrad retreated to his parents' new Alpine residence which they had built only a hundred yards from Dieter's home. A week later he rejoined the squad and immediately fell into a bitter disagreement with the trainer who, in bluntly ending the discussion, used some extreme language. It felt to Konrad as though a friendship had turned into a master-slave relationship. With Peter in Scotland recovering from his operation and Willy gone, Konrad felt very much alone. He persisted with the training for a few days then left for Scotland, needing desperately to talk to his ski friend.

He writes enthusiastically of the reception given to him at Struan and less so of the prospect which faced the two of them, of fitness training at Meadowbank in Edinburgh. On the drive down, a sheep attempted self-sacrifice in front of Peter's Lotus. The animal survived but the car's sump did not because a roadside rock took the main force of deceleration. Luckily Lisi was following and she took the two racers to the nearest garage but the duo were still three hours late. According to Konrad's account, Dieter greeted them sarcastically. He made no enquiries about Peter's operation; they were off to the worst possible start.

Konrad was so concerned about the deterioration in morale that he called the general secretary of the British Ski Federation to report. He was advised simply to get on with the training programme. The pair of them did so but with increasingly bad grace. There were arguments and episodes of open verbal abuse. All the joy had gone from the skiing lives of the two remaining Musketeers.

Nevertheless, the business had to go on and Peter was pleased, at least, that he had recovered sufficiently to begin snow training in Kaprun. He wrote home in November 1976 reporting; 'I did my first slalom courses today and considering everything they were quite good. The rest of the team are skiing pretty badly. I'll make my own travel arrangements home but I'll ring you up the night before so you can meet me in Inverness...'

Peter spent the Christmas holiday period back at Struan whilst Konrad faced the problems of mixing socially with Dieter and his family. In fact, relations were amicable, so much so that Konrad was mightily surprised when, for the first race of the season, Dieter broke a promise. Instead of being with the men's team, he went to the women. Konrad managed to finish but, due to a mistake which he attributes to emotional exhaustion, his time was poor. In despair he poured his heart out to the faithful John Samuel who, with Konrad's blessing, aired the troubles of the ski team in the next day's *Guardian*.

The authorities were not amused. The deputy trainer, Conni Ruprechter, who was looking after the men in Dieter's absence, told Konrad that he must ski in the next Europa Cup race in France. Fired with rebellious spirit, the dissident went instead to Kitzbuhel to have another attempt at the notorious Hahnenkamm. He knew that this was a risky move, given his poor form, and what he describes as a near nervous breakdown, but he needed to escape for a few days. The price he paid was a threat, from the Federation, of a two week suspension.

Angry telephone calls with Dieter eventually removed the injunction on the proviso that Konrad would take part in the next Europa Cup race in San Sicario under the guidance of a former Austrian coach called Sigi Bernegger. This was no penalty in Konrad's eyes and, although he was in no fit state to do well in the Hahnenkamm, he survived the course and then achieved a very creditable tenth place in the San Sicario race.

He found Sigi to be a coach to his great liking. Confidence came back and when Dieter unexpectedly agreed that Konrad could participate in the Canadian championships at Lake Louise, Britian's leading skier began to feel happy for the first time in months.

Then, inexplicably from Konrad's viewpoint, Dieter changed his mind. There was an explosion of abuse. In an attempt to make peace, Konrad's father went to see the trainer who claimed that Konrad was a disrespectful maverick. Mr. Bartelski mentioned the apparent mishandling of Willy Bailey's career and asked why Dieter had not been more supportive when his son and Peter had been recovering from serious injuries. No peace formula emerged from this initiative and Konrad then felt that he had no option but to write a detailed letter to the Federation. Acting properly, he sent a copy of the screed to Dieter.

The immediate result was no response from the officials and a 'sending to Coventry' by the trainers. Because Mr. Bartelski Senior had ended his conversation with Dieter on such bad terms, his wife offered to go to London to talk to Major-General Graeme, the Federation's secretary. The luminary was not in a conciliatory mood. He told Konrad's mother that the boy was 'bad' and that he had done poorly in South America because he had spent all his time womanising.

With rancour in his heart, Konrad had to attend the pre-season briefing for the team and trainers conducted by General Graeme. By this time Dieter was communicating, but coldly. Konrad voiced his case for improvement but, to his dismay, team members who had supported him privately failed to add their weight in public.

With this uneasy background, the 1977 season began.

Hoping that the surgery would give him a trouble-free year, Peter threw himself into the British Championships which were held that year in Val d'Isere. Konrad had pipped him twice for the top national honour and he desperately wanted to have his turn. Skiing better than he had for some time, Peter blazed his way to the championship. The *Press and Journal* rejoiced.

'The popular champion - he was runner up last year - had an overall time of 61.63 seconds. The margin might have been greater had he not skied into fifth place on the first slalom course, having lost time at a couple of gates where poles had previously been knocked away, but he still completed the course with speed and style.'

Soon afterwards Peter also won the Lowlander title. Prospects would have been good if only the leg had stood up to the pressure but gradually the pain increased until it was back to its former level. The surgery, as Eileen recalls with a shudder, had left a scar which, under the pressure of ski boots, refused to heal. The repaired tendon was partially exposed. Skiing was an excruciatingly painful business, even when special boots were made.

The ensuing season was a poor one for both of the main racers. There was never a time when Peter felt able to ski uninhibitedly and Konrad was beginning to experience problems of his own. There were worrying pains behind his left eye. It was impossible to decide whether these were caused by stress or whether they were a belated consequence of his terrible fall. By the exacting standards they had set themselves they were falling far short.

To compound their problems, there were renewed financial difficulties. Federation officials suddenly announced that unless the skiers themselves contributed to the costs of the team, their participation would have to be curtailed. Humiliatingly, the Britons missed the last races and went home with morale at a very low ebb.

Konrad decided to seek a meeting with the Ski Federation to give them a plain-speaking account of his views. He wanted to let the organisation know, without ambiguity, about his dissatisfaction with Dieter. He wrote the crucial letter and was offered a meeting with a specially convened committee.

The disaffected young man made his appointment with the neurologist for a date in April immediately after the Scottish championships and suggested to the Federation that their meeting should also be after this event. By coincidence, the Federation chose the same date for the meeting as Konrad's eye consultation. Neither of these dates could, it seemed, be changed. The clash served only to increase the pressure.

The Scottish championships were held on Cairngorm. Although small beer by the world measure, Konrad wanted to use the event as an opportunity to show that he was still the fastest Briton. An optimum result would be a timely reminder to the Federation.

Struggling even more than usual as the season drew to a close, Peter overcame the pain from his Achilles tendon to out-ski his friend and rival in the giant slalom. Sadly, the tighter turns of the slalom were too much for his exposed tendon but Konrad beat the field. Stuart Fitzsimmons was absent because of injury but obviously Konrad could do nothing about this. At a crucial time he had proved his point; he was the most accomplished British skier of all.

The meeting, a long one which had to be adjourned for the consulation with the neurologist, ranged over all the issues. Konrad felt that his views were heard with respect, even when he was expressing strong reservations about Dieter. One option which emerged was that Konrad should leave the team but continue to ski under a British licence. The drawback with this, from the aggrieved skier's point of view, was that the younger members of the team would continue to suffer what he regarded as less than satisfactory service.

On the next day, Konrad was called once more to the Federation offices, this time to see George Stewart, the Chairman of the Alpine Committee. This he found surprising because this was the father of Alan, whom Konrad had just beaten in the Scottish Championships. Had the meeting been a benign one, there would doubtless have been no question of a conflict of interest but it quickly emerged that there was nothing pleasant about what was taking place. To his astonishment and horror, Konrad learned that he was being sacked.

Bemused and angry, Konrad emerged onto the London streets. It was only when he had been walking furiously for a while that he realised; the persistent pain behind his eye had completely vanished.

In the *Guardian* of April 28th 1977, John Samuel gave the story of Konrad's dismissal publicity.

'Konrad Bartelski, Britain's leading downhill skier, has been dismissed from the national team by the National Ski Federation.

'The Alpine controller, Major General Ian Graeme, has written to

Bartelski saying: "You made it very clear to me that you were not prepared to be a co-operative member of the British team. In making plans for 1977-8 Dieter Bartsch (the British training director) and I have agreed that you should not be a member of the British Alpine team."

'Bartelski, aged 22, wrote to the National Federation in February criticising Bartsch and his assistant with the men's team, Conni Ruprecheter. Bartelski said yesterday: "I pointed out that Conni lacked experience for World Cup racing. I also felt that the men's team did not have enough support at Garmisch for the World Cup races, which were also important preliminaries for next year's world championships. When you are risking your neck in a world downhill you have to have complete confidence in your training set-up. General Graeme had earlier asked us to make our suggestions whenever we felt strongly and I took him at his word."

'Bartelski, whose mother is English and father, a KLM pilot, is Polish, was educated in Holland and now lives with his parents near Bartsch's new home at Zell-an-Zee in Austria. "It seems a complex background but I have always raced for England and feel strongly that as an Englishman I want to prove we can do as well in the Alps as the Austrians and the Swiss", he said. "I am most upset at being dropped, although I realise my criticisms were tough. With the biggest team, best organisation and equipment we have had since the war, this season's results are the worst since 1973. Obviously something must be wrong and I believe it is our training.

"For the first two or three years after Dieter took us over he did an excellent job in building up to the level of fitness where we could start to make a challenge. I was 15th in the 1974 World championships and Peter Fuchs was 19th.

"We have been unlucky with injuries since then. I had a bad fall at Megeve in 1975, but I do not believe, as some do, that it finished me. The reason why I did so badly in the 1976 Olympics was a knee bone operation which prevented any serious racing in the run-up. I also believe our training was going wrong at that point and experiences with the Canadian and other teams convinced me we have much to learn still.

"Dropping me from the team is bad enough, and in my view unjustified, but they have also denied me a start licence. It means I am forced to race for another country, which will exclude me from the Olympics. I have sacrificed almost everything for racing for five years, including university and a career."

'Bartelski is the only British skier rated among the top 100 in the world. This year his best performances were 26th in the World Cup at Laax, eighth at Cervinia and 10th at San Sicario. His downhill points, at 19, are easily the best of any Briton and he has also halved his slalom points.

'General Graeme said last night: "Konrad was not prepared to be a team member in the way we think necessary. He wanted too many of the resources for himself. We cannot issue him with a start licence in case he turns up at a World Cup race and takes one of the British quota which we want for a team member."

'Asked why no formal announcement had been made, General Graeme said the Alpine committee chairman, George Stewart, had decided it would not be necessary. It is likely, however, that some Scottish and Welsh critics of the national team set up will raise this and related subjects at the Federation Council meeting next month. For example, Ralph Jones, president of the Welsh Ski Council, believes that the federation should not encourage full-time racing without offering career or education security.'

Deprived of his livelihood, Konrad turned to the Dutch who welcomed him into their team even though they were unable to offer financial assistance. A ski equipment manufacturer, Salomon, came to the immediate rescue. Having to survive on very little, the new Netherlander called on the services of one whom he calls 'one of the world's great masters' of penny-pinching, his friend Peter. Though feeling desperately sad and disorientated by the turn of events, Peter did what he could to assist.

Konrad devised his own training schedule, one that he would enjoy and which would not leave him completely drained of energy as Dieter's had done. Using the cheap travel afforded by his father, and the mean money management skills taught by Peter, he went once more to

Argentina and lived frugually in a room in a private house. Nevertheless, Argentina's uncontrollable rate of inflation played havoc with personal finances and Konrad was compelled to sell some of his skis in order to survive.

Peter, still struggling with his injury, continued to hope that a peace formula would be found but when it became clear that Konrad was not going to be welcomed back he wrote to the Federation, explaining that he, too, could not ski under Dieter's management.

A correspondence developed, largely conducted from the Fuchs' side by Eileen. She was certain that the overt reason for Konrad's dismissal, that he was 'too keen on the girls', was a pathetic ploy. That autumn, on a holiday in Austria, she spent a substantial part of the time writing letters to everyone of influence in the matter. In her opinion, as in that of many others, George Stewart had had a clear and intolerable conflict of interest. As the correspondence developed it seemed to Eileen that she was experiencing similar treatment to that reported by Konrad. Mysteriously, crucial letters were allegedly not received.

John Samuel chronicled the events in *The Guardian*. He told of Peter's support and provided some detail of the eight point letter to the National Federation. Samuel continues:

'Fuchs refutes that Bartelski was unpopular with the majority of the team or that morale was threatened to the extent that he had to be sacked. He has asked for a licence to race independently, and this was due to be considered by the Alpine Committee in October. His letter said, "All I am asking for myself is an open start licence and the right to start where my FIS points justify me. If these are equal to or better than team members I think it would be reasonable to expect to be allowed to compete in the World Championships at Garmisch."

'The Carrbridge racer, 19th in the 1974 World Championship downhill, summing up his case, says: "I can see no real possibility of improvement in British ski racing if there are not radical changes in the near future. These would need to include a much improved and better thought out training programme, remembering that Great Britain has a completely different attitude to skiing to that of the major skiing nations.

"It is vital that our country stops internal bickering and each team member feels 'British' and that there is an end to personal grants, so that any funds can be given solely on merit and conversely that no-one can buy his or her way into the team. There are many young and promising skiers who may not be as lucky as someone being able to afford it, or find sponsors to do so." '

Using their considerable credit balance of power and influence, Karl and Eileen arranged a meeting with General Graeme. Eileen drew upon her rusty civil servant negotiating skills to present their case but the soldier was, in Eileen's word, 'impassive'.

Feeling helpless against the weight of bureaucracy and certain that he could not continue with Dieter, Peter reiterated his request for an independent licence. The response was that he should write yet again, with more detail, of the reasons for his decision and with a detailed programme of his summer training schedule. With great reluctance, but still wanting to find a way towards peace, Peter produced the document and, for safety's sake, delivered it by hand to the office of the Federation.

The organisation was housed in prime accommodation in London's Eaton Square. Peter was reminded of the time that he and the other young racers, on their way to the Alps and dressed in clothes suitable for travel, had been refused entry on the grounds that they were improperly attired. The contrast between the frugality of their lives and the opulence of the building had been upsetting and the memory of that did little to improve his mood. He pushed the envelope through the letter box with a shudder.

The Federation officials claimed, subsequently, that the document had never been received. For Peter this was the ultimate frustration.

The Fuchs family were furious. They were sure that Peter could not back down. If nothing else, loyalty to Konrad determined this. Long and difficult were the debates at Struan. It seemed absurd that matters could have reached a point where resignation seemed to be the only honourable option. Peter's entire focus was on ski racing. Without the Federation's endorsement the only events he would be eligible to enter would be the Scottish ones; small beer indeed after the glamour of the World Cup.

Every aspect was explored, every stratagem considered but in the end there was no escape. With a heavy heart, and feeling thoroughly victimised, Peter tendered his resignation from the team.

## 32. Fight

It might be felt that Peter's sacrifice in resigning in support of Konrad was a light one. His tendon was showing no signs of healing properly and it could be suggested that the honourable retreat might be a welcome release. In fact it was quite otherwise. Peter was still young, he was reigning British and Lowlander ski champion. The injury might have limited his scope in slalom but he could have looked forward to a few more exciting years in the downhill events. Far from being an easy way out, the resignation was a hard step which Peter took with a heavy heart.

But the fight was by no means over. The Fuchs camp felt that if Peter's noble action received the right kind of publicity, the Federation might be nudged towards a compromise. Karl and Eileen went to see John Samuel. He had become something of a friend but he was still very much the objective journalist. The September the 10th issue of *The Guardian* told all the sorry saga of Konrad's sacking and Peter's supportive sacrifice.

Central to the row was the allegation that the Federation, by insisting on contributions from individual skiers, was allowing people to buy into the team. George Stewart is quoted as saying, 'In the circumstances of our not having enough money we thought it not only necessary but entirely reasonable to call on racers for a contribution. Of the current team members only Peter Fuchs has not made a contribution.' At the end of a long, discursive piece Samuel's balanced conclusion was that not all of the criticism of the Federation could be ill-based.

Other newspapers gave the story of Peter's resignation a goodly number of column inches. *The Scotsman* of October the 5th featured the story prominently, as did the *Press and Journal*. The local newspaper article gave all the political detail and quoted the main players before revealing that Peter would be spending some of his freshly acquired spare time gaining ski instructor qualifications. The writer quoted Lewis Grant, the Scottish races convenor, as much regretting Peter's departure and saying that, 'Fuchs has been the best to come out of Scotland'.

The coverage was gratifying but the effect on the Ski Federation was negligible. When sufficient time for a reaction had elapsed, John Samuel wrote once again, on the 28th of October.

Samuel summarises the troubles between the skiers and the Federation and regrets that so much was kept under cover. This, it is suggested, hurt Dieter as much as it did the others. Dieter is cited as saying that several of Peter's complaints were justified but that it is not true that his injuries were ignored. He said, 'You know what difficulties we had in getting him to a doctor over his Achilles tendon trouble. And there were other things. But Peter has finished as a champion, which is no bad way to finish.' In the same article, Alan Stewart claims that team spirit was much better without the two disaffected members.

The 1978 season began. Ahead was the major event of the World Championship which, four years earlier, had provided Konrad and Peter with such encouraging results. Needing more than the Dutch could provide, Konrad persuaded the Austrian coach to allow him to train at Hintertux and, existing frugally in a cheap bed-and-breakfast establishment, the exile practised.

As the first races loomed, Konrad realised that he needed a coach. The Austrians had been very kind but they could not treat him as a full member of their entourage. Naturally, the Musketeer-turned-lone-ranger appealed to Peter who responded gladly, agreeing to donate his services until such time as he had to join the BASI teachers' course. The two of them worked hard, trying to achieve a reasonable race standard.

Despite problems with ski preparation, which resulted from not having proper back-up, Konrad performed creditably in the early season programme and began to look forward to the first World Cup event at Val d'Isère. A switch of ski manufacturer, and another bungled piece of preparation by an 'on loan' technician, led to a very poor result. Two of the official British team finished ahead of Konrad, a fact which was not pleasing under the circumstances.

Peter did his best to keep his friend's morale high but he was also under pressure. Karl and Eileen worked hard to keep their son's racing plight in the public eye and used, amongst other resources, the local papers to make their views known. One of them printed an article by Steve James based on an interview with Eileen. In part the jounrnalist wrote;

'Scottish ski star Peter Fuchs, dropped from the British team earlier in the year, is now claiming the National Ski Federation of Great Britain are preventing him from taking part in races - anywhere in Europe. He says their refusal to grant him an individual start licence - needed to compete in Europe and World Cup events - will prevent him from defending the Lowlands Championship, which he was the first Briton to win last year. Fuchs (22), Carrbridge, who along with former British ski captain, Konrad Bartelski, achieved higher world ratings than any previous countrymen, withdrew from the team after Bartelski was sacked. He also criticised the organisation of the London-based national federation, accused them of anti-Scottish bias and alleged team members had to pay £500 to 'buy their way in'. The allegations were denied by the National Ski Federation.

'Now Fuchs, believed by many to be the finest skier this country has yet produced, is kicking his heels in the Alps and helping his friend Bartelski to train for this year's World Cup series. This weekend, he has been at Val d'Isere, France. His mother, Mrs Eileen Fuchs, said yesterday her son had hoped to spend the winter on the Continent building up International Ski Federation points after injury, to enable him to get into European competition. But he was 'caught in a vicious circle', as he cannot compete without the start licence, and he cannot get the licence because of the British Federation's refusal. Mrs Fuchs said: "We will fight this until the Ski Federation admit they were wrong. They owe all of us an apology." '

For Peter, the non-racing life in the Alps was less than satisfying. It was frustrating to be amidst the circuit clamour yet to be excluded from the glamour of competing. The start of the BASI course brought honourable release. Vowing that he would continue to battle for his own reinstatement, Peter left Konrad to his own devices.

In the first race after Peter left, a World Cup event at Val Gardena, Konrad provided a vindication of the work they had been doing together by finishing sixteenth, the highest ever placing by a British skier. The 'official' British were a satisfyingly long way behind. Fate then brought Konrad together with a young freelance journalist called Mark Amis who, though almost devoid of ski racing experience, was keen and quick to learn. He agreed to become Konrad's 'assistant' and the lone ranger was no longer alone.

The World Championships were scheduled for early February. Whilst Peter spent his time learning to be a teacher rather than training hard for the event, a local paper poignantly speculated about Britain's prospects without its two stars. Alan Thompson wrote;

'Peter Fuchs, the 22-year-old British ski champion, has a diversion for a grey day on Cairngorm. He steers his Vielhaber skis over the Fiacaill Ridge cornice, takes a momentary hang-glider view of the Spey Valley and touches down on the snow-field 20ft down below. The elegant apparition then shrinks rapidly down the face towards the sliding dots in Coire Cas.

'Fuchs needs the stimulation. As the British team prepares for the start of the World Championship at Garmisch, West Germany, he is out in the cold, his racing career apparently at an end.

'For more than five years Fuchs, the son of an Austrian father and English mother with a hotel and ski school at Carrbridge, near Aviemore, has raced the pistes of Cortina, Val d'Isere and Kitzbuhel for Britain, excelling in downhill, a 70-m.p.h plus activity where mere reflexes and a skin-tight suit separate the competitor from what can easily become a fatal sequence of impacts. A badly broken kneecap and prolonged trouble with the scar of a tendon injury are his trophies of the chase.'

The article, after noting the then unusual fact that Peter wore a ring in his ear, goes on to explain how he requested an individual licence, was asked to provide an account of his training, how he hand-delivered the requested item and how the Federation claimed that it had never arrived. Eileen is quoted as saying, 'He lives for racing and his skiing life is now virtually smashed.' The newspaper piece continues;

'But in London yesterday Mr George Stewart, chairman of the Alpine Racing Committee and father of 22-year-old Alan Stewart, Britain's best all-round skier for the past eight years, said; "The door is still open for Peter Fuchs, I deeply regret what has happened. The tragedy is that we have no indication of Peter's training plans and so the matter must lie in abeyance. If he presents details of his racing intentions in the future, an individual licence would be seriously considered. I strongly deny that the licence has so far been refused." '

Alan Thompson observes that with Alan Stewart suffering from a severe rheumatic condition and unlikely to be a serious contender, the only remaining British challenger to the European giants was Stuart Fitzsimmons. He had been skiing well and had managed to reduce his FIS points to twenty four. The paper pointed out, however, that Konrad in the Dutch team was down to sixteen points and was clearly the leading Briton.

Thompson goes on to suggest that a disturbing sidelight is that Konrad, according to his friends, was likely to take suicidal risks in order to prove that he was better than anyone in the British squad. He goes on to say that; 'The irony is that their break from the team stems from a personality clash with a trainer who first taught at the Fuchs's ski school and was initially their private racing coach before being engaged by the Ski Federation.' Eileen is quoted once more; 'It is an awkward situation. We were close friends and often visited Dieter here and in Austria. It is sad we cannot all shake hands and get over this dreadful situation.'

It was difficult for Konrad to part with his amanuensis when Peter arrived, after his course had finished, to resume as coach for the World Alpine Championship races at Garmisch. Mark Amis had proved to be invaluable. Happily, his reputation in the ski world was by this time so high that the Canadian team promptly snapped him up.

With a clear conscience on Mark's fate, Konrad welcomed Peter. His ski morale was immediately boosted by the presence of someone who understood him, and the business of racing, better than anyone. As the big day approached they both had dreams of great glory. It would take luck as well as ability to win that coveted place on the podium but there was a secondary prize in the offing. If Konrad could not win a medal he would be mightily content if he showed the 'official British' that he was still the master.

In spite of having minimal technical backing and of having to cope with all the multiple pressures of his circumstances, Konrad hurtled to seventeenth place, beating dozens of the world's best skiers. It was an astonishing performance. The first of the approved British, Alan Stewart, was fifteen places behind. The rest were nowhere. The British had better showings in the combined results, with Alan Stewart seventh and Stuart Fitzsimmons ninth, but ski racing had become so specialised that few of the leading sportsmen aspired to be expert at both downhill and slalom.

Perhaps Konrad's demonstration of superiority acted as a catalyst for very soon after his brave showing the Federation's Alpine ski racing controller, Richard Berry, dramatically announced his resignation. Even more astonishingly, he cited dissatisfaction with Dieter's style of management as the reason. In February 7th's *Guardian*, John Samuel announced the shocking news, saying that Berry had come out in strong support of Konrad. Berry is quoted as believing that the Federation was willing to sacrifice anyone to ensure the continuation of Dieter as technical director. He said, 'Working first hand here at the world championships I can see the reasons why Bartelski and Fuchs rebelled. He doesn't want my experience and co-operation in rules and committee matters, though I have been a member of the International Ski Federation classifications committee since 1975 and will soon join the rules committee.'

Samuel suggests that the problems on the snow were just indicators of the underlying difficulties at the Federation. It was, he says, 'dragged into being' when the Ski Club of Great Britain gave up its responsibility for racing. He says that a few strong personalities have kept it going but that it has not been a good idea for the parents of skiers to be so closely involved.

A week or so later, John Samuel wrote another pertinent piece following a Press Conference called by the Federation. He explains that the Federation had announced an inquiry into the 'disappointing' results of the British team at Garmisch. Nonetheless, the officials were still not repentant. The chairman, Sir Richard Seligman, claimed that Berry's resignation came about because 'he just did not click with the team.' However, the good knight agreed that, 'when you start regretting your results and physical fitness, you have to consider very carefully what you do.'

From the pen of Ed Rattray, the *Press and Journal* of February the 23rd 1978 also provided its readers with an account of the latest developments under the telling headline; 'Scottish ski officials increasingly concerned over management methods.' The writer makes the additional, bitter point that Scottish newspapers had to fight for entry to the press conference at which Peter Seligman expounded his views on the Berry resignation. Focusing on the Scottish aspects of the affair, Rattray writes; 'While Scotland provides half the members of the unisex British team, and an increasing number of Espoir, or B squad trainees, many Scots officials feel that the national federation are totally Alpine oriented and pay little heed to the Scottish voice'.

Home again, and fired with enthusiasm after Konrad's success, Peter entered one of the few races that were still available to him, the East of Scotland Championships held in the middle of February. Berry's high profile resignation, and the growing criticism of Dieter's style of management, suggested that hope of reinstatement to the team was not misplaced. A good result at home might concentrate the wavering minds of the administrators.

Stuart Fitzsimmons was amongst the starters. Peter knew that his own recent lack of racing experience would put him at a severe disadvantage against someone who had just been competing against the best in the world but anyone who knew the racing scene at all would recognise this handicap and make due allowance.

He got, as the Scottish papers recorded, a dream start in the slalom. In the first run he was ahead of the field. Sadly, though predictably, he was just out-skied by Stuart Fitzsimmons on the second course and in the giant slalom but the overall result was extremely close. The newspaper headline which said, 'Fuchs finishes runner-up' was by no means dissatisfying.

The next event for which Peter was eligible was the North of Scotland championships which took place on Cairngorm. The competition was not of the highest quality but clearly there was nothing Peter could do about that. The important point was that Ben Watson, who was designated to take over as Secretary of the British Ski Federation following the resignation of Ian Graeme due to illness, was due to be a spectator.

Conditions for the races were appalling with rain, wet snow and thick mist. Peter's margin in the slalom was only half a second but in the giant version he was a clear one and a half seconds ahead of his nearest rival. The *Scotsman* of February the 27th carried the headline, 'Peter Fuchs wins both ski events'. It was an emphatic victory.

Just over a week later, the British ski world was turned, astonishingly for the rebels, upside down. *The Guardian* of the 9th March revealed the amazing news. 'Bartsch is retired,' cried the headline, a touch ambiguously. *Is* retired? Alan Thomson in *The Observer* of the 12th of March offered his analysis of the scene.

'Despite some confidence, not widely held, that British racers would make enough impact in Europe this season to firmly bury the controversial departure of Konrad Bartelski and Peter Fuchs from the national squad, results on the ski circuit in general and the world championships in particular confirm suspicions that much of the cream was ditched with the sour milk.

'Acrimony between Bartelski the Unruly and technical director Dieter Bartsch left the Alpine Race Committee with what they apparently felt was no alternative. Bartelski had to go. Unfortunately, the equally talented downhiller Peter Fuchs elected, in disgust, to depart with him. The outcome was painfully clear. Konrad would race in future for the Dutch and Peter subside quietly into his parents' ski school on Cairngorm.

'At least, that was the picture until earlier last week.

'A diplomatic communiqué from the National Ski Federation announcing the departure after six years of Dieter Bartsch from team management, in April, may have changed all that. Despite the proliferation of plastic boots in skiing, fear of toe-treading is pervasive. The Press were told simply that because the Federation feels it cannot raise the money to match Bartsch's plans for the 1980 Olympic build-up,'it had been mutually agreed' that he should retire. Dieter, of course, becomes an honorary life member of the NSF, an award 'that has been given to very few'.

After some speculation as to who might replace Dieter and Richard Berry the piece goes on;

'Ultimately, though, all the talent available in Britain is vital. The lack of in-depth ability is glaring. Bartelski's downhill performance in the world championships make it imperative that he is called in for the 1980 Olympics. Peter Fuchs told me, "I think the past could be forgotten. I know Konrad would be happy to race for Britain again, and in the circumstances, so would I."

'If that happened, a cynic might be excused for thinking that after all it was the British Ski Federation which departed, not Bartelski and Fuchs.'

All at once the prospect of reinstatement was available. Peter's appetite for competition was not diminished. Although it was something of a sideline, he entered the Scottish amateur freestyle championships, held on Cairngorm on the 13th of March, and won. More seriously for his racing career he took the West of Scotland Championship on the 20th of March to add to his 'North' title. He was well set to compete in the British Championships which, once again, were to be held on Cairngorm. An outstanding result in these would send an unavoidable message to the new rulers of the Ski Federation. It was sad that Konrad, the exiled 'Dutchman', had decided not to enter but there would be plenty of fierce competition. John Samuel previewed the event in *The Guardian.*

After noting how Scottish skiing had come of age, with a German world champion and a silver medalist amongst the female competitors, Samuel goes on to suggest that the outstanding interest would be to see whether or not Peter would beat of the challenge of the official team members. The reporter notes that Peter had had an outstanding domestic season, even though the main rivals were present for only one of the events. Samuel specifically suggests that Dieter's departure could pave the way for Peter's return and notes that many were sorry that Konrad had chosen not to compete.

The stage seemed to be set for Peter to surge back into the national team. It seemed that, allowing for the anticipated diplomatic noises designed to keep egos intact, he and Konrad had been entirely vindicated. A brilliant performance from Peter in the national championships would surely make a return inevitable but even with a failure, which can happen to the very best of skiers, the future looked assured.

But in fact, something very odd happened. As it turned out, Peter, perhaps feeling that he had too much resting on the result and trying too hard, failed to finish in either of the disciplines. It might be thought that, after all the pre-race prognostication, the reports would have referred to a minor setback in a resurrected career yet John Samuel's final word on Peter's ski racing career was;'There were two hard luck stories. One, relatively minor, was Peter Fuchs losing a ski on the first run with no apparent cause'. The other 'hard luck' story related to an accident involving one of the official cars.

*The Scotsman* went further. Their reporter wrote; 'Peter Fuchs, now ending his international racing career, was expected to push for results but crashed out of both races.'

Maybe the fact that his thoughts that season had been on gaining ski teaching qualifications had detracted from his competitive hunger; maybe the realisation had dawned that the torn Achilles tendon would never heal; maybe Peter could see that Struan, and his increasingly infirm father, needed him. Whatever the causes, it seemed that Peter's entire outlook shifted after those few days of Cairngorm racing. From being 'resigned' he became 'retired', like Dieter.

One oddness was that, after the Championships, the men's and women's teams provided Dieter with a farewell dinner. The erstwhile friend who had become almost an enemy was being feted in Peter's home territory. John Samuel wrote;'Whatever the ups and downs of his relationship with Konrad Bartelski and Peter Fuchs, Bartsch has done a tremendous job for British skiing in the past four years. He is an outstanding trainer and his main problem was in taking on too many varieties of jobs, as the Ski Federation now seem to be acknowledging.'

For Peter, the analysis was irrelevant. He had had his racing time, with its triumphs and frustrations but now he was moving on, starting a new phase of his life.

For Konrad, the case was entirely different. He had no immediate plans to settle. He decided to continue.

This might have been the time for an immediate rapprochement but, alas, the Federation officials were unwilling to concede readily to the reasoned arguments put by Konrad's father. Instead it was decided that the prodigal son should prove himself for another year before being admitted back into the fold. The result was that the last of the Three Musketeers spent the 1979 season still out in the cold.

Konrad records that the 'proving' year was a disappointing one for him, in spite of the renewed support of Mark Amis. The final disappointment came when the last race of the season in Canada, which they had made huge financial sacrifices to attend, was cancelled because of poor weather.

The 1980 season was Olympic time again. Restored to the team, and with Conni Ruprechter as trainer, Konrad began again. In his autobiography he reveals the surprising information that it was only at this stage of his career that he realised that winning high quality races was impossible without having precisely the appropriate skis.

To the uninitiated a ski is just a ski but there are many variables. Intermediates in the sport cheerfully accept whatever equipment the hire company hands out without stopping to consider whether the skis are, for example, of appropriate stiffness for their weight. On a once a year holiday the damage is not great. The person with inappropriate equipment might wonder why their skiing has deteriorated, or why others seem to find turning on moguls easier than they do, but mostly they will put all the 'blame' onto themselves. In the extreme business of professional racing, where fractions of a second separate the winners from the losers, this is not a healthy approach. The equipment has to be tailored precisely to the individual and to the prevailing circumstances.

Konrad undertook extensive testing and selection of skis prior to the Lake Placid Olympics and, partly as a consequence of that, finished twelfth in the Downhill, by far the best result ever achieved by a Briton in that competition, beating Jeremy Palmer-Tomkinson's excellent 1968 result by thirteen places.

Naturally Peter followed all of Konrad's doings, missing the 'buzz' himself but acquiring some of it vicariously. He was delighted on his friend's behalf when, during the northern hemisphere summer, Konrad scorched down a track in New Zealand to beat their close friend Ken Read who had already won two major races. The victory proved that they had not been fooling themselves during the years of struggle. With the right combination of circumstances any one of the Three Musketeers could have been standing proudly on the rostrum under a fluttering British flag.

With the New Zealand boost to his morale, Konrad had expectations of finally making his mark in the 'proper' racing but in the first of the new northern hemisphere season's events at Val d'Isère he achieved a miserable sixty-first position. With confidence suddenly back at its lowest point, and with his head full of a distressing cold, Konrad moved onto a World Cup race at Val Gardena.

His mind was hardly focused on the racing. In Poland there was civil unrest and many of his relatives were under threat. His beloved ski racing was all at once put into a different context. As always, he would do his best but with his head physically and mentally afflicted it would be gratifying just to post a reasonable time.

Perhaps because of this distraction he skied fluently. When the last runner had come down, when the times were put in the proper order it was revealed that Konrad had missed the gold medal position by eleven hundredths of a second.

It would have been easy to sour the moment by thinking of the thousands of ways in which that tiny margin might have been saved, a tighter line here, a lower tuck there, a fraction less edging, but this would have been to miss the point entirely. What had happened was that one of the once discounted Britons, one of the unfancied, under-budgetted, amateur-seeming Three Musketeers had achieved what they set out to do. An outright win would have been marvellous but those tiny fragments of time were an irrelevance. What Konrad had done was prove that a Briton could take on the best of the skiing world and beat them. At last he was, as they had dreamed, standing on the podium whilst, above his head, the flag of Britain fluttered.

## 33. Succession

Lisi's rapid transition from single woman to wife and mother took Karl and Eileen just as much by surprise as it did everyone else but they had always allowed their children freedom. They respected their daughter's decision and were utterly delighted by the swift appearance of grandchildren.

Equally they accepted without demur Peter's resolution to retire from racing. It was intensely disappointing, not because of the loss of reflected glory but because their son had been deprived of what he most wanted at that time. It was particularly frustrating that his decision had been partly caused by bureaucratic muddle. It would have been so much more satisfying had Peter been allowed to come unhindered to the end of this particular road.

But there were strong compensations for Karl and Eileen in Peter's move. For a long time they had nurtured the hope that one day either of their children or both would take over the running of Struan. Lisi's marriage, and an apparent and understandable determination to plough an independent furrow, had taken her out of consideration but Peter seemed to be moving towards the idea that his best future lay with the business.

The timing was good. The two founders had been working extremely hard for well over twenty years. Because they had started relatively late in life, the matter of age was becoming a factor. This was particularly so with Karl, whose health was not of the best. Tasks which once had seemed light assumed a different aspect when muscles were tired and bones weary. It would be excellent to spend a few years gradually shedding responsibility and watching their son commit his considerable energies to the development of the enterprise they had created. There would be problems, as ever, with the unpredictability of the Cairngorm weather and the vagaries of valley politics but, compared to the near void which had greeted them in 1954, there was a very solid foundation on which their son could build.

As far as the climate was concerned, Karl had already taken steps to mitigate the effects of wild weather. For years he had talked, often to the bemusement of partially-comprehending visitors, about building a plastic slope at the bottom of the garden. Given that the ground was uniformly flat this would obviously involve earth-moving and the building of structures. It would not be a simple matter but complexity and potential difficulty had never stopped Karl.

One early summer a bulldozer had roared its way to the bottom of the Struan garden and begun to create Karl's artificial hill. For the source of the material down which people would tentatively slither, Karl turned to one of his illustrious former instructors, John Shedden. The trunks of displaced trees were fashioned into huge tables and benches.

Thereafter, nobody had to leave Struan without the experience of trying out skiing no matter how foul was the weather on the hill or how sparse the snow cover. In practice, the artificial slope became more of a very useful créche facility than a poor weather fall-back. Young children could be left behind by grateful parents in the knowledge that they would be entirely safe and that they would be receiving instruction just as good as they would have done in the cold and mist above Coire na Ciste. Dez Barnes, who had long ago graduated from being the Struan barman to Ski School Manager, was for a while the acknowledged genius of the plastic slope. Like all good parent-figures, he was a benign disciplinarian. Children trusted him and they had extraordinary fun. At the bottom of the Struan garden, close to the encroaching forest, they played ski games on Karl's stretch of man-made slope and great and frequent were the gusts of happy laughter coming from that magic quarter.

An incidental benefit of all the earth moving was the creation of a tennis court which also became a great asset. Quite soon, some summer guests were coming specifically to play the game. Both the court and the plastic slope were, as Eileen records 'on the go all summer.' She recalls that, as always, 'the staff would join in with everything including some part of the ski team's summer training and many were the times when they would compete in swimming to the island in Loch Vaa.'

Peter had these significant assets on which to draw but also, in comparison to what his parents had faced, there was so much that could be taken for granted. Apart from a few dedicated environmentalists and the occasional disaffected customer there was almost no opposition to the further development of winter sports in the area. This was made evident when a Mr. Withers chose to air his conservationist views in a letter to a local newspaper which was printed late in 1976. If he, or the newspaper, anticipated a campaign they were disappointed and Bob Clyde, still the General Manager of the chairlift company, was able to make a spirited riposte.

'I would like to answer the criticism of the Cairngorm ski area made by Mr Withers in your paper of October 12. In an attempt to determine the value of his opinion I checked our records to find that he was employed as an unqualified temporary ski instructor with Glenmore Lodge for one week only in each season since 1971.

'From our logs I find that in early March 1971 he had very little snow and poor overhead conditions. His March visit in 1972 saw better conditions and better snow cover as most ski-tows were operating. Again in March 1973 overhead conditions varied from fine to stormy but with poor snow cover as only the upper ski-tows were operated. But he really did well in April 1974 with a week of sunshine and all machines operating other than one low level trainer tow. His visit in the first week of January 1975, coincided with some of the worst weather the Cairngorms have seen.

'On average he has been unfortunate with the weather and snow conditions. This makes me wonder why he came back year after year; and if we are such a poor resort why have we found it necessary to build a new chain of ski-lifts in Coire na Ciste to accommodate the numbers visiting us.

'Since our developments began in 1961 we have found it necessary to build 11 chairlifts and ski-tows on Cairngorm with a total uplift capacity of more than 8500 persons per hour. There are more than 150 qualified full-time ski instructors employed here each year; many of whom return to us year after year.

'In bad weather it is necessary to close some of the upper machines for the safety of our customers. When the snow recedes some of our lower machines have to be closed but given the snow and the weather every machine on Cairngorm operates. Does Mr Withers think that we close the machines on a whim?

'My remit on Cairngorm is to provide as much uplift as possible, as safely as possible and to suit the demand. I believe that we mainly succeed in doing this.

'Mr Withers also mentions how expensive skiing has become. Nobody deplores this more than our company but we have to be viable or we will not exist. We believe that a day ticket price of £5 is in keeping with modern prices but this is the maximum price. We have a full range of tickets available to suit the pockets of beginners, experts and family skiers. Skiers who take the trouble to investigate our ticket structure and buy wisely can get very good value for their money.'

The force of Bob Clyde's argument is irresistible. If conditions were so terrible then there would be no continuing demand. For many people the unpredictability of the weather was part of the charm. Those who had battled against the wind, or peered through swirling mists, and still had a good day on the slopes, knew that the rewards of such persistence could be much greater than those to be gained from perfect conditions.

As he gradually took over increasing amounts of responsibility, Peter had no reason to fear that the whole basis of the operation would be taken away. The development, and Struan's unique position within it, were assured. And neither did he have the burden of old feuds. Naturally, he understood his parent's reservations about Hans Kuwall but that had not prevented him being a regular user of the Hillend artificial slope in Edinburgh which Hans managed. The events of the early nineteen fifties were long in the past for Peter and he had no desire to keep old wounds open.

It was similarly the case in relation to Frith and BASI. In time, Peter took, and passed, all the three grades of examination. He accepted that

BASI had established itself as the relevant organisation for British instructors and that if he were to have credibility in the area he must possess their qualifications. With Frith he had no personal quarrel and he was able to watch, with a fair degree of detachment, as Karl's former rival ran into ski political difficulties of his own. Ironically, in view of the history, it was with Hans Kuwall that Frith began to have the problems which are recounted at length in '*The Ski Teacher*'.

Frith writes that the focus of his dispute with Hans, who was the BASI Director of Training in 1976, related to the issue of time-keeping. When Frith suggested that discipline could usefully be tightened Hans is reported as retorting, 'This is not the army'. Jack Thomson, Frith's erstwhile number one ally, sided with Hans. Towards the end of the seventies Frith had a hint from a former instructor of his, Ali Ross, who was teaching in Switzerland, that the knives were out. In a confusing sequence of events, Frith was cut out. Ostensibly the first official reason for severance was that the founder member was not teaching the BASI method. Later he was accused of 'conduct detrimental to the good name of BASI' At a meeting chaired by Clive Freshwater, Frith was expelled. He makes it clear, in his account, that he believes there was a hidden agenda.

The only area in which Peter might have been expected to encounter more problems than his father was in dealing with the high and mighty. Karl relished hierarchy, he doted on generals and loved the lordly gentlemen. Peter was diametrically opposite. Some time earlier, when a senior military man had graced Struan with his august presence Peter had been invited to join the official entourage for dinner. A message had been sent to the effect 'Tell him to put on a tie and join us'. Peter, happily ensconced in front of the television, had politely refused and no amount of diplomatic pleading from his parents could change his firmly composed mind.

Whilst Peter's final futile negotiations with the ski establishment were going on, he spent some of his time coaching Konrad but most of it at Struan. The only racing he had was within Scotland but it was clear to almost everybody that his future lay with the hotel and ski school.

This fact made Karl and Eileen focus on the thought that when Peter finally took over, possibly with a wife and eventually children to accommodate, he would need the house. A suitable place of retirement for the founding couple was needed. They located a largely derelict croft set back from the road which linked the Aviemore-Carrbridge thoroughfare with Grantown-on-Spey. The building, with extensive gardens, bore the noble name of 'Croft of Kinveachy' and it offered unparalleled views of the distant Cairngorms.

Without much hesitation they purchased the place. Karl and Peter set about the arduous task of renovation. As ever, they worked brilliantly together and without proper regard for trivial matters such as taking breaks.

*The croft, after renovation!*

In the June of 1977, Peter took time off from the building labours to help the staff in the Enzian bar. He had organised a ceilidh to amplify trade and the event was in magnificent flow. Unseen by the organiser, a solitary young woman came in. She knew the Spey Valley well but had been away for a time, in Canada, and for her it was a new thing for Struan to be humming at this time of the year. She wanted to see if the place lived up to its current reputation.

The crowd was so dense that she had to push her way through, excusing, pleading and apologising. The music, which she had to admit was excellent, made it difficult to hear anything but she was determined to acquire a drink and to spend some time soaking up the vibrant atmosphere.

There was a tall handsome young man with a dark bushy beard busy behind the bar. To Lisa he looked familiar. He also looked irresistibly attractive. Waving her Scottish pound note to attract attention, the customer tried to keep her emotions in perspective.

The man turned towards her. It was only then that she realised that it was Peter. Their paths had crossed a few times in the Sheiling or in ski lift queues but they had never had a significant conversation. Nevertheless, she would surely have recognised him sooner had it not been for the facial hair.

She could see that he, too, was struggling to put her into context. He nodded in a way that one would not to a complete stranger but it was evident that he could not decide who she was. Doubtless he had only ever seen her dressed in an all-concealing ski suit with her long, black hair captive under a thick woollen hat. In the summer, with flimsier clothing and glossy hair adorning her back, she looked somewhat different.

It was then obvious, as she shouted her order, that he had suddenly realised. This was Lisa, Lisa the instructor, very good skier, been away for a season. She saw, also, that she was no longer just another thirsty customer. His eyes readily betrayed him and her unsuspecting heart began an intolerable thumping.

With her drink, she stayed near the bar, trying to focus on the music. Probably, she thought, she had completely imagined an interest. Occasionally she glanced towards Peter but he was always busy. It was only when she had persuaded herself that she was being foolish that she found the man suddenly beside her.

The greetings were shy and laconic. The conversation was inevitably about skiing. Everything had to be shouted and voices grew hoarse. Perhaps with a strategy in mind or possibly purely acting on an impulse Peter steered the conversation to cars. It was a subject on which Lisa could readily hold her own. When he mentioned that in the Crannich garage he had not only an MG but a glittering Lotus her shining eyes let it be known that an invitation to view would not be refused.

It was in that Lotus, not many moments later, that they had their first kiss. Both of them were, from that initial physical contact, besottedly in love. Lisa remembers that there was no discussion and not one iota of uncertainty. It was just understood that, probably sooner rather than later, they would be married.

When they stopped to draw breath she told him some of her background. She was one of three girls, born in Dunfermline and with a disrupted childhood. When she was eight the family moved to Aviemore where she had been ever since, save for the times she had run away.

Much of Peter's story she already knew, as did most people in the area because of the constant media coverage, but she was not aware, until he mentioned it, that he had a significant other who lived some distance away. Even this presented no problems. He had made no long term commitments and it would be no act of betrayal to say, with due regrets, that things had radically changed. He made the telephone call immediately and the two new lovers were free.

The remainder of the summer they spent as much time together as possible. Lisa was working in an Aviemore shop and Peter was never short of a task either at the hotel or the gradually changing croft but against all his work instincts he made time, so strong was their need to be together. Very soon they were cohabiting and making wedding plans. They were both barely into their twenties.

Once more Karl and Eileen were faced with an astonishing replication of their own rapid romance. There was no case for caution in the Fuchs family. 'Find your partner and go for it!' was the family motto.

At this stage of his career, Peter was still acquiring the BASI qualifications. Coincidentally Lisa was also following that route. In November she resigned from her temporary job and both of them went first to Val d'Isère and then to Austria where they were due to take the second level of examination. Both passed without difficulty and by the end of January they were back in Scotland to be greeted by huge snow drifts which entailed the digging of deep channels through the hotel yard and helicopter deliveries of essential supplies. Struan was without electricity for four entire days. The only heating was provided by the open fires, the only cooking facility was a small gas stove. Everybody, guests included, pulled together and showed, once more, the special Struan spirit which could turn potential disaster into an enjoyable adventure.

Lisa began work as a Struan instructor, becoming immediately a part of the family. The season continued to deliver extreme conditions. In March temperatures fell to zero Fahrenheit and diesel froze in fuel tanks. One stranded motorist, unable to force the key into the door lock, applied his mouth to blow warm air. His lips became stuck to the metal and there he remained until an AA patrol man freed him with an application of ointment.

Everyone at Struan, Lisa included, worked hard to cope with the circumstances and to ensure that all of their guests enjoyed some skiing even if it was only on the Carrbridge golf course. *The Scotsman* was so taken with the impact of the fierce weather on skiing that it devoted five precious column inches to the story of a school party who were staying at Struan. The reporter wrote accurately enough about the conditions but could not, in true journalistic tradition, resist the deliberate mistake. With a final flourish, in an aside almost completely irrelevant to the story, the writer added, 'Karl Fuchs, incidentally, was one of those who set up the slalom course for the 1948 Olympic Games'.

Very soon the young couple announced to a delighted Karl and Eileen that another grandchild was on the way and that they planned to marry in May. As the 1978 season ended there were other exciting prospects to add to that of the wedding and pregnancy.

For some time, rooms in the ageing Annexe had been proving difficult to let in spite of significant sanitary improvements largely wrought by Peter. Extra accommodation was urgently needed and it so transpired that Mrs. Anderson, owner of the adjacent guest house, began to talk of retirement. Without the energy and ambition of their son, Karl and Eileen would not have dreamt of expansion in that direction but Peter was instantly full of ideas. With a relatively cheap linking building they could incorporate Crannich's rooms. All told, at least eight multi-bed units could be created. The dining room could be enlarged, as could the Enzian bar by taking in the television room. A cosy new lounge could be created in the Crannich part of the composite building. Peter's eyes sparkled as he talked of the Enzian which would then have a fire at one end and be wonderfully cosy and welcoming.

Naturally matters could not proceed quickly but a decision was made that a proper bid would be lodged for the next door residence if and when it came onto the market.

Peter and Lisa tried hard to find a Minister who would perform the wedding ceremony on Cairngorm but failed. Peter had just passed the highest grade of BASI examination and a mountain top service would have been most appropriate. Instead they made use of the tiny, picturesque church at Rothiemurchus, as near to the mountain as they could get. Characteristically, Peter refused to kneel. Under a headline 'Wedding slip-up for a ski star' a local paper reported;

'It's more down-to-earth than planned - despite a wedding arch of skis.

'Former British skiing champion Peter Fuchs, 22, wanted to marry Lisa Shields on the Cairngorm ski slopes. But they could not find a minister to join them there. Peter said "We have skied so often together on Cairngorm, we thought it a romantic idea."

'On Sunday, Peter, son of an Austrian hotelier in Carrbridge, and Lisa, 22 from Aviemore married in church at Rothimurchus. That's on the road to the slopes.'

*Press photograph of the happy day*

The reception was, inevitably, held at Struan and was, according to Lisa's fond memory, 'fantastic'.

When the child, Josef, was born on September 24th the new family moved to the croft which, by then, was almost completely refurbished. They stayed there for almost a year and then conducted a straight swap with Karl and Eileen. With the baby to look after, Lisa did no instructing but she worked in the hotel whenever she could, mainly in the bar.

With his commitment to Konrad fulfilled, Peter could devote all his time to the business. When Crannich became available it was immediately purchased and work began on integrating it with Struan. Eileen records the events;

'Mrs. Anderson, our friend and neighbour at Crannich, decided to sell her house. Our Annexe was becoming rather hard to let in spite of Peter's installing washbasins in all the rooms and Karli doing his usual tasteful redecorating, so we bought Crannich, acquiring after some alterations, another eight bedrooms and a lounge and games room. We were thus able to extend our Enzian bar to take in our own lounge (and its coal fire) and Peter made a splendid job of the wood-lined walls and ceiling and the copper counter.

'Karli was, by this time, already suffering from diabetes and the related circulation problems in his legs. Typically, on coming out of hospital on crutches, he started painting and varnishing and had to be readmitted to hospital suffering from crutch palsy in his arms through sheer over-exertion on the old-fashioned wooden crutches. The logical next step was to make a building linking Struan and Crannich and this Peter organised, again doing much of the interior work in the three new bedrooms and the wooden ceiling, walls and floor of the beautiful dining room extension. Here we were able to hold full scale functions such as dances and concerts.'

For Lisa life could not have been more fulfilling. There were times when she thought that her young husband's fifteen hour working days were too long as he strove, with Charlie and, when his illness permitted, Karl, to complete the enlargement of the establishment. But he was there, close by her, and many times during the day they would enjoy a few moments together. She remembers thinking, with a pleasant glow of bemusement, 'This is what life is like'. It was, oddly, not dissimilar to what life had been like for Karl and Eileen at the start of their marriage.

*Crannich after its incorporation*

There was, though, a difficulty for the Fuchs family which took away some of the gloss. Ever since Peter had devoted himself full time to the business it had been evident that there was no longer a full role for Charlie Walpole. Once the Crannich development work was over he and Peter would find themselves duplicating skills. With Karl usually fit enough to work in the ski shed and Peter able to undertake any maintenance task which came along there was no logical case for keeping Charlie on the pay roll. Even in the business of leading the summer walks, at which Charlie was a master, Peter was totally equipped. He had roamed the mountains since boyhood and knew every grassy mound and boulder.

It was a heavy business, especially for Eileen who was the one who faced the task of breaking the news. The gentle giant had become very much part of the Struan family, as had his dog Ricky, the faithful companion on so many otherwise solitary walks. Over and again they tried to work out ways of avoiding, or at least softening, the blow but in the end it had to be admitted that they were running a business. They had taken on huge new financial commitments with the croft and Crannich; there was limited scope for sentimentality.

Whilst they were agonising over the issue, an event occurred which made the matter a hundred times more difficult. Ricky, as though realising that his period of settled life and guaranteed attention was coming to an end, became ill and, shortly afterwards, died.

For many people the death of a long-loved pet is just as agonising as that of a human. Ricky had been for so long the reliable constant in Charlie's life. Absolutely loyal, reliably amiable, the creature had been more than a casual companion. The loss was devastating. Eileen, herself very considerably upset by the demise of her regular escort, delayed as long as she could but the task only became more difficult as time progressed. Just over a week after the bereavement, Charlie was informed that he had also lost his job.

The story for Charlie happily worked out well, however, for eventually he found a niche at Glenmore Lodge where his multi-faceted skills were much appreciated and where he could continue to live in his adopted home area. Although he was deeply saddened by having to leave Struan he fully understood that they could not afford to duplicate and that there truly was no point in having someone in Peter's considerable shadow.

The family might have reconsidered the decision about Charlie had they known that Peter was soon to be offered work as trainer to the British women's ski racing team, the first British man to be given this honour. He was already trainer of the Scottish espoirs, so all at once he was being called away from the hotel for prolonged periods. However, it was too late for Charlie to be recalled and the business had to learn to live without his omnibus skills.

Just as Peter was taking up his new role, BASI had finalised the details of a ski-race trainer's qualification. The two people involved in setting the scheme up, Hans Kuwall and Kenny Dixon, were deemed to have passed the test without formal assessment but Peter was the first to go through the process. Whether through a keenness to indicate that tough standards were in operation or because of a genuine evaluation, the initial decision was that Peter had not met the criteria. Not a little displeased, the former national champion forcefully argued his case and the judgement was reversed.

It was not ideal for Lisa nor for Struan to have Peter away in the Alps for weeks at a time but all concerned acknowledged that the training work was one way of mitigating the loss he felt at the premature end of his own competitive career. He still enjoyed the excitements of the racing circuit and, through his various charges, he could experience these vicariously.

With this minor reservation, the start of the eighties was a propitious time for those involved with Struan. The enlarged premises were mightily impressive. The Enzian bar, with its enticing fire and greater space, was significantly improved, whilst the much expanded dining room, the new lounge and the substantial Crannich bedrooms all gave the establishment an air of solidity. Guests felt that they were entering a substantial hotel rather than an expanded private house. It was even possible to get lost, albeit only momentarily, finding a way through some of the new territory. With Peter full of energy and ideas, with the Cairngorm ski scene set for steady expansion and improvements, the prospects were sparkling indeed.

## 34. All Good Things...

Peter's stock in the skiing world rose steadily. He was elected chairman of the Association of Ski Schools of Great Britain. He was also selected to travel to Japan for the eleventh Interski world conference with a BASI demonstration team which, in a sign of prevailing harmony, included Hans Kuwall, Iain Finlayson and a Glaswegian called John Hynds who had worked for both Karl and Frith in his instructing career. A newspaper piece on the event claimed confidently that, 'BASI trained instructors are held in high esteem throughout Europe'.

In the September of 1980 he was at home. The month had become the time of the Carrbridge Ceilidh, an event started by Bill Mitchell and which had developed into a major item in the folk music calendar. Eileen, abetted by David Hays of the local Landmark Centre, had persuaded the licensing authorities to allow late opening for the duration. Professional bands were engaged but there was also much informal music-making. Struan provided free Annexe accommodation for performers and the Edinburgh Ceilidh Band became resident as did a man universally known as 'Geordie', a brilliant accordionist, who had, many years previously, been on one of Karl's instructors' courses. They were augmented by 'Fiddler' Jennings who, musically speaking, lived up to his nickname and took over the organisation of the events based at Struan until Peter returned.

The highly successful ceilidh week had just ended. Peter had made many new friends amongst the musicians and everyone was talking about how much better the next year's event would be. Simon Tisdall had told *Guardian* readers about the atmosphere in the small village. He wrote of the impressive Landmark visitors' centre just across the road from Struan with its tree top trail, of the astonishing one thousand beds which the local people made available for travellers and of the piper who stood on the old bridge every evening to deliver a haunting serenade. In particular he had conveyed something of the Struan magic.

Although at this point Karl and Eileen were still very much the proprietors of Struan, Peter was taking on an ever-increasing portion of the management of the establishment. Eileen had made arrangements for him to take over the drinks licence when next it came up for renewal. Based in the house, on the spot, he was available to deal with all the crises and to take immediate decisions. Like everyone else, he relished the prospect of a lull before the non-stop winter routine started. It would be good to have some time to spend with Lisa, who was once more pregnant, and with baby Josef.

Karl and Eileen were expecting Maurice, John and Elfi and their children to arrive for one of their regular visits. On the Saturday after ceilidh week ended, Eileen drove the hotel minibus to Grantown to buy supplies for a family party to be held on the Sunday. Making her way back, she was rounding a bend in the road when she saw a van coming directly towards her.

Rather than crash headlong, she took quick, decisive action and veered off the road towards a steep embankment. But even with this evasive action, the van impacted, taking off a wing mirror and scraping a door. In the sudden stop at the bottom of the incline, the windscreen smashed and the vehicle tilted alarmingly. Recalling tales of fires after sudden stops, Eileen released her seat belt quickly and leapt out. It was her misfortune to land in a deep thicket of nettles. She was concentrating on escaping without too much pain when a bloody head appeared over the side of the road. It said 'Oh my god!' and vanished.

The embankment was too steep for Eileen to climb and she was greatly relieved when a motorist, who had been held up by the accident, took the trouble to haul her up. She saw, at once, that she had been right to dive off the road. The errant van, after scraping the minibus, had smashed into a following car. People were quite badly wounded but there seemed to be no fatalities.

The rescuer's wife, a nurse, looked at Eileen's badly bruised thigh and declared that it needed medical attention. The couple kindly offered to deliver her to Struan, where help could be summoned, but Lisi and Davie's house was only a few hundred yards away. Eileen decided to go to there. When she had recovered some composure, Lisi drove her to the hotel.

Feeling decidedly shaky, she went in. Karl was in the bar talking to a couple who had once run the Carrbridge Post Office and who had migrated to South Africa. Whilst they were there, their only son had been killed in a car accident. It was obviously not appropriate for Eileen to interrupt so she sought Peter who, it transpired, was having a bath. Rather than disturb him, and thinking that it would, after all, be better to be at her daughter's house, Eileen accepted the barman's kind offer to run her over.

Lisi telephoned the doctor who could not attend immediately because he was very much occupied stitching up the other accident victims. His advice was that the patient should take a bath, which she did. Peter appeared, having heard the news of the accident from his wife. He was, Lisa later revealed, deeply shocked by what had happened.

There being little that anyone could do to help the invalid other than offer tea and sympathy, Peter eventually went off to see to the recovery of the minibus. Lisi drove her mother home. Karl, still talking to the couple and completely unaware of the accident, waved for Eileen to join them for a drink. She would have loved to have done so but she was feeling decidedly shaky. There was a large lump on the back of her head, caused by she knew not what impact. Instead, she went into Peter and Lisa's house and reclined on the sofa where she read a bedtime story to little Josef.

It was not until nine o'clock that Karl heard about the accident. He came rushing in, demanding to know why he had not been informed earlier. Eileen stood quickly up to greet him, the words of explanation forming on her lips, and just as quickly subsided in a completely involuntary collapse. He promptly took her to the croft and did everything possible to make her comfortable.

The next day Eileen realised the true extent of the damage. The bruising was extensive and there was a lurid haematoma on the thigh caused, she imagined, by impact against the gear lever. Nonetheless, aided by her niece, Barbara, she prepared food for the family party. The event went very smoothly and the accident began to take on a slightly less troublesome perspective. When Peter called the next day to say that the police were convinced that she had done the right thing in veering off the road, she felt much better.

Later that day, Peter was in the Struan yard, on his back, peering under the newly-acquired second-hand Jaguar saloon which was his fresh automotive joy. Lisa came out with the toddling Josef and asked Peter to look after the child. She wanted to make a quick trip to Aviemore to see her mother. Though perfectly happy to do his parental duties, Peter pointed out that she had spent most of the previous evening talking to her mother in the Enzian bar.

This was true. They had devoted a good deal of the time to a discussion of how Peter had rapidly matured from wild boy into a responsible father and how they were profoundly impressed by the manner in which Peter, though in some ways shy, had forced himself to interact with guests. He would never have Karl's absolutely natural ease with people but he was on his way to developing some of Eileen's great skills of remembering significant pieces of information and deploying them appropriately.

She patiently offered an explanation as to why further contact with her mother was necessary, which Peter accepted. He seemed more interested in the exhaust pipe on the Jaguar which, he said, was quite badly corroded. He told Lisa that he would take it down to the garage and have it welded. Leaving Josef happily 'helping' his daddy, Lisa went off.

Lisi was at Struan, helping with the cooking of the evening meal. She stepped out of the kitchen to fetch something from one of the storerooms and saw that her brother was painting preservative on some slalom poles. For reasons which she could not identify, Lisi felt suddenly anxious about Josef. She urged Peter to keep a close eye on the boy and was told, not unkindly, that everything was under control. Objectively, Lisi knew that there was no particular danger but she felt a very strong urge to offer to take the child into the kitchen. She knew, though, that any suggestion on these lines would annoy Peter so she bottled her anxiety up and went back to work. She finished the immediate tasks by about two o'clock and then went home.

Lisa returned to Struan, a bit later than planned, at about half past five. She learned that Peter, impatient of waiting for her and anxious to get the car from the garage before the mechanics went home, had taken their son with him. Lisa wandered happily down the road and found her husband just on the point of taking the car for a test drive. She thought for a moment about going with him but then decided that she should get Josef home and feed him. Mother and child waved happily in farewell as Peter set off.

Lisa gave Josef his supper and put him to bed. Whilst she read a familiar Peter Rabbit story, the little boy, exhausted by the effort of 'helping' daddy, fell asleep.

Moggs came drifting in, looking for his close friend. Lisa explained the absence and the young man wandered unconcernedly off, saying that he would call later.

At around half past six Lisa began to feel anxious about Peter's non-appearance. She peered out of the window towards the Crannich garage where the Jaguar was normally kept. There being no sign of activity, she went distractedly out and looked down the road towards the village. At the time she felt that this was a pointless thing to do but the need was compulsive.

The gesture was nowhere near enough to calm her anxiety. Making immediate short-term baby-sitting arrangements with one of the staff, she slipped into her car and drove the short distance to the garage. To an extent the mechanic, still working, reassured her. Peter loved his new car and was, the man suggested, probably just enjoying cruising down the smooth village by-pass.

Feeling better, Lisa drove back to hotel. She could readily understand that her motor-loving husband might have been enjoying the drive so much that he had gone further than originally intended. He had probably lost track of time.

She parked her own car and went into the house kitchen. To her surprise the local doctor, Angus McNeil was there. She said something light such as, 'This is an unusual time to be making house calls,' but did so with a dreadful sense of foreboding.

The baby sitter was loyally there, watching Star Trek on television. Clearly nothing could be amiss. Politely, Angus McNeil asked the baby-minder to leave. There was a hint of panic in Lisa's mind but still she was unwilling to face anything like reality. The doctor suggested that she might like to sit down. Still seeking escape in humour she said, 'No, I won't because if I sit down you'll tell me something bad.'. It was obvious that everything must be fine with Josef yet Lisa's barely contained panic was all about her baby. Finding that there was no longer strength in her legs, Lisa collapsed into a chair.

Dr. McNeil hesitated for just a moment but realising that there was no way of softening the impact, no technique for hiding nor disguising the disgusting tragedy, he bravely and truly broke the news. Peter had been in a terrible accident. He was dead.

To the immediate family, to those who had known and intensely loved Peter, the news was literally incredible. Of course, the blunt fact had eventually to be accepted but it seemed utterly impossible that he would never stand foursquare, arguing his point, nor spend hours wrestling with some problem of Struan maintenance, nor hurtle heart-wrenchingly down the Cairngorm slopes, nor cuddle and kiss his loved ones.

A loyal Struan worker, Christine, who had heard the sound of the crash from her home close to the A9, had made enquiries and learned the dreadful news. She came rushing over and could at least relieve Lisa of the immediate task of taking care of Josef.

Karl and Eileen were in the croft. The local policeman, off duty but loaded with the impossible task, came to tell the literally incredible. In instant shock, Eileen resorted to making tea.

There was then the nightmare of breaking the news to Lisi. Eileen picked up the telephone. She was unsure as to whether or not she would be able to speak and was mightily relieved to hear Davie's calm voice. 'Thank God it's you', Eileen said.

It was said to Davie and he said it to Lisi but still it seemed impossible.

John and Elfi were still on their holiday which had suddenly turned so sour. John came, as soon as he heard the news, to console Eileen.

Together they went to Struan where Lisi and Davie were waiting. Eileen rushed in to Lisa and found that Elfi was already there. She had gone over, in all innocence, 'for a chat' and landed in the lake of misery.

Neither Karl nor Eileen slept that night. Karl said heartbreakingly, over and over, 'Never mind, we still have Lisi'. The radio began to carry the news of Peter's death on its bulletins. There was no escape.

The next day Karl insisted on driving Eileen to the scene of the crash. He knew that it was necessary to acknowledge the reality as fully as possible. On the road was a crude, shocking, piece of evidence, a dark mark perhaps a quarter of a mile long made by deposited rubber.

The next day local newspapers allowed no denial of reality. 'Two car drivers killed in A9 crash' said the stark headline. The text ran;

'The drivers of two cars were killed last night in a collision about half a mile north of Carrbridge on the new A9 road in Inverness-shire. It is not known if there were any passengers in the cars.

'One of the victims was top Scottish skier Peter Fuchs (25). He won the Scottish junior championship when he was 15 and many other championships and honours followed. When he was 18 he took second place in the British men's championship and the following year he won the Scottish senior championship. In 1976 he was a member of the British team in the Winter Olympics. In 1977 he won the downhill at the British Alpine Ski Championships and went on to take the overall Elswick Hopper British Alpine Ski Championship. In 1977 he resigned from the British team in support of his friend Konrad Bartelski who was in dispute with the authorities.

'Peter was married with one son, Josef. His wife is expecting their second child. His father, Mr Karl Fuchs, is a former Austrian Olympic skier. He was one of the pioneers of skiing in the Cairngorms and runs the Austrian Ski School and the Struan House Hotel, Carrbridge.'

The Ski Federation just happened to be in the midst of a meeting when Peter's friend and erstwhile rival, Fraser Clyde, telephoned to tell them what had happened. They stood in silence, demonstrating their respect.

Konrad Bartelski was in London. The pleasure of his British record-breaking performance in the 1980 Olympics was still with him. He had spent part of the summer in New Zealand and had there beaten the formidable Ken Read. Relationships within the British team were better than they had been for years. He felt as though, after a decade of dedicated struggle, he was on the verge of achieving that elusive goal of a place on the top step of a World Cup podium.

On the way back from New Zealand he had stopped over, with Ken Read, in the tropical dream of Rarotonga. All the anticipated features had delighted him. Restored by the swimming and the glorious sunshine, he was brim full of energy and excitement for the forthcoming season. He had spent almost three days on the telephone, setting up the arrangements for the new round of races. When the business was over, his thoughts turned to Peter. He writes;

'However, on about the third day, I got a strong, almost eerie, feeling and just had to ring him. We talked for an hour. He was happy, his wife and child were well, and he had just acquired a new Jaguar XJ12. He was jolly, bouncy and keen to hear all the stories of my trip, and his infectious breeziness found its way to me.

'That was a Sunday night. I couldn't stay in London very long, as I had to go to Annecy to test boots for the Salomon factory, so I left on the Monday morning. The following morning, Tuesday, I had a telephone call from Mark Amis. He said; "Peter..." My heart sank and I felt dizzy. I knew already what Mark was going to say. There had been a head-on car smash and Peter, in his sparkling XJ12, had been killed instantly.

'It was the worst news I have ever had in my life. For about nine years Peter and I had been as close as brothers. More than that, we had been friends and colleagues in a sport not noted for very close friendships between racers. Ever since the Three Musketeers days we had shared each other's highs and lows. We had spurred each other on and supported each other whenever a bad patch came along. We were human, of course, and there were many times when we didn't quite see eye-to-eye, but those times were few and easily forgotten. All my memories of Peter are good ones; his talent, his love of fun, his loyalty as a friend and his willingness to put himself out are aspects of his personality which I shall always treasure. Without Peter there was something lacking, some element missing, from my skiing career. Put quite simply, I had lost my best friend.

'My first impulse was to jump on a plane to go to Peter's wife and parents but I couldn't, at least for a short while, just drop my business with Salomon. I rang Peter's parents and my own - Peter's so that I could commiserate with them and mine to give myself someone to talk to. Despite knowing many of the people at Salomon, Peter's death had made me feel quite alone.

'As soon as my business was finished I took the first plane to London. I had booked to fly alone but I was pleased to find myself travelling with Peter Hankey from Salomon. His words of comfort were a godsend.

'Once in London, my first thought was to travel straight to Carrbridge but I had several long-standing engagements, some of which involved speaking to clubs, and I met all of them before travelling north. Naturally the temptation was there to cancel them but I knew that Peter would have disapproved of that and I knew he would have wanted me to carry on and get on with achieving the goals which I had set myself. Peter was on my mind throughout those few days and I finally got up to Carrbridge on the morning of the Thursday, the day of the funeral.

'When I got back to the snow of Hintertux after the funeral nothing was quite the same. Memories of Peter were everywhere and racing friends, young and old, kept coming up to me to say how sorry they were. Everyone was very kind but all I wanted to do was get on with the job. Years before Peter and I had started along a road and now I wanted to finish the journey - for his sake as much as mine. To do this I had to train harder than ever before, reach hitherto undiscovered levels of determination, and show the world that the dreams we had as young boys starting out could be realised.'

The funeral brought together virtually everybody who was of significance in British skiing. The Bell brothers, beginning to show their considerable promise as racers, were there with their parents as were dozens of Struan 'graduates' who had made names for themselves. General Leathes came, along with very many military men. Eileen was surprised, and mildly disconcerted, by the presence of George Stewart, the man at the British Ski Federation with whom she had had such a torrid battle over Peter's racing licence. After the bitter ceremony he cautiously approached. Eileen felt obliged to acknowledge his courage in being there and said, in response to his overtures of peace, that an apology would be a good start. The words were duly uttered but in the terrible context they had scant effect.

Once the funeral was over there came the analysis. What had caused the accident? Could anyone be blamed? Was there some rational explanation of an apparently senseless piece of slaughter?

Nothing was totally resolved. The bare facts seemed to be that Peter was overtaking the local AA man in his van on the Carrbridge by-pass. Seeing an approaching saloon, he had braked and skidded sideways. The ferocious impact between the front of the on-coming car and the side of the Jaguar had crushed the other driver and simply, neatly, astonishingly, broken Peter's neck. On his body there had been no marks whatsoever.

Some people suggested that the main factor was that Peter had been unfamiliar with power-enhanced brakes. Anyone who has stamped on a servo-assisted brake pedal, forgetting the mechanical multiplication of effect, will testify to the alarming consequences. Just a touch is all that is needed and anything more produces deceleration of magnitude easily great enough to cause a skid.

The AA man's recollection of the shocking event suggests that Peter had been adjusting something on the dashboard, probably the radio, as he overtook. This may have been a contributory factor but Peter was an experienced and highly skilled driver. It seems unlikely that pure inattention could have been the primary cause.

There are other, indeterminate, considerations. Lisi is convinced that there was a letter in the glove compartment of Peter's car relating to a fault with one of the tyres. There was, she believed, something about a missing piece of casing. Could there have been a blow out?

Through all the agonised, angry, tearful debates which followed the tragedy, people sought ways to deal with their misery. For Moggs it spelled the end of skiing. The joy of the sport had been extinguished, the point clinically removed.

For Lisa, the heavily pregnant widow, there was an extra, unexpected factor. Although everybody did their utmost to acknowledge her special position, she found that she felt largely excluded. All Peter's true intimates, the family of course, Moggs, Konrad and a few others, had known him for all or significant segments of his life. She was an incomer. There was still a good deal about her husband which she had not had chance to discover. It felt almost as though she had no proper right to be grieving. She was the only one of the immediate mourners who had felt unable to look at the reportedly unblemished body. In a distant, desperate fashion, she felt that she was slowly losing control.

Whilst those most directly affected by Peter's death battled to deal with despair others wrote considered obituaries. One of the leading ski magazines published a fulsome tribute. It told some of the personal history and paid special tribute to the recent work he had done as trainer to the Ladies Team. He had, the piece avowed, built up, ' a level of team rapport, integration and enthusiasm that was boding well for their continued development and success'.

In another publication, Major General Leathes, who had come to know Peter well through his involvement with the British Ski Federation, gave his assessment;

'A little over ten years ago Peter Fuchs had already made his mark in junior ski racing and was progressing fast through senior, indeed international, competitions. I remember him in this early day period at the start of a Lowlander Downhill on the OK course at Val d'Isere. I was very impressed by this tense, eager and determined young man, as he literally leapt out of the starting hut to attack that difficult downhill course, with all the dash, nerve and courage that were so much part of his character.

'Peter had everything that goes to make a natural world class downhill racer, as he was to show the world at the age of 19, when he came 19th in the World Championships in St Moritz in 1974.

'At that time there was a good deal of controversy over the manner of training and management of British ski teams, just when the young racer needs all the support and encouragement he can get. Unsettled by this controversy, and dogged by a persistent injury to a tendon in his leg,

Peter battled on with characteristic courage and determination. But in the end his injury proved too great a handicap.

'A natural leader with truly infectious energy and enthusiasm he very soon found another outlet for his vitality, lively talents and very considerable racing experience at world class level.

'In a very short time he was training young racers and such was his ability as a race trainer that he had already achieved the distinction of being the first British trainer to be appointed to train one of our national teams. At the time of his tragic accident he was all set to take the British Women's Team through to the 1984 Winter Olympic Games.

'Our deepest sympathy goes out in full measure to Lisa, his wife, and to Karl and Eileen Fuchs, who themselves have done so much for skiing in Scotland. Their loyal and enduring support and ever present encouragement meant so much to Peter. In their sad loss we must hope they take some comfort in the knowledge of and extent of, Peter's many achievements in the short time that was allotted to him. Not the least of these being the tremendous number of his friends who will cherish his memory with respect, esteem and affection.'

Yet another publication persuaded Konrad to write his own, more personal, appraisal;

'It is now many months since I was struck with the tragic news of Peter's death, yet I still find it difficult to write about the vacuum that he left.

'Peter was a young man with exceptional character. He had strength in his beliefs and tastes and a tremendous appreciation of life. These strengths carried him through many unpleasant situations forced upon him by the politics of sport yet in the end he would always emerge wiser and stronger. The appreciation was reflected in the warmth and friendliness he radiated to everyone around him.

'His contribution to the sport in the years that he was involved with British skiing was remarkable. He had a tremendous power for learning and also for sharing his knowledge. What he could have done is irreplaceable.

'It is impossible for me to write in a few words what would really fill a book, yet I am thankful that I had the pleasure to share an important part of my life with him. In the short life that he had, he experienced, enjoyed and accomplished more than many in a full lifetime. For how he helped those around him, and certainly myself, thank you.'

On the 28th of October, on what would have been a day of celebration for Peter's birthday, Lisa began to experience the first symptoms of imminent childbirth. She was taken to hospital the following day. Her sister Stella, who had made the long journey from Canada to provide support, went with her. As the time for delivery drew nigh Stella, at Lisa's request, stayed by the bedside. A doctor intervened, asserting that only fathers-to-be were allowed to be present at births. Lisa pleaded and was firmly told that it was only under the most special of circumstances that exceptions could be made. Lisa thought, 'My husband has just been killed in a horrific accident, I'm having his child, my sister, to whom I am very close, has travelled thousands of miles to provide support; how much more special can you get?'

Stella took up the case. The white-coated woman was extremely reluctant to shift. It took the combined determination and strength of character of the two sisters to win the concession. Stella was, in fact, holding her sister's clenching hand as Helene, a beautiful, healthy, vigorous baby came into the world.

Peter's family was complete.

## 35. Life Must Go On...

Money had been borrowed to finance the Crannich expansion; there was no option but to continue. Reluctantly Karl and Eileen concluded that they would have to move back to the hotel but they were very wary of impinging upon Lisa with her two very young children. They decided to take over two of the rooms on the second floor of the linking wing, making do as best they could.

Eileen records the aftermath of her son's tragic departure.

'After Peter died, although Karli carried bravely on with the ski school in spite of his increasing physical infirmity, I lost my enthusiasm, as did Lisa. We had wonderful support from the locals, both customers and staff and from our New Zealanders and from Davie who took on much work and responsibility in the bar. Most of all we were helped by Lisi who took on the cooking, did incredible amounts of washing up and turned her hand to every other job which came along including doing the bar on Monday nights when we always had music and a late licence.'

Eileen remembers that the villagers, in particular, were good to her and Karl far beyond the call of duty. The extended family closed protectively about them and they felt wonderfully cherished. It seemed that nothing was too much trouble. A hint was sufficient to bring immediate action but more often than not, needs would be anticipated and met even before the bereaved parents had realised that they existed.

Another helpful circumstance was that the hotel became very busy in an unusual way. One of the army groups organised a large scale training exercise which involved their taking over of the entire establishment during the week. They brought their own kitchen staff and provided regular army food. This reduced the work load whilst ensuring that income levels were satisfactory. At weekends, the military men departed and Struan returned to normal. It was a felicitous arrangement.

In proper keeping with the Struan family tradition, John and Elfi's son, Frank, came up for the summer season bringing three of his school friends. This 'fire brigade' performed any and every task and brought a well-considered, sensitively expressed cheerfulness which raised everybody's spirits.

It was whilst they were there that Eileen took her father and Lisi's little David on a familiar excursion to Loch an Eilein. Maurice was at last showing true signs of ageing. His short term memory had deteriorated and he had difficulty walking. When they reached the loch, Eileen suggested that he should stay within easy reach of the car whilst she took the child for a short ramble. 'If you try to come with us, you'll break your leg', she said.

Grandmother and grandson wandered along the well defined track. It was in Eileen's mind to introduce the little boy to the delights of reaching a summit. At a suitable point she struck off and began the ascent. It was only a hillock but there would be a view from the top and the exhilaration of achievement. David had picked up a stick which he waved about in a way which worried Eileen. Infant eyes seemed to be in danger. Keeping a close watch, she failed to spot a dip in the ground and in an instant she was falling. She knew, immediately, that she had once more broken a leg.

She called David over. The stout stick instantly became an asset rather than a liability. Using it, Eileen raised herself gingerly to the vertical. There was acute pain but she thought that she would be able to hop and hobble back to the car.

Feeling foolish, especially with the memory of the remark she had made to her father, Eileen inched her way back with David watching solicitously and making helpful comments which, under less agonising circumstances, would have been comic. Maurice might have been triumphalist but in fact he was immediately solicitous. Happily, the car had automatic transmission so it was possible for Eileen to bring the expedition back to base.

In the context of the bereavement, the accident was a minor inconvenience. Eileen and Karl somehow survived the aftermath of Peter's death. For Lisa the time immediately after the tragedy was more manic. Life seemed unreal. It was crazy to be carrying on as though nothing had happened but she acknowledged, of course, that there was little other that could be done. We each find our own way of dealing with traumatic events. Some retreat, some suffer breakdowns, some become ill, some resort to addictions. For Lisa the natural route was diversion, escapism, a turning away from that which was impossible to contemplate. Some, at the time, those who did not fully understand how humans behave when deeply wounded emotionally, saw her bright, brittle, hectic life as disrespectful, as evidence of uncaring. This was very far from the truth. She was only partially alive and she would turn to almost any alluring object or activity to deflect attention from the unthinkable.

She thinks, from a much later perspective , that she went through the motions of looking after her children but that she was almost totally incapable of providing the full emotional support that infants need. Had she opened up these avenues then she would have been unable to continue to repress the grief which, had it been released, might have destroyed her.

Some of her diversionary tactics involved attending wild parties and drinking to excess. She knew that she was, to a considerable extent, failing her children but felt incapable of correcting her behaviour. Her assessment is that she 'fell to pieces' and is entirely grateful now that her own mother and Peter's were there to fill some of the void for Josef and Helene. Her primary thought was that if she could find a substitute father for the children quickly enough then the world might right itself and she reached out to anyone who seemed as though they might take on the burden. At length she met a man who lived in Tomatin who seemed appropriate. Two years after her husband's death she moved out of Struan, leaving most of her belongings in the house.

Her relationship with Karl and Eileen disintegrated. Deep in their bottomless pit of grief it was hard for them to accept the wild behaviour and the apparent lack of consideration for the welfare of the children. All contact between the separated parts of the Fuchs family ceased for a time. When it became clear that Lisa would not be returning, the Struan proprietors reviewed their circumstances. Eileen remembers;

'We could not cope with the very large establishment we had by then become and we could not justify the expense of keeping on Crannich. So we divided it off and sold it. There were still many happy times to come with mostly good New Zealand staff at first and great support from my nephew and his friends who spent a summer working and who brought much music and gaiety joined every now and then by Ceilidh week friends and musicians. Miree, Jessie's daughter, took over the day-time bar and many other things and Pete Evans and his brother Geoff also did much bar work. In the winter our last and longest serving New Zealander, Annabel and an English girl, Julie Berry, together with Pete Evans and Lisi when she had time, joined in the high tradition of ski instruction while Karli directed operations from his ski hire shed.'

*Helene, Lisa and Josef*

The 'happy times' included the visits of groups of schoolchildren from Glasgow and Northern Ireland. New Zealander barman Larry, an expert twelve-string guitarist, proved himself to be excellent with the youngsters. The Edelweiss was turned from bar into tuck shop, staffed by the accompanying teachers but with profits accruing to the business. There was also a dramatic change to the menu. Children demanded burgers, fish fingers and mountains of chips. Wanting to keep the adults happy, Eileen and her helpers laboured as usual to produce the delicious and nutritious Struan meals until one of the beneficiaries hesitantly approached to say that they, too, would prefer the children's fare. This was a surprise, but no problem; it was far easier to grill a hundred burgers than to create schnitzel and strudel.

In the post-Peter years there were also three wedding receptions, including that of Jessie Hewlett's granddaughter, Iona. There was also a huge party for Maurice's 90th birthday. Lisi was very much a part of this phase of Struan's history. Her Davie had constructed the house to a point where it was comfortably habitable and had then taken the new opportunity of working on the oil rigs to bring in some much needed money. Lisi made her financial contribution, and kept the potential loneliness at bay, by working in the Struan kitchen and dining room.

No doubt the continuing close family involvement in the venture for the four years after Peter's death was a healing factor but it was evident to Eileen, at least, that they could not continue indefinitely. Karl's health was steadily deteriorating and for her, the endless chores of running the establishment were becoming increasingly irksome. She records the end simply;

'But the sparkle had gone from the hotel and when, in 1984, a young couple said they wanted to buy Struan I felt an immense sense of relief. Karl was devastated at the thought of leaving but agreed on condition that he kept the ski school. So we were finally able to retire to our beloved croft.'

Karl's devastation extended to the point where he refused to sign the contract of sale. When it came to the actuality of parting with their creation he could not bring himself to do the deed. Every logical argument reached the conclusion that selling was the only viable option but the emotional ties and the memories were far too strong. Eileen was, of course, just as much affected but, as always, she was steering the practical course through the mists of romanticism. She had to recruit several powerful 'persuaders', people whom Karl deeply respected, before he put the fateful pen to paper.

For the estranged Lisa, life was also taking a dramatic turn. The week that Struan was sold, she was separating from her Tomatin partner. Still seeking escape, she embarked on another relationship which also failed. It was only then, she recalls, that 'reality came crashing in'. She stopped searching for a Peter substitute, cut out the excesses in her life and began to regain control. In the new circumstances, contact was re-established with Karl and Eileen. Lisa stepped out on the long and difficult road to recovery.

There was, of course, a huge, typically Struan, retirement party in June 1984. The Carrbridge villagers took up a collection to provide farewell and 'thank you' presents and all the local papers carried the story prominently.

*Eileen on her bike*

Karl commuted from croft to hotel for two seasons but spent some of his time building what Eileen describes as, 'a typically attractive but workmanlike hire shed in our old steading'. She adds: 'He had one very happy and successful season there before his health broke down too much for him to work a commercial ski hire service. Although he could no longer take any physical part in skiing, he spent time at the meetings of the Association of Ski Schools in Great Britain, of which he had been president for many years, and tried to put over his views on how skiing could best be organised and developed and on the need for unity. He was always passionately interested in this and was bitterly disappointed at the disputes and rivalries and jealousies which developed.'

Karl's final retirement attracted much media attention. The Strathspey and Badenoch Herald of December the 10th used the headline, 'Fuchs Family leaves its mark on Scottish Skiing, Karl signals end of an era'. The article recounts Karl's history and achievements and comments;

'Karl Fuchs has dedicated his life to skiing with remarkable and outstanding results. He was responsible for starting the ski school movement in Scotland; trained the Army's ski instructors to ski and teach; and can count many famous and successful international skiers, including the Bell brothers, Martin and Graham, and local cross country star Ewan MacKenzie among his long list of outstanding pupils.

He was also well known in Carrbridge, which was his home for 30 years, for his work with local children. Determined to see them ski, he transported them to the slopes, provided equipment and taught them free of charge.'

In a subsequent piece the same paper reported another retirement honour for Karl;

'The Spey Valley's Grand Old Man of skiing, Mr Karl Fuchs, who is retiring on health grounds, was honoured by British ski instructors last week. At a ceremony at the Red McGregor Hotel, Aviemore, he was presented with an engraved glass mountain bearing a skier, which was specially made by Caithness Glass. The presentation was made by Mr Rudi Prochazka, of Kingussie, who is chairman of the Association of Ski Schools in Great Britain.'

Engraved on the mountain were the simple, immensely satisfying words, 'You started it all, Karl.'

The family, including Lisa and her children, attended Konrad Bartelski's wedding, where they were treated as guests of honour. Five year old Josef was a pageboy and the groom explained, in his speech, that Peter would have been best man had he lived. Willy Bailey, who was deputising, was in no way upset by this remark; he knew that Konrad and Peter had had a very special closeness.

The reunification of the immediate family brought immense relief for Karl and Eileen. Both derived huge pleasure from their rapidly growing grandchildren. There was also great solace to be gained in the interaction with the wider kinship group which had grown up around Struan. Eileen tells of Karl's post-retirement days in all their richness.

'Even though in the end hardly able to drag himself round on two sticks and with his right arm virtually useless, he eagerly watched Coire Cas through his binoculars. He did incredibly hard work chopping winter wood, mowing our three lawns, turning part of the garage into a garden shed and clearing up on his tractor any snow that fell. In the enforced intervals of resting on his seat in the garden he listened to and observed his beloved birds and watched the sheep and cows and occasionally roe deer that surrounded us. He enjoyed being visited by his friends and going for short trips in the car up to Glenmore and to Loch Insh where he organised canoeing and windsurfing lessons for his grandchildren. He made new friends among the district nurses who looked after his feet so skilfully and kept him mobile and every one of them had some connection with skiing and he was able to stimulate their interest. Typically he loved bringing them presents from Austria and making Christmas and Easter parcels for them. He organised racing and jumping in the garden for the grand-children using his old slalom poles to set dry courses on the lawn and was able vicariously to enjoy skiing through watching them.'

Even though movement became difficult for Karl he still insisted on making visits to Austria and he had, as Eileen recounts, 'the tremendous pleasure of watching the family ski with one of his early instructors and great friends, Franzi Stock, on the glacier at Hintertux. We introduced them to Austria not as tourists but as children with Austrian blood and heritage.'

*Karl with family in Austria*

In June 1987, Eileen's father, 'Grandpa' to hundreds, maybe thousands, Maurice Knowles to the rest of the world, died at the age of almost 95. For the last few years his memory had become so poor that he was no longer safe to be out and about on his own. With great reluctance his children had arranged accommodation in a beautiful, very caring home close to Inverness. His end came there and the cremation was arranged at the nearest available venue, which happened to be in Perth.

His son, John, was abroad at the time. The ceremony was attended by only a few but soon after John returned, a commemorative gathering was arranged at the croft. The day was happily sunny and the event took place outside. Many of Maurice's favourite songs were sung, entirely as he would have wished.

By this time, Karl's own health had deteriorated even further. Primarily he was suffering from diabetes but he had two small strokes which, amongst other things, took away his ability to smile, a handicap which he hated more than the difficulty which he had with mobility. Operations to his frostbitten foot, which removed two toes and some bone, had quite badly affected his ability to get about.

In the early summer of 1990, Karl and Eileen made another trip to Austria, visiting friends in Obergurgl and Finkenberg and being visited by several more, including Konrad's parents, Lisi, and Lisa and their children. Norbert and Shona met the party at Munich airport and took everyone to a delightful celebration lunch. In a specially hired minibus Norbert drove them all to Obergurgl. On the way back they stopped for a while in Kufstein where Karl had started his army training. It was an emotional excursion.

Karl and Eileen came back, gladly as always, to the place they had made their home. There were exciting developments. With money hard earned on the rigs and devotedly saved, Lisi and Davie had purchased a plot of land next to the croft. There they began the mammoth task of building a large restaurant. Karl, delighted by the development, full of support and excellent advice, turned his favourite garden seat round so that he could watch the progress.

One day, Charlie Walpole, former Struan stalwart, was helping with the building of a garage at the croft, laying down sand as a base for concrete slabs. Whenever an opportunity arose, Karl chatted with the worker, taking an acute interest and clearly regretting that he could not help. When he had seen and talked enough, Karl made his way back indoors and went, as always, early to bed.

It was his last day. Eileen provides the simply, moving account of the great man's passing.

'Karli died peacefully in his sleep on September 30th 1990 leaving everything in perfect order like a good soldier and with many projects still in mind, never abandoning hope.

'He was a man extremely sensitive but with great physical and moral bravery, tough and unyielding but gentle and kind to anyone in pain or trouble, serious and a perfectionist in his work but full of fun and anecdotes, loving and loved by all children and animals and above all a man who loved nature in all its aspects and his own family.'

Knowing that it was entirely what Karl would have wanted, Charlie appeared that day with a friend. After conveying his sincere condolences, the old Struanite pitched into hard work, intending to finish the garage foundation. When it was not, in fact, completed, he and his companion worked through the night. It was their act of respect and homage to the departed.

The media response to Karl's death was extensive. Myrtle Simpson contributed a long piece headlined, 'Man with a lofty vision', which neatly summarised her 'Skisters' account of Karl's work. There were many other eulogies, all with their own banner, amongst them; 'Skiing pioneer Karl Fuchs dies, 'Father of Cairngorm skiing dies', 'Prince's skiing instructor dies'

The piece with the royal allusion managed to suggest that Karl was the first head instructor at the Hillend artificial slope and then claimed, with perhaps similar accuracy, that, 'Prince Charles cut short a fishing holiday in Sutherland to return to Balmoral. He is believed to have been upset by the news of Mr. Fuchs' death. He is expected to call on Mr. Fuchs' wife and daughter.'

In the 'Father' piece, Eilif Moen is quoted as saying, 'When I first came here there was only really one ski school - Karl Fuchs'. He set the path for us all and was very professional and accurate for skiers in finding the right areas. Struan was a unique centre sought by skiers in Britain. Karl was absolutely dedicated. I had great respect for the man.'

The *Inverness Courier* in its obituary quotes Rudi Prochazka's words when Karl was honoured in 1988 by the Association of Ski Schools of Great Britain; 'Without Karl, commercial skiing in the Cairngorms would never have happened the way that it did.' An anonymous contributor is reported as saying, 'Anybody who is anybody in the ski business started with Karl.'

In the December/January edition of *Ski Survey*, John Samuel recounted his history of friendship with Karl from the moment in 1967, on his first ski trip to Scotland, when he was advised by all and sundry that he had to visit Struan. He writes;

'It was almost a cultural shock to come across Struan, a grey Victorian pile on the Carrbridge road, illumined with red and white Scottish Austrian ski school livery and, inside, the kitchen and bar, hugger-mugger of a St. Anton keller.

'What would they brew up here? It was dominated by the massive figure of Karl, exploding with joy or wrath over some twist or turn of Highland ski training or politics, ordering 'noch ein Scotstrian pint' for his guests and happy to see his profits gurgling down their throats as long as his passionate love of skiing went down with them...

'Illness much reduced Karli's involvement in the Seventies and Eighties but he was loyal to his adopted Cairngorms to the last. If any man could claim to be the father of Scottish ski racing it was Karli.'

The funeral was arranged for Wednesday 3rd October at 1.30pm. It had been decided to hold the ceremony outside, in the extensive front garden of the croft. People, travelling from far and wide to pay their respects, looked at the exceedingly dark skies and the frequent heavy showers and wondered about the wisdom of this but as the time for the simple service drew near, a most extraordinary gap appeared in the thick belt of clouds. Astonishingly, some sunlight angled down. There was in fact no rain during the service but the Cairngorm wind was there, of course, having its last playful tussle with the master. Flowers there were a-plenty, Eileen's favourite wreath being of red carnations sent by the New Zealanders with the message, 'From your Struan family.'

The space, though large, was crowded. People who had known Karl since the first days of Struan mixed with young folk who had recently benefited from his advice or generosity with ski equipment.

A minister read his text and then people who had known Karl well delivered homilies according to Eileen's programme; one spoke of him as a family man, another as the community spirit, another as the teacher, yet another as 'mine host'. Rounding off, summarising, the minister spoke around the theme of 'Karl the man'.

At Peter's funeral, a senior soldier, Tony Forbes, who was much involved with ski training and racing, had personally led the cortege, playing the pipes. For Karl he arranged for a Regimental Sergeant Major in full ceremonial uniform to do the honours. The hearse, followed by a long line of cars, moved slowly to the entrance to Carrbridge cemetery then, with the music lifting and lilting, the coffin was carried along the paths, through the dark trees, to the place of burial. The bearers, taking turns were, appropriately, old bar comrades, ski colleagues, former barmen, Jessie's son, Eileen's brother and two grandsons. In an almost unbearably poignant moment, the coffin was lowered into a grave next to Peter's.

The letters and telegrams of condolence flooded in. The medical team at Raigmore Hospital, some of whom had grandfathers whom Karl had taught to ski, said how much they would miss him. The letters referred glowingly to special days, the joys of Struan's extended family, the pioneering work in Scottish skiing, and Karl's unusual, completely unforgettable character. John Samuel, Sir Russell Johnston MP and many other well known people made their contributions. Many of the letters from the army of Struanites refer to life-changing experiences associated with the place.

Alex Newton fondly recalled Karl's great love of nature and respect for the mountains. He wrote;

'I recall still, so clearly, my first trip with Karly and the New Zealand girls on a wee cross-country tour to Ben Macdhui. How we examined and wondered over animal tracks and how always he was ever conscious of changing weather patterns. Later he told me of the times he'd been to Macdhui in an attempt to sight a rare Snowy Owl, but without success.

'I remember the summer too, when he took the guests on the 'walky walkies'. There were frequent sightings of red and roe deer and one very particular time where Karl believed an osprey pair had nested. In this regard he induced in me a burgeoning interest which remains strong today in natural history.

'Certainly Karli influenced me in my approach to ski teaching. He showed the importance of teaching the basics of sideslip and traverse and of the ability to select ski terrain within the capabilities of the class. He insisted that an attitude of patience and empathy was just as important as the technical skill of good demonstration.'

A former 'housemaid', writing from Spain, echoed Alex's remarks about Karl's ability to communicate his love for nature and his unmatched skill as a ski teacher. She adds;

'Even though I'm in a fairly mountainous area and go walking every week with a mountain group, I've found that I've been homesick. Often when I'm high up on the mountains I can hear a snippet of something Karl has said or taught me. I feel most fortunate to have been taught by him and for my time with you at Struan (golden days). I still have a postcard from the shop at Struan of you and Karl when you were young. Your story is filled with romance, sadness and happiness which has touched us all.'

A man called Andrew acknowledged his particular debt;

'I will never forget the very friendly family (and Austrian) atmosphere developed at Struan which was a unique product of Karl and yourself. It was with much pleasure that I introduced the Bank of Scotland (Edinburgh and District) Ski Club to Struan and we were delighted when Karl agreed to become Honorary Vice President of the Club - he is not replaceable! I may say that Club members still regularly recount their fond memories of the great days at Struan which are acutely missed by us all. Scottish ski-ing is tremendously indebted to Karl for his enthusiasm, drive and foresight, without which, frankly, I do not consider that we would have seen the progress which is now evident.'

A former pupil of Karl's called Donald commented that, 'You and he made us all feel part of the family, and the lessons that I learnt were certainly not all on the ski slopes'. He added;

'It may not have been easy at times to live with such a char-ismatic man, I don't know. If we who found him so fascinating stole a little of him away from his family, then I'm sorry. His sense of fun, and his 'larger than life' presence have a place among my warmest memories. I know that there will be people like myself all over the world who would want to share with you not just their sense of loss, but their gratitude for having known Karl.'

The Secretary of the Carrbridge Community Council wrote to express the belief that the establishment of the first Scottish professional ski school in the village helped greatly to turn the place into a tourist attraction and thereby much increased the prosperity of the inhabitants. He added;

'Karl's achievements in the ski world are widely known and acknowledged. What Karl did for the children of Carrbridge may not be so public. That Karl, through his own generosity, taught and encouraged so many of the village children to ski, is testimony to the kind of man that Karl Fuchs was. Thus it will be that Karl is remembered by many families and his friends in Carrbridge.

'In recognition of his achievements to the village and Scottish skiing, the Community Council would like to establish a memorial to Karl within the village. We therefore seek your permission to raise a subscription to fund such a memorial.'

Many others wrote, all of them commenting with huge enthusiasm on the quality of life at Struan and the enrichment of their lives which Karl had brought through his ability to generate a deep love of winter sport. One related that he had skied up to the age of seventy and would still be on the slopes but for an accident which ended his fun.

A woman sent a long letter which included the paragraph;

'Karl and you, Eileen, are synonymous with many happy years of both Anna's and my life. Between you, you brought all the joys of skiing and friendship, the opening up of wonderful Cairngorm and all the exhilaration and joys of the early days that are magic to look back on. The White Lady and Coire Cas, Norbert and Ludwig, the cosy and laughter-filled Struan house, Mrs Anderson's Crannich, and Karl ever patient and ever smiling and with his roguish sense of humour. Anna and I still ski, but what can match those early days. No one who skis can ever forget Karl.'

Soon after Peter's death, Karl had presented a quaiche to the Carrbridge Golf Club for a memorial tournament. Latterly, Peter had been very interested in the sport. The Association of Ski Schools of Great had also presented a cup for the winner of the Instructors' Race in honour of Peter. Similar honourings of Karl soon followed his death.

The Carrbridge Community Council erected a granite stone opposite Struan with a very touching inscription and arranged a splendid unveiling ceremony. Rudi Prohaska and Clive Freshwater addressed the gathering and Eileen uncovered the stone. Afterwards there was tea in the village hall and music by the band from RAF Kinloss and Lossiemouth who were disguised, to hide them from the IRA, as the Cairngorm stompers.

Norbert and other Austrians arranged for a plaque to be made with the inscription, 'In loving memory of our dear friend Karl Fuchs - Ruhe in Frieden ', to be put up on the wall of the car park restaurant facing one of Karl's favourite teaching slopes. Norbert, Franzi and

Othmar Preissl came over to unveil it at an informal ceremony arranged by the chairlift company. who invited about twenty of Karl's earliest pupils. Many other old friends and, of course, all the family, were there for the occasion. Not to be outdone, the New Zealanders set up a memorial race at a South Island resort with suitably inscribed trophies.

*Charlie Walpole and Eileen close to the Karl Fuchs memorial plaque on Cairngorm.*

With the perspective of almost a decade, Clive Freshwater, who owns and runs a substantial water sports centre on the shores of Loch Insh, sees Karl as part of an extraordinary generation of individuals who ran 'charisma-driven' organisations. He cites Colin

Sutton, David Johnson and Bill McConachie as a few examples of the many who gave Speyside an extraordinary potency from the mid-fifties until the late 1980's. Even the chairlift, under the direction of the redoubtable Bob Clyde had, he suggests, a unique character. In the place of these powerful people have come trained, professional, salaried managers who are doubtless efficient but who can never generate the atmosphere, the kinship and the loyalty produced by the likes of Karl.

Clive recalls fondly how Herr Fuchs would almost always be there, in and around his hotel, usually in his ski boots. He was the visible father of the house, a man who worked extraordinarily hard for the benefit of everyone, who gave generously of time and resources, who generated the kind of loyalty which made staff want to stay in the establishment after their work was finished. His 'We'm a familie' motto was never just a form of words and in his family he generously included any creature, animal or human, who wished to be associated.

He was a most unusual man.

## 36. Epilogue

Whilst Karl was still alive, plans were being made for a reunion of Struanites. The main impetus for this came from those New Zealanders who had returned to their country and the several British people who had migrated to the other side of the world. In spite of the distance and cost, an impressive number from the northern hemisphere committed themselves to the idea.

When Karl died, a few months before the event, some of the organisers thought that Eileen might find the prospect of the gathering too daunting but they reckoned without the Knowles spirit. She made the journey gladly, as did Dez Barnes, Charlie Walpole, Rosie Bell and many more of the Struan stalwarts.

The Skier magazine, published in New Zealand, celebrated the Christchurch reunion with an article which began;

'An Austrian ski school, based in Scotland, staffed by a bevy of young Kiwis, frequented by handsome, hard-drinking mountain climbers - and patronised by Royalty. That may sound like the script for a raunchy television series, except it is all perfectly true. Just ask the more than 100 people who have already promised to attend a Struan House reunion in Christchurch - yes, Christchurch - in mid-January.'

The article goes on to recount the history of Struan and its long involvement with New Zealand and to celebrate the many marriages between Europeans and New Zealanders.

The reunion, held at the University Staff Club in Christchurch, was superbly organised. The committee produced an excellent brochure, mounted a large exhibition of photographs, contrived to locate an ancient, Struan-style mangle and cunningly re-created something of the

Carrbridge atmosphere. With a conversazione, a formal dinner and dance and a family barbecue there was ample opportunity for people to renew acquaintanceships and to catch up on gaps in personal histories. Participants were, of course, sad that neither Karl nor Maurice had survived to see the heart warming evidence of Struan's continuing power but Eileen's strength of spirit was an example to all. The event was so successful that it was made very evident that the northern hemisphere contingent were duty bound to organise something similar. It was informally agreed that a five year time span was appropriate.

Among the many topics of conversation in Christchurch was Eileen's plan to establish a memorial fund for Karl and Peter with the aim of doing something practical to enhance skiing, something of which Karl and his son would have thoroughly approved. Eileen's dream, at that early stage, was of a large plastic slope somewhere on the mountain, perhaps served by one of the existing lifts.

Back home she established a steering committee. Clive Freshwater, Eric Langmuir and Eilif Moen were automatic local choices. John Blyth, a retired quantity surveyor from Edinburgh and former manager of the Espoir team, agreed to help. Peter had always rated him very highly and his daughter had been, along with Eric Langmuir's, in the British Ladies Team which Peter had coached. The family lawyer, Douglas Graham, was willingly recruited and he immediately proved his worth in the tricky negotiations for charitable status which involved a degree of unfortunate obstruction from Inland Revenue officials. Finally but indispensably, Tom Mackenzie's widow, Audrey, took on the role of secretary.

The Badenoch and Strathspey District Sports Council gave enthusiastic support. It soon emerged that the costs involved in the creation of a plastic slope would be beyond the limits of the anticipated income so some lesser targets were set. Eileen wrote to everyone she knew.

The letter summarised Karl's distinguished history and told of Struan's unique contribution to the development of skiing in Scotland. Eileen continued;

'These are the bare facts of Karli's work in Scotland. But the many, many friends he made remember him as a man of striking personality and great humanity, who wanted to pass on to everyone he met his own passionate love of the mountains in all seasons, and of skiing in all its aspects. Even in his last years when he was cruelly handicapped by illness, his greatest pleasure was to give help and advice to those who came to hire his skis, making sure their boots were warm and comfy and that they went to the skiing area best suited to them so that they would get the greatest possible enjoyment.

'A very large proportion of today's senior instructors and of the ski world's administrators have at some time learned to ski or worked with Karli and he has introduced many people to the joys of skiing in the Alps, particularly in Austria. He is especially remembered for his uniquely graceful yet powerful style, his ability to teach and give enjoyment on any kind and amount of snow, anywhere and for the imaginative tours he led at all seasons into the remote hills, always bringing his pupils safely home.

'He was robbed of seeing his work carried on by his son Peter who was killed at 24, a member of the 1976 Olympic team, the first British trainer of a national team (the British Girls) and chairman of the ASSGB. I feel that his friends would wish to see some permanent memorial to Karli and to Peter, and am therefore setting up a fund which can be used both to help ordinary people, especially families with children, to learn to ski and start a lifetime of enjoyment of the sport; and also to help those who excel to share in its competitive side.'

Eileen then revealed two schemes which were being considered, one of which involved the setting up of a crèche at the Lecht ski area. The other, more ambitious, was for the building of a short ski tow on the Fiacaill Ridge for use by trainee slalom racers.

The appeal was addressed to Karl's personal friends and former pupils, to local businesses and to ski clubs and the racing confraternity.

A brochure was produced with colour pictures of Karl and Peter and brief biographies. Those who could responded with cheques of anything from a few pounds to hundreds. The total grew steadily.

Whilst this was going on, fate played one of its cruel tricks. Frith Finlayson's son, Iain, one time racing rival of Peter's, had been living and working in the French Alps. Frith and his wife Jean visited as often as they could. Like Karl and Eileen they derived great pleasure from seeing their son carry on the family involvement with skiing. Then, very suddenly, without any prior indication of a problem, the young man died.

Frith writes very movingly of the tragedy and goes on to relate, 'In Glasgow I visited Sandy Greaves of Greaves Sports. He was very interested to hear how things had worked out in Les Deux Alpes. He made an observation that two of our best skiers were gone. He was talking about Peter Fuchs. Peter had been killed sometime past. He was right, they were two of the best.'

As these things do, it took time before the Memorial Fund was in full operation and by the time it was, the focus had shifted again. It had been decided to devote all income from the fund to ski-educational purposes. Eileen wrote to all the donors, telling then that the charity had been registered under the name, 'The Karl and Peter Fuchs Educational Trust.' The broad aim, she revealed, was to help Speyside youngsters to learn to ski. The plan was to advertise each October in the local papers and to allocate grants in December. The first awards went to the Parent Skiing Support Group for the children of Carrbridge, to Deshar (Boat of Garten) and Abernethy Primary schools to pay for weekly transport to the ski slopes for their ski classes, and to the Cairngorm Ski Club to help with training abroad. The trustees felt sure that these projects would have been close to the hearts of Karli and Peter.

When the five years from the Christchurch reunion had all too rapidly passed, Dave and Marg Will bravely took on the task of organising the Scottish version of the event. In addition to his work as a solicitor, Dave had, by this time, become Chair of the Scottish Football Association and a leading light in FIFA, the international ruling body for the world's favourite game. In spite of these heavy commitments he and Marg exerted a huge amount of effort arranging venues, contacting possible participants and collecting money. As in New Zealand, the local press saw the event as a newsworthy item and it is heartening to note that fact and fiction continued to be mixed in the best journalistic tradition of Struan reportage;

'More than 130 people are expected to descend on Carrbridge this week-end for a reunion party for friends of the Austrian Ski School, run for many years by the late Karl Fuchs and his wife Eileen. The week-end is being organised by Mr David Will and his wife Margaret, regulars of Struan House Hotel, headquarters of the ski school back in the late 1960's and guests are expected to come from as far afield as New Zealand.

'The Austrian Ski School was a favourite stopping-off point for New Zealand ski instructors from the '50's onwards and two years ago Eileen Fuchs was invited out to New Zealand to meet some of the many people who had passed through Struan over the years. During her time there, she was instructed that she must hold a reunion at Carrbridge and she is looking forward to meeting old friends this weekend.

'Events kick off with a reunion party in the Struan House Hotel on Friday evening, move on to a dinner in the Dalfaber Golf and Country Club in Aviemore on Saturday night and end with Sunday lunch at Lisi's Country Kitchen. Lisi is the daughter of Karl and Eileen Fuchs and well known to all the weekend guests.

' "We are expecting quite a number from New Zealand although all those who hoped to get here won't manage the weekend," said Eileen. "We also hope to see people who were associated with Struan from as far back as 1955 so there will be lots to talk about."

'It will also be a special weekend for David and Margaret Will. They met at Struan and will be celebrating their silver wedding this weekend.'

The guests assembling at Struan quickly discovered that the place had changed. The couple who bought the establishment from Karl and Eileen had turned it into a 'proper' hotel. The Edelweiss bar had been converted into a reception area by knocking down a wall. There was an impressive fireplace and a regulation reception counter. Upstairs, by a cunning trick of architecture, all of the rooms had been given integrated bathrooms.

The perpetrators of all these changes had moved on and the new proprietors seemed to be of the type that might have kept things as they were but it had to be admitted that the modifications were impressive. Struan life was noticeably more comfortable than it had been in the Fuchs' days.

People congregated in the dining room. It seemed that at least half of the 'Manchester boys' were there with representatives from most of the other 'gangs'. Not a few had, of course, died or become too infirm to travel. Strange it was to stand in that place, talking to people last encountered ten, fifteen, in some cases forty years ago. The atmosphere was convivial but few could miss the undercurrent of profound emotion. Naturally much of this was concerned with lost youth, with memories of glorious times, with sadness at the thought of those who, once brilliantly alive in that unique spot, had died.

*Norbert, Lisi and Eileen at Karl's Cairngorm memorial plaque*

Strong in the minds of those who gasped in astonished recognition, or attempted to summarise a life in five minutes of hoarse yelling, was the shade of Karl. His phrases echoed; 'You haf your ski?', 'Im bus please', 'Make a pretty picture'. Some fondly recalled his 'Mah, like de bottle today, I could not ski!'

It was always kind of him to say it. Those of us nursing bruised flesh and deflated egos were boosted by this confession of fallibility by the master but we knew that he was speaking with an extreme degree of relativity.

We could not cope with the conditions. Karl could always ski, on ice, through spring porridge, across wind crust, down cliffs, across valleys, through the clouds, into the occasional brilliant blue. His innate skill, his instinctive bonding with the natural world, would take him anywhere.

It may, to some, seem trivial, this celebration of a life devoted to what, after all, is a slightly crazy pastime but it is not so. It would be a poor existence for us all if there were nothing but drudgery. For life to be bearable there have to be sports and entertainments; activities which are pursued for the sheer pleasure which they bring.

And Karl's greatest gift ('gift' in the sense that it was something that he possessed and also in the sense that it was something that he freely passed on to others) was his ability to communicate the pure joy of things. This was not limited to skiing but extended to the antics of snow hares, the cry of the curlew, the furriness of 'kettles', the crashing flight of the startled capercailzie, the contour of a mountain, the cosiness of home. These and many, many other good things were brought, by Karl, to people's attention. He forcefully showed that in the love of the natural world, and in the loving interaction of human beings, there was more than sufficient reward to make it easily worth coping with the setbacks.

He was an instinctive environmentalist, a natural humanitarian. Of course he had his share of frailties but he was, to an extraordinary degree, a good man who gave unstintingly.

With Eileen, he created a place called Struan which brought untold enjoyment and positively influenced very many lives.

It was a noble act.

## Postscript

Lisi and David duly completed their second major feat of construction and now run a fine log cabin restaurant which serves superb food, in a warm, welcoming ambience and which offers one of the best views of the Cairngorms from its windows and large balcony. They also sell high quality pottery and wood carvings, some of them made by David.

Lisa worked for a number of years as Publicity Officer for the Eden Court Theatre, Inverness. She is now doing a degree in sociology and lives with a long-term partner in Aviemore.

Peter and Lisa's son, Josef, followed Karl in his love of team games, especially rugby which he played for the local Strathspey Club. But the ski bug is also a part of him; he went for a year to Whistler in Canada where his mother's sister lives. Thereafter, he spent a year at James Watt College in Greenock doing a course in sports coaching and management where he was elected 'student of the year'. He is now taking a sports degree at Jordanhill College, Strathclyde University. He coaches underprivileged children in rugby, plays for Glasgow Academicals, and takes an active part on the committee of the Karl and Peter Fuchs Memorial Fund. He intends to take the BASI skiing qualifications when time permits!

Their daughter, Helene, has worked for two years as an instructor for the Scottish Norwegian Ski School on Cairngorm and is now following a foundation course in Inverness. She plans to go on to a degree.

Davie and Lisi's son, David, is artistic and musical. He trained as a stage manager at RSAMD in Glasgow and, like his cousin, won a prize as best student in the drama department. He spent a year at the Bristol Old Vic Theatre School where, reminiscent of his Uncle Peter, he showed a penchant for challenging some received opinions and systems. After a time working as a waiter and then functions manager for a prestigious catering firm, he went to work in the theatre on *QE2* and *Oriana* cruises to the Mediterranean, the Caribbean, the Canaries, South America, South Africa, Indonesia and Australia.

*Eileen in Cambridge, summer 1998*

Their daughter, Kris, is studying sports management and coaching at Telford College, Edinburgh. She taught skiing for two seasons at Franz Stock's school in Finkenburg where she qualified as an Austrian-approved instructor, including the passing of a written examination in German. Her main love is snowboarding and she has gained an Austrian qualification in this, too. She teaches at Hill End in Edinburgh at weekends but, like her grandparents, she loves Austria and plans to work and probably settle there.

Eileen spends summers at the croft, being visited by an endless stream of Struanites, and the winters travelling and staying with yet more members of the extended family. In 1998 she attended a celebration in Cambridge of the 50th anniversary of the granting of degrees to women where crowds lined the streets and all the graduate survivors from those times were treated like heroes.

Karl would be proud of all of them.